The Committee and Its Critics

* * * A CALM REVIEW OF THE HOUSE COMMITTEE ON UN-AMERICAN ACTIVITIES by William F. Buckley, Jr. AND THE EDITORS OF *National Review*

G. P. Putnam's Sons, New York

THE COMMITTEE AND ITS CRITICS

*A Calm Review of the House Committee
on Un-American Activities*

For Esther Chambers

"...my gentle wife for whom in her loneliness that dark moment was darker than for me."

—WITNESS

* * * The contributors to this volume are, for the most part, associated with *National Review,* as editors, associates, or contributors. We are especially grateful for the participation in this volume of Messrs. WILLIAMS, FERMAN and CROCKER, who are not connected with the magazine. * * * WILLIAM F. BUCKLEY, JR., editor of *National Review,* is the author of *Up From Liberalism* and other books. * * * JAMES BURNHAM, formerly professor of philosophy at New York University, is the author of *The Managerial Revolution* and a half dozen other books, of which the most recent is *Congress and the American Tradition.* * * * WILLMOORE KENDALL was formerly an associate professor of political science at Yale University. He is the author of *John Locke and the Doctrine of Majority Rule,* and of the forthcoming *The General Theory of Freedom of Speech.* * * * WILLIAM F. RICKENBACKER is a graduate of Harvard (*cum laude*), and an editor of *National Review.* * * * KARL HESS is now press editor of *Newsweek,* and co-author of *Crime Without Punishment.* * * * RALPH DE TOLEDANO, editor of *Washington World,* is co-author of *Seeds of Treason* and several other books, of which the latest is *Lament for a Generation.* * * * M. STANTON EVANS is editor of the Indianapolis *News,* and author of *Revolt on the Campus.* * * * C. DICKERMAN WILLIAMS has been visiting Sterling lecturer on the law at Yale University, was a director of the American Civil Liberties Union, and former general counsel to the Department of Commerce. He has written extensively in the scholarly journals on the Fifth Amendment and other subjects. * * * IRVING FERMAN was formerly chief counsel for the American Civil Liberties Union and has frequently contributed to the scholarly journals. * * * GEORGE N. CROCKER is an attorney, and author of *Roosevelt's Road to Russia.* * * * ROSS D. MACKENZIE is an undergraduate at Yale University studying history and is vice-chairman of the *Yale Daily News.* * * *

CONTENTS

THE COMMITTEE AND ITS CRITICS

*A Calm Review of the House Committee
on Un-American Activities*

The legislation under which the House Committee on Un-American Activities operates is Public Law 601, 79th Congress [1946], chapter 753, 2d session, which provides:

Be it enacted by the Senate and House of Representatives of the United States of America in Congress assembled, * * *

PART 2—RULES OF THE HOUSE OF REPRESENTATIVES

RULE X

STANDING COMMITTEES

*   *   *   *   *   *   *

17. Committee on Un-American Activities, to consist of nine members.

RULE XI

POWERS AND DUTIES OF COMMITTEES

*   *   *   *   *   *   *

(q) (1) Committee on Un-American Activities.

(A) Un-American activities.

(2) The Committee on Un-American Activities, as a whole or by subcommittee, is authorized to make from time to time investigations of (i) the extent, character, and objects of un-American propaganda activities in the United States, (ii) the diffusion within the United States of subversive and un-American propaganda that is instigated from foreign countries or of a domestic origin and attacks the principle of the form of government as guaranteed by our Constitution, and (iii) all other questions in relation thereto that would aid Congress in any necessary remedial legislation.

The Committee on Un-American Activities shall report to the House (or to the Clerk of the House if the House is not in session) the results of any such investigation, together with such recommendations as it deems advisable.

For the purpose of any such investigation, the Committee on Un-American Activities, or any subcommittee thereof, is authorized to sit and act at such times and places within the United States, whether or not the House is sitting, has recessed, or has adjourned, to hold such hearings, to require the attendance of such witnesses and the production of such books, papers, and documents, and to take such testimony, as it deems necessary. Subpenas may be issued under the signature of the chairman of the committee or any subcommittee, or by any member designated by any such chairman, and may be served by any person designated by any such chairman or member.

★

Chapter
1.

THE COMMITTEE AND
ITS CRITICS

THE idea of this book grew out of a personal experience of the editor with ignorance. It was a college gathering, and in the course of the proceedings someone entered a ritual crack at the House Committee on Un-American Activities with great effect upon the audience. The surprise did not lie in the audience's instinctive animosity toward the Committee (every college sophomore knows one must disdain *any* organization so un-chic as to chase down un-American activities), but in the quality of the jibe that provoked it. There was no wit or precision in the taunt, no special passion; in fact, I even forget the exact words. The experience threw me back to my college days, which began during the euphoria after the war, when if you said anybody else was a Communist, or a pro-Communist, or that any organization was, or ever had been, or ever would be, a Communist front, why you were a witch-hunter, and everybody knew what to do to witch-hunters in those days—namely, burn them.

Then, in 1948, poor Mr. Henry Wallace permitted himself to be run for the Presidency of the United States by a group of pros who hugged the Communist Party line even as you and I, edging our way across the peak of the Matterhorn, would hug a defile. Simultaneously, Stalin was gobbling up the satellites, stealing our secrets and showing at every opportunity, with which he was amply provided, his contempt for the bourgeois notion that the alliance could survive the war. The climate changed; the existence of an undercover international Communist apparatus was garishly revealed by a succession of informants who submitted to the rack—testimony to the FBI, appearances before Congressional committees, books, articles, personal appearances; and it became generally accepted that, in the words of Dwight Macdonald, in fact there were loose in our society little witches like Judith Coplon, and little wizards like Alger Hiss; and for a few years the community settled down to accepting the realities the enemy imposed.

It seems as though we must go through it all again. For in the past few years, for complex reasons, we are back to something that resembles the general indifference to the problem of Communist subversion which beset us during the immediate postwar years. There are differences, notably the general agreement on the fact of Soviet intransigence. But along with it goes the fixed conviction, so frequently avowed by our governors of opinion, that the threat is exclusively "external," that those who talk of an "internal" threat are at best deluded, at worst suffering from paranoia; that therefore the existence of a Congressional committee devoted to the internal dimension of the Soviet threat is at best an affront upon reality, at worst a continuing agent of confusion. And quite apart from the irrelevance of such an agency in the present situation, they reason, we should oppose its existence because it does positive damage to our way of life, and belies our implicit commitment to the idea of the free society.

These are important criticisms, which this volume attempts to analyze. The contributors to it share a number of common premises. One is that the Soviet world threat is real, a noncontroversial assumption held in common by the entire spectrum of non-Communist opinion in this country. But we go further to say that in the final analysis, the distinction between the internal and the external threat is unreal: that the scope of the Communist effort transcends the conventional boundaries, and that therefore the conventional vocabulary is anachronistic. Thus—we reason—the activities of the Congressional investigating committee cannot be detached from the activities of the CIA, or the FBI; or, even, those of the Pentagon, the United States Information Agency, some of the foreign aid agencies, or any of the manifold enterprises whose common purpose is to ensure the security of the Republic.

Even if that assumption is accepted, we are left with residual problems which anyone concerned with the preservation of freedom must face up to. Assume the need for an all-out response to the Communist threat, and excuses can be made for reordering the entire structure of American life. We often hear the rhetorical cry for a "total" response to the Communist challenge. And no doubt the American people, if it proved necessary, would make "any sacrifice whatever," to use the phrase of President Kennedy, to survive the threat. But after all, that is rhetoric. We are free men, and we accept impositions upon our freedom only as they prove necessary. We do not want to sacrifice a single freedom which we need not sacrifice in order to safeguard the Republic. We fight, after all, not only for the future, but for the here and now. The Communists may, before they are done with us, force us into a garrison state, a government-managed economy, the suspension of civil liberties —the totalist response. But the best instincts of American freemen demand that we stay as free as we can possibly stay, consistent with the stability of the ship of state. It is wrong to sacrifice a single freedom heedlessly. We are, as a people, generally agreed that we must tax ourselves hideously to maintain our armed services; that we must pay the bill of the CIA, and of the USIA, and, to the extent necessary, of foreign aid, military and economic, for our allies. We accept conscription—that drastic curtailment of liberty which is, in its generic form, proscribed by the Constitution under the name of involuntary servitude. We accept a Federal Bureau of Investigation which (albeit with decorum) necessarily traffics in tapped telephones, secret informants, and all that grimy business that goes against the grain of a people who value highly the importance of privacy. The question has arisen in serious quarters whether we ought also to accept a House Committee on Un-American Activities.

The purpose of this book, and more narrowly of this introductory chapter, is to crystallize the arguments against the Committee and to analyze them in the light of our dual commitment to our national defense and to our free society. I should have said that another premise shared by the contributors to this volume is this: that the state wants constant watching, because it is, notoriously, the principal instrument for the oppression of free men. It, exclusively, wields the conclusive weight: for it has at its disposal the police power. The contributors to this volume, I think it safe to generalize, have in recent years resisted with a consistency they would match up against that of any other half dozen persons, the accumulation of power in the government of the United States. Their deliberations on the matter of the House Committee on Un-American Activities should be viewed in this light. We are, every one of us, disposed to resist the accumulation by the state of any power which is unnecessary to the insurance, by reasonable measures, of the survival of our society.

It is in this context that we seek to illuminate a number of questions, which I shall attempt to deal with generally in this chapter, and which the writers will take up in their respective chapters. The principal questions are: (1) Does HUAC (the House Committee on Un-American Activities) perform licitly? (2) Does it perform a necessary function? (3) Does it harmonize with our free institutions? And (4), if not, should it be abolished? Or should our free institutions move over far enough to accommodate it?

The principal enemy of purposive thought is of course ignorance, and this book seeks—honestly, I believe—to enlighten. It is not easy to exaggerate the depth of the ignorance in critical quarters concerning the Committee and its work. I do not make this judgment invidiously. I was myself stupendously ignorant of the scope of the Committee's work even at the moment when I undertook to put this volume together. Somewhere along the line, I had been put on the Committee's mailing list, and in the interstices of my bookshelves volumes upon volumes of the Committee's publications are wedged—which I never looked at, and most of which even now I am unfamiliar with. Yet I am deeply involved in the anti-Communist enterprise. It hardly behooves me, under the circumstances, to expatiate upon other people's ignorance or laziness. But the ignorance of particulars, from which I suffer, becomes an ignorance of generalities where others, so quick to criticize the Committee, are concerned. I have no doubt that many of our *tricoteuses* would modify their demands for the Committee's bloody execution if they actually took the time to survey the Committee's work. I do not suggest for a minute that all those who patiently examine the Committee's work will become the Committee's supporters. Some will probably feel, even after measuring its work against the exigencies of our tormented age, that on balance HUAC is a liability rather than an asset. But their opinion on the matter will then be responsibly taken, whereas now it is, in many cases, ill-advised; prejudiced, to use the dread word.

I have before me a thickish pamphlet put together and mimeographed by the Kenyon (College) Council to Abolish the House Committee on Un-American Activities. It contains a most valuable semi-impromptu symposium by members of the Kenyon faculty concerning HUAC. No less than 33 professors contributed their feelings, in 500 words or less, on HUAC, and of these all but five favored its abolition, or radical reform. It is a useful condensation of intellectually popular misconceptions. Professor A. begins by announcing that *"Since HUAC is not a judicial body but a fact-finding one, a special set of rules should be formulated controlling its investigations...."* (a) HUAC is *not* merely a fact-finding body. It is also an *evaluative* body—a factor of considerable importance. And (b) it *has,* and has had for several years, a special set of rules, patterned after recommendations by a committee of a bar association, and by the members of the House of Representatives. In fact it is the first Congressional committee to adopt formal rules of procedure. (See Chapter 8, A.)

Professor B. (the professors' names, along with their comments, are given alphabetically) is against HUAC because it is engaged in *"stigmatizing unpopular ideas and intimidating those who believe or express such ideas."* One wonders, is pro-Communism the "unpopular idea" Professor B. has in mind? Or does he have in mind the Committee's persecution of non-Communist unpopular ideas? But on the record (see Chapter 10) HUAC has gone after pro-Communists or suspected pro-Communists, or apparent victims of Communist influence only (and here and there a pro-fascist, or "hate" group). It may be that in going after Jones the Committee falsely attributed pro-Communism to him—but that is a different charge from the one Professor B. makes. The difference is between an honest mistake on the part of the Committee, whether caused by sloppiness or stupidity, and a conscious, hypocritical abuse of HUAC's implicit mandate. Has HUAC been stigmatizing non-Communist ideas? Have Liberals about whom it could not reasonably be shown that they got involved in some way or other with Communists, or pro-Communist enterprises, felt the Committee's lash? Where are they?

Professor C. asks for abolition. *"The necessary function of a House committee is to draft legislation, and in all the years that the Committee has been in existence it has not done this or else very little of it."* It is not a necessary function of a House committee to draft legislation (see Chapter 2). A House committee may, without drafting a single piece of legislation, occupy itself usefully in overseeing the operations of government, or in examining attempts to influence government, or in apprehending the need for legislation—and needs no other warrant. But in fact (see Chapter 9), HUAC has created a considerable body of legislation, including the omnibus Internal Security Act of 1950. Professor C. may not consider this an important act of legislation. But the Communists do, and have fought it bitterly for years. It is, for all its shortcomings, an extremely ambitious attempt to hinder the activities of professional subverters with minimum molestation to the freedom of nonconspiratorial dissent.

Professor D. remarks: *"If the Federal Bureau of Investigation is not at present adequately financed for the control of subversion within the country, then I think its budget should be increased by the sums of money now appropriated to the House Committee."* Leaping lizards, professor! Are we, in the name of the extension of freedom, going to ask the Federal Bureau of Investigation, a semi-secret extension of the police arm of the State, to a) hold hearings on, evaluate, and recommend legislation to the House of Representatives; b) interrogate witnesses (in open session?) in connection with matters which are not clearly proscribed by the law, but which relate to the internal security; c) maintain and make widely available to legislators and agencies of the government, files and reports on pro-Communist activities? Would the professor really prefer that the police within the soundproofed walls of their ministries of love, undertake the work at hand? Let him read the description (see Chapter 8, A) of the way the Canadians handle *their* subversive problem. . . .

Professor F. wants to know just what it means to be "un-American," and generalizes that *"in practice [HUAC's] activities . . . have been devoted almost entirely to the harassment and intimidation of persons and institutions whose views are noticeably to the left of those held by Everett Dirksen, William Buckley, and Barry Goldwater."* Does he really believe that, poor man? Will the professor, who must live in dreadful torment, after reading this book (especially Chapter 10), find peace? *"I have not heard that the Committee has ever questioned the objectives of the Ku Klux Klan. . . ."* But the Committee has; see, e.g., Special Com. on HUAC Vols. 1–6, 9–12, 14; Exec. Hearings, made public, Vols. 1, 2, 6–7. Appendix I, IV, and divers references, 1946–1960. ". . . *Their hearings are not hedged about with such basic protections as the right to consult counsel. . . .*" Not only are witnesses entitled by the Committee's rules to counsel, meetings have even been suspended when witnesses appeared without counsel (see Chapter 8, B). Not that Professor F. doubts the necessity for an occasional Congressional investigation, nor is he himself confused about the composition of un-Americanism: *"If we must have an HUAC [sic—F.* is a professor of English, no doubt] *it might well look into the real intentions and methods of the people who financed Joe McCarthy and are sponsoring Mr. Welch."*

Professor H. also disapproves the designation "Un-American" (as do I—see below). *"Surely,"* he comments ruefully about the land of Huey Long, Carmine De Sapio, Harry Truman, Kissin' Jim Folsom, and Wayne Morse, *"we have the right to expect a higher degree of political sophistication from the men who represent us."* A different Professor H. fears that *"the methods adopted by the Committee have done much to destroy faith in the principles of democratic government."* Really? Where? A third Professor H. faults the Committee for failing to make the distinction between *" 'Communism' as an economic and social system and treasonous loyalty to foreign powers."* I have not found that distinction slurred, or coarsely dealt with (see Chapters 5, 7, 10). *"HUAC makes flagrant denials of constitutional rights."* But in fact it does not (see Chapter 8, A). . . . Professor R. objects because HUAC seems to be arguing that *"whatever pleases the Committee therefore and necessarily has the force of law which binds conscience."* What *can* he have in mind? Professor S. says, *"If the reputation of even* one [his emphasis] *honest, innocent individual has been tarnished by the Committee, then I feel that whatever good, if any, which the Committee might have effected has been more than counterbalanced, and the Committee has thereby outlived its usefulness."* Does Professor R. also believe that if even *one* honest, innocent individual has been sent to jail under the common law, we should abandon the common law, as having outlived its usefulness? . . . Professor S. announces that *"The chief effect of the House Committee on Un-American Activities has been to enforce silence or despair upon conscientious and intelligent persons."* Indeed? The Committee no doubt wishes to frustrate, and to cause to despair, those persons who conscientiously and intelligently plot the overthrow of our free institutions. Is it their despair the professor is mourning? Surely not: he must mean other people's despair, the despair of free and loyal men. Are *they* silent? Surely not all, for there is much noise in the air. Certainly they are not silent at *Kenyon!* Do they, however, despair? Perhaps. But is there *cause* for them to despair? If they knew the truth about HUAC, would they despair less?

I profoundly believe so, as do the authors of this book, one of whose principal purposes is, I repeat, to isolate the real from the unreal criticisms of the House Committee, and to rescue the discussion of it from frenzy, to which level the putatively best-informed, most sophisticated, and most discriminating members of the community have, despairingly, consigned it.

With what specific criticisms of HUAC might a supporter of the Committee agree? I do not undertake to speak for all the contributors to this volume, not having canvassed their views; nor is there any need to add my voice to theirs on a number of specific objections raised in different chapters of this book. But it seems to me that on at least one important theoretical point, the Committee's critics are correct.

Criticism of HUAC falls into three general categories. The first is generic criticism: of the mere existence of a Congressional agency which consciously seeks the means by which to neutralize the political activities of a particular group. That argument is easily disposed of on the traditional grounds of the clear and present danger argument, fortified by the distinction Professor Sidney Hook has elaborated in his book, *Heresy Yes, Conspiracy No!* But under that category falls the more sophisticated criticism of the Committee's name: How, Professor Henry Steele Commager (for instance) asks, is anyone to say, and on what authority, what is an un-American activity?

It seems to me Mr. Commager has a point, though not perhaps exactly the same point he seeks to run off with. Confronted with Mr. Commager's objection, Professor Sidney Hook observed: "If it is impossible to say what is un-American, then it is likewise impossible to say what *is* American. In which case, how come Professor Commager undertook to write a book called *The American Mind?"*

A clever point, more than merely useful to the debater. Indeed, Mr. Commager's title is his own tacit recognition that every country has its own traditions and even, broadly speaking, consensus—with reference to which an anthropologist or historian can responsibly, even if a little arbitrarily, generalize that this custom or that, this innovation or that, is un-American, or un-French, or un-Iroquois. Certainly it should be safe to say that a call for the abolition of the monarchy in England would be un-English—to say it as a plain, observable, empirically and historically verifiable fact. But it is quite another thing to say that a royal commission should be established to persecute those who hold to such un-English views on the monarchy. It might indeed be held that to charge a royal commission with devising the means to discourage even concededly un-English activities, is in itself an un-English thing to do, so that whereas we are agreed that antimonarchist agitation is un-English, so is it un-English to proscribe antimonarchist agitation. And whereas the offender in the first instance is an individual or a group of individuals, the offender in the second instance, speaking with the authority of the House of Commons, is the graver offender. It is too bad if John Jones undertakes un-English activities; it is shocking if Her Majesty's Government undertakes un-English activities. . . .

We should, I think, reject Mr. Commager's notion that a dynamic and changing society, which governs itself pragmatically, and is continually experiencing and assimilating the disorderly demands of history, cannot therefore responsibly decide what is and what is not un-national. It is all too clear that many national ideas change, and that what is un-American today was not necessarily un-American yesterday, nor will be tomorrow. But the historically unimpeachable fact that a people's customs and traditions and mores change perceptibly, does not commit a society to the doctrine that it should hold lightly its current commitments. A proper historical skepticism is one thing: quite another is the anomy of the uncommitted, unrooted man. Even if we should take it for granted, considering the turbulent movements of history, that tomorrow our society will believe differently, we do not believe less strongly today, nor cease to assert our views, or protect them, by the use of the common sanctions, legal, moral and social, by which a society shields its own institutions and personality.

If, then, Professor Commager, or Professor Vernon Parrington, or whoever, may as historian and critic pronounce on what is, and what is not, typically or profoundly or congenitally "American," has Congress the corresponding right to use the word "un-American" and mean something by it? Perhaps. But Congress should proceed with a moderation greater than that which Messrs. Commager and Parrington have shown in their apodictic dispositions. Even granting the intellectual validity of the effort to distinguish the "American" from the "un-American" at any particular point in time, this is not a game Congress should play. When the professors are mistaken, the mischief is limited to the influence they exercise. Not so with Congress. In time of emergency Congress may exercise emergency powers, and declare implicitly what is and isn't un-American—it has done this every time it passes a conscription law, overreaching the objections of the pacifist or revolutionary, in behalf of the survival of the nation, understood as the survival of a nation implicitly dedicated to a set of values. But I agree that Congress should proceed very reluctantly to act as fugleman for what-is, and what-isn't American, or what-is or what-isn't un-American. In the popular usage, "un-American" is simply a term of opprobrium, hurled mostly by indiscriminate polemicists against those with whom they disagree. Harry Truman called HUAC itself un-American, critics of HUAC call Southern segregationists un-American, opponents of the social security law have called *it* un-American—and no doubt the day will come when an official of the Committee for a Sane Nuclear Policy will call un-American those who would rather be dead than Red.

But we are not concerned here with the use of the term as a

knuckle-duster, but with its use when it carries, even rhetorically, the great leverage of the law. I side with those who believe that HUAC's designation is too broad. The Committee should not, in my judgment, consider itself free to explore "un-American activities," because when a semi-autonomous Congressional Committee has a running license to investigate any and all un-American activities, it is given, without the reassuring processes of public and Congressional debate, standing and plenipotentiary powers to fix the meaning of un-Americanism.

The Committee's critics are constantly warning the people of the United States not only that HUAC will, almost certainly, end up denouncing as un-American everything that doesn't conform with its most freshly baked bias, but that in fact it has already gone a long way in this direction. The latter charge does not happen to be true, as this volume proves. But the potential is there. In the past, HUAC has confined itself to investigating people and groups of people who, prima facie evidence indicated, were acting in behalf of the Communist conspiracy, or who were being victimized by it. The exceptions are investigations of racist and neo-fascist activity. I happen to believe that true fascists, e.g. Fritz Kuhn of the pre-war Nazi Bund, or Lincoln Rockwell of the American Nazi Party, are un-American in the provable sense: their ideals and manners do not have historical antecedents in respectable American practice. Racism, on the other hand, if by that is meant white supremacism and its accompanying mystique, is not un-American in the historical sense. It is despicable—but there we go, and there the Committee might go: that which is despicable is un-American—so let's investigate? . . .

Lots of ideas are despicable, but those of us who favor limited government want to let despicable ideas be disciplined by the market place. It is not despicable movements—or even un-American movements, in the sense of mutational movements, or movements clearly unrooted in the American tradition—that we want to see watched over by a committee of Congress. It is any despicable idea (whether historically un-American or not) which *(a) is being sustained by foreign and powerful enemies of the republic or (b) threatens explosive internal crises.* It was correct for the Dies Committee on Un-American Activities to hold extensive investigations into the activities of Fritz Kuhn, who was actively attempting to influence American foreign policy in behalf of a foreign dictatorship, and doing so by the use of intrigue, false propaganda, espionage, and subversion. It would, I think, be preposterous to investigate systematically the activities of George Lincoln Rockwell and his two dozen swastikaed cretins who go about plying their pathology in the fever swamps of the crazy-Right. If, per impossibile, Lincoln Rockwell's movement were to grow to the point where, as an arm of a robust international conspiracy, it provoked the responsible curiosity of the Congress of the United States, it should then be investigated—by a committee especially mustered to look into the neo-Nazi movement: a committee mandated, after full discussion in Congress on whether the need appears to have arisen, to investigate, and to consider legislation designed to inhibit, the growth of the neo-Nazi movement.

It is ironic that in the discussions leading to the formation of the House Committee on Un-American Activities, it was understood that to use the term "un-American" was a concession to the Left. The idea was to counter the suspicion that an essentially conservative Congress would show itself opposed to the Communist conspiracy, while indulgent toward conspiratorial movements arising from the Right. But then there *was* such a movement from the Right during the thirties. And Congress should have responded by setting up a committee to investigate Communist and Nazi activities. By seeking a generic cover for Communist *and* Nazi, Congress came up with the unfortunate word "un-American," which now tends to make a great many nervous liberal professors feel personally insecure, from one day to the next.

Accordingly, I deplore the Committee's name. I believe we should have a standing House Committee on Communist Activities. I believe the durability and resourcefulness of the Communist movement justifies, as a matter of efficiency and economy, the use of a standing committee, as opposed to an *ad hoc* committee. I'd like to see such a committee die the day after the Communist threat ends, but so would I like to see the Armed Services Committee die the day after we can cease to worry about the possible need for armed services. Meanwhile, the Communists exist (see below), they continue to do mischief (see below), we have yet to find perfect legislative instruments for combating them (see below), they are an integral part of the international Communist conspiracy (see below) and must be engaged by the agency entrusted by the Constitution to provide for the common defense (see below)—so then let us have the Committee, but let us make a sensible concession to right-minded critics who fear the loose, omnipotent rubric.

The second category of criticisms it is the principal business of this book to discuss. It is said, as by the professors at Kenyon, that HUAC is out of harmony with the American tradition, that it is abusive of individual rights, that it has assumed uniquely judicial functions, and so on. The contributors consider these charges, and distinguish between those that are and those that are not informed and serious.

As to the third general charge, we make no comment, because it is outside the scope of this inquiry. The charge is that the Committee's work has by and large been done by self-seeking vulgarians, ignorant of or indifferent to the decent restraints of power. This book does not attempt to evaluate the performance of the members or staff of the Committee. On the abstract question, anyone would agree: if better men can be found to run the Committee, we are all for finding them. If better men can be found to run the White House, we are all in favor of finding *them,* too. The House of Representatives elects its own captains, and that is the way it will probably continue to be.

It seems only fair, however, after reading through a ton of the material issued by the Committee, to make a few general remarks that relate to this criticism. What would we like to see in the administrators of such a committee as HUAC? The temper of a judge. The disposition of a dove. An indifference to the sordid demands of political life. And the professional background of a doctor of political science.

But such men do not exist in any quantity, and are not likely to turn up in Congress. It is all very well to enjoin upon the members of HUAC a judicial disposition toward Communists. But *no* man who will read through one year's hearings by HUAC—any year's hearings (see e.g., Chapter 5)—will expect so detached a bearing, or even, I think, commend it. The Committee is a fact-finding and evaluative body: but it does not pretend to be impartial in respect to the (remember: un-American) work of the enemy, whose deceits and stratagems and violence it is professionally engaged in probing. . . . Investigators report that Jones, identified under oath as a member of the Communist Party, has established a cell in the ganglion of a major industrial union, in an industry doing vital defense work for the government. Jones is subpoenaed. He arrives with his lawyer, an old-timer practiced in contumely against anti-Communists. To get to your office, you must pass picket lines denouncing you as an inquisitor, a warmonger and a fascist. . . . You question Jones. Just a minute, he has a statement to make. It denounces you and the Committee and all your works and its, as a plot to bring fascism and militarism to America. You are an enemy of due process, a cynical betrayer of your oath to the Constitution, in league with the forces of hate, you loathe liberty, decency, order, progress, Negroes, Jews, Catholics, peace. . . . There is a demonstration of approval in the audience —you call for order, and ask Jones whether he is still a member of the Communist Party. He consults his lawyer and refuses to answer, opportunizing on every question to discourse upon your immorality, cowardice, and unconstitutionalism. . . . You direct him to answer. . . . He replies, in effect, go to Hell, taking the First Amendment. He and his lawyer and his retinue flounce off, and the question whether he should have answered works its way through the Speaker of the House of Representatives, to the House, to the Justice Department, to a grand jury, to a court. If Jones is very unlucky, he will be sentenced to spend up to a year in jail. But before then he will tour the country abusing you and the Committee, and everywhere he will receive standing ovations. Committees of scholars and literati will sign petitions in his behalf. Then perhaps the Supreme Court will, on a technicality, void the conviction. . . .

Such experiences as this do not make for irenic dispositions, and I am not even sure I could warm to the iceberg who succeeded in absolutely curbing what should be a passionate resentment of the impudence and treachery of declared enemies of the Republic, or a bitter dismay at their success in commending themselves to so many of their innocent countrymen.

I do not know what principle of decorum or dignity requires a legislator to feign indifference to the abuses of freedom by which the Communists continue to practice their malevolent designs upon us. I tend to feel rather that we are lacking in the passion for justice which true anger can effectively express, and I shall not criticize the man who engages the Communists and occasionally, by rhetorical accent or barbed word, betrays his sense of outrage.

They should not behave as politicians? I grant the more general proposition, that politicians should not behave like politicians, but until that law is enacted (and where will you find the politicians to vote for it?) it is, as Mr. James Burnham indicates in Chapter 2, foolish to expect otherwise. The members of the House Committee unquestionably will mint political credit out of what they do (and suffer the complementary liabilities), as would the members of a housing or antimonopoly committee. It hardly seems fair to demand of a Congressman that he renew his mandate every two years, that he spend a considerable amount of his time during those two years on the problems of internal security, and that he should desist, in his public relations with his constituency, from publicizing his own Committee's work, and his role in it.

If one seeks a more human explanation of the concentration by the members of HUAC on the Committee's activities, let us reflect on the truism that most men become engrossed in the work they are doing, tend to attach to it a significance that may be out of proportion in considering the sum of the human predicament. For instance, there are in our midst men who devote almost full time to the derogation of the House Committee on Un-American Activities, who pronounce its abolition the single most important Congressional reform on the agenda of progress. It is strange that many of these persons should in turn be surprised at the zeal with which those Congressmen who are members of the Committee insist on the Committee's continuing importance.

And the final argument against the personnel of the Committee: that they do not know enough. Once again it becomes necessary to admit that nobody really knows enough—and certainly that would seem true of those who had a hand in shaping American foreign policy during the period when the Communists engorged a third of the members of the human race.

But beyond that I venture to say, always with due respect to the professional academicians who have contributed to this volume and many others, that the Committee on Un-American Activities is responsible for the development of more serious information, of a didactically useful kind, than the typical department of political science in the typical university. The reader who is shocked by what appears so exorbitant a claim should, before rejecting it out of hand, read closely the extraordinary chapter that concludes this book, which is simply a catalogue, a drastic truncation of the hearings held by HUAC during the past fifteen years, and of the reports it has published. The scope is astonishing. What is the current strength of the Communists in the waterfront unions in Hawaii? What connection do the Communists maintain with organized gambling in Miami? How much money is the Soviet Union probably spending on paid propaganda in the Western Hemisphere? What is the opinion of a dozen Soviet experts on the impact of the Twentieth Congress on Communist thought? What loopholes have the Communists uncovered in the immigration laws? What is the role of political assassination in the advancement of Communist revolution? What is the biographical background of the dramatis personae of International Communism? What does Professor David Dallin's extensively documented graph of the movements in the Party line suggest is in store for the West? How does Professor Gerhart Niemeyer reckon the current bearing of Marxist-Leninist ideology on Soviet policy? Hundreds of hearings, a thousand publications, a library of expert testimony, qualify the work of the Committee as a supremely valuable repository of expert knowledge on the scope and meaning and particularities of the Communist enterprise, a source more valuable by far than what the typical student, taking every course in the curriculum, is likely to come up against in a major university in his quest for a profound understanding of the most vital problem of our time. Supplement it with a reading of the relevant works of Koestler, Camus, Burnham, Meyer Chambers, Sperber, Orwell, Malraux, Conrad, and you will arrive at something like true understanding. How one wishes that the last three Presidents of the United States had read and understood some of the literature HUAC has made available!

The scholar may scorn some of HUAC's reports as simplistic, but these are, in the main, merely simple expressions (as in an elementary catechism) of profound studies to which some of the best-informed minds in the country have contributed. All of the members of the House Committee on Un-American Activities may not be qualified to earn doctoral degrees in political science. But they seem nevertheless to have shown an intuitive apprehension of Communism which by empirical standards seems truer than that of some of our most conspicuous and learned academic and journalistic Kremlinologists. No doubt it would do the members and staff of HUAC good to spend a year at Harvard perfecting their knowledge of the history and theory of Communism. But it might be more in point for some of the professors at Harvard—and Kenyon—to spend a year studying the literature of the House Committee on Un-American Activities—or, even better, a year sitting through the Committee's hearings, and reflecting on their context.

We grope, finally, for the critical delinquency of the intellectuals as it relates to the House Committee on Un-American Activities and the national effort against internal-external subversion. There has been, I believe, a default by the academic profession, which has failed to put its enormous intellectual resources to work on the problem of how to craft sensitive and relevant and enforceable legislation which *can* be counted upon to make the necessary distinction between the heretic and the conspirator, to guide a Committee which, for all its experience, has failed to come up with truly satisfactory legislation aimed at encumbering and neutralizing the operations of the Soviet apparatus, covert and overt. The legislation that has been passed at the instigation of the Committee is, to be sure, much of it useful. But much of it is not, and a certain amount of it is a mess. It took *eleven years* for the Supreme Court to render a decision on the constitutionality of the Internal Security Act. Yet even now, it is by no means ascertained whether the law will prove an enforceable impediment against the Communists in an age when subversion is so critical an instrument in international affairs. Here is where the intellectual community might have come to the nation's rescue by putting forth its best efforts, much as it tried to do in attempting to prepare the postwar world for the special problems of international government, and continues to try to do with respect to the problems of public policy as regards the relationship between the races, and the workings of the economy. The literature on the problem of internal security has been almost exclusively antagonistic and irrelevant: a mechanical and abstract projection of the platonic principles of John Stuart Mill's open society, a hostile and ideologized refusal to understand that the problems of internal security do exist, that they are real, that the members of Congress are truly and justly concerned with the morphological innocence of our present laws in an age of scientific revolution. The intellectuals might, in a word, have helped the Committee along more than they have done. Instead, their operating premise (cf. the works on the subject of Robert Carr, Henry Steele Commager, James Wechsler, Alan Barth, Zechariah Chafee, Telford Taylor, *et al.*) seems to be: How shall we make it painless for an American citizen to contribute to the subversion of his country?

The profoundest question at issue is whether the open
society can tolerate an unassimilable political minority if it is
in league with great and powerful and hostile foreign forces;
specifically, whether the open society can tolerate Communists-
at-large. The answer one most often hears at centers of elevated
thought is a complacent pooh-pooh—based on the conspiracy's
admittedly small membership. Another response, more con-
gruent with reality, some of us believe, focuses not on the
exiguous membership of the Communist Party, but on its
capacity, considering always its great international resources
and contemporary concentrations of power, to do irreparable
damage. In his dreams, Archimedes could not have fancied a
lever greater than modern technology has given to the critically
situated saboteur. The relatively new science of opinion subversion (see Chapter 3) can have—indeed, has had—lethal consequences for millions of people. There are fewer Communist
Party members in America today than twenty years ago, but
America is in greater peril from Communists in general, and as
the power of the enemy abroad increases, so necessarily does his
arm here, unless we chop it off. It may be that the West is going
to lose this one because of an organic sickness of which the
First World War was the most drastic symptom. Marxist
theology may be wrong in its diagnosis of the causes of the
Western decline, while still being right in believing that the
West's illness is terminal. One of our problems is our enslave-
ment to abstractions. It is an empirical question, not to be
answered by liberal dogmatic invocations, whether a Western
nation can pursue a truly effective pro-Western policy (as Mr.
Irving Ferman maintains in this volume it can do) while ad-
hering to conventional libertarian attitudes toward the rights
and privileges of dissent. Our Republic was forged on the assumption—to be sure, explicitly skeptical—that nearly all points
of view are, if not equally honorable, at least equally tolerable.
Yet even Jefferson lifted himself up from some of his abstractions about the free society far enough to denounce some of
his contemporaries and their views as "swinish," and to consider
tampering with the judiciary in order to diminish their influ-

ence. Lincoln arrived painfully at the conclusion that some points of view were intolerable. These were men who, notwithstanding their devotion to the generally useful principle of freedom for dissenters, even for conspiratorial dissenters, acknowledged, with their pragmatic turn of mind, that requirements of reality transcend at the margin the abstract imperatives of the free society. It is only in our time that the idea of the open society was transmuted into Holy Writ, put forward as the first loyalty of free men. Before, the first loyalty of free men was to freedom—and freedom is not served by extending to the enemies of freedom, freedom to mine the city and whistle while they work. It is an ancient problem, how free men deal with the enemies of freedom. The superstition that the hounds of truth will rout the vermin of error seems, like a fragment of Victorian lace, quaint, but too brittle to be lifted out of the showcase. The tragedy is that at this moment, when the State is so gravely threatened, we find ourselves frozen in inaction by lofty and otherworldly pronouncements of John Stuart Mill. We need to make definitional strides forward in a political theory of freedom suitable to a world in which things like Communists and atom bombs exist. It is nothing short of preposterous willingly to tolerate an active conspiracy in our midst: and if the Constitution is not, as presently understood, resilient enough to cope with the contemporary requirements of survival, then the Constitution should be modified, as it has been before. The Congressional investigating Committee which is the object of this book writhes under the dilemma, and needs understanding and help from those who, desiring the perpetuation of freedom, will realize with Macaulay that "a nation may be placed in such a situation that the majority must either impose disabilities or submit to them, and that what would, under ordinary circumstances, be justly condemned as persecution, may fall within the bounds of legitimate self-defense."

WM. F. BUCKLEY, JR.

Stamford, Conn.
December, 1961

Chapter | THE INVESTIGATING POWER
2. | OF CONGRESS

THE *questions are raised: Has Congress, in authoriz-*
ing the House Committee on Un-American Activities, licensed a
Congressional body with extraordinary powers, the likes of
which have not been exercised by other Congressional com-
mittees in American constitutional experience? Have other
committees dealt in exposure to the extent this one does? What
if any are the limits to the so-called informing power of
Congress? Does the debate over HUAC bear on the continuing
tension between the legislature and the Executive for supremacy?
What techniques are being used by the executive to press its
claims, and do they contravene traditional requirements for the
separation of powers?

Many of its admirers as well as most of its critics believe
that HUAC is an exceptional or even unique institution. This
premise, indeed, is one of the factors that make a rational discussion of HUAC so difficult. The truly unique is not discuss-
able, since no abstract or general terms apply to it. Confronting
the unique, we can respond only by direct intuition, feeling and
taste. Concerning tastes, we have learned, there is no discussing.

The premise of uniqueness is, however, mistaken. Except for the bare quantity of the words, spoken and written, that have been devoted to it, there is nothing very special about HUAC. It is a member of a large and familiar class, just one legislative committee among thousands of legislative committees past, present and to be, that have come and gone as part of the working apparatus of republican and parliamentary governments. In the House of Representatives, HUAC is one of nineteen regular ("standing") committees that are given routine approval and appropriations at the opening of each new biennial Congress. There is nothing about HUAC's origin, composition, interests, methods, which cannot be matched in the history of a dozen or a hundred other committees of today or yesterday. Nor is there anything exceptional—except again, perhaps, in volume and persistence—about the heat of the public controversies that have raged around it.

HUAC is one of the organizational instruments devised by Congress to exercise one of the attributes of sovereignty that is usually called "the investigatory power" or "power of inquiry." Where sovereignty is divided among several institutions, or "branches," as in our governmental system, this investigatory power, or attribute, has been generally understood to inhere in the legislature. Naturally enough: for how could the lawmakers legislate wisely if they did not have the power to assemble, and if necessary uncover, the relevant facts? The Fathers of our own Constitution took for granted that the power of investigation and inquiry is implicit in the legislative function. The power being self-evident, there was no need to mention it in the written charter that issued from the Philadelphia convention. From the earliest years of our government under the Constitution, and ever since, legislative investigations have been an active part of our governmental system.

The Fathers continued in this, as in so much, the prior tradition of the English Parliament and the assemblies of the separate colonies. Formal parliamentary investigations in England date back at least to the sixteenth century. The first—into certain election disputes—is dated by most authorities about 1571.[1]

In the seventeenth century, parliamentary investigations were of fairly common occurrence, and the records of a number of them still exist. In the 1604 case of Sir Francis Goodman, Parliament gave a committee the crucial authority to summon witnesses and require the production of records. In 1681, Sheriff Acton was sentenced to the Tower of London for lying to a "Committee for the Examination of the Merchants' Business." As early as 1666 the Commons had set up a supervisory committee similar to our own Senate's present-day Committee on Government Operations.

In 1689 the Commons appointed a Select Committee "to inquire who has been the Occasion of the Delays in sending Relief over Ireland, and particularly to Londonderry"; and in the same year a committee—in the direct line of HUAC's ancestry—was authorized to investigate espionage in the Irish wars, with power "to send for persons and papers." This power to send for persons and papers, it should be noted, included the corollary power to punish the persons if they failed to come when sent for, or refused to produce the papers and to talk when they did appear. In the years following, other committees were appointed to supervise administrative agencies and their personnel.

The colonial assemblies in America assumed the investigatory power as a normal part of their business, and were sustained therein by the courts. Accounts of colonial investigations survive from most of the colonies, especially Massachusetts, New York, Pennsylvania and Virginia. In 1722, the Massachusetts Assembly summoned a Colonel Waltin and Major Moody for questioning on the military operations in Maine. As a result, both officers were retired from the service. Still earlier, in 1691, the New York Assembly had imprisoned the French minister, Mr. Dally, for refusing to answer questions. A few years later, it imprisoned George Webb for insulting, and R. Richards for assaulting, a member. The thirteen constitutions adopted during the revolutionary period by the newly independent colonies expressed in nine cases, and in the other four clearly implied, the power of the legislature to punish for contempt.

Under the federal Constitution the first formal Congressional investigation was undertaken by a select committee of the House in 1792. A military expedition under General Arthur St. Clair had been almost annihilated by an Indian ambush in the Northwest Territory. There was widespread popular concern, talk of possible treachery as well as incompetence, and a demand for a public accounting.

The House voted an "inquiry into the causes of the late defeat of Major General St. Clair." In the discussion before the vote was taken, some members argued that it would be insulting to President Washington, and that he should be requested to conduct the investigation through the Executive branch—a proposal echoed in our day by those critics of HUAC who insist that its functions ought to be performed by the FBI or some other Executive agency. On that first appearance of this point of view, in 1792, Representative H. Smith of South Carolina, in rejecting the alternative, expressed the conviction of the majority: "This House is the grand inquest of the nation."

In the hearings that followed, the Secretaries of the Treasury and of War were among the witnesses. General St. Clair was found to have displayed "coolness and intrepidity," and was exonerated of any personal guilt, but study of the testimony led to a number of changes in War Department policy and procedures.

Only three subsequent Congresses have failed to initiate investigations. There had been about thirty by 1814 and, according to Professor Dimock, three hundred and thirty through 1928. Since then, as the investigatory power has increased its relative strength in the weakening Congressional arsenal, the rate has so greatly quickened that there have been more than twice as many investigations in the generation following 1933 as during the government's entire preceding history.

It would be hard to name a topic of even the smallest public concern that has not been the target of a Congressional investigation.* The departments and major agencies of the Executive—

---

* Congress has, of course, often investigated the election qualifications of its own members, or the conduct of government officials in connection with possible impeachment proceedings. These two cases differ from other types of investigation, in that they are pursuant to explicit clauses of the Constitution, which herein assigns Congress a plainly judicial function.

to which investigations were more or less confined until 1827 —have all been investigated, most of them many times. Each of the nation's wars, except for the Spanish-American War (which was in a sense Congress's own conflict), has been diversely investigated. There have been investigations of all major branches of the economy: railroads, shipping, oil, banks, housing, insurance, utilities, munitions, agriculture, mining, investment and banking, communications, real estate, drugs, lobbying. In early days, the Post Office Department, which then operated in large part through subcontracts with private individuals, was a favorite and rewarding subject, as military departments and their procurement practices have always proved to be. For a century the customs houses periodically enticed investigatory ardor. Often Congress has instituted special investigations of scandals, riots and disasters: such as the investigation of the New Orleans riots in 1866 (or the San Francisco riots in 1960), the Crédit Mobilier scandal (1872–73), the Jay Cooke bankruptcy (1876), the Star Route mail contract scandals in Grant's Administration or the airmail scandals in the 1920's, the Alaska Purchase scandal, the Teapot Dome oil contracts (1924), various kinds of racketeering in recent years, the railway strike of 1886, irregularities in Daniel Webster's books (1846), or General Andrew Jackson's conduct of the Seminole War (1818).

Investigations of alleged conspiracy, espionage and subversion are by no means a mid-twentieth-century novelty. In many of the early English and colonial investigations, such possibilities were at issue, as they were directly in the General St. Clair inquiry, and indirectly at least in numerous of the investigations mentioned in the preceding paragraph. Before 1800, espionage in relation to France and Spain was several times a subject of Congressional investigation. In 1810 a committee was instructed to inquire into a reported conspiracy through which General James Wilkinson "corruptly received money from the government of Spain or its agents," and more generally into the relations with foreign agents. Full-scale investigations probed the Aaron Burr conspiracy (1808) and John Brown's raid (1859).

The roughest of our present-day investigators of Communism are models of courtesy compared to some of their predecessors. Fletcher Pratt describes Senator Ben Wade, chairman of the famous Committee on the Conduct of the [Civil] War (which concerned itself frequently with charges of subversion, treachery and conspiracy): "Barrel-chested, vulgar, shrewd, and violent, [he] kept a sawed-off shotgun in his desk . . . and tried every means he knew to provoke some of the Southern fire-eaters into calling him out, for he was a deadly shot." [2]

John Quincy Adams tells in his diary how a witness named Reuben Whitney was handled by an 1837 investigating committee: "[Representative] Bailie [Balie?] Payton, of Tenn., taking offense at one of his answers, threatened him fiercely, and when he rose to claim the committee's protection, Mr. Peyton, with due and appropriate profanity, shouted: 'You shan't say a word while you are in this room; if you do I will put you to death.' The Chairman, Henry A. Wise, added: 'Yes, this insolence is insufferable.' As both of these gentlemen were armed with deadly weapons, the witness could hardly be blamed for not wanting to testify again."

Of Adams' own inquisitorial abilities, a colleague admiringly observed: "He has . . . an instinct for the jugular and the carotid artery, as unerring as that of any carnivorous animal."

2

The investigatory power of the legislature, both federal and state, has been developed further within the American than within any other political system. The British Government also disposes of a formidable power of inquiry, exercised through parliamentary committees, royal commissions and "special tribunals." In the past this was a rod often used to chasten the King and his agents; but within the structure of modern "responsible" (i.e., Cabinet) government, it does not have much effect on the general power equilibrium. In non-Anglo-Saxon nations, the development of an independent investigatory power—where it exists—in all cases falls much short of the American level.

The investigatory, like the treaty power, is "an extraordinary power, liable to abuse." [3] Although it is interpreted formally as an expression of the legislative function, in actuality it has also, in some cases, quasi-judicial and administrative—that is, executive—aspects. Investigating bodies cannot, like courts, convict and punish a defendant for crimes of substance, but they can and often have created situations that lead to subsequent conviction and punishment. Even without later court action, the publicity attendant on investigations has been the cause of social, economic and political sanctions against witnesses; and sometimes, when the publicity has been favorable, of rewards rather than sanctions. Moreover, by disclosures, political threats and other pressures, investigations can indirectly intervene, sometimes rather intimately, in the administrative process. Such consequences as these are not something novel that appeared on the public scene with the advent of HUAC. They have always been involved in the investigating process, and have been well known for centuries.

In order to understand the investigatory power, it is necessary to define the precise conditions under which that power attains its full flexibility and amplitude. The essential conditions are three. First, the investigator (individual, committee or other corporate body) must have the power of compulsion, the power to compel the presence and testimony of persons, and the production of documents. This of course implies the power to punish a refusal to appear and to testify, or to produce documents on order. Second, the investigator must himself have personal immunity for his conduct of the investigation. He must not be subject to any legal, police or any other official reprisal for anything that, as investigator, he may do. And finally, he, or the body of which he is a member or agent, must have autonomy with respect to the investigation: that is, must not be restricted in the exercise of the investigatory power by any other person or institution.

Congress has traditionally claimed that all three of these

conditions—the power of compulsion, immunity, autonomy—hold for its investigatory power; and Congress has never formally acknowledged any limitation on any of the three. They hold, on the traditional view, for investigations into the acts of any and all persons within the jurisdiction of the United States, except possibly the President and the Justices of the Supreme Court. Even this minimum restriction has never been formally admitted, and does not in any case apply to an investigation that might be motivated, or be said to be motivated, by the possibility of impeachment. Nor has Congress ever acknowledged any limitation (except as may be self-imposed) on the subject matter that may be inquired into. It has always been recognized that the strict courtroom rules of evidence and procedure do not hold unqualifiedly for the nonpunitive and necessarily looser type of inquiry undertaken by an investigating committee. In early years, in fact, some members of Congress maintained that the first ten (Bill of Rights) Amendments do not apply to Congressional investigations. It was more than a century after adoption of the Constitution before anyone suggested that a Fifth Amendment "privilege against self-incrimination" was relevant to a Congressional investigation.

In 1860, during the Senate debate over the inquiry into John Brown's raid on Harper's Ferry, Senator William P. Fessenden of Maine—though a Northerner and altogether out of sympathy with that inquiry's objective—asserted in unshaded terms the traditional claim of Congress to investigatory autonomy: "Congress have appointed committee after committee time after time, to make inquiries on subjects of legislation. Had we not the power to do it? Nobody questioned our authority to do it. We have given them authority to send for persons and papers. . . . Have we not that authority, if necessary to legislation? Who is to be the judge as to our duties necessary to legislation? [The people] have made us their Legislature. . . . The people [and only the people] have power over us." [4]

This extreme interpretation of the investigatory power is rigorously logical. The first section of the first article of the Constitution vests *all* legislative powers in Congress. If the investigatory power is—as it is granted to be—a legislative power, then, in pure logic, it is for Congress and Congress alone to decide how the investigatory power is to be used. Of course, like any other power, this will be subject to the provisions of the Constitution; but—again by pure logic—it will also be for Congress to give its own interpretation to these provisions. To submit the investigatory power to restrictions and interpretations issuing from the courts or from the Executive means to deny the exclusively legislative character of this power, which is granted in the premise.

Such a rigorous, univocal, abstractly logical application of any political premise is, however, contrary to the genius of the American tradition. In practice, rules and limits governing the exercise of the investigatory power have been gradually formed over the years. Most of these have been imposed by the two Houses of Congress on themselves. Congress has accepted others—whether cheerfully or not—from the courts or (for inquiries concerning the Executive) from the practice of the Executive. In neither case, however, has Congress ever formally admitted the right of the other branches to intervene in what it continues to assert as its own exclusive prerogative.

3

The specific power to compel testimony by the threat of appropriate sanctions is of the essence of a true investigatory power. Prior to 1857 and occasionally thereafter, Congress itself punished witnesses for contempt, without turning them over to the lengthy processes of court trial and appeal. A resolution would be passed: "That the Speaker do issue his warrant directed to the Sergeant-at-Arms attending the House, commanding him to take into custody, wherever to be found, the body of So-and-So, and the same in his custody to keep, subject to the further order and direction of the House." The contumacious witness would then be brought, physically, to the bar of the House (or Senate). If he refused to purge himself of his contempt (by answering the questions that had been put to him, if that was the issue), he would be "incarcerated" in "the common jail" of the District of Columbia.

This procedure was challenged in 1819 by one John Anderson, who sued Thomas Dunn, the then Sergeant-at-Arms of the House, for assault and battery, and false imprisonment, in having brought him under duress to the bar of the House to be "there reprimanded by the Speaker for the outrage he [had] committed" in trying to bribe a member. The Supreme Court, in *Anderson v. Dunn* (1821), rejected Anderson's charges and upheld the investigatory power of Congress, though the Court maintained, plausibly, that the derivative power to incarcerate a contumacious witness lasted only until the adjournment *sine die* of the session of Congress that had suffered the contempt.

In 1857 Congress enacted a law under which witnesses in contempt could be prosecuted. Thereafter, such prosecution rather than direct Congressional action became the usual procedure, and has never been challenged in principle.

In *Kilbourn v. Thompson* (1881), a case that grew out of the Jay Cooke bankruptcy, the Supreme Court asserted a limit to the right of Congress to inquire into private affairs unless these were charged with public interest. But in this decision no answer is given to the problem of who is to decide whether public interest is at stake. *In re Chapman* (1897), confirming the contempt conviction of a Senate witness, declared that a legislative intent must be presumed in a Congressional investigation: "We cannot assume on this record that the action of the Senate was without a legitimate object, and so encroach upon the province of that body. . . . It was certainly not necessary that the resolutions should declare in advance what the Senate meditated doing when the investigation was concluded." As the Court further observed in *United States v. Bryan* (1947): "The exact scope of an investigation cannot always be charted and bounded in advance with the precision of a survey."

In *McGrain v. Daugherty* (1927), an aftermath of the Teapot Dome investigation, the Supreme Court summed up the traditional doctrine of the investigatory power in a sweeping affirmation of Congress's extraordinary prerogatives:

We are of the opinion that the power of inquiry—with process to enforce it—is an essential and appropriate auxiliary to the legislative function. It was so regarded and employed in American legislatures before the Constitution was framed and ratified. Both Houses of Congress took this view of it early in their history—the House of Representatives with the approving votes of Mr. Madison and other Members whose service in the Convention which framed the Constitution gives special significance to their action—and both Houses have employed the power accordingly up to the present time. . . .

A legislative body cannot legislate wisely or effectively in the absence of information respecting the conditions which the legislation is intended to affect or change; and where the legislative body does not itself possess the requisite information—which not infrequently is true—recourse must be made to others who do possess it. Experience has taught that mere requests for such information often are unavailing, and also that information which is volunteered is not always accurate or complete; so some means of compulsion are essential to obtain what is needed. All this was true before and when the Constitution was framed and adopted. In that period the power of inquiry—with enforcing process—was regarded and employed as a necessary and appropriate attribute of the power to legislate—indeed, was treated as inhering in it.

Anderson v. Dunn, the first of these judicial comments on the investigatory power of the legislature, had found, in effect, that the protection of the rights and liberty of citizens against the abuse of that power rested basically, not on the courts or on "the balance of powers," but on the representative and responsible nature of the legislative body: "Where all power is derived from the people, and public functionaries, at short intervals, deposit it at the feet of the people, to be resumed again only at their will, individual fears may be alarmed by the monsters of the imagination, but individual liberty can be in little danger."

This same conception, which implicitly singles out the investigatory power as unique among the powers of the American government, was repeated as late as 1948, in *Barsky v. United States,* a case decided by the District of Columbia Court of Appeals, and implicitly accepted by the Supreme Court by its refusal to review it on appeal: "The remedy for unseemly conduct, if any, by Committees of Congress is for Congress, or for the people. . . . The courts have no authority to speak or act upon the conduct of the legislative branch of its own business, so long as the bounds of power and pertinency are not exceeded."

4

From the formal standpoint which has usually been assumed by the courts in this country, the investigatory power is an expression or adjunct of the legislative function. In order to determine whether a new law is needed or whether an existing law needs changing, Congress requires relevant information. But since Congress is the body exclusively charged with the making and unmaking of laws, Congress cannot properly rely on any other person or body for such information. Congress must get its own information, in its own way and on its own responsibility; and it must have the power and resources to do so.

This legislative function may be further analyzed in terms of four related aims or purposes: (1) to gather information on the enactment, amendment or repeal of laws; (2) to check the consequences on the public weal of laws previously enacted; (3) to check the performance of the Executive and the bureaucracy in administering the laws; (4) to check how public moneys lawfully appropriated are actually being spent.

It is a fact that investigations have served these legislative aims, have been indeed virtually indispensable to their fulfillment. As a direct or indirect result of its investigations Congress has enacted, amended or repealed many laws on many subjects. This has been true throughout the nation's history: from the postal contract investigations of the early 1800's that brought reorganizations of the Post Office, through the 1860 Covode investigation of graft in printing contracts that led to the establishment of the Government Printing Office; to the New Deal probes of the 1930's that prepared for new banking acts, the Securities and Exchange Commission, and the National Labor Relations Board; to the inquiries of HUAC and the Senate's Internal Security Subcommittee that resulted in the Smith Act, the Internal Security Act, and so on (see Chapter 9). It should be added that investigations which reach the negative conclusion that no change in existing laws is necessary are also performing, often very sensibly just because negatively, a legislative function.

However, no matter what strict theory and court pronouncements may say, the investigatory power has never limited its operations to the legislative function in any strict or narrow meaning, but has been an active ingredient of the social and political process in a considerably wider sense. In this country, Congressional investigations have played a critical and repeated role in sustaining the delicate equilibrium that marks the traditional American system of government. On the stage of a major investigation, with the Court watching from the wings and the public in the stalls, the actors of the governmental drama—Congress, the Executive, the bureaucracy, the lobbyists, and individual citizens selected by accident or design to embody a force or a cause—issue their challenges and defiances, cross swords, join hands also, make and break pacts with and against each other, expose wrongdoing and boast of achievement.

In particular, the investigations have been the setting for the encounters of legislature and Executive, whose eternal conflict and co-operation, wedding and divorce, are an intended and inescapable part of the American political system. Although most Congressional inquiries dealing with problems of administration have been critical of the Executive, others have been friendly and some subservient. Agents of the Executive have themselves requested investigation of their own departments, following an example set by Oliver Wolcott when he withdrew in 1800 as Secretary of the Treasury. The need for this or that investigation has sometimes been suggested by the Executive. In Woodrow Wilson's first three years and (still more notably) Franklin Roosevelt's first six, Congressional investigations became almost an operating arm of the Executive in advancing the policies of the White House; and this has again been the case with some of the investigations conducted during the first period of the Kennedy Administration. If investigations have been more naturally and frequently an occasion for conflict between legislature and Executive, they have also provided a device for communication and mutual aid.

Performing a legislative function and helping to sustain the governmental equilibrium do not exhaust the range of the investigatory power. It has been well understood from early days that the investigatory process can be used to foster political ambitions. The 1819 investigation of the Arbuthnot and Ambrister court-martial, decided in Andrew Jackson's favor, launched him toward the White House. Daniel Webster used investigations to expand his fame and to try to rouse a call for his own Presidential services. The "Covode Inquisition" into the Buchanan Administration helped prepare Lincoln's election. Senators Thomas Walsh and Burton Wheeler made their public mark as inquisitors of the 1920's. Few had heard of the young Ferdinand Pecora until the New Deal banking investigation, with its roll call of the mighty, and the circus dwarf on the elder J. P. Morgan's lap. It does not seem likely that Hugo Black would sit today on the Supreme Court, there so strict a censor of current inquiries, if he had not headed so spectacular, and so ruthless, an investigation; or that Harry Truman would have been picked to run with Franklin Roosevelt in 1944 if it had not been for his wartime record on the Senate Special Committee Investigating the National Defense Program. It was the televised inquiry into gambling and big-city rackets that got Estes Kefauver his Vice-Presidential nomination. Robert Kennedy's role in a big-scale investigation of labor and management malpractices gave a powerful boost to his brother's candidacy for the White House. Martin Dies, Pat McCarran, Joseph McCarthy and Francis Walter became nationally known, for better or worse, through the investigations of subversion. The frequency with which investigations have become the path toward public fame is a consequence not only of the drama to which such hearings naturally incline, but also of an intuitive public awareness of the importance of the investigatory power in our political system.

Just as investigations are sometimes used to advance the public fortunes of an aspiring inquisitor, so can they serve as a weapon against an opponent or victim. The disclosures of investigating committees, though without judicial force, can virtually compel the prosecution of exposed witnesses, or their discharge from their jobs. Without any subsequent official action, some witnesses have suffered the adverse social consequences of a battered reputation. As a traceable result of the Teapot Dome investigations in the 1920's, three Cabinet members were compelled to resign, of whom one went later to jail and one died while awaiting trial; two witnesses committed suicide; four oil millionaires skipped the country; and numerous other individuals were jailed or fined sums up to several million dollars.

This spectacular aftermath was probably a record, but on a more modest scale sanctions against individuals have been common enough. Investigations of lobbying, gambling and racketeering have led to many indictments. In the early 1950's, the committees investigating subversion developed a routine technique through which witnesses with "sensitive" jobs in defense industry who "took the Fifth" [5] at a committee hearing would then be fired by their employers. Both Alger Hiss and Whittaker Chambers lost highly paid jobs, and Hiss ended up in prison, as a result of a HUAC investigation. Scores of persons, both citizens and aliens, scampered abroad, and scores more were barred from government posts, in the wake of Internal Security Subcommittee and HUAC inquiries into the Institute of Pacific Relations and wartime espionage. A number of State Department officials—such as John Carter Vincent and John Paton Davies—lost their posts in consequence of their testimony before Congressional inquisitors. The cause-and-effect relation is sometimes astonishingly abrupt: as when in 1957, M. S. Pitzele was discharged from his jobs with both New York State and the McGraw-Hill publishing company immediately after he received unfavorable publicity from his testimony before the Senate committee investigating labor rackets.

When Congressional investigations are made part of a process that leads to the imprisonment or fining of individuals, or to the firing or job reassignment of employees of the government's Executive branch, then the investigating committees are performing judicial and executive rather than purely legislative tasks. When they injure (or inflate) the reputation or livelihood of individual private citizens, they become part of the apparatus by which public opinion, through its complex arsenal of social pressures, approvals and threats, tries to keep individuals within certain implicit customary and moral boundaries. By critics of the investigatory power the first two extra-legislative side effects are regarded as "encroachments" on the constitutional provinces of the courts and the Presidency; and by the third, as a form of public relations or psychological terror. However judged or prejudged, they are further witness to the high social potential of the investigatory process.

Investigations are also a principal means by which Congress exercises "the informing function," which, though not mentioned in the Constitution and never recognized formally by the Supreme Court, is so integral an attribute of the legislature of a representative government that Woodrow Wilson concluded it "should be preferred even to its legislative function." * Even in ordinary debates, of course, Congress is incidentally carrying out an informing function which can be more deliberately exercised through an investigation focused on a subject matter of public importance. Through public investigation Congress informs the citizens about the nation's problems at the same time that it is informing itself.

The subject matter of investigations divides into two types that are often though not always linked in particular inquiries: first, the activities of private citizens or groups of citizens en-

---

* Cf. *Congressional Government* (Houghton Mifflin, 1885). Wilson's judgment here, as often, echoed Walter Bagehot, the great analyst of the British Constitution. See Chapter 8, B for a more extensive analysis of the informing powers of Congress in the light of the civil rights of witnesses.

gaged in economic, political or social pursuits having or felt to have a public interest; second, the activities of administrative (and occasionally the judicial) officials and employees of the government itself.

With respect to the first type (into private activities), Congressional investigations have often been one of the most important sources of public information concerning the great problems that have arisen in one field after another during the course of the nation's development: banking and finance, transport, communications, mining, power, education, labor relations, lobbying, subversion, shipping, charity, etc. HUAC and its predecessor of the 1920's (the Buchanan committee) were much in advance of any agencies of other branches of the government and of all but a handful of private individuals and institutions in giving serious attention to totalitarian subversion, espionage, infiltration and political warfare, which constitute probably the crucial problem of our century.

With respect to the second type (into governmental administration), Congressional inquiry is often the only method by which the conduct of the Executive and the bureaucracy can be brought into the light. In Woodrow Wilson's words:

There is some scandal and discomfort, but infinite advantage, in having every affair of administration subjected to the test of constant examination on the part of the assembly which represents the nation. The chief use of such inquisition is, not the direction of those affairs in a way with which the country will be satisfied ... but the enlightenment of the people, which is always its sure consequence. . . .

Unless Congress have and use every means of acquainting itself with the acts and the disposition of the administrative agents of the government, the country must be helpless to learn how it is being served; and unless Congress both scrutinize these things and sift them by every form of discussion, the country must remain in embarrassing, crippling ignorance of the very affairs which it is most important that it should understand and direct. . . . The argument is not only that discussed and interrogated administration is the only pure and efficient administration, but, more than that, that the only really self-governing people is that people which discusses and interrogates its administration.[6]

5

In the past, Congressional investigations have been frequently and sharply attacked. The 1923–24 investigations into the oil industry and the Departments of the Navy and Justice were condemned by Owen J. Roberts (later a Supreme Court Justice), speaking before the American Bankers Association, as mere "propaganda for nationalization." The *Wall Street Journal* dismissed them as a "political smokescreen." *The New York Times* declared that Congress was "investigation-mad," and was trying to introduce "government by clamor [and] hole in corner gossip." The *Times* (in February 1924) upheld Attorney General Daugherty as a sturdy patriot who was defending "decency [and] honor... the honor which ought to prevail among gentlemen, if not among politicians." * In the same month the Communist *Daily Worker* created the label "smelling committees."

A few years earlier Walter Lippmann, in his book *Public Opinion,* had described investigations as "that legalized atrocity ... where Congressmen, starved of their legitimate food for thought, go on a wild and feverish man-hunt, and do not stop at cannibalism." In 1925 the influential legal authority, J. H. Wigmore, characterized the investigators as "on the level of professional searchers of the municipal dunghills." The investigators to whom Wigmore was thus referring (Senators Walsh, Wheeler, Borah and La Follette) were also termed, in the contemporary press, "scandal-mongers," "mud-gunners," "assassins of character." Their inquiries were described as "lynching bees," "poisoned-tongued partisanship, pure malice, and twittering hysteria," and "in plain words, contemptible and disgusting."

* Within six months Daugherty had resigned in disgrace, after the investigators had shown that during his two and a half years in Washington on a $15,000 salary, his personal holdings had shifted from a $19,000 debt to a $100,000 fortune.

A decade later the New Deal inquiries into investment, banking, utilities, and munitions were the targets for denunciations comparable in content though less colorful in rhetoric. Long before, Congressional investigating methods had been eloquently criticized even from the floor of Congress itself. In 1860, during the course of the Senate inquiry into John Brown's raid, Senator Charles Sumner defended a contumacious witness, Thaddeus Hyatt, who had been "incarcerated in the filthy jail" for having refused to answer the committee's questions: "To aid a committee of this body merely in a legislative purpose, a citizen, guilty of no crime, charged with no offense, presumed to be innocent, honored and beloved in his neighborhood, may be seized, handcuffed, kidnapped, and dragged away from his home, hurried across State lines, brought here as a criminal, and then thrust into jail." [7]

Senator John P. Hale of New Hampshire, agreeing with his colleague from Massachusetts, declared: "I ask ... if there ever was a despotism on earth that could define its position more satisfactorily than that? ... If Louis Napoleon has more than that I think he would be willing to give it up readily."

Sumner's rhetoric, in antiphony, swelled still higher: "For myself, sir, I confess a feeling of gratitude to the witness [Hyatt], who, knowing nothing which he desires to conceal, and chiefly anxious that the liberties of all might not suffer through him, feeble in body and broken in health, hardly able to endure the fatigue of appearing at your bar, now braves the prison which you menace, and thrusts his arm as a bolt to arrest an unauthorized and arbitrary proceeding." (The critics of HUAC would seem to be offering nothing new in content, and to have declined considerably in the vigor of their rhetoric.)

Generally speaking, as these prominent instances suggest, and as is natural enough, it is not unusually the gored ox that bellows. Whether well-grounded or not, lively Congressional inquiries usually threaten institutionalized as well as individual interests. The spokesmen and friends of these interests, along with the individuals directly involved, fight back as best they can. Usually the best defense, in a public polemic, is to drop the question of one's own private concern out of sight, and to counterattack either with *ad hominem* grapeshot or with seemingly general considerations of propriety, morals and political philosophy.

It was natural enough that the *Wall Street Journal,* the American Bankers Association, *The New York Times* (as edited in the 1920's) and the Hearst press (with large Hearst mining interests in the background) should look with initial disfavor on a probing of oil leases by a partisan and already suspect Public Lands Committee. The established banking and investment interests, the utility holding companies, and the great industrial corporations that had armed the nation for the First World War could not, even though cowed by a long depression, welcome the inquiries of the 1930's into their carefully unpublic ways. Naturally the drug industry does not relish Senator Kefauver's examination of its exceedingly involved pricing policies; and naturally the Communists, fellow travelers and dupes who are the primary targets of HUAC's explorations dislike HUAC. John Brown was a martyred hero of the abolitionists, who had provoked and financed his raid on Harper's Ferry. The abolitionist Senators from New England could hardly have been expected to favor an investigation, headed by a Senator from Virginia, which was likely to confirm the formal case against Brown and to uncover the links in the conspiracy. It was no doubt natural also that the committee chairman from Virginia, James M. Mason, and Senator Jefferson Davis from Mississippi made the replies that Senators Sumner and Hale might have formulated if the interests at stake had been reversed:

Jefferson Davis: "How shallow the plea is, when a witness is brought here for great purposes, that he should say his conscience was too tender to tell the truth. What criminal, or what man who had been in a conspiracy, criminal in all its ends and aims, would not shelter himself, when commanded before a Committee to testify, if his tender conscience at the last hour, when steeped in crime and treason, might plead against the right of a Committee to know from him the truth?"

James Mason: "The matter inquired into here . . . was matter

affecting the very existence of this government—treasonable purposes; and if there is any citizen in the land who can give information on the subject, he is bound by every obligation of honor,
of duty, of loyalty to his country, voluntarily to come; not to
seek to avoid this duty by evasion, or subterfuge, or pretense
that his conscience will not allow him to give his testimony."

On that particular occasion, in the passions of that debate, it
happened to be two men of the South who explained the duties
of the Congress and the citizens when dealing with "matter
affecting the very existence of this government—treasonable
purposes." But whenever in our history Congress has been faced
with that "matter," there have always been voices to give utter-
ance to those same imperatives, and the Congress as a collective
body has never failed to listen.

6

I do not mean to suggest that all of these past criticisms of
Congressional inquiries have been biased or hypocritical. It
may be presumed that Dean Wigmore was concerned primarily
with the investigative procedures that are too coarse for so
judicially oriented a mind as his was. Mr. Lippmann has been
long and persistently critical of investigations differing widely
in subject matter and political direction. Many good citizens
have criticized the inquiries into subversion not from any
softness to world Communism but out of a sincere if sometimes
confused or obsessive worry over freedom of speech and association.

Until recent years, most of the attacks on investigations, like
the defending replies, have been specific in their impetus:
against this particular inquiry or related set of inquiries. The
legislative inquiry as an accredited institution of the American
political system has not been in dispute. The critics did not
question Congress's right to investigate, with adequate compulsory sanctions, in its own way and on its own sovereign
authority. In the Senate debate over the Harper's Ferry inquiry,
the critics made their appeal for gentler treatment of Hyatt to

the Senate itself. They did not suggest superseding recourse to the courts or to the Executive. Senator Hale, recognizing that he and Sumner would lose the vote in the Chamber and not questioning its power to act as it saw fit, directed his words to what was logically the only supreme tribunal of a sovereign legislature: "You may imprison him; you may lock him up; you may make his bars and his bolts fast, and turn your key upon him; but I tell you that the great *habeas corpus* of freemen, the ballot, will reverse your judgment, and pronounce sentence of condemnation, not on him, but on you."

During the past fifteen years, the perennial attacks on Congressional investigations, or on some of them, have widened their range. Although they have been mounted for the most part in relation to the inquiries dealing with Communism and other forms of subversion, they are no longer specific and limited. In fact, they are no longer attacks on investigations, but on the investigatory power, and they have come from many directions: from journalists, cartoonists, publicists and academicians; from the courts; from the Executive; and even from within Congress itself.

The postwar attacks have centered on the inquiries dealing with subversion, and have thus been directed primarily against HUAC, the Internal Security Subcommittee of the Senate Judiciary Committee, and on occasions—especially when Senator Joseph McCarthy was its chairman—the Subcommittee on Investigations of the Senate Committee on Government Operations. This focus is significant for an evaluation of the attacks. Undoubtedly these three committees have from time to time been guilty of procedural excesses and other abuses of their power. But this has been true of many other investigating committees of the present as of the past. Senator Estes Kefauver's conduct in his probes, a few years ago, of gambling and racketeering, and in his more recent pricing and antimonopoly inquiries; the questioning of Bernard Goldfine and his associates by the House Subcommittee on Legislative Oversight; Robert Kennedy's methods both inside and outside the committee room in the investigation of labor and management malpractices—conspicuously including his dealings with the press—these are examples from the list of recent investigations that have offended due process, the rights of witnesses and the trust of the public more grossly than the three target committees dealing with subversion.

The primary target of the attacks, then, is a particular set of committees dealing with the particular subject matter of subversion. But for the very reason that the nature and methods of these committees does not differ in any significant way from those of the other Congressional committees of the present and past, an assault on these few becomes inevitably, in its implications, an assault on all. That is, the persisting attacks on these particular investigations become, implicitly, attacks on the investigatory power.

7

The opponents and critics of the Congressional investigations seldom call explicitly for the abolition of the investigatory power; that is, they do not state that Congress should be altogether deprived of the right and power to make investigations. Their public argument is, rather, that the investigations should be curbed, limited and controlled in such ways as to protect due process, and to prevent what are held to be demagogic exploitation of the investigative process, encroachments on the Executive or Judiciary, and violations of the rights of privacy, freedom of speech, belief and association.

It was explained above that the investigatory power can operate with full flexibility and amplitude only if the investigator possesses the three essential conditions of autonomy, immunity, and the power of compulsion. The net effect of most of the critical proposals is to weaken one or another of these conditions, and thereby dilute the investigatory power itself. For example, it is obvious that the acceptance of the Fifth Amendment plea as a valid ground for refusal to answer questions in a Congressional inquiry—a modern innovation—weakens the investigator's power of compulsion. It would be much further weakened, indeed almost destroyed, if pleas of the First Amendment (freedom of speech and belief) and of "privacy" were allowed, as has been repeatedly proposed in both good and bad faith—in connection, for instance, with questions about former associates in subversive organizations, or about personal adherence thereto.

In the censure proceedings against Senator McCarthy, the immunity necessary to a plenary investigator was at least indirectly involved, since he was being tried or judged in part for actions performed in an official capacity as a Congressional investigator. But in that affair Congress was at any rate itself judging itself, so that the autonomy of the investigatory power was not brought in question. When the courts intervene to prescribe for the investigation, or when the Executive defies an investigating committee, this autonomy is also, in one or another degree, violated, and the investigatory power is to that extent thwarted or destroyed.

As pictured by Communist and by many Liberal cartoonists, led by Herblock, Fitzgerald and Mauldin, the typical Congressional investigator is either a gangster, a Star Chamber hanging judge, or a rubber-truncheoned fascist. Over the past fifteen years, thousands of editorials, articles, monographs, lectures and sermons have condemned the investigating committees, their methods, their results and their most prominent members. In 1955 two general books—Alan Barth's *Government by Inquisition* and Telford Taylor's *Grand Inquest*—broadened the adverse critique that had been undertaken by such preliminary studies as Professor Robert K. Carr's *The House Committee on Un-American Activities*. In 1961 Frank J. Donner renewed the direct onslaught on HUAC with a book, called with disarming simplicity *The Un-Americans,* that is dedicated to the proposition that HUAC must be immediately abolished.* Besides the Communist Party itself, and a variety of its *ad hoc*

---

* The author of *The Un-Americans* has been identified under oath by three witnesses as a member of a Communist cell of lawyers that operated in Washington and in the National Labor Relations Board. In testifying before HUAC, he took the Fifth on all directly worded questions concerning Communist associations.

fronts, a number of non-Communist organizations—among them Americans for Democratic Action, the American Civil Liberties Union and the Committee for an Effective Congress—have in these recent years made the defects of investigations and investigators a principal element of their public agitation.

Concurrently with this massive campaign in the press, the schools and other organs of public opinion, the courts made a significant turn in their attitude toward the investigatory power. For more than a hundred and fifty years following adoption of the Constitution, the courts, led in this by the example of the Supreme Court, had deliberately shied away from intervention in the legislature's investigatory power. During that entire period, only a handful of cases arising out of investigations were even heard by the Court.[8] In 1927 the Court's traditional recognition of legislative autonomy with respect to the investigatory power was summed up by its sweeping decision in *McGrain v. Daugherty.* In the late 1940's, by refusing to review three lower court decisions that affirmed Congressional autonomy in investigations [9], the Court held fast to *McGrain v. Daugherty* against the anti-investigation clamor that was beginning to be heard in public.

Then, in a series of decisions that began with *Christoffel v. United States* (1950) and reached a high point in *Watkins v. United States* (1957), the Supreme Court asserted what could become by implication a general right to define the rules, limits, methods, scope and sanctions of the investigatory power. Most of these cases were appeals brought by various defendants (principally Communists or fellow travelers) against convictions for contempt of Congress for having refused to answer certain questions put to them by Congressional investigating committees—usually HUAC or the Internal Security Subcommittee. The Court did not attack the investigatory power directly. However, it threw out many of the convictions on such grounds as that due process had not been observed in the committee procedure, or that in the case of the disputed questions put to the defendants, "legislative intent" had not been demonstrated.

Now the real political and historical issue here is not whether due process and legislative intent were in some abstract sense defective. The most ardent defenders of the investigatory power of the legislature readily grant that inquiries should have, broadly at least, a legislative intent, and that their conduct should be in accord with relevant rules of due process. But the basic question is: Who shall decide, who shall say, whether due process and legislative intent are present? In the seven-year series, 1950–57, from *Christoffel* to *Watkins,* the Court was suggesting, if not quite saying, that *it* and not the Congress had the final say: from which it would follow that the Judiciary, not the elective legislature, has the final control over the investigatory power. In several subsequent (1960–61) decisions, such as *Barenblatt v. United States, Wilkinson v. United States* and *Braden v. United States,* the Court seems to have receded somewhat from the full implications of the *Christoffel-Watkins* series. But as for the meaning of *Watkins* itself, dissenting Justice Tom C. Clark believed it accurate to write that through the *Watkins* decision the Court was appointing itself "Grand Inquisitor and supervisor of Congressional investigations."

8

From the point of view of political meaning, the distinction has been made above between two quite different types of legislative inquiry: investigations into the activities of private citizens, associations and institutions, on the one hand; and on the other, investigations of the administration of government—that is, of the Executive branch and the bureaucracy. A particular investigation may and usually does combine the two types. HUAC and the Internal Security Subcommittee, for example, inquire into possible subversion as it may affect both private organizations and governmental agencies, since both cases concern the public interest. Indeed, this double character holds for most major investigations, especially in modern times when both governmental and nongovernmental activities are operative within nearly all major fields. Nevertheless, the functional distinction remains clear.

Most of the formal public arguments against investigations, and most of the cases that come before the courts, concern, primarily or exclusively, the first type of inquiry. It is alleged that the civil rights or personal life of private citizens who appear as witnesses are violated, and that the protection of these private rights is a duty that takes precedence over the possible public gains from investigating this or that subject matter. That is to say, the argument, whether justifiably or not, is cast in the form of: individual liberty *vs.* despotism.

For Americans, an argument in this form has roots in both tradition and rhetoric. It is persuasive to many citizens even apart from their opinion on the particular subject matter of the investigations which provoke the controversy, and the considerable arguments that appeal to the existential requirements of the state, and the traditional rights of the collectivity when it is threatened, fall on deaf ears, as we have seen. But inquiries into the doings of the Executive and the bureaucracy are of a different order, in which private and individual rights are only coincidentally at stake; and even they are now being challenged.

Traditionally it has never been questioned that the legislature possesses the power, as it was put in the early years, "to inquire into the honesty and efficiency of the Executive branch." Under the American system it is this that is the heart of the investigatory power. It is conceivable that, without a major constitutional transformation, Congress could cede all investigations of the affairs of private citizens to the Executive and the Judiciary. But if it lost the power to investigate the Executive, Congress would retain only the name of legislature.

The late Senator George Norris, once the dean of liberals, remarked during the disputes of 1924: "Whenever you take away from the legislative body of any country in the world the power of investigation, the power to look into the executive department of the government, you have taken a full step that will eventually lead into absolute monarchy and destroy any government such as ours."

Woodrow Wilson's distaste for many practices of Congress

did not lead him to obscure the basic relations. He repeats in numerous contexts the gist of his words quoted earlier:

Quite as important as legislation is vigilant oversight of administration. . . . An effective representative body [ought] to serve as [the nation's] eyes in superintending all matters of government. . . . There is some scandal and discomfort, but infinite advantage, in having every affair of administration subjected to the test of constant examination on the part of the assembly which represents the nation. . . . Congress is the only body which has the proper motive for inquiry. . . . It is the proper duty of a representative body to look diligently into every affair of government and to talk much about what it sees. . . .[10]

Professor McGeary has put the situation still more bluntly: "An administrator's knowledge that at some future time he and his activities might be subjects of congressional investigation has probably been the principal external deterrent to wrong-doing in the executive branch." [11]

Scholars who have taken refuge in the United States from totalitarian regimes have been still more deeply impressed with the crucial role of legislative investigations into the operations of the Executive. Dr. Henry W. Ehrmann, a refugee from Nazism, concludes that a lack of this power was a prime factor both in the failure of German pre-Nazi parliamentarism and in the bureaucratic sclerosis of the French political system. He recalls the judgment of Germany's great sociologist, Max Weber: "In his criticism of the political situation in Imperial Germany, [Weber] attributed greater responsibility for the unsatisfactory results of constitutional life to the lack of parliamentary investigations than to any other single factor. The German parliament was condemned to dilettantism as well as ignorance."

It is against this background that we may evaluate the progressive undermining of the investigatory power during the past generation by the Executive as well as by publicists and the courts. The Executive under Presidents Franklin Roosevelt, Truman, Eisenhower, and currently under President Kennedy, has challenged the investigatory power in the most direct of ways: with respect to an ever-expanding mass of data, the

Executive has simply refused to supply information to the investigating committees.

These refusals have been formally motivated by: the doctrine of "the separation of powers"; the need for secrecy; various laws, and in particular a "housekeeping act" of 1789 originally passed to authorize executive departments to set up files and records; an alleged traditional practice within the American system. These considerations were systematically stated in a memorandum submitted in May 1954 by then Attorney General Herbert Brownell to President Eisenhower, and countered by a Staff Study of the House Committee on Government Operations, dated May 3, 1956.

The Executive's argument from tradition is undoubtedly specious. It is true that a number of Presidents, beginning with the first, have denied the universal right of Congress to call for testimony and documents from the Executive branch. Among them have been Presidents otherwise so various as Andrew Jackson, John Tyler, Abraham Lincoln, Grover Cleveland and Calvin Coolidge. Washington would seem to have declared—in theory—a complete Executive immunity to the investigatory power: "The Executive ought to communicate such papers as the public good would permit and ought to refuse those, the disclosure of which would injure the public." Jackson, when Congress wished to look more closely into the working of his Spoils System, replied indignantly: "For myself, I shall repel all such attempts as an invasion of the principles of justice, as well as of the Constitution; and I shall esteem it my sacred duty to the people of the United States to resist them as I would the establishment of a Spanish inquisition." Even Calvin Coolidge denounced with unwonted sharpness the investigatory feelers directed by the Couzens committee at Secretary Andrew Mellon's administration of the Treasury Department.

But if we look more closely at the precedents in the pre-Franklin Roosevelt past, we will observe that they have little bearing on the Executive practice that has become established since 1933. In the first place, the earlier incidents were exceedingly rare. Attorney General Brownell's memorandum [12] states at the outset that "American history abounds in countless illustrations of the refusal, on occasion, by the President and heads of departments to furnish papers to Congress, or its committees." In fact, however, he cites only twenty-six instances in all, of which fifteen are from the Franklin Roosevelt and Truman Administrations.

Moreover, nearly all the pre-1933 instances have certain common characteristics. They almost invariably concern either appointments or treaty negotiations. The papers or information that the Executive refuses * are the record of confidential, often informal discussions and reports—in which, as a rule, the President has himself been personally involved—that have entered into preliminary stages of treaty negotiations, appointments, or diplomatic missions. Constitutional niceties aside, the Presidents were taking a reasonable and common-sense position when they argued that administration of the public business, or of any business, would be impossible if the chief administrator could not have confidential preparatory talks with his immediate subordinates and agents.

The same message from Washington, quoted above, that claimed an executive privilege to withhold certain material, explicitly recognized that Congress "might call for papers generally." Grover Cleveland had more of a contest on this score than any other pre-1933 President, but in the incident concerning appointments that Mr. Brownell cites from his Administration, Cleveland declared in his formal communication to the Senate: "The Senate is invited to the fullest scrutiny of the persons submitted to them for public office. . . . I shall furnish, at the request of the confirming body, all the information I possess touching the fitness of the nominees placed before them for their action." He objected only to the transmittal of "letters and papers of a private and unofficial nature." [13]

This earlier occasional practice—which like so much in the older American tradition commends itself to ordinary common sense—has now been blown up into a polished routine. By an administrative fiction, the "confidential" relation between Pres-

---

* Or merely claims the right to refuse. In several cases, including one of the two that Mr. Brownell cites from Washington's Administration, the President, having made the claim, supplied the data nevertheless.

ident and subordinates—which in the past meant a literal personal relation between man and man—has been extended to the entire bureaucracy, so that the Executive now claims a right to order any official or employee of the bureaucracy to refuse to testify to an investigating committee, or to withhold almost any sort of document or record pertaining to any department or agency.

In explaining Congress's 1958 attempt to restore the traditional interpretation of the 1789 housekeeping act as a mere authorization to preserve public records, Representative John E. Moss of California commented:

"The 'housekeeping act' has been twisted and tortured by federal officials seeking to withhold information from the public and from the Congress. . . .

"A few of the recent examples of misuse of the act include the withholding by the Treasury Department of information about imports and exports; the attempt by the Agriculture Department to impose censorship as the price for co-operation in the making of newsreel and television films about agricultural subjects; the withholding of information by the Farmers' Home Administration and the Rural Electrification Administration on loans of public money."

Mr. Moss added a revealing datum: "Each of the ten Cabinet departments opposed this amendment to restore the traditional interpretation." [14]

With the shibboleths of secrecy, security and "classification," the Executive has still further darkened the screen constructed out of the claims of constitutional privilege and separation of powers. Whenever the Executive (or the bureaucracy) wishes to hide information from Congressional scrutiny, it is only necessary to declare it "classified." Sometimes, granted the conditions of our age, this procedure is justified—as, for example, in the case of advanced military experiments, or the Federal Bureau of Investigation's "raw" (i.e., unevaluated) security files on individuals *—but the secrecy labels have been extended

---

* Common sense would agree that it would be improper to turn over such files to a large and factionally minded Congressional committee. But even in this case there are solutions other than total executive immunity: e.g., the

over a considerable portion of the nation's ordinary business, which thus becomes removed from Congressional (and thereby also from public) scrutiny.

The results are sometimes curious. The Executive, for example, will call on Congress to vote appropriations for foreign aid, but will decline to furnish the information about what has been, is being and is intended to be done with the foreign aid, or what sort of persons have been doing it. On the basis of a special commission study, like the 1957 "Gaither Report," the Executive will demand certain armament funds; but will not show Congress the report which supplies the motivation. The Executive will insist on Senate confirmation of a military treaty, like those establishing the North Atlantic or the Southeast Asia treaty organizations, without disclosing the commitments that the treaty entails. The Executive will demand additional funds for the Information Agency, but will not show Congressional committees the field reports on the Agency's personnel and results.

It would be wrong to exaggerate the stage already reached in this long and perhaps cyclical process. The investigatory power has been bruised and shaken, but it is still vigorous: the overwhelming votes given each session of Congress to HUAC, by far its most heavily attacked embodiment, are proof enough of that. In fact, it is just because the investigatory power is so vigorous, because it retains more vitality than any other of the Congressional powers, that it is so sharply under attack in an age of the growth of Executive power. It becomes easier to see why Dr. Ehrmann, reflecting on the experiences of many nations, concluded his study of investigation with the summary judgment: "Certainly 'government by investigation is not government,' but government without investigation might easily turn out to be democratic government no longer."

JAMES BURNHAM

British practice of showing the confidential material to a small parliamentary committee of authoritative and trusted members. Something of this sort was done in Washington during the 1953 conflict over the appointment of Charles Bohlen as Ambassador to Moscow.

Chapter

3.

SUBVERSION IN THE
TWENTIETH CENTURY

A COMMITTEE *of the Congress as conspicuous as the House Committee on Un-American Activities must, to justify its flamboyant experience, represent a serious answer, however imperfect, to a peculiar need of our time. The questions are whether subversion by the Communists is a large or a small matter. Is the commonweal affected by the success, or lack of it, of the concerted agitations of the enemy? In espionage? In the subversion of public opinion? Can one actually point to decisive steps taken by the Government of the United States in a direction contrary to its own best interests, which might not have been taken but for the influence of Communist propaganda upon our affairs? Can we, in the last analysis, distinguish between the internal and the external threat, or are the two, considering the compression of global affairs, indistinguishable?*

My purpose in this chapter is to discuss the role of subversion in the struggle in which we are presently engaged, to single out some successful ventures in the subversion of American policy and to argue the continued relevance to the national defense effort of an organization with the powers of a Congressional committee, a broad mandate, and a continuing curiosity about the operations of the Communist movement.

The twentieth century is called, rightly, an age of revolution. It is, by that token, also an age of subversion, which frequently precedes successful revolution.

One meaning of subversion is the overturning or overthrowing of existing governments or institutions. Another and more prevalent meaning is the undermining of a people's allegiance or faith in its institutions, which is often the precondition for the overthrow of those institutions.

Western democracy, resting as it does upon a moral consensus, the free exchange of ideas, and the understanding that one set of ideas prevails over another by a process of reasoned discussion, is poorly equipped to deal with the new (i.e., Communist) type of subversion. Communist subversion, let us note at once, is not a simple thing. Its mechanics and pace vary, most particularly with changes in the growth and allocation of Soviet military power. Invariably, however, subversion takes place in three stages. First comes the corruption of accepted ideas, and the substitution for them of views consonant with Communist objectives (we may call this the stage of intellectual and spiritual infiltration, and say of it that it demands, of those who would prevent or forestall it, notably more, in the way of sophistication and resourcefulness, than either of the other stages). Second comes a stage during which the Communists seek to manipulate the policies of the target government in such fashion as to favor Communist goals. Finally comes the stage of overt individual and collective action (espionage, sabotage, insurrection, etc.), under Communist guidance or direction.

The Bolsheviks, seizing power in Russia in 1917, began at once, against the day when the world situation might become more propitious, to ready themselves for expansion. They created a world-wide network of Communist Parties, and initiated a massive domestic training program for future collaborators in other countries, including the United States. The idea was to exploit any visible weakness in the enemy's regime or institutions, and to drive home invidious comparisons with

Soviet society. This requires, simultaneously, the exaggeration
of the enemy's faults and the exaggeration of Soviet virtues. The
recognition of such propaganda themes by the leaders of the
free world and their constituencies is, therefore, necessary to
the proper ordering of anti-subversion policy. Ideally, it should
be the intellectuals and the press of the free world that spot,
and quash, the incipient themes of Communist propaganda.
Actually, however, it is difficult for them, even assuming their
willingness to undertake the task, to cope fully with this responsibility, most particularly because they do not have the power
to compel testimony. You and I may know it is the intention of
the Communist Party to foster internal dissent by exaggerating
the misery of the Southern Negroes, or inducing a state of
tension between white and Negro; and we may proclaim the
fact, based on a projection of our knowledge of Soviet tech
niques and on impressionistic evidence garnered from the ac
tivities of the Party here. But our case is made much more
forceful when a Congressional committee reveals, let us say
that thousands upon thousands of dollars were spent during
such and such a period on false and exaggerated propaganda
that Negroes' houses were burned down by Communists as an
act of provocation; that John Jones and Harry Smith traveled
last year to Moscow, and were lectured to there by Ivan Ivan
ovitch on the techniques for increasing racial strife.

In 1928, the Communists announced their first Five-Year
Plan, and pointed to it as proof that they had not only genuine
insight into the political future, but also a concept of industrial
and economic development destined to bring a new world into
being. By their good fortune, this first massive venture in state
planning began almost simultaneously with the Great Depres
sion in the principal target countries, so that the Five-Year
Plan could fall far short of its announced objectives and still be
passed off as a "success." Thus: the capitalist economies were
"stagnating," while the Soviet economy was blazing trails into
a future in which stagnation would be unknown and unthink
able. These contentions beguiled many people. They might
have beguiled far fewer if competent testimony had been put

lished comparing, say, the lot of the depression-ridden American farmer and that of the liberated kulak.

Many impatient Western intellectuals accepted the Soviet Union as the model of future economic and social relations, so much so that not even the bloody purges of the late thirties could disturb their image of a "decadent" capitalism projected against the background of a "progressive" Communism. The "locomotive of history" charged forward, with many of them safely aboard.

Hitler attacked Russia; the United States joined with Russia —and, in the passion of our embrace, Russia seemed to us a fine catch. "Harry [Hopkins] says that Stalin doesn't want anything but security for his country, and I think that if I give him everything I possibly can, and ask for nothing in return, *noblesse oblige,* he won't try to annex anything and will work with me for a world of democracy and peace." * Thus the President of the United States, who four years before had denounced the House Committee on Un-American Activities which, *noblesse oblige,* had labored to inform the country, and its President, of some of the enduring truths about the Communist movement.

Or consider the "bring-the-boys-home" campaign. Obviously it was not the Communists who kindled the desire of American mothers and wives to bring their men home. But a national policy uninfected by Communist misrepresentations, while not loving the boys less, would not have dismantled our military machine at a moment when it alone could have checked the Communist irruption into eastern Europe and southeast Asia.

And so on, through the tragic years.

Successful subversion is, I repeat, a matter of bringing about a fundamental change in a people's attitude toward its society and its government, and Communist subversion has raised to a high degree of perfection techniques for speeding up and directing the process by which a people moves from one set of attitudes to another. It has developed an instrument appropriate

* William C. Bullitt, quoting from a conversation with F.D.R. *Life,* August 30, 1948, p. 94.

to these techniques; namely, the Communist Party. Its task is to locate and aggravate conflict within the target society, to pit elements of that society against one another, and to promote crises as a means of affecting governmental policy, even far in advance of the moment for any future attempt to seize governmental power. And we possess now a rich literature about the structure, the strategy, and the tactics of the Communist Party.

The Party, seeking always to block action hostile to the Soviet Union and to induce action favorable to its purposes, lets no opportunity go by to enlist the assistance of non-Communists who want something that will in any way contribute to these purposes. The announced objective of the satellite organization may be anything you like, but it will always be found to have a bearing, however hidden, on Soviet foreign policy.

The Principal Targets of Communist Subversion

The Communists describe themselves as a party of and for the masses. Many persons have, therefore, supposed that the unique and final aim of their operations is to indoctrinate everyone with Marxist-Leninist beliefs. Nothing could be further from the truth. Communism is an elite movement. It seeks to subvert actual or potential members of the ruling groups within the target country, and these in turn will gain control of and dominate the masses. Even in Communism's motherland—the Soviet Union—only some three or four per cent of the population is deemed qualified to belong to the Communist Party, and take part in controlling and influencing the development of Soviet society.

Communism considers as most available for its purposes men and women who feel superior to their own society, its institutions, its accepted values. Rebecca West made this point convincingly in her book, *The Meaning of Treason,** which describes the Canadian atomic spy ring that was uncovered by the defection of Igor Gouzenko, the Soviet cipher clerk. The ring's members apparently cherished none of the ordinary moral obli-

* Rebecca West, *The Meaning of Treason* (New York: Viking, 1947).

gations toward their Canadian society, and therefore "felt no qualms whatsoever, but great pride and pleasure, in handing over to the representative of the Soviet Union any information required of them, no matter how brutally this treachery might conflict with their duty to their employers, public or private, or what dangers it might bring down on their fellow countrymen."

The Communists are forever on the lookout for men and women who have repudiated traditional sentiments of patriotism toward the society that has nurtured them. The liberal societies of the West, say the Communists in framing their appeals to foreigners for help, are smashing themselves on the shoals of their own contradictions, but subversion can hasten the progress that leads to the inevitable final disaster. That being the case, the "duty" to subvert stands, paradoxically, high in the scale of Communist "moral" obligations. That is why the Communists, although determinists, often behave more like believers in indeterminacy, in free human agency, than we who actually profess belief in it.

The enlisted agents of Communist subversion, then, have always been numerically few, however great their impact upon events. The few must in turn lead the many. The Communists know that takes time, and are prepared to think and plan in terms of a carefully orchestrated campaign of subversion that may take many years to complete. Ideally, as they recognize, they must shift the mind of an entire people from one set of convictions to another, and this calls for seizing upon particular issues as they arise, and so handling them as to cause key groups to accept current Marxist interpretations of "objective, scientific truth." Above all, it calls for convincing everyone, everywhere, that like it or not the Communist system is riding a wave that must and will wash upon the shore of complete victory, while its enemy, the West, is slated for final and ignominious defeat. That explains why the Communists concentrate first on the elite group of the country they seek to subvert. It molds and sets public opinion, so that anything cast upon its waters is indeed likely to come back a hundredfold. First the writers, the scientists, the professors, the teachers, the artists. If they can be brought around, they can be counted on to force all other doors, and so carry Communist influence into all walks of life. These are simple truths, but they are still widely ignored for all that the House Committee on Un-American Activities (see Chapter 10) has copiously documented them, and communicated them to many Americans. What a pity we did not know, in 1944 when we might have averted catastrophe, as much about Soviet Far Eastern policy as many Americans now know, thanks in large part to HUAC, about Soviet "peace" campaigns.

After the Russian victory at Stalingrad in June 1943, nobody could doubt that the Allied coalition would win the war. Stalin therefore turned his attention to the task of advancing the postwar position of Communism, preferably at the expense of, or if necessary in direct opposition to, the interests of his Western comrades-in-arms; and, as we should expect from the above, he reached first for the weapon of subversion, turning it upon the United States. The two most pressing goals of the resulting campaign were (a) to shift United States policy from support of the Nationalist Government of China over to acquiescence in a Communist take-over in that country, and (b) to obtain, by whatever means but in any case quickly, America's atomic secrets. The first of these, the shift of American policy from active support to betrayal of the Nationalist Government of China, called for a sustained effort over a long period: co-ordinated actions, propaganda, above all the planting of elaborate misinformation in numerous diplomatic and political forums throughout the world.

Within the United States itself, these tasks were entrusted to three groups: First, the Communist Party, which during the period of our wartime alliance with the Soviet Union had been highly influential in the circles that distribute news and form public opinion, and whose influence was to outlive the shooting war by several years. The Party, with membership at an unprecedented peak and with a wide variety of influential fronts at its disposal, could, at the end of the war, deeply affect American thinking when and as it needed to. Second, a number of Communist dupes who held high posts in certain strategic areas within the government of the United States: Alger Hiss, for instance, who became the first General Secretary of the United Nations; Harry Dexter White, who was Undersecretary of the Treasury; and Lawrence Duggan of the State Department. Third, the Institute of Pacific Relations, which was to prove a remarkably effective instrument for the purpose in hand. The IPR's role in the molding of United States Far Eastern policy is, no doubt, today generally forgotten. That is a pity—and it would repay anyone's time to review the detailed hearings of the Senate Internal Security Subcommittee from July 1951 to June 1952 (the task might well have fallen to HUAC) covering the IPR's activities. What the IPR did by way of promoting the interests of the Soviet Union in the United States, and bringing American Far Eastern policy in line with Communist objectives, is a model of the USSR's *modus operandi* in these matters. Only by understanding how it worked can we hope to learn how to prevent a repetition of the entire episode, or to ferret out less ambitious and less concentrated attempts to accomplish similar objectives—as, for example, in Latin America or the Near East.

The IPR found room in its organization not merely for a wide range of Communist sympathizers and dupes, but for Communist espionage agents as well—Michael Greenberg, for example, a British-born Communist who in 1941 became managing editor of IPR's *Pacific Affairs*. (By 1942, Greenberg was the proud occupant of an office in the White House.) IPR's reliance on persons with Communist affiliations who also had close ties with the State Department is fully documented in the IPR hearings.*

The IPR was in considerable part responsible for the proposal, finally put forward by the United States, that Chiang Kai-shek form a United Front coalition government with the Communists. Chiang, to be sure, knew from the first that the coalition in question would be only a first stage in an eventual

---

* *Institute of Pacific Relations*, Report of the Senate Committee on the Judiciary, 82nd Congress, 2d Session.

Communist take-over of China: he resisted the proposal at every turn, and only under constant pressure from Washington officials, who were in turn being prodded by IPR, was he induced to yield, little by little, on first one point of substance, then another. During the celebrated China civil war truce engineered by Ambassador George Marshall, for example, Chiang found himself stripped of nearly all forms of military assistance (he was refused ammunition for the very weapons the United States had placed in his hands). "I was informed by the Chinese Government officials that they had ceased to receive war equipment manufactured in the United States," General Chennault subsequently testified. "When I inquired why, they said that General Marshall had forbidden its shipment from American-held islands and from the United States." * The Chinese Communists, of course, made the most of the truce— to build up their army with equipment that the Soviets had captured from the Japanese-Manchurian army and turned over to them.

We must not oversimplify or exaggerate: a number of forces had to be combined in order for the Communists to win in China. But it was the IPR that accomplished the first essential victory, which was to pull the wool over the eyes of Washington officials, and enable the Communist strategy of conquest in China to develop until it was too late to do anything about it. Nor is there any doubt that the IPR operation was masterminded from the Kremlin itself and, at the same time, effectively supported by the simple technique of keeping up the appearance of correct and formal diplomatic relations with the Nationalists, while at the same time directly encouraging and covertly aiding the Chinese Communists.

Above all, it was the IPR that invented—and put across— the convenient myth that the Chinese Communists under Mao Tse-tung were not really Communists, but "agrarian reformers," dedicated to the ideal of genuine democracy for China. Anything to discredit Chiang Kai-shek in American eyes; and,

---

* Hearings on the Institute of Pacific Relations, testimony of General Claire Lee Chennault, May 29, 1952.

as we know, the final result was a Washington policy that contributed to Chiang's ultimate defeat on the mainland. Even as early as November 1945, Secretary of State James F. Byrnes was saying, "The wise course would be to try to force the Chinese government and the Chinese Communists to get together on a compromise basis, perhaps telling Generalissimo Chiang Kai-shek that we will stop the aid to his government unless he goes along with this." * But the main point is this: A systematic and diversified campaign of subversion finally persuaded the United States Government to accept, in general, the Communist position about China as the basis for its own policy decisions.

If the evidence regarding the IPR is compelling, so is the evidence concerning the group of American, British, and Canadian scientists who handed the secrets of the atomic bomb over to our avowed enemy. We are, to be sure, told that their largesse was of little use to the Russians, since the latter would have discovered the same atomic secrets anyway, perhaps even at just as early a moment. But the available data point to the opposite conclusion. The report of the Royal Canadian Commission, published June 27, 1946 (and viewed from another aspect later in Chapter 8), sets forth the findings of an exhaustive inquiry into the matter, and leaves no room for doubt that the Communist spy ring in question operated successfully over a long period not only in Canada, but in the United States and Great Britain as well. "It is clear," states the report, "that the information sought was considered of the greatest importance by the Russian espionage leaders, and that alone might be a fair test on the question of value. . . . [much] secret and valuable information was handed over, some of it is so secret still that it can be referred to only obliquely and with the greatest care, and this is especially so in the case of certain secret information shared by Canada, the United Kingdom, and the United States." † Dr. Allan Nunn May, whom Rebecca West described as "one of a close corporation of the most

---

* *The Forrestal Diaries* (New York: Viking, 1951), pp. 1-3.
† Report of the Royal Commission, p. 616.

inconvenient kind of traitors any community ever had to fear," never specified the amount of information he handed over, but he did say that it was more comprehensive than that to be found in the authoritative Smyth report,* which was not published until considerably later. Thus M. Rubenstein, no doubt accurately informed of the successes of his country's spy rings, could write, in 1947, "The secret of the atom bomb has long ceased to be a secret, and America's temporary monopoly of the atomic weapon is becoming a thing of the past." † Klaus Emil Fuchs, who was convicted for his participation in atomic espionage in Great Britain in 1950; Ethel and Julius Rosenberg, who were sentenced to death in 1951 for parallel espionage as a result of the testimony given against them by Ethel Rosenberg's brother, David Greenglass—they and their fellow conspirators did incalculable harm to American—and Western—interests. Soviet nuclear technology gained, in consequence, not less than three years, and possibly as many as four. It is unlikely Stalin would have initiated the Korean aggression (cost: 157,000 casualties) if the United States had still possessed an atomic monopoly.

Nor is that all the experience we have of how the Soviet Union has used scientists as instruments of subversion. Scientists have prestige as well as secrets. As we have watched the USSR build atomic weapons that they could not have built without personnel in the Manhattan project, we have also watched the USSR conduct a world-wide campaign, to a considerable extent through the medium of the world's scientists, to paralyze America's development of its nuclear potentiality by the cessation of tests. It is unlikely that a sophisticated student of Communist technique—e.g., someone who is familiar with, and has absorbed the meaning of, the hearings of the House Committee on Un-American Activities—would have walked into the trap set by the Soviet Union in the fall of 1958 (when we were per-

---

* H. D. Smyth, *Atomic Energy for Military Purposes* (Princeton University Press, 1945). This book was authorized for release in August 1945, and is the official report on the development of the atomic bomb. The work was prepared at the request of Major General Leslie R. Groves, U. S. Army.

† *New Times*, M. Rubenstein (No. 50, December 10, 1947), "A New Sect of the Atomic Religion," p. 7.

suaded, without assurances of any kind, that the Russians would do likewise) to cease testing; and unlikely that, in the absence of pressures built up by the engines of Communist propaganda all over the globe, "World Opinion" should have succeeded in disarming President Eisenhower.

Semantic Subversion

Another distinctively Soviet method of undermining a people's political ideas and institutions is through what we may call "semantic subversion"—that is, seeking to obfuscate and destroy the stable meaning of the words men use in communicating with one another in the process of arriving at political choices. Consider what has been done to "democracy," "peace," "war," "neutralism," "imperialism," "capitalism," "socialism," "colonialism." All these have been co-opted by the Communist slogan mongers for their special uses. They will never, in our time, regain their pristine meaning.

The first victims of semantic subversion, as originally practiced by the Bolsheviks, were paradoxically not the bourgeois or capitalist elements of the West, but the socialists. Ever since Lenin, the Communists have claimed that *their* movement, and their movement alone, looks to genuine socialism (wherefor the "bastion" of Bolshevik Communism is officially called the "Union of *Socialist* Soviet Republics"). This word juggling has, moreover, worked: by unfurling the banner of Western parliamentary socialism as if it were their very own, the Communists have been able to carry with them a great number of European intellectuals and workers who venerate the principles of socialism much as we Americans treasure the Bill of Rights.

The Communists, like many other observers, had foreseen that the State would play in modern industrial society a vastly more important role than in the agrarian societies of the past. The fact that the modern liberal is in some degree a "statist" has, accordingly, contributed to the success of the Communist masquerade. The Communist concept of the State, since it is totally totalitarian, does differ fundamentally from that of the typical liberal. But the Communists have been able to identify themselves conspicuously with liberal programs, which they have wished to do, partly, to distract attention from the illiberalism of their own conduct when in power. Their duplicity can best be appreciated when one compares simultaneously events on the two sides of the Iron Curtain. Behind the Curtain, successive big brothers have used force, internal propaganda, or organized social compulsion to ensure compliance with their will. Yet outside of their own domain, they continue to pose as progressive; that is, as liberals and democrats. The "dialectic" makes understandable their working of both sides of the street; but it is their own skill that enables them to do so with such effect. Thus the Communists advocate general and universal disarmament—and practice cold-blooded nuclear blackmail; they support wars of national liberation—and reject historical nationalism once they have themselves acquired power; they put themselves forward as champions of peaceful coexistence—and engage in permanent war. And these are the three issues that are likely to dominate the Cold War in the years ahead. Let us, then, glance at the concepts the Communists are sure to use in their attempt to subvert the free world's resistance.

The Nuclear Trap

The Soviet exploitation of the nuclear weapons issue has been intensified *pari passu* with the increases in the USSR's nuclear stockpiles. Prior to their acquisition of their first nuclear device, the Soviets' sole objective was to see to it that the United States should never employ nuclear weapons as a defense against Communist expansion—as witness Molotov's 1946 proposal that the United Nations establish a control commission to execute the U.N. decision to prohibit the use of atomic energy for military purposes, and the Soviets' concurrent rejection of the United States offer (the "Baruch plan") to place America's atomic secrets in the custody of an international organization. Though clearly terrified at the thought that the United States might use nuclear weapons against Soviet power, their domestic propaganda simultaneously (a) pooh-poohed such weapons as ineffective, and (b) applauded the Western scientists who were asserting that atomic weapons, once brought into play, would destroy the human race. Typical of such Communist double-talk was Molotov's statement to the General Assembly on December 14, 1946:

The honor and conscience of the freedom-loving peoples demand that the atomic bomb be outlawed, for the United Nations will never assume the responsibility for any plans to use atomic energy for the purpose of wholesale destruction of people, and in general use it to the detriment of mankind.

Once, however, the Communists had acquired their first atomic bomb, and with increased emphasis after they had added hydrogen weapons, they moved promptly to a different position —that of the champions of nuclear disarmament *and* the principal practitioners of nuclear blackmail. Apart from a temporary heresy on the part of Malenkov (according to which nuclear weapons might be destructive to both Communist and capitalist societies), the Communists have never since abandoned their thesis that revolutionary conquest of the world cannot be accomplished without some application of violence— although (they add) if nonviolent techniques are applied successfully, the amount of violence required in a specific situation may be reduced. And they have repeatedly implied that their system, based as it is on a high degree of discipline, can absorb a nuclear attack better than any capitalist nation.

It has become increasingly evident in the course of the vain and endless East-West negotiations on arms control that the fundamental barrier to real agreement is ideological. Any effective system of arms control requires an effective inspection system, which the Communists cannot and will not accept. Accordingly, by Soviet logic, the demand for arms-control measures must be made into an important ideological and propaganda weapon. Thus they reason: If the West ever accepts, on a permanent basis, any degree whatever of arms control or test-banning, it will, in doing so, increase the relative strength of the Communist powers. Khrushchev has never proposed demobilization of his political warfare machine, for the obvious reason that the Kremlin can never give up its role as direct organizer, and spiritual preceptor, of world revolution. Khrushchev has openly asserted, as recently as January 1961, that he intends to use arms negotiations as a means of undermining Western military power, especially the United States'. Notwithstanding, the influence of the Unilateralists grows.

Lord Bertrand Russell's slogan, BETTER RED THAN DEAD, superordinates survival over any other value. Mr. Adlai Stevenson has noted the phenomenon. "Millions of persons," he said in a speech on May 23, 1961, "appear to be groping for new ethical guidelines as if they had never before been traced, or as if the old ones were no longer relevant. This seems to me curious, and I wonder if we can trace this uneasiness and search for a new ethic to the nuclear power-balance between East and West. Certainly, men everywhere are now living under a shadow of fear as horrendous universal implications of nuclear holocaust become more apparent."

Mr. Stevenson would, however, limit the causal connection to the nuclear aspect of the struggle; that is, to fear. But this is not the only possibility and, in the United States (where people in general have remained remarkably calm in the teeth of authoritative pronouncements concerning the horror of nuclear war), perhaps not the most interesting one. Some observers, for example, speak of a crisis in the soul of Western man himself that long antedates the discovery of atomic weapons—a crisis whose "causes" are to be sought not in external historical events, where Mr. Stevenson seeks them, but in the autonomous realm of the spirit itself; a crisis, indeed, that far from being caused by the struggle between East and West, itself produced that struggle.

Our struggle against the collaborationists and pacifists is no less urgent than our struggle against Communism itself, and the Bertrand Russells are not so different, in the pinch, from those Western statesmen who, while they do not speak as the Russells speak, often act much as the Russells wish them to act. It remains true, nuclear weapons or no nuclear weapons, that "where there is no vision the people perish"; and, conversely, that where there *is* vision, the people must be prepared to sacrifice life itself in defense of it. Russia's leaders appear to understand this better than ours: they encourage and foster nihilism and defeatism among other people but do no such thing at home. Perverted though their values are, from a sane Western point of view, the Russian leaders do not permit those values to be challenged from within the USSR, and punish draconically all who so much as hint at the possibility of defeat or abdication. One cannot imagine *On the Beach,* for all that it has done to weaken the will to resist in the West, being shown at Soviet movie palaces * which, we may be sure, are reserved for morality plays that inculcate the virtue of *courage,* as that virtue was once understood in the West. As for ourselves, the correct answer to the Russell slogan is always the battle cry that Russell was surely paraphrasing: "It is better to die on your feet than to live on your knees."

The Strategy of National Liberation

Communist strategy seems to be relying, in the sixties, on "wars of national liberation" much as, in the thirties, it relied on the "Democratic Popular Front"; and importantly situated men and women in the West seem as little able to see through the one as the other. The politically deluded fail adequately to understand (a) that the Russians use their support for colonial peoples merely as a cloak for Communist expansion, and (b) that the West is not simply anticolonial, but *suicidally* anticolonial. Wars of national liberation, Khrushchev assures us, are "just," thus "justified . . . [and also] inevitable, for the colonialists do not fully bestow independence on the peoples. The peoples win freedom and independence only through struggle, including armed struggle." † Among such wars of national liberation, Khrushchev cites the Communist take-over in North Vietnam, the uprising of the Arab people against the

* At the instance of the American producers, who designed world-wide simultaneous premieres, the film was shown once only, to Soviet film workers, at their own Domkino Theater, presumably to satisfy a professional curiosity.

† Nikita S. Khrushchev, address, January 6, 1961.

French in Algeria, and Castro's seizure of Cuba, which he describes as "an uprising against a tyrannical regime, backed by U. S. imperialism." Such wars, he continues, will go on as long as imperialism exists, and "the Communists support just wars of this kind wholeheartedly and without reservations. . . . [They] march in the van of the people fighting for liberation."

The doctrinal basis for current Communist strategy in this area was laid down in Lenin's book, *Imperialism, The Last Stage of Democracy*. Marx, Lenin contended, had been wrong in thinking that declining capitalist profits **must** plunge the workers of the advanced countries into ever-growing poverty. Marx had overlooked a second possibility, namely: the profits brought into the industrial countries through their exploitation of the colonial areas. These might temporarily avert the decline and so postpone the (ultimately unavoidable, of course) pauperization of the workers. But this siphoning off of the colonial people's wealth, despite its beneficent results in one direction, comes with a hidden price: the bourgeoisie, by maintaining and living off a feudalistic system, signs its own death warrant. The execution of that death warrant is a major Communist responsibility, which must be discharged if the workers are to be led into the new world of plenty and freedom. The proletariat must take over the erstwhile task of the bourgeoisie —as Lenin put it, must carry through the "bourgeois-democratic revolution," which has now been translated into the "National Liberal Democratic Revolution," with which the Communists spearheaded their entrance into the former colonial areas. In general, however, the Communist line on this topic has changed little in the past forty years, as witness almost any Communist pronouncement on the colonial countries. This, for instance from *New Times,* August 23, 1953: "[The people of the colonial countries] are not inclined to reconcile themselves any longer to the colonial system which robs and exploits them in the interest of a few 'advanced' capitalist countries."

The important thing to grasp here is the bearing of national liberation on the strategic interests of the USSR. The latter's strategy calls for the splintering of the non-Communist world into units, each too weak to defend itself, and too demoralized to combine with other units in the general defense. But for that, national liberation would be an extremely dangerous game for the USSR to play, since if the American doctrine of "self-determination of peoples" were to be strictly applied the world over, the USSR would fall instantly apart into a great number of independent nations. And the same goes, of course, for Red China.

The process of Communist subversion through support of movements for national liberation will, predictably, go on at an accelerated pace, and for many years, in Asia, Africa, the Middle East, and Latin America. And national liberation will continue to serve the Communists in any number of ways. It will unite the active nationalist elements in the colonial areas and in the "unadvanced" independent countries, and urge upon these elements extreme action. Thus the Communists will hope simultaneously to make friends among the backward countries, which in due course they will the more easily communize, and to weaken the "colonial" powers, who happen to be the USSR's probable enemies in any future war. And national liberation will provide the Soviet propaganda mills with an endless supply of grist: All social ills in the colonies and former colonies have their nests in imperialist exploitation, and can be indefinitely and profitably exploited for propaganda purposes. "Throw the imperialists out" becomes an appropriate propaganda slogan everywhere, good not only until the imperialists are thrown out, but also until the last reminder of their earlier presence has been snuffed out. (If, after they go, political chaos and economic stagnation ensue, the imperialists can still be blamed for both.) If, as is alas all too likely, the expelled imperialists get a case of bad conscience and offer to help, they can be denounced for trying to get back in and re-establish "colonialism"; they must be rebuffed, and the case for rebuffing them also makes good propaganda, since what just man wishes to see them "perpetuate ... oppression ... by foreign capital"? *

* *New Times*, No. 33, August 5, 1953, editorial, p. 3.

The Lure of "Peaceful Coexistence"

We turn now to "peaceful coexistence" as a technique of Communist subversion.

The Communists invented the term "peaceful coexistence"—along with its twin sister "relaxation of tensions"—to describe a peculiarly deceptive transitory phase of their struggle for world power. The purpose, put in its crudest terms, has been to persuade non-Communist leaders everywhere that "coexistence" with Communism is now the only course open to the free world. And here, as with the other techniques, we can measure the effectiveness of the stratagem by asking ourselves how many people all over the world believe that Communism, like the poor, will always be with us, and must be lived with on terms that it chooses to dictate. To ask the question is to answer it, and to shudder at what the answer implies. And here, as with their other techniques, we can understand what is involved by keeping attention fixed on the totality of the Communists' behavior. That will enable us to see that the term means to the Communists exactly the opposite of what, on other lips, it might seem to say.

Peaceful coexistence is neither "peaceful" (it calls for peacefulness from only one side in the world struggle, always for unlimited aggression by the other side) nor "coexistence" (only the Communists are intended to keep on existing). Once again the "dialectic." Herewith four expressions of it,* each contributing a dimension in our understanding: (1) "It does not at all follow from the fact that we stand for peaceful coexistence and economic competition with capitalism, that the struggle against bourgeoisie ideology, against bourgeoisie survivals, can be relaxed." (2) "The only correct and reasonable principle of international relations is the principle of peaceful coexistence of states with different social systems advanced by Lenin and further elaborated in the Moscow declaration and in the peace

---

* The first is incorporated into a statement issued by the 20th Congress of the CPUSSR, the remaining three are by Khrushchev in his January 6, 1961, speech, *op. cit.*

manifesto of 1957.... [But] the slogan of the fight for peace by no means contradicts the slogan of the fight for Communism. The two go hand in hand...." (3) "Peaceful coexistence promotes the growth of the forces of progress.... In the capitalist countries it facilitates the work of the Communist parties and other progressive organizations...." And (4) "The policy of peaceful coexistence is, then, as far as its social content is concerned, a form of intense economic, political, and ideological struggle between the proletariat and the aggressive forces of imperialism in the world arena."

In short: "Kindly put your pistols away, because we are going to shoot you with ours."

"Coexistence" is a temporary phase of Communist strategy, though we may not hear the last of it for many years. What the Communists intend is to go on nibbling up the countries located in the power vacuums of Asia and Africa, and to refrain from direct attack on the West for so long as suits their purposes. The West must not, according to the rules of "peaceful coexistence," do anything so "unpeaceful" as, for example, actually to block Communist infiltration into the free world. The West must write off millions who are already Communist slaves, and it must look on, unmoving if not unmoved, as new areas are led to the slaughter. The rules are simple, and the West has merely to abide by them to remain safe from war.

The Balance Sheet

The United States and the other Western democracies have not shown much skill in waging the "war called peace." Yet the nature of Communist subversion, as we have insisted, changes over the years only in detail; what varies is merely its intensity. Its invariable purpose is to promote confusion in the ranks, and even the high command, of the free world, to paralyze our action, and to twist policy in a direction favorable to the Communists' interests and designs. As a tool of the Soviet state, subversion marches hand in hand with Soviet military and political power. Both operate within a moral framework that was succinctly defined by Radio Moscow some years ago:

"At the root of Communist morality, said Lenin, lies the struggle for the consolidation, for the completion, of Communism. Therefore, from the point of view of Communist morality, only those acts are moral which contribute to the building up of a new Communist society."

Communist subversion strikes first, and most energetically, most craftily, at our capacity to *judge*, to choose rationally, to opt for the course that is "right" in the twofold sense that it reflects true morality and that it takes genuine reality into full account. The Communists know that no one, individual or nation, can choose rationally unless, to begin with, he knows— knows and remembers—that some things are "better" than others, and which things are better and which worse. They know, too, that no one, individual or nation, can choose rationally unless he or it sees reality clear and sees it whole. Wherever, then, there is today confusion amongst us, whether about moral principle or about the true character of the situation we face, we are well advised to ask whether, or to what extent, it is the result of a deliberate Communist-subversive effort to create it. Confusion amongst us there certainly is, of both kinds, and more certainly than at any earlier moment in our history. And these, I submit, are urgent matters, of proper concern to a Congress charged with the common defense.

Take, for instance, the existence within our ranks of the three schools of thought: (1) that which agonizes over the internal Communist threat to our security, but seems blissfully unaware of any external threat; (2) that which is willing to devote unlimited resources to meeting the external threat, but dismisses the existence of an internal one; and (3) that which concentrates exclusively on social and economic problems, for the solution of which it will contemplate any sacrifice, however great, but gives no thought to Communism's threat to our own security, internal or external.

This is not a matter of healthy democratic disagreement about policy. It can be explained only on the grounds that there are those among us who are either unable to recognize reality, or unable to refer it to what we have always regarded as acceptable moral concepts—or both. It is analagous not to the momentary indecision of the troubled but clearheaded man, but the successive phases of euphoria and depression in the schizophrenic. Some of us are terribly wrong on the foregoing issues and, all too probably, because Communist subversion, working diligently in all corners of the world, under every guise, taking advantage of every situation, has successfully changed the appearance of reality. Is there an internal Communist threat? Is there an external threat? Should we act vigorously against any and all threats? These questions are surely capable of being soberly investigated and soberly decided; yet the continuing debate about them seems to get nowhere.

On Monday, June 5, 1961, the Supreme Court upheld the Internal Security Act of 1950, which requires the Communist Party in this country to register as the agent of a foreign power. The Court upheld the requirement in question, as also the further requirement that the Party divulge its membership, by citing the Party's secret and conspiratorial character and its domination by the Soviet Union, as established over the years by Congressional investigations. Overnight the nation's leading newspaper hit back: "The sustaining of the Smith Act's membership clause ... could only serve again to divert public attention to the virtually nonexistent internal Communist threat. The real Communist challenge is from abroad." *

There is sufficient evidence by now to demonstrate the ultimate impossibility, in the age of subversion, of distinguishing clearly between the "external" and the "internal" threat. Is it an "external" or "internal" victory of the Communists when the President of the United States is moved (by the euphoria following the "relaxation of tensions" period after Stalin's death) to say, as Mr. Eisenhower did in Geneva in 1955: "I believe the Soviet Union wants peace every bit as much as we do"? How much of a hand did Soviet propaganda have in the planting of that hallucination in the mind of the principal leader of the West? Was the resulting imbalance in American

---

* *The New York Times,* editorial, June 7, 1961.

foreign policy, which accepted the Spirit of Geneva as the new cornerstone, "externally" or "internally" induced? And as for espionage, how many spies does it take to put sand in the machinery? What did Martin and Mitchell, who disappeared from their jobs with the National Security Council in the spring of 1960, to surface a month later in Moscow, tell the Russians? Did they take along, as is widely suspected, the vital information on the U-2's? Did they, in a word, make possible the Soviets' apprehension of the U-2, and thereby change the course of history?

In the few weeks before and after the *Times*' blasé dismissal of the internal threat, the Government of Israel was shaken by the exposure of Israel Baer (it is as though Bernard Baruch had been shown to be a Communist spy), the Government of England by the exposure of George Blake, Henry Houghton, Peter and Helen Kroger (alias Morris and Lola Cohen, both Americans), Gordon Arnold Lonsdale, and Ethel Elizabeth Gee. Meanwhile, the United States was wrestling with the problems posed by its most recently apprehended spies: Dr. Robert Soblen, Irvin C. Scarbeck, and Miroslav Nacualec and Karel Hlasmy.

The Congress of the United States has shown wisdom in creating machinery to investigate and expose the nature and scope of Communist subversion in the United States. Communist subversion, as we have said, seeks to twist U. S. policy in the direction of Communist designs. This is done by bringing one or more U. S. officials to make, wittingly or unwittingly, decisions that forward Soviet objectives. So much is obvious. It is less obvious that no governing group, no Administration, is ever eager to recognize that one of its trusted officials, even one not highly situated, has played into the Communists' hands. Its instinct for political self-preservation naturally disposes it to defend any suspected employee against such a charge even, as we know, when the adverse evidence is overwhelming. The Executive, in short, cannot be counted on to police itself in this regard, which means that either someone else polices it, or that it goes unpoliced. Under our form of government Congress has the power necessary for such work—has, indeed, broadly interpreted, a constitutional duty not only to oversee the execution of policy, but to inquire into the pressures that go into the formulation of policy—whether pressures by monopolists, or pressures by Communists. Many instances of Communist-tilted decision making would never have come to light but for Congressional scrutiny of decisions and decision makers. And had they not come to light, officials sympathetic to Communism might, with impunity, have gone right on serving Soviet interests. Examples are legion: the one-sided advantages frequently given the Soviets in the Cultural Exchange Program; the sale of wheat to the USSR at bargain prices during the height of the 1961 Berlin crisis; the semiofficial status of Owen Lattimore in Outer Mongolia during an intensive campaign, and his attempt, fortunately aborted, to rush recognition of that Soviet satellite. For a knowledge of this kind of thing, Congress relies mainly on the Committee, and will, predictably, continue to do so, since the Committee's function is bound to be more important as the pace of the Cold War is stepped up. "The showdown with the Communist world conspiracy is on," writes Eric Sevareid in the *New York Post* (July 9, 1961). "We have entered the final stage of the long struggle to determine if we can hold our world position short of a great war. We are in that stage because Khrushchev has decided we are. He will act accordingly, which will force us to act accordingly—if we can clear our heads."

WILLMOORE KENDALL

Chapter

4.

A SHORT HISTORY OF

THE COMMITTEE; AND A

CHRONOLOGY, 1946–1960

WHAT *domestic or external developments caused the formation of the House Committee on Un-American Activities? Did it grow out of an impulsive public demand, issuing from panic, for a Congressional response to the dramatic, but essentially pacific, social developments that followed in the wake of the revolution in Russia? Is the Committee a spastic response by Congress to social epiphenomena which might better have been dealt with by the customary laws of toleration for dissenting opinions? Who actually crafted the Committee, and what was it designed to do? What did it do during its early years? How did it come to achieve the status of a standing committee? How has it spent its time and energies, particularly since 1946, when it became a standing committee?*

Running along the crest of the gentle slope that forms the east bank of the Hudson River north of Tarrytown, the traces of an old path may still be found. Although an historical monument stands near the main road down by the river, the event it commemorates took place, according to local tradition, here on the path along the ridge. Somewhere in these woods, between the undulating fieldstone walls built by the early farmers, thirty miles north of New York City, on the path I've walked so often, Major André was captured, in the autumn of 1780, while the leaves were turning. The career of the "young and debonair artist, poet, satirist, and man of fashion" [1] stopped not a mile from where I now sit, engaged in writing a summary of my country's efforts to defend itself against espionage and subversion and treason.

Preludes

The states have had treason laws on their books from the earliest days.[2] Indeed, the history of governmental reaction to seditious activity stretches back to the trial of Socrates. Surely, said Aristotle, governments have a duty to investigate such things: "And since innovations creep in through the private life of individuals also, there ought to be a magistracy which will have an eye to those whose life is not in harmony with the government, whether oligarchy or democracy or any other." [3] And such an investigation is not discordant with liberty. In perhaps the noblest plea for freedom of speech that has ever been written, John Milton granted the necessity of governmental investigations: "I deny not, but that it is of greatest concernment in the Church and Commonwealth, to have a vigilant eye how books demean themselves, as well as men." [4] That thread of thought, like André's path, may be traced along the ridge of history. A century after Milton it was Edward Gibbon who said, "It is the undoubted right of every society to exclude from its communion and benefits such among its members as reject or violate those regulations which have been established by general consent." [5] Fourteen years after André's capture Alexander Hamilton defended the sternly repressive action of the Federal Government during the Whiskey Rebellion: "Those, therefore, who preach doctrines, or set examples, which undermine or subvert the authority of the laws, lead us from freedom to slavery. They incapacitate us from *a government of laws,* and consequently prepare the way for one of *force,* for mankind must have *government of one sort or another.*" [6]

So it was not strange that in the year of André's capture New York State should establish a committee to investigate and crush the subversion of the day—the Loyalist conspiracies.[7] (Two generations later Macaulay was writing, "A nation may be placed in such a situation that the majority must either impose disabilities or submit to them, and that what would, under ordinary circumstances, be justly condemned as persecution, may fall within the bounds of legitimate self defense." [8])

"Under ordinary circumstances"—of course. As a matter of fact, since the Congressional investigation of General St. Clair's disastrous expedition in 1792, Congress has instituted almost a thousand special investigations,[9] very few of them connected with espionage or subversion or treason. (A happy exception: the legislative inquiry in 1810 that discovered General Wilkinson's part in the Burr conspiracy.[10]) But in the year 1919, were the circumstances exactly ordinary? Consider:

On April 30, 1919, a vigilant postal clerk in New York discovered twenty bombs set to explode the next day, May Day.[11] In Washington a bomb intended for Attorney General A. Mitchell Palmer (who had taken office on March 3rd) exploded as it was being delivered to his house. The man carrying it up the steps was obliterated. Across the street, Assistant Secretary of the Navy Franklin D. Roosevelt came out of his house and found bits of blood and flesh on his doorstep.[12] Another bomb intended for a Senator from Georgia amputated the hands of his Negro maid.[13] Communism and anarchism had—I say it seriously—exploded onto the national scene.

On March 26, 1919, the New York State legislature established a joint committee of six, under the chairmanship of Senator Lusk, to investigate seditious activities and to make reports to the legislature.[14] The Lusk Committee published its report the next year: a four-volume study called *Revolutionary Radicalism*.[15]

In 1919 and early 1920 various Congressional committees and the Department of Justice were investigating Bolshevism.[16] In 1919 the Senate adopted a resolution to inquire into "any effort to incite the overthrow of the government." [17] In the same year there were 36 bills on subversive activities pending before the House and 32 before the Senate.[18] The Senate had authorized an investigation of "the brewing industry and German propaganda" during the First World War; this was now broadened to include Communist activities.[19] After the outbreak of bombings Senator Miles Poindexter of Washington offered a resolution demanding that the Department of Justice explain why it hadn't taken legal action against those citizens and deported those aliens who advocated the overthrow of the government by force and violence.[20] After this "ultimatum" [21] from Congress, Attorney General Palmer instituted his infamous and ill-starred raids. The first was scheduled for November 7, 1919, the second anniversary of the Bolshevik Revolution. Most of the aliens taken were released for lack of evidence, but 249 of them were deported, four days before Christmas, aboard the S.S. *Buford.* In January 1920, the Department of Justice seized 2,500 more and treated them with incomprehensible inhumanity. By April the Labor Department had canceled 3,000 of the 4,000 arrests made to date. In May, twelve eminent lawyers, among them Felix Frankfurter and Roscoe Pound, charged Attorney General Palmer with four violations of the Constitution. Palmer was forced to resign.[22] The conflict was now clearly stated between the rights of citizens and the duty of the government to defend itself.

In the noonday crowd on Wall Street, on September 16, 1920, a bomb exploded just outside the main office of the J. P. Morgan bank. Thirty people died; three hundred were injured.[23] The scars on the exterior wall of the House of Morgan remain to this day. New York has been the seat of subversion, whose physical mementos can be traced from André's path to the shrapnel signature of the anarchists; and as a result New York has led the counterattack—from the legislative investigation of conspiracies in 1780, to the Lusk Committee of 1919, to the earliest predecessor of HUAC, the Fish Committee of 1930.

The Predecessor Committees

On May 22, 1930, Congressman Earl C. Michener of Michigan offered a resolution (modeled on one by Congressman Hamilton Fish of New York) to appoint a committee of five members of the House to investigate Communist propaganda in the United States and "particularly in our educational institutions." The committee was also to investigate "the activities and membership of the Communist Party . . . and all entities, groups, or individuals who are alleged to advise, teach, or advocate the overthrow by force or violence of the Government of the United States, or attempt to undermine our republican form of government by inciting riots, sabotage, or revolutionary disorders." [24]

The principal opponent was Congressman C. William Ramseyer of Iowa, who complained he hadn't had fair notice of this resolution. He said the chief job of Congress was to combat the depression, not to indulge in "witch hunts." He feared the members of the proposed committee would use their positions to gain political prominence. He informed the House that the witch-hunters of Salem "not only hunted" their victims, "but burned them." (The victims were hanged, not burned; and the opposition to HUAC has seldom risen, during the last three decades, above the accuracy or intellectual level of Mr. Ramseyer's remarks.)

Mr. Fish of New York drew the attention of the House to the recent decline in anti-Communist activity. "Only fifteen Communists have been deported in the last four years," he said, concluding with this plea: "The main question before the House is to see to it that this revolutionary activity . . . that has its fangs in every industrial section of the country, is brought out into the open so that we may know who our enemies are; and as to these aliens who are criticizing and denouncing our form of government and urging revolutionary methods, is there any sane reason why we should compromise with them?"

The resolution was adopted, by a vote of 210 to 18, and the Special Committee to Investigate Communist Activities came into existence. Mr. Fish assumed the chairmanship. An appropriation of $25,000 was voted. Before it issued its last report on January 17, 1931, the Fish Committee reported that there were 12,000 dues-paying members of the Communist Party in this country and about a half million sympathizers. It denounced the American Civil Liberties Union as a bulwark of Communism. It proposed legislation: to prohibit the sending of Communist matter through the mails; to create a special section of the FBI to investigate subversive activities and to watch individuals; to send Treasury agents to Russia to study forced labor; to declare illegal the Communist Party or any party that advocated the violent destruction of our govermnment.[25] (Opponents of HUAC and its predecessors often isolate the proposal to send Treasury agents to Russia and criticize it as a sample of the Fish Committee's entire work.)

After the Fish Committee dissolved, there was only one committee of the House that could effectively concern itself with the problems of subversion: the House Committee on Immigration and Naturalization. Soon after the rise of Hitler, the chairman of that committee, Mr. Samuel Dickstein of New York, noticed with anxiety the spread of Nazi activities in this country. He offered a resolution, introduced in the House by Mr. Eugene E. Cox of Georgia, on March 20, 1934, to establish a committee of seven members to investigate: "(1) the extent, character, and objects of Nazi propaganda activities in the United States; (2) the diffusion within the United States of subversive propaganda that is instigated from foreign countries and attacks the principle of the form of government as guaranteed by our Constitution; and (3) all other questions in relation thereto that would aid the Congress in any necessary remedial legislation." [26]

During the debate Mr. Dickstein listed 20 aspects of Nazi subversive activity in this country, using information that had resulted from an informal investigation conducted by a subcommittee of his Committee on Immigration and Naturalization. Much of the debate was concerned with the possibility that this might be a piece of anti-German legislation. Eventually the word "Nazi" was amended to read "foreign." Mr. Dickstein announced that his resolution had the support of the American Federation of Labor, the American Legion, the Veterans of Foreign Wars, and the Disabled American Veterans of the World War.

The resolution was adopted by a vote of 168 to 31. John W. McCormack of Massachusetts became the chairman of this Special Committee to Investigate Un-American Activities, and Mr. Dickstein vice-chairman. The McCormack-Dickstein Committee functioned until February of 1935. Although it was principally concerned with Nazi activity, its report ("Investigation of Nazi and Other Propaganda") included some analysis of Communist activities as well. As a result of the legislative recommendations made by the committee, Congress passed the Foreign Agents Registration Act in 1938.[27]

When the McCormack-Dickstein Committee disbanded, the problem of subversion went once more to the Committee on Immigration and Naturalization. It became clear after three years (and in the midst of a wave of sitdown strikes instigated by Communists) that this committee could not cope with the problem. A resolution by Mr. Dickstein to form an investigative committee was introduced but voted down.[28] Vice-President John Nance Garner called Congressman Martin Dies of Texas and asked him to gather support for an Un-American Activities Committee that would have "substance and specific duties." [29] On May 26, 1938, Mr. Dies offered a resolution to establish a committee of seven members with duties almost identical to those outlined in the Dickstein resolution of 1934; but instead of "foreign propaganda activities" the new resolution said "un-American propaganda activities," and instead of "subversive propaganda" it spoke of "subversive and un-American propaganda."

Mr. J. Will Taylor of Tennessee, in support of the resolution, argued that the proposed committee would help to overcome the difficulty of controlling subversion through the immigration laws. "For instance," said Mr. Taylor, "in 1932 there were 19,426 deportations of aliens, whereas in 1934, under

Mme. Perkins, Secretary of Labor, the number had dwindled to 8,879; and yet there are nearly a million—some estimates say more than 3,000,000—aliens in this country illegally, from whose ranks the Communist Party draws a considerable part of its following." (Hamilton Fish had used this argument in 1930.)

Mr. Harold Knutson of Minnesota, who had argued against the 1934 resolution, rose up to ask the House what accomplishments could be attributed to the previous (McCormack-Dickstein) committee. Mr. McCormack answered, "It brought to the attention of the American public the damnable efforts that were being made in this country. It aroused public opinion. As a result, several pieces of legislation have been enacted into law. Several bills are now pending. . . . One requires propagandists in the employ of any foreign agency to register so that the American people will know who these paid propagandists are."

Mr. Dies found it necessary once more to explain that the resolution was not a piece of anti-German propaganda. He went on to list 26 patriotic organizations that endorsed the resolution. And he charged that there were 32 Nazi camps in this country and 480,000 Nazi Party members. "I regard Communism and Nazism and Fascism," said Mr. Dies, "as having one underlying principle—dictatorship—the theory that government should have the right to control the lives, the fortunes, the happiness, the beliefs, and every detail of the life of the human being, and that man is a pawn of the government, rather than the American conception that government is created for the benefit of mankind."

Despite Mr. Dies's precaution of disavowing at the outset any anti-German thrust in the resolution, Maury Maverick of Texas took it upon himself to defend the entire German-American population (but more particularly, one suspects, the thriving German settlements in Mr. Maverick's district around San Antonio). Having looked after the honor of his constituency, Mr. Maverick went on to belittle the subversive problem in terms that anticipated President Truman's by a full ten years: "Of course, others will drag the red herring around and talk of Communists and the 'red menace.' "

But Mr. John J. O'Connor of New York drew the applause of the House when he said, "Why, Mr. Speaker, I saw 50,000 people march through our streets with the red flags of Communism. They were of all races and colors. We in Congress here are the only ones who can do our duty to our established Government by investigating this monster and stopping this conflagration before it sweeps us out of control of our Government. . . . Let us save this country . . . before the hour becomes too late." (Lord Chief Justice Treby, in Vaughn's Case, 1696, said, "And after this kind of reasoning, they will not be guilty, till they have success; and, if they have success enough, it will be too late to question them." [30])

John Rankin of Mississippi, who was to move successfully to make HUAC a permanent committee in 1945, opposed the 1938 Dies resolution at first—most probably on personal grounds, for he withdrew his opposition when he learned that Mr. Dies and not Mr. Dickstein would be the chairman of the proposed committee.[31] And J. Parnell Thomas, who was later to serve as chairman of HUAC, also opposed the Dies resolution in 1938—and also withdrew his opposition, after informing himself of the extent of Bund activities in his state of New Jersey.[32]

The Dies resolution was adopted, 191 to 41, and the Special Committee on Un-American Activities came to life.[33] Chairman Dies asked for an appropriation of $100,000 but was voted only $25,000.[34]

Through an unbroken chain of committees in each succeeding Congress this Committee stands as the direct ancestor of the present HUAC. The present Committee is often accused of straying far from the duties originally assigned to it. This charge finds little support in the historical record. Starting in 1919 the principal subversive activity under Congressional consideration was that of the Communists. In 1930 the Fish Committee was created to look into this specific area. By 1934 the attention of the country focused on Hitler, but even then the McCormack-Dickstein Committee was to investigate not "Nazi" but "foreign" propaganda and subversive activity. Finally, in

1938 the Dies Committee came into being to investigate not "foreign" but "un-American" activities, and the less than dominant role played by the fear of Nazi subversion can be inferred from the reception the House gave to Mr. O'Connor's evocation of the American spirit against the Communist marchers, and Mr. Dies' accurate summary of the underlying similarity of Communism and Nazism and Fascism. The legislative investigation of subversive activity evolved slowly from 1919 to 1938 —from temporary reaction against specific threats, to generalized action along the whole front of subversion from whatever source it might derive. This is a type of evolution not uncommon in human affairs. What prophet, watching the antics of the Boston Tea Party, could have foreseen the ultimate codification of that expression in the Constitution?

HUAC, 1938–1944

The House voted to continue HUAC in every succeeding Congress. In 1939 the appropriation was raised to $100,000. It ranged between $100,000 and $150,000 until 1944, dropped to a low of $50,000 in 1945, reached $200,000 in 1948, and has been in the neighborhood of $300,000 a year since then.[35] Opposition to HUAC in the House has declined, as measured by the votes on appropriations: [36]

	Ayes	*Nays*
1942	291	64
1943	278	66
1945	315	54
1946	240	81
1948	337	37
1949	353	29
1950	348	12
1953	352	2
1954	363	1
1956	385	1
1961	412	6

(In years not shown, the House took no roll call.)

In its first year HUAC exposed the activities of the German-American Bund, showing how it distributed Nazi propaganda in the United States and identifying its reserve force of 5,000 uniformed storm troopers.[37] After HUAC exposed the Communists and fellow travelers in the Federal Theater Project and the Federal Writers Project, the Congress abolished those projects. Chairman Dies in this year published a report on "radical and Communist activities" that were "rampant among the studios of Hollywood"—the precursor of the 1947 and 1951 investigations.[38] HUAC produced a detailed analysis of Communist activity in front organizations; of Communist finances; propaganda centers; publications in English and other languages; Communist schools and camps; and Communist infiltration into educational institutions, the Army and Navy, youth organizations, the unemployed, minority groups (Negro and other), the theater, farmer groups, and many more. Also in 1938 the opposition mounted one of its earliest formal assaults on the Committee.

It all came about after Dr. J. B. Matthews (former fellow traveler, and the man who coined that term) testified on August 19th: "The Communist Party relies heavily upon the carelessness or indifference of thousands of prominent citizens in lending their names for its propaganda purposes." Mr. Matthews gave as an example the Communist-owned French newspaper, *Le Soir,* which "recently featured hearty greetings from Clark Gable, Robert Taylor, James Cagney and even Shirley Temple. ... No one, I hope, is going to claim that any one of these persons in particular is a Communist." [39]

Mr. Matthews was too sanguine. Heywood Broun and Frances Perkins joined the wild halloo. Harold Ickes set the tone: "They've gone to Hollywood and there discovered a great Red Plot. They have found dangerous radicals there, led by little Shirley Temple. Imagine the great Committee raiding her nursery and seizing her dolls as evidence!" [40] (Question: Did Matthews say Shirley Temple was a Communist?)

In its first annual report HUAC said, "Our committee has only scratched the surface."

In 1939 the direct and indirect results of HUAC's work were manifold. Fritz Kuhn, leader of the German-American Bund, testified before the Committee in August and October.[41] As a result he was convicted of larceny and deprived of citizenship; and the Bund was discredited. Ralph Townsend, exposed as a Japanese agent, was convicted under the Foreign Agents Registration Act. Earl Browder, then General Secretary of the Communist Party, and William Weiner, its financial secretary, and Nicholas Dozenberg, a Communist spy, were convicted of passport fraud. Fraser S. Gardner, secret agent of Silver Shirt leader William Dudley Pelley, was convicted of perjury. Bookniga, a Soviet propaganda agency, pleaded guilty of violations of the Foreign Agents Registration Act. Arno Rissi and Mrs. Leslie Fry, leaders of Fascist groups on the West Coast, fled the country. HUAC published the names of 563 government employees who were members of a single Communist front, the American League for Peace and Democracy. HUAC published a 967-page report on the nature and aims of the Communist Party, its connection with the Soviet Union, and its advocacy of force and violence.

In 1940 the Committee's work led to the dissolution of Pelley's Silver Shirts and his apprehension for unlawful acts in North Carolina. Congress passed a bill, introduced by Committee member Jerry Voorhis of California, to require foreign-controlled agencies to furnish public reports of certain pertinent facts. HUAC exposed the fraud and corruption in election petitions filed by the Communist Party; as a result, a hundred indictments were handed down, leading to more than fifty convictions. The committee published a 414-page report on Nazi activities (cited later by President Roosevelt when he shut down the German consulates [42]) and a 60-page report on Axis propaganda arriving at the West Coast on Japanese ships: a report that led the Post Office to seize all such material. Leaning on information gathered by HUAC, Martin Dies was able to publish in 1940 one of the first and best-documented (and least-known) books on Communist subversion.[43] And in 1940 the opposition attempted a second formal attack on HUAC.

Congressman Frank E. Hook of Michigan announced to the House that he held in his hand (where have we heard this phrase?) photostats of letters proving that HUAC and Martin Dies were in league with the Silver Shirts. HUAC's chief investigator, Robert Stripling, showed that the letters were forgeries by one David Dubois Mayne. The forger confessed and was convicted. Mr. Hook's case against HUAC collapsed.[44]

In 1941 the Committee exposed the Communist affiliations of four highly placed O.P.A. officials and informed the Justice Department that 1,124 other federal employees were members of subversive groups. It showed that Communists had instigated the sabotage strikes in a number of defense plants and municipal operations. Its 178-page report containing original documents of the German-American Bund led to the trial and conviction of G. Wilhelm Kunze, one of the Bund leaders. In another long report it showed the Communist control of the Transport Workers Union. Before the Japanese attack on Pearl Harbor the Committee was ready to release a 287-page report on Japanese intelligence about U. S. Navy vessels, Japanese intelligence about our fleet positions at Pearl Harbor, Japanese naval officers serving aboard radio-equipped fishing smacks, and action committees in Hawaii and on the West Coast. But the Justice Department, after consulting with President Roosevelt and Secretary of State Cordell Hull, refused to co-operate; and HUAC held no public hearings on the subject and published no report.[45]

In 1942 the Committee sent to the President a list of 17,000 workers in defense industries whose associations gave rise to reasonable doubts as to their ultimate allegiance. After the Japanese attack on Pearl Harbor, the Committee found Washington receptive enough to its lengthy report on Japanese espionage activities. One apparent result of this report was the lamentable deportations of the Japanese population from strategic areas along the West Coast—an action that drew very little fire from the most vocal critics of the Committee.

In 1943 the Committee continued its investigation of Japanese relocation centers, investigated Communist activity in

West Coast aviation plants, and issued a 260-page report with a comprehensive listing of Axis agents and groups in this country and a handbook on Japanese subversive activities. As a result of its investigations a rider was attached to the Deficiency Appropriations Act of 1943, forbidding payment of salaries to three federal employees whose records intertwined with the activities and front organizations of the Communist Party: Robert Morss Lovett, Goodwin Watson, and William E. Dodd, Jr. (Many years later Dodd's daughter and her husband were to defect to Communist Czechoslovakia.) The Supreme Court in 1946 ruled this part of the bill unconstitutional as a bill of attainder.[46]

In 1944 the Committee issued a special report on Communist domination of 21 CIO unions. It cited 160 organizations as fronts of the Communist Party. The rapidly growing files of the Committee were consulted for almost a month by officials of the Justice Department while preparing their case in the mass trial of 29 alleged pro-Axis seditionists in Washington, D. C.

HUAC, 1945–1960

As the war drew to a close, there seemed to be less and less reason to fear subversion at home. The Axis, after all, was crumbling; and was not Russia our ally? The investigations in recent years had produced less and less. The Committee had seldom met in 1943 and 1944. The House reduced HUAC's appropriation from $150,000 in 1943 to $75,000 in 1944. The chairman, Martin Dies, announced in May 1944 that he would not seek re-election in the fall.[47] Toward the close of that year only a few people still believed in the mission of HUAC.[48] Among them was John Rankin of Mississippi.

It was at this same time that the infiltration of Communists in the Federal Government reached its highest point of success. There is more than a superficial relation between the strength (or influence) of the Communists and the disfavor into which HUAC was falling.

Also at this time the opposition revived the point first raised by C. William Ramseyer of Iowa during the floor debate in

1930 over the proposed Fish Committee: the possibility that Committee members might use their positions for their own political advantage. This charge, which is still encountered today, deserves some notice. It is enough, I believe, to admit openly that service on the Committee has been a political asset that the members have exploited, more or less. But a major reason for the desirability of Committee posts is that public opinion polls since 1938 have shown a strong popular demand for investigations of subversion. If the people want this, then politicians will vie for the honor of giving it to them; just as politicians vie for the honor of introducing "welfare" measures they think the people want. The critics of the Committee never complain that politicians use welfare programs to enhance their political careers; they would, I presume, urge upon us politicans of welfare but dollar-a-year men in antisubversion.

Out of this complex of accusations and hypotheses emerged the feeling that HUAC was doomed. But, on January 3, 1945, as the House was organizing itself, just after Mr. Adolph Sabath of Illinois had offered a resolution to adopt the rules of the 78th Congress as the rules of the new 79th Congress, John Rankin arose to offer an amendment, the meaning of which was to increase HUAC to nine members, make it a standing committee of the House under the name of House Committee on Un-American Activities, and give it the same duties as the Dies Committee had had, with the added duty of reporting its results to the House and making any recommendations it deemed advisable.

Mr. Sabath moved that the amendment be referred to committee. Mr. Rankin made a point of order: "An amendment to a pending motion cannot be referred to committee." The Speaker of the House concurred. The House had to vote on Rankin's amendment.

Most of the floor debate concerned the unorthodox manner of setting up a permanent committee under an amendment to the rules. Mr. McCormack, past chairman of the McCormack-Dickstein Committee, said that he had voted in favor of HUAC every time it had come up, that he would vote for it again, that he supported the work it was doing; but he objected strongly to the "procedure that in one-hundred-and-fifty-odd years of constitutional history, no Congress, no membership of this body, has ever followed to establish a permanent committee of this kind."

Nevertheless, Mr. Rankin stuck to his guns, insisting that the important thing was to preserve the records of the Committee. For they were valuable: they had been visited by other agencies of the government more than 5,000 times. And they were in jeopardy: for their normal destination if the Committee were disbanded would be the Library of Congress, whose Librarian, Archibald MacLeish, was frankly hostile to the Committee. "Some of the men," said Mr. Rankin, "who went over there to look over those papers were prepared to remove them and said they would like to throw them into the Potomac River. I want to see that these records are kept; that is the one thing I am striving for."

In a voice vote, the amendment appeared to have lost. Mr. Rankin, correctly guessing that some Congressmen didn't want to be on record as voting against HUAC, called for a division. In the division, the amendment passed, 208 to 186.[49] HUAC was permanent. The floor debate on the Fish Committee occupies six pages of the *Congressional Record;* the McCormack-Dickstein Committee 15 pages; the Dies Committee 19 pages. John Rankin made HUAC permanent, and the debate fills only four pages.

That the enormous and carefully cross-indexed files of the Committee are important has been amply proven. Representatives of federal agencies have been visiting the HUAC files at the rate of about 3,000 visits per year since 1945. The Committee staff itself makes about 1,500 requests a year to the reference service. Members of Congress in the last decade have made about 2,000 requests a year for information from the files.[50] There is no "typical" request. The reports made by the reference service in response to requests from properly authorized officials may vary from a verbal report to a reproduction of original documents to extended reports on individuals, organizations, and general topics. All reports by the reference service are thoroughly documented, and they are not accompanied by any attempt at evaluation: that is done only in official reports of the Committee.

The first chairman of HUAC in 1945 was Edward J. Hart of New Jersey. In July he was succeeded by John S. Wood of Georgia. In this least active year, with an appropriation of only $50,000, the Committee confined itself to investigations of radio programs conducted by the government, and to hearings on Communist Party activities (Earl Browder and William Z. Foster testified).

In 1946 Mr. J. Parnell Thomas of New Jersey assumed the chairmanship. In the Legislative Organization Act the Committee's permanence was reaffirmed. The Committee investigated the financial arrangements of the Communist Party and identified the Joint Anti-Fascist Refugee Committee as a subversive group. Eighteen leaders of that group were cited for contempt of Congress and convicted by District Court juries in Washington. Louis Budenz testified voluminously. Gerald L. K. Smith was questioned about his racist propaganda. Richard Morford, Director of the National Council of American-Soviet Friendship (a Communist front), and George Marshall, chairman of the National Federation for Constitutional Liberties (another Communist front), were cited for contempt of Congress, convicted by District Court juries, and sentenced to prison.

In 1947 the Committee exposed Gerhart Eisler as the principal agent of the Communist International in this country. He was convicted of contempt and passport fraud; he fled the country aboard the S.S. *Batory,* and returned to eastern Europe. Leon Josephson, exposed by HUAC as the official source of false passports for Communists, was convicted of contempt. Hanns Eisler, Gerhart's brother, was exposed as a member of the Communist Party in Germany who had concealed his affiliations when he entered this country. The Committee recommended deportation; Hanns Eisler left voluntarily. Eugene Dennis, General Secretary of the Communist Party of the United States, was sentenced to jail for contempt. In October the Committee held extensive hearings at which ten Hollywood writers and directors refused to affirm or deny charges that they were Communists, despite the documented evidence held by the Committee. (They pleaded the First Amendment guarantee of freedom of speech; the Fifth Amendment was first invoked before HUAC on July 23rd of that year, during the testimony of Robert C. Black, whose counsel was Joseph Forer—notorious as an attorney for Communists.[51]) The "Hollywood Ten" were cited for contempt and eventually jailed. The Committee investigated Communist infiltration into labor unions (Local 248 of the United Auto Workers; the United Electrical, Radio, and Machine Workers of America—which we shall meet again in 1955; and Local 22 of the Food, Tobacco, and Agricultural Workers). It issued reports documenting the Communist Party as an agent of a foreign power, which reports, in addition to others of similar purport, were to be cited by the Supreme Court in 1961 as evidence justifying the McCarran (Internal Security) Act.[52] In other reports it exposed the American Youth for Democracy as a Communist front; and exposed the Southern Conference for Human Welfare and the Civil Rights Congress as Communist fronts.[53]

In 1948 the Hiss case erupted into full public view (see Chapter 6). On August 3rd Whittaker Chambers testified that J. Peters was the head of a Communist underground apparatus in this country. J. Peters, alias J. V. Peters, alias Alexander Goldberger, alias Isador Boorstein, alias Steve Lapin, alias Roberts, alias Pete Stevens, alias Steve Miller, alias Alexander Stevens, was summoned to appear before the Committee. He refused to answer any questions. Deportation proceedings commenced. The Committee continued its investigation of Communist activity in labor unions. The House voted (301 to 29) on April 22nd to direct Averell Harriman to produce the letter sent to him dated May 15, 1947 (when he was Secretary of Commerce) by J. Edgar Hoover, which discussed the loyalty status of Dr. Edward U. Condon, then Director of the Bureau of Standards and scientific adviser to the Special Committee on

Atomic Energy. But the Executive Branch (President Truman) ordered Harriman not to release the letter. That information denied, HUAC held no public hearings on the Condon matter.[54] (The opposition holds that HUAC intentionally smeared Dr. Condon, then refused to hold hearings.) The Committee reported, and the House passed, the Mundt-Nixon bill, requiring Communists to register; but the bill died in the Senate Judiciary Committee.[55]

In 1949 the chairman, J. Parnell Thomas, was convicted of malversation (he put into his own pocket money the government was paying as wages for fictitious or supernumerary employees). Mr. Wood of Georgia assumed the chairmanship for the second time. The Committee continued its investigation of Communist activity and infiltration in minority groups. It investigated charges that a certain scientist had turned over some atomic secrets to a Communist spy, and it recommended that the scientist, Joseph W. Weinberg, be prosecuted for perjury. (He was prosecuted—and acquitted, on March 4, 1953.[56]) During the year the Committee distributed about 2,000,000 copies of its publications, the bulk of which were copies of its pamphlet, *100 Things You Should Know About Communism*, a revised edition of which was planned for publication in 1961. The Committee recommended, among other things, an extension of the statute of limitations in espionage cases (Hiss's loophole), and a redefinition of the treason statutes in view of modern methods of subversion.[57]

In 1950 the Committee, after extended hearings, reported out a bill similar to the Mundt-Nixon bill of 1948, requiring Communists and front groups to register, denying passports to Party members, and excluding them from employment in the government or in defense industries. The House passed the bill (354 to 20); it was combined with a Senate bill and was enacted, over President Truman's veto (September 20th), as the Internal Security Act of 1950 (the McCarran-Wood Act).* In a case

* The full title of this act is the McCarran-Wood Subversive Activities Control Act of 1950. It is also known as the Anti-Subversive Act, the Internal Security Act of 1950, the McCarran Act, and various other titles combining the elements above in different ways.

growing out of his testimony before the Committee in 1950, William W. Remington was tried for perjury, and convicted (January 20, 1953 [58]). The Committee held hearings concerning the charge that valuable materials and information relating to the manufacture of an atomic bomb were shipped out from the United States at Great Falls, Montana, and heard the testimony of ex-FBI agent Matthew Cvetic concerning Communist influence in the Progressive Party. Extended hearings were held in Hawaii which revealed a serious penetration by the Communists of the labor union movement. Other investigations included the circumstances surrounding the assassination of Leon Trotsky, and their bearing on immigration and counterespionage laws. During the year the Committee added more than 300,000 items of information to its files.[59] By the end of the year it had heard some 1,300 witnesses and issued 71 publications and reports since its founding.[60] Writing in 1951, an author not known at the time for his sympathy toward Congressional investigations had this to say of the Committee's files: "No comparable source of published data on American Communism exists anywhere else in the world." [61]

In 1951 the Committee held about 200 hearings, more than half of them public. It investigated the extent of Communist infiltration in farmers' and veterans' groups and found it refreshingly slight. Once again it looked into the motion picture industry (partly in response to criticisms that the "Hollywood Ten" were not Communists), and once again it labeled the Hollywood Ten Communists—along with 300 other persons associated with the industry. The Committee investigated Communist infiltration into areas of vital defense industries (Baltimore, Boston); and from further testimony by Whittaker Chambers it uncovered the curious connections of Oliver Edmund Clubb, then a foreign service officer with the State Department. Clubb was relieved of his duties pending a review by the State Department's Loyalty Board. The Committee issued a report, *Guide to Subversive Organizations and Publications,* that listed 624 organizations previously cited as Communist or front groups, and 204 "Red-tinged" publications.[62]

By now another antagonistic writer had to admit that the Committee had done some good, though he sang his paean in the minor mode: the Committee had "promoted awareness" of the Communist purpose, it had "put the public on its guard," and it had exposed, in 1948, "certain pre-war espionage activities" within the government.[63]

In 1952 the Committee, continuing its investigations of Communism in vital defense areas (Detroit, Chicago, Philadelphia), published the names of several hundred persons identified as Communists in those areas. In Philadelphia the Committee uncovered the existence of a city-wide Communist underground apparatus. In Los Angeles the Committee uncovered Communist cells within the medical, legal, and journalistic professions. Continuing its investigation of Communism in the motion picture industry, the Committee reported that as a result of its exposures "the extensive financial reservoir which had existed in Hollywood for Communist purposes had been greatly diminished." The Condon case (1948) came up again when a member of Congress charged the Committee with failure to hear Dr. Condon. The Committee invited the scientist to appear; he declined. The Committee then subpoenaed him; he appeared, denied any knowledge of the espionage activities of persons he had associated with, and denied having been a Communist.

During the year the Committee distributed almost a half million copies of its hearings. Among its legislative proposals were the recommendation to make it a crime to transport in interstate commerce, without authorization, any classified government document; and a recommendation to restrict government employment under the Civil Service Act to citizens or to persons who owe allegiance to the United States.[64]

In 1953 Mr. Harold H. Velde of Illinois assumed the chairmanship. The Committee held 154 sessions during the year, with hearings in Washington, Los Angeles, New York, Albany, Columbus, Lansing, Philadelphia, and San Francisco. Although the Committee's investigations revealed new information on Communist infiltration of defense industries, its principal effort during the year was the continued investigation of conspiratorial Communist activity within the general areas of entertainment and education. Testimony before the Committee revealed that the Communists had made a determined (and often successful) effort to infiltrate into the educational system. Testimony in New York disclosed the successful efforts of the Communist Party. Several witnesses reported on efforts to infiltrate into the shipping industry and the waterfront unions. Bishop G. Bromley Oxnam made a theatrical appearance in his own behalf.* Harvey Matusow gave testimony on his prodigious career as an informant. During the year the Committee distributed almost a quarter million copies of its publications (in greatest demand: the committee's *Organized Communism in the United States*). In its annual report it recommended legislation to strengthen the oath provision of the Taft-Hartley Act to prevent Communist infiltration into labor unions, and legislation to deny to subversive publications the use of the United States mails under second-class privileges.[65] (The Fish Committee had proposed substantially the same thing in 1931.)

In 1954 the Committee held hearings in Washington, D. C., Albany, Chicago, Dayton, Flint, Lansing, San Diego, Seattle, Portland (Ore.), and Miami. (It is worth mentioning that the opposition to HUAC often rails at the Committee for its travels about the country, accusing it of unnecessary "junketing"; yet, when the Committee stays in Washington and summons witnesses from distant places, the same opposition rails at the Committee for placing undue hardship on the witnesses.) During the year the Committee heard testimony from nearly 600 witnesses. By 1954 the Committee had made 47 recommendations, all but eight of which had been favorably acted upon by Congress or the Executive. The Committee issued several reports, among them a summation of its years-long investigation of Communist penetration into defense industries, *Colonization of America's Basic Industries by the Communist Party of the U.S.A.*; an informative booklet on the work of the Committee,

* For further information see page 304.

This Is Your House Committee on Un-American Activities (which met such strong demand that the supply was almost immediately exhausted); the result of an investigation into crackpot non-Communist groups, *Preliminary Report on Neo-Fascist and Hate Groups*; and a report, *The American Negro in the Communist Party*, in which the Committee took note of the "infinitesimal" success of the Communists in engaging the allegiance of Negroes.[66] Early in November Francis E. Walter of Pennsylvania, who was scheduled to be the next chairman of the Committee, announced that he would propose to the House that HUAC be abolished as an independent committee and that its function be carried on by a subcommittee of the House Judiciary Committee.[67] Within two weeks, however, Mr. Walter announced he might withdraw his proposal—probably (according to one press report [68]) because he had been advised that it would not attract the necessary support from Republicans.

In 1955 the Committee held hearings in Washington, D. C., New York, New Jersey, Illinois, Wisconsin, California, and Washington State. As a result of his appearance before the Committee, John T. Gojack, an official of the Communist-controlled United Electrical, Radio, and Machine Workers of America, was cited by the House for contempt. From the hearings the Committee proved that this union siphoned off the workers' dues for Communist Party purposes. The Committee discovered ten Communist cells that had previously operated within the Executive and Legislative branches. It exposed the Communist control of several summer camps; and one was closed up by midyear. Mrs. Mildred Blauvelt, a former secret agent of the New York City police department, helped the Committee put together a complete picture of the subversive nature of "neighborhood" Communist clubs in the New York City area. In a series of hearings the Committee was able to show that the National Committee to Secure Justice in the Rosenberg Case was a Communist front, and that much of the $300,000 raised by that organization was used for Communist purposes. The several chairmen of HUAC, the Senate Committee on Government Operations, and the Senate Internal Security Subcommittee reached an agreement under which they would seek to avoid overlapping or duplication in their investigations. The Committee issued a cumulative index to all hearings and reports from 1938 through 1954. It made ten legislative proposals, most of which had been made in previous years; one of them was that the government be allowed to prosecute for perjury a witness who makes willfully contradictory statements under oath, thus relieving the government of the burden of proving which of the two contradictory statements is false.[69]

In 1956 the Committee conducted hearings in San Francisco, Youngstown, New Haven, Los Angeles, St. Louis, Seattle, Chicago, New York, Denver, and Washington. Frank Donner, author of an anti-HUAC book published in 1961, testified on June 28, 1956, invoking the First and Fifth Amendments when questioned as to his membership and activities in the Communist Party. Almost 400 witnesses testified before the Committee. Looking into Communist attacks on the security programs of the Federal Government, the Committee found that 180 Communist front organizations had been created to balk the security provisions of the Immigration and Nationality Act alone. One witness reported that in 1955 the Port of New York alone handled almost 2,000,000 pieces of mail suspected of containing political propaganda. The Committee conducted a somewhat inconclusive investigation into "the curious posture of a major United States 'educational' foundation, the Fund for the Republic, Inc., some of whose practices have provided great aid and comfort to the Communist apparatus, particularly in the vital area of mass communications and entertainment." After the testimony of Sidney Hatkin, who was approached for subversive purposes by one Vladimir Mikheev posing as a student, Mr. Mikheev was relieved of his duties at the Soviet Embassy and recalled to the Soviet Union. During the year the Committee filled requests for more than 350,000 copies of its hearings and reports. Among its publications during the year were *The Great Pretense,* an analysis of spurious anti-Stalinism in the Soviet Union; *The Communist Conspiracy,* an analysis of the interna-

tional Communist movement; *Trial by Treason,* an analysis of
Communist front activity in the Rosenberg case (demand was
so heavy that the supply was exhausted a few days after publication); and *Soviet Total War,* an analysis of Communist use of
violence and deceit (also "sold out" a few days after publication).[70]

During 1957 the Committee uncovered new areas of Communist infiltration in industry and the arts, and exposed the
Communist penetration of the communications systems of several government agencies. Hearings were held in San Francisco,
New Orleans, New York, Chicago, Buffalo, New Haven, Baltimore, Newark, and Washington. The Committee distributed to
the public 285,000 copies of its reports. During the year it issued
a report on Communist political subversion; also *Operation
Abolition* ("The Campaign Against HUAC, the FBI, and the
Government Security Program by the Emergency Civil Liberties Union and Its Affiliates"); and a series of reports on World
Communist leaders. The *Watkins* decision of the Supreme
Court was handed down on June 17th, requiring that legislative inquiries make "undisputably clear" to witnesses the pertinence of their questions. One day later 29 witnesses in San
Francisco relied on that decision when they refused to answer
Committee questions; but, after Committee counsel explained
the pertinence of the questions, 28 of the witnesses gave up
their sole reliance on *Watkins* and (don't be half safe) took
the Fifth.[71]

In 1958 the Committee held hearings in Gary (Ind.), Buffalo,
Boston, Atlanta, Newark, Los Angeles, and Washington. At
the Atlanta hearing, where the Committee was investigating
Communist influence on propaganda aimed at the South
(through the Emergency Civil Liberties Committee and other
fronts), Frank Wilkinson and Carl Braden refused to answer
any questions. They were cited for contempt, convicted, and
eventually sentenced to a year in jail. Other contempt citations
were voted on Edward Yellin, Robert Lehrer, Alfred Samter,
and Victor Malis (all of whom refused to answer questions as
to their having concealed their superior educational back-

grounds when applying for production-line work in the steel industry in Gary, Ind.); and Sidney Turoff, Sidney Ingerman, and Paul Rosenkrants (who refused to answer questions about their involvement in Communist cells in the metals industries). The Committee printed 424,000 copies of its hearings, consultations, and reports during the year; in response to direct requests it distributed 136,000 copies of reports of previous years.[72]

In 1959 the Committee took extended testimony on Soviet espionage, terror, and internal security operations from a former officer in the Soviet state security system. In two separate hearings it continued its investigation of the Communist Party in California. In Pittsburgh the Committee studied the current strategy and tactics of the Communist Party, the problems of industrial security, and problems arising from denaturalization and deportation proceedings. In Chicago the Committee held hearings in its continuing investigation of Communist penetration of basic industries. In Washington the Committee held the first of a series of hearings on the Communist training operations. During its hearings in New York the Committee gathered information on "a $100 million Communist propaganda campaign to penetrate the Spanish-speaking countries of the Western Hemisphere, with Puerto Rico as a 'nerve center.' " Frank Donner, by now general counsel of the Communist-influenced United Electrical, Radio, and Machine Workers of America, testified again (he had previously appeared before the Committee in 1956). Three former Communists had identified Donner as a member of the Communist Party. Asked whether he had resigned technical membership in the Party, Donner said, "I never resigned and you have no evidence I joined, so there you are." During the year the Committee issued several reports: a 75-page study of the activities of Communist lawyers; a report on the reorganization of the Southern California District of the Communist Party; a report on Communist lobbying in Washington, D. C.; and the first volume (by Professor Gerhart Niemeyer) in the two-part series, *Facts on Communism*. During the year the Committee distributed 450,000 copies of its current hearings, consultations, and reports; and 200,000 copies of Committee publications of earlier years.[73]

In 1960 the Committee held hearings on the case of the Air Reserve Center Training Manual that had been withdrawn after there had been a wave of protests against its assertion that the Communists had infiltrated into some churches and church groups. Dudley C. Sharp, Secretary of the Air Force, testified that the revised manual would again point out that the Communists were trying to infiltrate into the churches, and said, "If it were not in the manual, we would be very derelict in our duty to inform our people." The hearings on Communist training centers continued. Lt. Col. Frantisek Tisler, chief of Czechoslovakia's military intelligence operations in this country from 1955 until his defection in 1959, testified on the Communist use of diplomatic officials for espionage (anticipating, by just one year, the exposure of the espionage operations of a member of the Czechoslovakian Embassy). In May the Committee held hearings in San Francisco to investigate the Northern California branch of the Communist Party—in terms of tactics, leaders, and techniques to avoid detection. It was these hearings that drew the riotous demonstrations that were part of the campaign to destroy HUAC. The Committee continued its hearings on Communist activity on the waterfront and in radio communications. During the year the Committee issued a report on the San Francisco riots; issued the film *Operation Abolition* on the same subject; issued the first volume of a selective chronology of the World Communist movement (1818–1945); and issued volume II (by Dr. David J. Dallin) of *Facts on Communism,* a study of the Soviet Union from Lenin to Khrushchev. During the year the Committee printed about 332,000 copies of current hearings, consultations, and reports.[74]

At the end of its report for 1960 the Committee had this to say: "We must not permit the incident of exposure, necessarily involved in legislative activity, to be degraded by Communist name-calling, which has for its purpose the suppression of discussion and understanding. The time calls for knowledge and action. Relentlessly, we must continue to breathe down the stiff necks of traitors and enemies within, until that better day is born—which is the fondest hope of America—when the lion lies down with the lamb, and all this will no longer be necessary."

WILLIAM F. RICKENBACKER

★

Chapter
5.

A YEAR'S WORK (1958)

IF *one wants more than a general impression of the Committee's activities, an informed idea of whether or not it devotes its time in pursuit of its mandate to mischievous, or nonmischievous, relevancies or irrelevancies, why not focus on its activities during a given year? Let us say, 1958.* What actually did it do during 1958? *Did it do work in faithful pursuit of its mandate? If so, is its mandate precise enough? Did its work add to the sum total of the public understanding of the activities of the Communists? Did it gain knowledge from which the Congress might clarify or illuminate the problem in hand, and therefore discuss more fruitfully appropriate legal responses to the particular character of the threat? Did it wander too far afield, and if so, is its mandate too vague?*

The purpose of this chapter is to turn the camera on the actual operations of HUAC—to watch the Committee *in action,* and try to understand its true significance in terms of what it *does.*

Which actual operations? How to choose from among the multifarious investigations that the Committee has conducted over the years (see Chapter 10)? One might pick and choose among the various operations, and fix attention on those that have been most talked about, or those that demonstrably yielded the most pay dirt, or those that, from this point of view or that, might seem most typical—whereupon, however, the critic might say: You have picked and chosen with an eye to beefing up a set of favorable theses about the Committee. In the act of including, you have also excluded. Had you included this investigation or that one, your generalization would fall to the ground.

It seems wise, therefore, to take all the operations over a specified period of time. Arbitrarily, let us turn to the annual report for 1958.

The Committee itself—witness the size of the volume—was neither notably more active that year nor notably less active than in most years within easy historical memory. No Big Case leaps to the consciousness in connection with 1958. We shall find the Committee up to things which, if the fight against Communism were less important or the Committee's investigations less central to it, we might call routine, "business as usual," matter of course. It held hearings in a number of cities; it looked into Communist propaganda, Communist subversion in government, Communist influence in the labor movement and the entertainment industry—all of them topics it had handled before and would return to again. It issued staff research reports on a spy thriller, published the biographies of some outstanding leaders of Communist parties in other lands, called together a panel of knowledgeable men to discuss the Soviet proposal for a summit conference, heard a general describe over-all Communist plans for world conquest, prepared an introductory report on brainwashing, obtained contempt citations against nine persons, and offered specific proposals for legislation.

*　　*　　*　　*　　*

Time: February
Place: Gary, Indiana
Topic: Communist infiltration of a basic industry.[1]

Gary's "basic industry" is steel, and Big Steel at that. The witnesses are highly placed members of the Communist Party of the United States, so what we learn is going to come, you might say, from the horse's mouth.

Take John Lautner, for example. He served as an organizer and official in West Virginia and New York State, close always to a certain underground leader who was busy organizing classes for industrial "colonizers." He was expelled from the CPUS in 1950.

Or take Joseph E. LaFleur. He was an FBI undercover agent in the CPUS for ten years. Party "missions" kept him in constant touch with infiltration operations right here in Gary, all through the 1940's. We should not be surprised, then, if other witnesses prove to be persons Lautner or LaFleur "named as a Communist."

Listen a moment to the Committee's summary of Lautner's testimony...

The plan began as far back as 1932 when the Communist Party decided to concentrate first on basic industry, such as steel. Key factories and shops were the next step, and from there the plan evolved to key departments within the factories and key people within the departments. By 1948, between 400 and 500 industrial branches were established throughout the country by the Communist Party....

In a frantic effort to build its power within the American labor movement, the Communist Party at this time adopted a policy of "colonization" whereby the Party instructed its members, including intellectuals and white-collar workers, to migrate to certain industrial areas and obtain employment in specific industries for the purpose of building Party units within that industry.[2]

Many of the colonizers, Lautner tells us, were organized and trained in regular classes by J. Peters, one of the Party's top underground functionaries. Prospective students had to satisfy two interesting qualifications: they must be college graduates, and they must be capable, once on an assembly line or in a mill, of concealing the fact of their being better educated than their fellow workers (as, of course, they would conceal their Communist Party membership). Their job was not to be that of winning adherents for Communist doctrines, but that of enhancing "the Party's position in labor by discrediting anti-Communist union leadership and creating dissension within non-Communist unions so that, at the very least, individuals who will tolerate Communist activities in the labor movement will again be selected for union leadership."[3]

Ex-agent LaFleur adds some details, and also names some names (those of 32 CP members in the Gary area) and, in general, confirms Lautner's testimony. Of the persons named by the two of them, twelve are called to testify, eight of whom refuse to answer questions about the Party's activities in the steel mills, two of whom admit that they have been Party members, two of whom deny Party membership. Of those who refuse to answer questions, two will be cited for contempt—for refusal to answer not on Fifth Amendment grounds but on First Amendment grounds, and interestingly enough, refusal to answer not only about Communist Party membership but about their educational backgrounds as well. Both, we learn, did in fact list no college background when applying for employment in the steel mills, though the first, Edward Yellin, had attended both City College of New York and the University of Michigan, and the other, Robert Lehrer, was a graduate of Rutgers. Why conceal these proud achievements? No answer.

* * * * *

Time: February
Place: New England, Boston especially
Topic: CPUS activities.[4]

The principal witness is named Armando Penha, former member of the National Textile Commission and the New England District Committee of the CPUS, former section organizer for the Party in Bedford (Mass.), former chairman of the Bristol County (Mass.) Communist Party, former chairman of the Regional Section Organizers Committee, and a man whom there is still reason to regard as a CPUS officer. Once on the stand, however, he reveals that he has all along been an undercover agent for the FBI (the revelation, our report points out, "abruptly ended his career in the Communist Party"). He has, he says, known some 400 Party members, most of them in New England. And he names 200 of them. Penha's testimony reminds us of what we heard in Gary, from Lautner and La-Fleur: the Textile Commission's task was to provide colonizers for the textile industry in the South. But the details are different, and we may profitably pause over some of them. . . .

Some members [Penha says] completely divorced themselves from the open apparatus of the Party and, in most instances, completely separated themselves from their families. They assumed false identities and used various devices to alter their physical appearance. They lived in the homes of trusted Party members and all contact with the open apparatus was handled through couriers.

Another witness is the Attorney General of New Hampshire, whom the Committee hears in connection with another part of its mandate from the Congress. He is Louis C. Wyman, and the questions concern the omnibus security bill (H.R. 9937) now pending before the Committee. All in all, 32 witnesses appear, 29 of whom are asked questions about their alleged membership in CPUS. Two of them deny that they are now Communist Party members, but refuse to answer questions as to whether they have been members in the past. Two admit that they are Party members. One refuses to answer questions about Party membership, on First Amendment grounds, and twenty-four refuse to answer questions about Party membership on Fifth Amendment grounds. (Two of the latter, who admit that they are not citizens of the U. S. although they have been residents of the U. S. for several decades, will be called to the attention of the Immigration and Naturalization Service for possible deportation.)

*　　*　　*　　*　　*

Time: May-June
Place: New York City
Topic: The entertainment industry.[5]

Is it true, the Committee asks in effect, that there are Communists who have penetrated the entertainment industry, and have used other entertainment personnel to promote Communist fronts? Have these fronts furthered the foreign policy of the Soviet Union? Have prominent persons in the entertainment industry contributed funds that have financed Communist operations in the United States? [6]

We soon see, and recognize, a familiar face—John Lautner, whom we met in Gary. He speaks now of the Cultural Division of the CPUS, as he knew it from the standpoint of a Party functionary:

> First of all, members of the Cultural Division are members of the Communist Party as such. The only special consideration they receive is one of security, one of concealing their identity as Party members, and the reason for that is a very simple one.
>
> If a Party member in any of the cultural activities, whether it be theater or television or radio or movie or whatever it is, if his identity would be known as a Party member, his effectiveness to do Communist work would be practically nil. Therefore, concealing Party membership adds so much more to the effectiveness of that individual in carrying out Communist Party work. But he is a Party member and he must carry out the policies of the Party. The Party policies—tactical policies today—are very closely linked with ... the tactical policies of all Communist Parties, whether it be in the United States or wherever else.[7]

Another witness is Paul Mann, actor-director-teacher, who has been named to the Committee as a member of the Communist Party. But he does not wish to discuss any questions the Committee is interested in. He is, on the other hand, eminently willing to unburden himself of his opinion of HUAC itself:

> You want your standards to determine who shall be permitted to act, direct, sing, dance, and play music in the American theater— even to dictate policy on plays and productions. Whoever disagrees

with you or does not conform to your way of thinking is blacklisted, deprived of his livelihood, smeared and publicly inquisitioned or threatened. . . . As a member of the American theater I need no seal of approval from this committee. . . . I refuse to permit the standards and political view of this committee (composed of politicians elected for a temporary term) to supplant the Constitution of the United States and its Bill of Rights, and to hack away at the culture of my country. . . .[8]

Twelve other persons employed in the entertainment industry imitate Mann, and refuse to answer questions regarding Communist Party activities in or out of show business.

*   *   *   *   *

Time: July
Place: Atlanta, Ga.
Topic: Communist infiltration of industry.

We have already heard of colonization, of the training of colonizers, of the CPUS's special interest in concealing the college training of its colonizers (so that they will be placed in the shop, not in the office), and of its further interest in, specifically, the Southern textile industry. Now we meet an alleged colonizer, Madge Spurny Cole, of Greensboro, N. C., but formerly of New York. She works, she says, in a textile mill, as a "spare hand in the spinning department." Her application for employment in the mill (so we learn from a photostatic copy) describes her as having had no education beyond high school, but now, under oath, she says she holds an M.A. degree from Syracuse University. As to whether her activities at the mill include those of a Communist Party agent, she is less helpful: invoking the Fifth Amendment, she refuses to answer.[9] So, also, do several other college-trained mill hands.

The next witness is Eugene Feldman, the editor, we are told, of a publication called the *Southern Newsletter,* and our first reaction may well be, What has this got to do with the colonization of textile mills? We soon learn. The *Southern Newsletter,* now two years old, is always loaded with Party-line material slanted for Southern readers, most especially materials likely to ease the path of the colonizers in the textile mills. And we get an indication of how the bits and pieces the Committee picks up in one investigation point the way to other investigations. The Committee first heard of Feldman, we discover, from our old friend Penha, who had named him as a member of the Party's Industrial Commission at High Point, N. C., and as a former colonizer.

Feldman—for we are learning to expect this from a high percentage of witnesses who turn up in that way—refuses to answer questions about Party membership, and refuses also to say whether or not he is the editor of the *Southern Newsletter*—refuses even when shown a photostatic copy of his application, on behalf of that publication, for a post office box. He refuses, finally, to answer questions about the *Newsletter*'s contributors, all of whom had been named to the Committee as Communist Party members. Carl Braden, for instance, who also appears and declines to answer questions (the Committee will later cite him for contempt, and he will be sentenced to a year in jail).

One thing, as we have just observed, leads to another, and the Committee, still questioning Braden, moves on from the *Newsletter* to the Emergency Civil Liberties Committee, which is of interest to it because, throughout the Atlanta hearings, it was busy making public protests against the Committee and its activities (Braden refused to answer questions about it). And from the ECLC to its spokesman, Frank Wilkinson, who two years earlier had been named by an FBI undercover agent as a Communist Party member.[10] The Committee calls Wilkinson, who turns out to be an innovator of sorts. He does not "refuse" to answer questions; he pleads no Fifth Amendment, no First Amendment; he merely counters all questions with "I am answering no questions of this committee." [11] (He will, in due course, be convicted of contempt of Congress and, like Braden, will be sentenced to a year in jail.)

The Committee has other sources of information about ECLC, which figured in one of its 1957 reports. Its leading members have been named as members also of the CPUS; its major task has been the raising of funds and the recruitment of counsel for Communists being tried under the Smith Act and other statutes directed against internal subversion.

* * * * *

Time: September
Place: Newark, N. J.
Topic: Communist infiltration of industry, especially
manufacturing plants.[12]

Our first—well, not witness, because he refuses to appear; rather, our first focus of attention is Harvey O'Connor, who in two respects reminds us of Wilkinson in Atlanta. He is a spokesman for ECLC, and he has been organizing protests, including one public rally, against HUAC and HUAC's conducting hearings in the locality.

The nature of those hearings is itself instructive. Two defectors from the Communist Party, and one man who had joined the Party as an undercover agent for the FBI had named certain other persons as Party members who had been given assignments underground. Robert J. Dixon, Jr., who had defected after being a member for five years, had told the Committee of his recruitment into an "industrial group" of the CPUS at a time when he was employed in the General Electric plant at Bloomfield, N. J. His group, he had testified, had included employees of other electrical plants in the Newark area, all of them "always" able to "pass on information that the Party could pick up and use," and each of them able to promote organization within his own plant. (He himself, for example, had been president of the union local that held bargaining rights for the very plant in which he was employed while he belonged to the Party—a local, as we might have guessed, of the United Electrical, Radio and Machine Workers of America.) The other defector, Bernard Zick, had been an employee of a Tung-Sol plant in Bloomfield, a member of the Communist Party, and a member of the same "group" to which

Dixon had belonged. He, too, had testified as to the effectiveness of Party members in enhancing their usefulness by becoming officials of UE locals. Dennis James, the FBI undercover
agent, had testified largely as to the operations in the Newark
area of the Labor Youth League. All three of the witnesses,
however, had agreed that the Party was playing down public
activities in favor of activities underground.

On the strength of Dixon's, Zick's, and James' testimony,
HUAC subpoenas three persons whom they had named as
having switched from open to covert operations in and around
Newark. The Committee speaks of them as follows:

> In the late 1940's Kate Heck was observed to be operating as a
> county organizer for the Communist Party in the Newark area,
> where she was also openly employed by the Communist-con-
> trolled United Electrical, Radio and Machine Workers union. In
> the 1950's, she had moved to Boston, where, under the alias of
> B. Brosser, she was assigned as courier and disciplinarian in the
> Party underground. She participated in these conspiratorial
> activities in New England until 1957, when she resumed resi-
> dence in Newark.
>
> Miss Heck was questioned extensively regarding her role in
> the Communist underground operations. She persistently in-
> voked the Fifth Amendment, however, and indicated that even
> a grant of immunity from criminal prosecution would not
> persuade her to divulge information regarding the important
> Party work with which she had been identified.
>
> Similarly adamant in their refusal to discuss recent under-
> ground assignments for the Communist Party were Louis
> Malinow and Emanuel Cantor. Their repeated invocation of
> the Fifth Amendment also applied to any discussion of their
> previous open Party activity. Both Malinow and Cantor, before
> the Communist Party strategy shift toward increased under-
> ground operation, had run for public office in New Jersey on the
> Communist Party ticket. Malinow also had been identified as
> organizer for the Essex County organization of the New Jersey
> Communist Party, while Cantor served in a similar capacity for
> the Party in Mercer County, N. J.[13]

*   *   *   *   *

Time: June–September
Place: Washington, D. C., and elsewhere
Topic: Communist propaganda, especially from
abroad.[14]

The star witness is Irving Fishman, Deputy Collector of Customs in New York City, who describes the inflow of Communist propaganda from foreign sources, which in 1958 will, he thinks, total 10,000,000 individual pieces. Testifying during the New England hearings, he states that 80,000 pieces, unquestionably Communist in origin and tendency, and all addressed to New England, have cleared the Port of New York in a bare two months. Nor, he adds, is it easy to stop the flow by legal enactment based on "country of origin"; much of the material is sent to the United States from non-Communist countries. At the New Jersey hearings, he produces samples of propaganda disseminated in that state, which ranks fifth among the states as a target for overseas propaganda pieces, dealing with anything you like from capitalist war mongering in the Middle East to United States Army atrocities in South Korea.[15] The originators of such propaganda, Fishman observes, can only write it, print it, and ship it to the United States; the rest (since direct mailings from abroad have proved impractical) is up to U. S. Communists and Communist sympathizers. To Fishman, this sort of redistribution was "absolutely necessary" to the success of the propaganda efforts.[16]

* * * * *

Time: March
Place: Washington, D. C.
Topic: Communist treason in the U. S.[17]

The chairman of HUAC, Representative Francis E. Walter, holds in his hand a Committee report, *Chronicle of Treason,* the result of months of hearings, research, and analysis by Committee members and their staff. The report drives home two points, each directed at a major pocket of ignorance and misunderstanding on the part of the American public and its elected representatives: First, the world Communist movement has benefited enormously from treasonable acts committed by citizens of the United States, mostly native born. Second, by no means all the traitors are Communist Party members (i.e., Communist agents are often instructed *not* to join the Party). And we readily see that the general ignorance of the role of treason in international affairs is itself an enormous asset for the world Communist movement (e.g., much criticism of HUAC itself has its roots in the critics' unwillingness, or incapacity, to trust the evidence rather than their own preconceptions). The cases cited in the report, we find, offer us evidence aplenty. Harry Gold, Philadelphia chemist, turned over a packet of atom bomb information to Klaus Fuchs, a German-born physicist who had become a British subject—in the crucial year 1945. (Gold was convicted of atomic espionage and sentenced to thirty years' imprisonment in the same series of trials that brought to justice Julius and Ethel Rosenberg, who were sentenced to death.) Judith Coplon passed secret U. S. Government documents along to Valentin Gubitchev, a Soviet engineer employed by the United Nations. (Though twice convicted, Judy Coplon, now a married woman resident in a large American city, is still free.) And the report chronicles other cases, all to the same effect, each conclusive on one or both of the points at issue.

* * * * *

Time: May
Place: Washington, D. C.
Topic: Soviet espionage.

The Committee is again releasing a report, the result of months of digging and sifting and, this time, in an area where the truth has been peculiarly elusive. That report will tell us the story (as the title indicates) of Erica Wallach, though we are ourselves more likely to have heard of the matter in connection with the name of Noel Field, not Erica Wallach.

Noel Field had been an employee of the State Department and the League of Nations. He had directed relief work in Europe, representing the Unitarian Service Committee, during

World War II. But he had also belonged to a Communist spy ring and one day in 1949, while in Prague, he disappeared. When his wife and his brother went to Prague to look for him, they also disappeared—as, in 1950 in Berlin, did his adopted daughter, whose name was Erica Wallach.[18] These front-page facts come back to us as we listen to the report, and we eagerly await the sequel: The name of Noel Field figures prominently in the treason trials conducted behind the Iron Curtain in the early 1950's, where he is exposed as a spy not for the USSR but for the U. S., and is sent to jail. There he remains until 1954 when, inexplicably, he is released and, equally inexplicably (he is, remember a U. S. spy), seeks and obtains political asylum in, of all places, Hungary, where he takes a job as a propagandist specializing in anti-Western tirades. A year later, Erica Wallach turns up too—first in Moscow, then in Berlin, then in England, where her mother lives, and, in due course, as an applicant for entry into the United States. Her application, because her name is associated with Field's and because she has been a known member of the German Communist Party (1946–1948), is turned down. In 1957, she is approached by HUAC investigators, who find her willing to talk, and before long she is giving testimony at an executive session of the Committee. (Because of this testimony, the Committee chairman will recommend her admission to the United States as a defector from Communism.)

Erica Wallach's executive session testimony filled in many long-missing details concerning Field's espionage, and threw welcome light on Soviet police methods, especially those used in getting "confessions." But it also enabled the Committee—again we notice how, in the case, investigation of x yields up data, often quite unexpected, about y—to link the name of Noel Field with a name far more famous: that of Alger Hiss. For it had learned that when Noel Field lost his job at the League of Nations in 1940, he was recommended for the post of executive assistant to the U. S. High Commissioner in the Philippines, and that the man who recommended him was Hiss himself.

We may note, in passing, several other Committee releases in 1958. We see, for example, *Organized Communism in the*

United States, a 153-page detailed history of the serpentine ins-
and-outs and ups-and-downs of the CPUS Party line over the
years (the one constant: support of Soviet foreign policy). We
see a series of brief biographies of Communist leaders (Vicente
Lombardo Toledano, Carlos Prestes, Enver Hoxha, Gheorghe
Gheorghui-Dej). And here a booklet of questions and answers
concerning HUAC itself.[19]

We see, finally, a report, the last of the year as it happens, in
which the Committee offers the complete facts-to-date regarding espionage activities by Communist-bloc diplomatic personnel serving on American soil.[20] Eight of the cases covered are
new—that is, have never before been brought to light. The
report names 28 Communist diplomatic representatives and
U. N. employees, some of them still about, some already expelled, as active espionage agents, and in each case justifies the
naming beyond any reasonable doubt. It stresses the fact that no
less than 442 Soviet citizens are officially stationed in the United
States, over against some 80 American citizens stationed in Moscow; that six satellite missions in the United States have a total
staff of 468 of their own nationals, over against the 258 Americans who staff U. S. embassies in the relevant six countries; and
that the six U. S. diplomatic missions in question employ 364
Communist nationals, against the 10 U. S. nationals employed
by the corresponding missions in the United States. The Committee concludes from these data—not, one would have thought,
very daringly, for all that certain quarters were quite shocked—
that the United States should tighten its regulations concerning
Communist missions in the United States, and step up security
precautions in U. S. missions everywhere.

* * * * *

Time: Off and on through the year
Place: Washington, D. C.
Topic: World Communism.

We pick up a different kind of scene—not a hearing in which
information, "leads," evidence, are elicited from witnesses

"friendly" and "unfriendly"; not the release of a report in which the Committee communicates its findings; but a "consultation," in the course of which the Committee listens to an independent expert on the USSR and Communism, as he presents the results of his diligence and his penetration into one or another aspect of the Communist problem. A consultation is, briefly, a "think" session, intended to deepen, to fertilize, and to illuminate the Committee's whole investigative effort. In the very nature of the case it rarely gets the headlines on the day it occurs, any more than the academician or world traveler or book writer would get headlines for a lecture anywhere, so that few people are aware of this intensely serious phase of the Committee's work.

Here, for example, is a consultation with General Albert C. Wedemeyer, former commander of the China-Burma-India Theater, wartime Deputy Chief of Staff, on the Communist program for world conquest.[21] General Wedemeyer is concerned —as, we now realize, he might well have been in 1958—about Soviet strength in certain fields of scientific endeavor that have a military bearing, about Soviet military strength in general, and about recent Soviet successes in the political, economic, and psychological Cold War spheres. If these successes continue, he thinks, the Soviets will never have to engage in a shooting war to win their objectives. He points up the contrast between the USSR and the United States, which does not define its objectives, cannot therefore co-ordinate its actions, and so loses progressively in the Cold War. What should the United States do, then? Well, it might start out by offering greater encouragement to potential defectors from Communism, and by giving genuine support to the peoples of the satellite nations in their struggle for freedom. The opposite, that is to say, of what the United States did at the crucial moment in Hungary, which the General cites as a major U. S. failure.

The camera shifts and picks up Edward Hunter, Far Eastern correspondent, author of *Brainwashing in Red China,* World War II propaganda specialist with the OSS. His topic is Communist psychological warfare,[22] including Communist psychological conditioning techniques as demonstrated in Korea during World War II—but let us listen to Mr. Hunter himself, as he zeroes in on our Cultural Exchange Program . . .

American students, professors and businessmen, who wander through Red countries in the eyes of the people there, confirm the Communist propaganda line that there is no hope; that the free world, especially America, the symbol of the free world, has given in to the Reds. That was the Communist purpose at the much-publicized Bandung Conference, when the Asian and African countries met. The broadcasts to the people of China by the Peking regime stressed that all this proved that the outside world had recognized that Red China is here to stay. Any time an American student walks down a street in Red China, he is conveying one message to the silenced people who see him, and that is, "Don't look to the outside world, don't look to America for help in your hour of need. We have let you down. We are betraying you." There is no hate so fierce as the hate of a friend who feels he has been betrayed, and that is the theme of the whole world Communist propaganda program today; to convince the people inside Communism, who hate it, that we have betrayed them, while convincing the people outside of the Communist world, principally in America, that there is a future for what they call, in their double-talk, co-existence.

Next comes Milan Jakubec, president of a group of 18 Canadian ethnic groups that represent the satellite states of Eastern Europe. His topic is twofold: Communist activities in Canada, and the impact in Europe of Communism's campaign to force "realistic" acceptance of its conquests. We may remember him, in part, for a pun that he makes to point up a grave thesis: From the standpoint of psychological impact, he says, future "summit" conferences might well be called "submit" conferences; their purpose, as understood by the Communists themselves, is "to show the American people that the Communist leaders are down-to-earth, good fellows, who can be trusted and with whom we can get along." But for the people behind the Iron Curtain, he says, they have a different meaning —that of a death knell for their hopes for the survival of freedom in the free world.[23] All this, of course, before Paris, before Vienna, before the building of the wall between West and East Berlin.

The next consultant is Constantin W. Boldyreff, Russian-born, reared in the Russian Military Cadet Corps, former teacher at Georgetown University, now the full-time representative of the National Alliance of Russian Solidarists, whose purpose is nothing less than the overthrow of Communism in the Soviet Union. He, too, thinks that our failure to help the Hungarian Freedom Fighters was, to quote a famous phrase, something worse than a crime, namely a blunder, which can now be undone only by a "great and, if necessary, 'unconventional' effort ... to reach [the satellite peoples] and win back their confidence." He adds a warning—to which, we note from the urgency in his voice, he attaches enormous importance: American anti-Communism must not be permitted to become "anti-Russianism." The people of Russia, he insists, are a proud people and a great people; and it would be disastrous to give them the impression "that the free world's hatred of Communism has gradually waxed into hatred of Russia and everything Russian. This feeling of suspicion, of apprehension of the free world's ultimate designs, I have found to be common in varying degrees to practically every single Soviet citizen with whom I recently had a chance to talk. This misconception must be removed at all cost. This should become one of the foremost objectives of the free world." [24]

Next, an old acquaintance—at least for those of us who have vivid recollections of the front pages over the years: Maj. Gen. Claire Lee Chennault, who commanded the now legendary Flying Tigers (it being 1958, he is already under sentence of death, and this is one of the last blows he will ever strike in his long, always aggressive, never defensive fight against Communism). He also has Summit Conferences on his mind, and he also thinks their effect is to deepen the despair of the peoples already enslaved by Red troops. In order to turn the tide, he thinks, America needs more active *grass-roots* representation around the periphery of the Iron Curtain—representatives capable of working *with* native leaders in carrying out, and bringing to good political purpose, American aid programs. In passing, he strikes down a piece of Red Chinese propaganda that has for years had wide currency, and made great difficulties both for the Chinese Nationalist Government and for its defenders in the United States, namely: that U. S. military aid to the Nationalists, back when they were supposed to be fighting the Communists, was all wasted, because corrupt Nationalists black-marketed the weapons to the Reds. Ridiculous, says Chennault, and for the very simple reason that the Reds weren't in the market; the Soviets had turned over to them a Manchurian stockpile of arms large enough to keep a million-man army for ten years.[25] He turns, finally, to the question of admitting Red China to the United Nations, and his words are passionate: "It would mean taking over all of the Far East by the Communists. We would pull back our efforts to Hawaii and the West Coast. The people in the Far East are sitting on a fence watching; and whenever we show signs of weakness, many of them immediately fall off on the Communist side. If we recognize Red China, there will just be an avalanche. They would all go Red. They could not resist it."

Next in order are four consultants whom the Committee, prompted by the warnings it has received, wishes to hear on the specific topic "What Is Behind the Soviet Proposal for a Summit Conference?" They are David J. Dallin, author of *The Changing World of Soviet Russia, Soviet Russia's Foreign Policy, Russia and Postwar Europe, The Rise of Russia in Asia,* and other highly respected volumes on the USSR and Communism; Anthony T. Bouscaren, then associate professor of political science at Marquette University, and lecturer at the National War College; James D. Atkinson, associate professor of political science at Georgetown University and director of a special course in psychological warfare in the university's graduate school; Francis J. McNamara, vice-chairman of the All-American Conference to Combat Communism, who formerly edited a periodical newsletter called *Counterattack,* published by a group of former FBI agents. Each brings to the problem in hand a particular point of view and a special kind of *expertise,* so that the resulting symposium is balanced, nuanced, and impressively authoritative. But we must content ourselves with hearing the over-all conclusions that the Committee was able to draw from their arguments, as follows:

Four eminent authorities on international communism warned against another summit conference with the leaders of the Soviet Union. They listed the following motivations for the Kremlin demand that another such conference be held:

1. To avoid attempts to settle major differences between the Communist and free worlds in the U. N. because (a) the USSR has recently been losing propaganda debates in that organization, and (b) the U. N. today is "old hat" and does not have the publicity value it once had as a propaganda forum.

2. To play the role of the most dynamic force in the world today, the initiator of far-reaching moves for peace.

3. To disarm the West psychologically by convincing it that the Soviet Union truly wants peace and disarmament, that Soviet power is no cause for alarm, that everything can be settled by talk, and that peaceful coexistence is truly possible (i.e., there are no irreconcilable elements between the free and Communist worlds. All differences can be negotiated. By implication, this means that Moscow does not believe in forcible overthrow of free governments).

4. To convince the world that the Kremlin's leaders are "reasonable" men, that they can be trusted, and that lasting, amicable agreement with them is possible.

5. To achieve an aura of legitimacy and respectability in the eyes of the world. A summit conference tends to give this to them and to add to the stability of their regime.

6. To create the impression among the enslaved peoples that the free world recognizes the legitimacy of Soviet control of its entire empire, including the satellites; to convince these people that the free world has abandoned them and thus crush their spirit of resistance and hope of winning freedom.

7. To give encouragement to their followers in all parts of the world. The first summit conference was actually held in response to an intense and prolonged Communist agitation and propaganda drive. It was a victory for communism. A second summit meeting

demanded by Communists in all parts of the world, would be another victory for them and a symbol of their great power and influence.

The four specialists on international Communism also quoted official reports to the effect that the first summit conference of 1955 had disastrous results for the United States and the free world because it promoted apathy and neutralism in Europe and Asia and thereby weakened NATO, SEATO, and the whole free world defense effort. They also warned of the danger inherent in any U. S. agreement to halt the testing of nuclear weapons and to giving in to Communist proposals for "disengagement," that is, the withdrawal of the U. S. and Soviet forces from certain areas in Europe.

The following major steps were proposed to change the course of the Cold War and bring victory to the free world:

1. The United States must increase its military power until it has a force second to none in the entire world.

2. The people should stop talking about reductions in taxes and make up their minds to tighten their belts and put even greater effort into the fight against communism on all levels.

3. A much more effective and hard-hitting propaganda program must be devised.

4. The will to resist communism must be strengthened. The American people must stop being escapists and face the fact that there can be no real peace while Communist power remains in the world.

5. The free world must switch from the defensive to the offensive.

6. It must place all possible pressure on the Soviet empire, feed the discontent that exists within it, and aid anti-Communist underground movements, thus weakening Communist power.

7. An effective education program designed to give the people of the free world an understanding of the true nature of communism and the hard facts of life in today's world must be undertaken.

8. There should be no further concessions to the Soviet Union.

9. The United States should reward its allies and stop giving as much help to neutralists and appeasers as it does to those who stand firmly against Communist aggression.

10. The United States must make it clear to the entire world that it is on the side of the people enslaved by communism and that it will do what it can to help them.[26]

We hear, next, Professor Robert Strausz-Hupé, director of the Foreign Policy Research Institute at the University of Pennsylvania, and two of the Institute's research fellows, Alvin J. Cottrell and James E. Dougherty, who in another "collective" consultation outline a "Communist Strategy of Protracted Conflict"; then Dr. Charles Wesley Lowry, chairman of the interfaith Foundation for Religious Action in the Social and Civil Order, who directs attention to the differences between "God-centered" and "State-centered" ideologies; then Professor Gerhart Niemeyer of Notre Dame University, who presents his research findings on the "irrational" aspects of Communism; then, finally, Dr. Alex N. Dragnich, former USIS officer in Belgrade and professor of political science at Vanderbilt University, on the topic "Titoism" (Tito, he insists, remains "neutral" on the side of the Soviets).

Professor Niemeyer strikes a note upon which we may very well conclude our account of HUAC's activities in 1958. Here is the Committee's summary of his concluding remarks:

Negotiating a solution to the present conflict between the Communist and free worlds is "out of the question," Dr. Niemeyer said, because of the Communist belief that "the basic reality in all historical societies is class war, and that class war is in its very nature irreconcilable." For the same reason, "peaceful coexistence" is possible only as a breathing spell for Communist leaders until they have accumulated enough power to crush other societies. Because of their fundamental beliefs, a "genuine will to peace" or an acceptance of non-Communists' right to exist is impossible on the part of Communists.

The battle between the Communist and the free world, Dr. Niemeyer said, has often been described as a battle of ideas. He granted that this is true to a certain extent, but pointed out that the "ideas" of communism have become a "mortal danger" to us by the accumulation of great power on the part of the Soviet Union. Therefore, our only hope of escaping subjection to this power lies in building superior military might. There is "no substitute" for this.

If the free world is to cope successfully with the forces of international communism, Dr. Niemeyer said, it must next strengthen its will to resist and then divest itself of the following false notions:

> the idea that we live in a peaceful world;
> the idea that peace with communism can be had for a reasonable price;
> the idea that communism is a rational force or that its leaders are merely cynical power seekers;
> the idea that we can't be defeated because "we are right";
> the idea that Communists would come over to our side "if they only knew us";
> the concept that we can afford "less than a supreme effort" in the battle against communism because "truth will prevail."

"Above all," he said, "in this period of 'soft' Kremlin policy, we are tempted to fall into the error of believing that when Communists appear to be doing the same as other people, it actually *is* the same thing. The truth is that when Communists appear to be doing the same thing as other people (in art, education, science, etc.), they are mostly doing just the opposite—actually pursuing their own destructive objectives through seemingly nonpolitical means. When engaged in apparent cooperation with others, they are actually fighting the struggle which to them is "the law of laws." [27]

Well, there it is—the work of HUAC in the course of a single, not untypical, year. And we may fairly ask, in view of all the hoop-de-la in certain quarters about the Committee, its own alleged "un-Americanism," its alleged untender disregard for individual rights (to freedom of thought and speech, to privacy, etc.): What does this record for one year, now we have it before us, enable us to say by way of passing judgment on the Committee?

One might be tempted to say, at first blush: Pretty paltry stuff, and if that's all the Committee can find to do in a whole calendar year, it clearly isn't needed: a few persons not hitherto known as Communists get named as Communists; a few persons named as Communists get cited for contempt, some of whom are sent to jail; a little light gets thrown on how Communists infiltrate industry and the mass communications; a few reports, reflecting research the Committee performed prior to 1958, and suggesting that similar research was probably in progress in 1958, get published and, one supposes, distributed to interested persons; a few college professors put in their two bits' worth, which might just as well have been an article in the *Times Magazine,* on national policy, and that also gets published and distributed; a few proposals are put forward for future legislation. Are "un-American activities," if indeed there are any, any the less likely to go forward in 1959 because of what the Committee did in 1958, or in 1962 because of the (presumably similar) things the Committee did in 1961?

In the main, we may concede the factual point embodied in such an objection to HUAC, provided we accept certain underlying premises: The Committee doesn't do much in any single year and, taken by itself, the little it does in any single year might, granting certain assumptions, be made to seem very small potatoes. Only, however, on these certain assumptions, which let's get right out into the open:

1. There is no serious internal Communist conspiracy.

2. Participation in the Communist conspiracy is not an un-American activity.

3. The American way is to depend on the "free market in ideas" for the elimination of Communism.

4. We can make an adequate response to the Communist conspiracy on something short of the fullest obtainable information about it.

5. Full information about the Communist conspiracy can be obtained by methods other than those of bit-by-bit investigation.

6. The bit-by-bit investigation needed for full information goes forward constantly in better hands than those of HUAC, and is best confided to those better hands.

7. The achievements of a bit-by-bit investigation can be judged by some criterion other than that of the total information acquired over a long period of years.

Those, I think, are the assumptions that underlie the kind of attacks on HUAC that hit at the alleged "triviality" of its findings, the alleged "duplication of effort" involved in its inquiries, the alleged busy-busying about matters that are already sufficiently well known (but not, of course, because HUAC has made them known!). And those assumptions are the points that need arguing about; they are logically and temporally prior to any argument about the merits of the Committee and its findings.

Get agreement about the issues to which these points address themselves (which, since issues are not really debatable, should be, but never is, easy), and there will be no two opinions about the Committee—or, to return, the Committee's work in 1958.

Let's turn the points around, replacing each by its contrary, and see what they add up to in the way of a catechism for defenders of HUAC:

1. There *is* a Communist conspiracy, international in scope but incessantly active among *us,* in our own backyard, save as we move to prevent its activity. It is unified, brilliantly organized, and intelligent.

2. Participation in the Communist conspiracy *is* an "unAmerican" activity, because it is an anti-American activity, and in two senses: The world Communist movement recognizes the United States as its major foe, and is pledged to destroy it. And Communism as a domestic movement seeks, in every way possible, to undermine the beliefs and institutions by virtue of which America is America.

3. We can *not* depend upon the free market in ideas for the elimination of the Communist movement: the Communists do not, not any longer at least, compete in that market; their business is not persuasion but subversion.

4. Every gap, every inadequacy, in our information about the Communists—who and where they are, what they are doing—constitutes a further area in which the Communists can operate without let or hindrance.

5. Communist operations, though they go forward under unified control, are (if only to make them difficult to ferret out,

though for other reasons too) widely dispersed; they can be apprehended only by widely dispersed investigation which, because of the tightness of Communist security, *must* proceed bit-by-bit.

6. It is *not* true that if HUAC does not keep after our domestic Communists, someone else will; much less is it true that someone else is already doing so. Our scholars, for the most part, implicitly and even explicitly deny that there is a serious domestic Communist problem; and the FBI has work of its own—akin to that of HUAC, but by no means the same—that makes infinite demands on its scant resources.

7. Because the Communist movement, though dispersed, is also unified, the bits of information we pick up through patient investigation do fit together; if we had *all* the bits they would, we may be sure, fit into an orchestrated and comprehensible whole (which is why, as we have seen above, one bit tends to lead to another). Our judgment of the continuing investigation should, therefore, turn exclusively upon whether, over the long pull, it gives us a picture complete enough to inform an adequate legislative counterstrategy.

Besides which: in so far as our picture is deemed incomplete, the correct inference is that HUAC should redouble its efforts.

KARL HESS

★

Chapter | **THE HISS CASE**

6.

AT *a more specific level, what exactly was the role of the House Committee on Un-American Activities at its most publicized moment, when it brought together Alger Hiss and Whittaker Chambers? What exactly did the Committee have to do with flushing out the case? Did it act in pursuit of its mandate, or was this merely an excursion into notoriety for its own sake? Might another agency of government have done the job, assuming it was worth doing, as well, or better? As a matter of historical interest, did the Committee behave courageously, or well, or creatively, or was it merely buffeted about by chance currents of the public scene, whose meaning it did not know, nor care about? Was it an integral part of the great drama of the Witness versus the Establishmentarian?*

What is now known as the Hiss Case exploded across the nation's front pages on August 3, 1948. On that day, Whittaker Chambers—a short, stocky man in a rumpled gray suit—began a series of public disclosures which shocked the nation and finally led to prison and disgrace for Alger Hiss. For the first time, the American people saw plain the bland face of treason—

and in the stark conflict of two men focused on the root problem of our times. Forces and implications affecting the entire body politic and reaching across three decades of history were involved behind the scenes, but what touched the public was the human drama on a stage provided by the House Un-American Activities Committee.

From the start, the case was a compound of ironies. To begin with, Alger Hiss's involvement in the Communist espionage conspiracy was no secret to official Washington. Nine years earlier, Premier Daladier had informed the American Ambassador in Paris, William Bullitt, that according to French Intelligence reports Alger and Donald Hiss were Soviet agents. Shortly thereafter, Whittaker Chambers had told the story of a Communist cell in the government to Assistant Secretary of State A. A. Berle who communicated the information to President Roosevelt and, in 1943, turned over careful notes of the conversation to the Federal Bureau of Investigation. Isaac Don Levine had labored in agonizing frustration to interest federal officials and newspapermen in the Chambers account. FBI Director J. Edgar Hoover had tried to budge the stubbornly antagonistic President Truman in 1945 and 1946.

So well were the Hiss activities and sympathies known that the *Christian Science Monitor* could write in 1946: "More than one Congressman, whenever the subject of leftist activity in the State Department is mentioned, pulled out a list of suspects that was invariably headed by Mr. Hiss." There was a second major irony in the case: Whittaker Chambers was called to the stand by the House Un-American Activities Committee as a kind of afterthought, yet he opened the door to the most sensational and significant case in its history. Only because its chief investigator, Robert E. Stripling, recalled a two-year-old conversation with a high-ranking security official at State who had described Hiss as "the Communist who runs the department" was Chambers called—and then to buttress the testimony three days earlier of Elizabeth Bentley, a former Soviet espionage agent.

On that hot August morning when Chambers answered "I do"

to Acting Chairman Karl E. Mundt's "Do you solemnly swear," the newspapers were far more interested in Miss Bentley's detailed story of a wide-ranging espionage apparatus, with sources in almost every sensitive federal agency—an apparatus for which she served as courier. The reporters covering the hearing had no inkling of what Chambers would say—and in this ignorance they were joined by most members of the Committee. At the press table, there was a flutter of amusement that a senior editor of *Time* should be on the receiving end of a Congressional investigation. That amusement quickly changed to astonishment —or bitter anger among the more politically committed—once Chambers had moved past the preliminary questions and into his prepared statement. For it was immediately apparent that the Committee, so often bogged down in the minutiae of Communist subversion, had blundered on a man of stature, deep sensibility, and broad perspective, personally reluctant to speak but historically committed to probe the cancer in the bosom of Western civilization. The names he mentioned were secondary to the diagnosis of the disease.

That prepared statement was the opening gun of the Hiss Case. To the fallible members of the Committee, to the hostile press corps, and to a nation beginning to feel the first chill of the Cold War, it understated what would be meticulously documented in all its terrible detail at later hearings, before a grand jury, and at two trials. In a voice so low that reporters had difficulty catching his words, Chambers began the long travail of his witness:

Almost nine years ago—that is, two days after Hitler and Stalin signed their pact—I went to Washington and reported to the authorities what I knew about the infiltration of the United States Government by Communists. For years international communism . . . had been in a state of undeclared war with this Republic. With the Hitler-Stalin pact, that war reached a new stage. I regarded my action in going to the government as a simple act of war, like the shooting of an armed enemy in combat.

At that moment in history, I was one of the few men on this side of the battle who could perform this service.

I had joined the Communist Party in 1924. No one recruited me. I had become convinced that the society in which we live, Western civilization, had reached a crisis, of which the First World War was the military expression, and that it was doomed to collapse or revert to barbarism. I did not understand the causes of the crisis, or know what to do about it.... In the writings of Karl Marx I thought that I had found the explanation of the historical and economic causes. In the writings of Lenin I thought I had found the answer to the question: What to do?

In 1937 I repudiated Marx's doctrines and Lenin's tactics. Experience and the record had convinced me that communism is a form of totalitarianism, that its triumph means slavery to men wherever they fall under its sway, and spiritual night to the human mind and soul. I resolved to break with the Communist Party at whatever risk to my life or other tragedy to myself or my family.... For a year I lived in hiding, sleeping by day and watching through the night with gun or revolver within easy reach. That was what underground communism could do to one man in the peaceful United States in the year 1938.

At this point, it became obvious that Whittaker Chambers was not scratching in the kitchen middens of the Communist Party. To those with any knowledge of Communist organization, the brief description of his break was an overt confession that he had once been a part of that complex alliance of Red Army Fourth Bureau (Intelligence), Soviet secret police, and the Comintern. Only the faceless men of espionage risk death when they "surface"—the technical term for resuming a place in society. As Chambers continued to read his statement, he carefully underscored this point in a manner which would alert U. S. security forces and serve notice on the men he named:

I had sound reason for supposing that the Communists might try to kill me. For a number of years I had myself served in the underground, chiefly in Washington, D. C. The heart of my report to the United States Government consisted of a description of the apparatus to which I was attached. It was an underground organization ... developed, to the best of my knowledge, by Harold Ware. ... I knew at its top level a group of seven or so men, from among whom in later years certain members of Miss Bentley's organization were apparently recruited. The head of the underground group at the time I knew it was Nathan Witt, an attorney for the National Labor Relations Board. Later, John Abt became the leader. Lee Pressman was also a member of this group, as was Alger Hiss, who, as a member of the State Department, later organized the conferences at Dumbarton Oaks, San Francisco, and the United States side of the Yalta Conference.

The purpose of this group at that time was not *primarily* espionage. Its original purpose was the Communist infiltration of the American government. *But espionage was certainly one of its eventual objectives.* Let no one be surprised at this statement. Disloyalty is a matter of principle with every member of the Communist Party.... [Emphasis added.]

In the course of the somewhat disorganized questioning that followed, Chambers described how the underground apparatus operated, where it met, and who its members were. He told how, under orders from J. Peters, leader of the underground activities in Washington, members of the apparatus who "were going places in the government" were detached for security reasons and how, from that point on, did not meet as a group. It was his assignment, Chambers testified, to be the link between these men and J. Peters. A direct inquiry from Chief Investigator Stripling brought in the name of Harry Dexter White who in the 1940's became Assistant Secretary of the Treasury and Secretary Henry Morgenthau, Jr.'s most influential adviser. White, though not a member of the original cell, was "going places" too—and he was assigned to Chambers.

If there was any focusing of attention on Alger Hiss, it was the Committee's doing. Chambers could testify more fully about him because, by his own account, the two men had become close friends. By 1948, all the men named had left government employ, but Hiss had moved on to the ultrarespectable position of President of the Carnegie Endowment for International Peace. Representative Mundt, moreover, singled him out for special attention.

"Mr. Chambers," Mundt said, "I am very much interested in trying to check the career of Alger Hiss.... As a member of the

Foreign Affairs Committee, the personnel committee, I have had some occasion to check the activities of Alger Hiss while he was in the State Department. There is reason to believe that he organized within the Department one of the Communist cells which endeavored to influence our Chinese policy and bring about the condemnation of Chiang Kai-shek, which put Marzani * in an important position there, and I think it is important to know what happened to these people after they left the government. . . ."

From an investigative standpoint, the hearing had demonstrated the continuity of two Communist underground groups—one operating in the 1930's and the other during the war. Harry Dexter White had not only worked with Chambers, he was an integral, though remote, part of the Bentley apparatus and known to its members as "one of us." Miss Bentley's testimony had, however, admittedly been hearsay—the shop talk of espionage. Chambers could nail the accusation home. But it was the mention of Alger Hiss that sent the jungle into an uproar. The late Elmer Davis, a man so dense about the problem of infiltration that he spent much of his career as director of the Office of War Information protecting the jobs of crypto-Communists, filled his nightly newscasts over the American Broadcasting network with righteous protestations of Hiss's innocence and countercharges that the Chambers testimony was an attack on the New Deal, and a Republican plot. *The New York Times* inveighed against "false accusation"—seemingly unaware that until all the facts were in it might itself be falsely accusing Chambers. Liberal cartoonists and commentators had a field day with the tar brush.

On August 5th, Alger Hiss made his triumphal appearance, at his own request, before the Committee. The hearing room was packed with friends and well-wishers, and at the press table the reporters waited expectantly for the flat denials which

* Carl Aldo Marzani, a State Department official, was convicted of falsely swearing in a government application that he was not a Communist. It is interesting to note that neither Mundt nor Stripling was aware that Hiss had been called as a witness before a federal grand jury investigating Soviet espionage in 1947.

would destroy Whittaker Chambers. Urbane, smiling, and patronizing, Hiss took the stand and read as categorical a statement as the Committee had ever heard. "I am not and have never been a member of the Communist Party. I do not and have never adhered to the tenets of the Communist Party. I am not and have never been a member of any Communist front organization. I have never followed the Communist Party line, directly or indirectly. To the best of my knowledge, none of my friends is a Communist.... To the best of my knowledge, I had never heard of Whittaker Chambers until in 1947, when two members of the Federal Bureau of Investigation asked me if I knew him. ... So far as I know, I have never laid eyes on him...."

Then he rapidly ticked off the names of the other members of the apparatus supplied to the Committee by Chambers: "I have known Henry Collins since we were boys in camp together.... Lee Pressman was in my class at the Harvard Law School.... Witt and Abt were both members of the legal staff of the Agricultural Adjustment Administration.... Kramer was in another office of the AAA and I met him in that connection. I have seen none of these last three men I have mentioned except most infrequently since I left the Department of Agriculture. I don't believe I ever knew Victor Perlo.... The statements made about me by Mr. Chambers are complete fabrications." Curiously, he did not deny the flat assertion of the Committee that the Communist connections of these people was a matter of common knowledge. He did not even feel "qualified" to "testify absolutely" that his brother Donald was not a Communist—and even about his wife Priscilla, he watered down his answer by stating that "so far as I know" she was not a member of the Party.

Before the hearing had ended, the Committee began to flounder. Mundt noted plaintively that he was puzzled as to why Chambers "should come before this Committee and discuss the Communist apparatus, which he says is transmitting secrets to the Russian Government, and he lists seven people—Nathan Witt, Lee Pressman, Victor Perlo, Charles Kramer, John Abt, Harold Ware, Alger Hiss, and Donald Hiss ..." The

witness was so much in control of the situation that he interrupted Mundt loftily to correct him. "That is eight," he said
and later, ominously, "I wish I could have seen Mr. Chambers
before he testified." Representative John Rankin, who had been
most enthusiastic over the Chambers testimony, switched completely. "After all the smear attacks against this Committee and
individual members of this Committee in *Time* magazine, I am
not surprised at anything that comes out of anybody connected
with it." (Laughter.)

By the hearing's end, Committee members were busily apolo-
gizing for having inconvenienced Hiss and he was graciously
accepting their apologies. Reporters and spectators rushed to
Hiss, shaking his hand and congratulating him. Among the
few in the room who abstained were Representative Nixon and
Chief Investigator Stripling. In a memorandum prepared for
this writer, Nixon described the reactions of the Committee
to the morning's reversal.

I would say that 90 per cent of those who attended the hearing,
including 90 per cent of the press, were convinced Hiss was telling
the truth. The impression Hiss had successfully conveyed was that
the name Chambers and a picture of Chambers meant nothing to
him whatever and that this was simply a case where he had been
indiscriminately smeared by a man he had never known before. Hiss
on that day was a convincing witness because the Committee had
no facts on which to cross-examine him which would in any way
shake his story.

Immediately after that hearing the Committee went into executive session and virtual consternation reigned among the members.
Mundt, along with all the members of the Committee except myself,
said that it was quite apparent the Committee had been taken in
by Chambers and that unless the Committee was able to develop a
collateral issue which would take it off the spot and take the mind
of the public off the Hiss Case, the Committee would suffer a great
deal of damage. [Representative F. Edward] Hébert insisted that
the only way to handle the problem was to send the file containing
the testimony of Chambers on August 3 and the testimony of Hiss
on August 5 over to the Attorney General and to ask him to determine who was lying. I objected to that decision, and Stripling sided

with me. I insisted that although the Committee could not determine who was lying on the issue of whether Hiss was a Communist, we could at least determine which of them was lying on the issue of whether Hiss knew Chambers. I suggested that we immediately go to New York, contact Chambers, and get him in executive session to tell everything that he knew about Hiss. Stripling suggested that there was a witness in the Bentley Case who also lived in New York and that the Committee might interview him at the same time.

The Nixon strategy was at once simple and ingenious. He hoped to pump dry the Chambers well of memory, to get on the record every single fact which could be known only by a close and long-standing friend. If these minutiae were later corroborated by Alger Hiss and/or the Committee's investigators, it would establish that Hiss was lying when he carefully denied knowing a man *named* Whittaker Chambers and, by a rule of law governing testimony, tend to impeach his other denials. If, on the other hand, Chambers' account of his personal association with the Hisses turned out to be fiction, the case would collapse. Acting Chairman Mundt and the Committee reluctantly agreed to allow Nixon to pursue this course, though the pressures for an immediate whitewash of Hiss were very great.

At that moment, the Nixon plan called for considerable courage. Even friends of the Committee were dubious. Nixon recalls that right after Hiss's first appearance, he was told by Mary Spargo—a reporter on the Washington *Post*—"Here's a chance to win some liberal support by repudiating Chambers and clearing Hiss." When Nixon demurred, she said, "Well, go ahead. But I warn you, you'd better be right or you're a dead duck." Antagonists of the Committee were already blasting away. Dean Carl B. Spaeth of the Stanford University law school, Francis Sayre who represented the U. S. at the United Nations, Clarence Pickett of the American Friends Service Committee, former Secretary of War Robert P. Patterson, Senator Herbert H. Lehman, Acting Secretary of State Will Clayton, Ralph Bunche, Chairman H. H. Fisher of the Hoover Library, Mrs. Eleanor Roosevelt, and many others had written Hiss deploring the investigation and pledging their faith and support.

The Committee's decision to allow Richard Nixon to continue the investigation had one effect: from that point on it was his show. For better or for worse, he was inexorably tied to the course of the inquiry. It made him a national figure, and it might have destroyed him. For the friends of Hiss—left, right, or center—never forgave him. Like all men who have met the Communist conspiracy head on, he was marked for life as the target of smears, lies, half-truths, and outrageous assumptions. But it was not all opposition. Very early in the investigation, Bert Andrews, bureau chief of the New York *Herald Tribune,* saw a good story and moved in as an unofficial adviser to Nixon. The Andrews role in the Hiss case has been exaggerated, but there is no doubt that his moral support of Nixon was a tremendous factor. Kenneth G. Crawford and Samuel Shaffer, both of *Newsweek*'s Washington bureau, ran full stories.

From this point on, Richard Nixon took control of the Hiss case. With the full, able, and dedicated backing of Robert Stripling, Research Director Benjamin Mandel, and the Committee staff, he helped make the investigation a classic of its kind—careful, thorough, and unbiased. On August 7th, in Room 101 of the Federal Courthouse on New York's Foley Square, Nixon began his questioning of Chambers. In the cold print of the official transcript, Nixon's language seems harsh and uncompromising. And, in a sense, he was too. His purpose was to get at the facts and to do so he used the techniques of cross-examination. Step by step, he took Chambers along the old dry path of his former associations with Hiss. With Representatives Hébert and John McDowell breaking in now and then, Nixon bore in to elicit the details of Hiss's home life, the nicknames used by Alger and his wife Priscilla, the kind of car they owned—an old 1929 Ford with a hand windshield wiper—that Hiss had bought a new Plymouth in 1936 and turned over the old car to the Communist Party.

Chambers told the Committee about Hiss's personal habits, boyhood anecdotes ("I remember he told me as a small boy he used to take a little wagon—he was a Baltimore boy—and walk up to Druid Hill Park, which was at that time way beyond the civilized center of the city, and fill up bottles with spring water and bring them back and sell it"), Priscilla Hiss's background and where she came from, that she was a Quaker. In the course of this testimony, Chambers casually mentioned one episode which was to be the clincher for many people. To a question by Mandel, "Did he have any hobbies?" Chambers answered:

"Yes, he did. They [the Hisses] had the same hobby—amateur ornithologists, bird observers. They used to get up early in the morning and go to Glen Echo, out on the canal, to observe birds. I recall once they saw, to their great excitement, a prothonotary warbler."

"A very rare specimen?" McDowell asked. "I never saw one," said Chambers—and most Americans had never even heard of the species. When Hiss later corroborated the fact that he had seen such a bird and more than ten years later was as excited about it as he had been when the incident happened, it was a dead giveaway.

For Nixon, and for the Committee, the secret session in New York was a clincher. It was obvious that Chambers was not talking of a man whose life he had studied, but of a onetime friend. There was just too much about Hiss that was not on the public record—some of it not known to any of his friends. In the nine days between this hearing and Alger Hiss's second appearance before the Committee, Nixon continued his marathon inquiry into what Chambers knew and what his motives had been. He even made several trips to the Chambers farm in Westminster. "On these occasions," Nixon later said, "I asked Chambers innumerable questions concerning his relationship to Hiss and his answers to them were in all cases forthright and convincing." On the matter of motive, Nixon realized what was gradually seeping into the minds of some of the less biased reporters: In destroying Hiss, Chambers was also destroying himself.

On August 16th, when Hiss took the stand in the Committee's hearing room in the Old House Office Building, he could sense a different atmosphere. The members had studied the Chambers testimony. Nixon's hunch had turned into conviction. The staff had checked out every fact at that time susceptible of proof and had found that Chambers was telling the truth. Hiss's former arrogance now turned to wariness and the change in manner was not lost on the Committee. As Nixon led Hiss step by step to corroborate what Chambers had said about him, his wife, and his home life, the witness began his long retreat from the categorical statement that he had never seen Chambers. "The face," he said in typical government jargon, "is definitely not unfamiliar." He also very carefully repeated that he had never known a man *"by the name of Whittaker Chambers."* But this gambit no longer impressed the Committee. Thereupon, Hiss changed his tactics. Aware that Chambers had furnished damaging detail of their past association, he launched into a pettifogging attack on the Committee, accusing its members of bad faith. His charge that the testimony he was giving would be leaked to Chambers, giving him "ex post facto" knowledge, was quickly demolished when Stripling and others pointed out that Chambers had been the first to supply the incriminating details, and that Hiss was merely corroborating them.

At this point, Hiss made what lawyers have since called his most serious error. He grudgingly identified Chambers, subject to confrontation, as one "George Crosley"—according to the Hiss account a free-lance writer to whom he had supplied public information and sublet an apartment, and whom he had befriended in 1934 and 1935. This gave him the opportunity for confirming part of the Chambers story, for explaining how Chambers came to know so much about him, and for avoiding the charge of perjury. But it also placed on him the onus of pinning the "George Crosley" personality on Whittaker Chambers—something he was never able to do. And it also trapped Hiss in a major lie which was to be his undoing. This trap was of Hiss's own making. For having been warned—reportedly by a friend in the Justice Department—of Chambers' comments on the old Ford, Hiss had to tailor his story to fit his purported dealings with the "deadbeat" Crosley.

Suddenly turning voluble, Hiss testified that he had sublet his apartment to the "Crosleys," that until their furniture arrived he had put them up in his new home, and that he had "thrown in" the old Ford which he no longer needed since he had a new Plymouth. The Ford, said Hiss, "had been sitting out in the streets in the snows for a year or two. I once got a parking fine because I forgot where it was parked. We were using the other car." He set the date for these transactions at July 1935, certain that the date of transfer could not be traced. The date, and the unnecessary detail, lived to haunt him as the hearings progressed.

It was not until several days later that the Committee realized the importance of the car testimony. What jolted them most was the brief exchange about the prothonotary warbler which Chambers had casually mentioned. When Hiss admitted to an interest in ornithology, Representative McDowell asked casually: "Did you ever see a prothonotary warbler?"

HISS: I have right here on the Potomac. Do you know the place?

THE CHAIRMAN (sharply): What is that?

NIXON: Did you see one . . .

HISS: They come back and nest in those swamps. Beautiful yellow head, a gorgeous bird.

The Committee dropped the subject. But the balance of the scales had shifted definitely and irrevocably. Subsequent outbursts of righteous indignation by Hiss that the Committee equated the value of his word with that of Chambers, which but eleven days before would have given the Committee some pause, merely led to acrimonious debate. The Committee made it clear that it was not going to be impressed by Hiss's efforts at proclaiming innocence by association with famous men or by his anger that the testimony of a "self-confessed former Communist" and "self-confessed traitor" was being taken seriously. The session wound up when Hiss and the Committee agreed that a confrontation between the two principals should be arranged. But before this, Hiss had been damaged further by his reluctance to take a lie-detector test.*

---

* In his August 7th testimony, Chambers had agreed readily to such a test. The idea had been suggested by Bert Andrews to Nixon. Much was subsequently made of Hiss's refusal in later testimony to agree to submit to the lie detector.

The qualified admission by Alger Hiss that he had known Chambers as "George Crosley" changed the focus of the investigation. The newspapers still continued their litany of "Who is lying, Hiss or Chambers?" but the public—through leaks to the press from Committee members—now knew that at least part of the Chambers story was true, and that Hiss had been less than candid in his first appearance before the Un-American Activities investigators. Repeated attempts by President Truman to discredit the inquiry as a "red herring" and the anguished outcries of much of the liberal community only served to stimulate the public interest. In accordance with its promise to Hiss—and its own desires—the Committee arranged for a secret confrontation of the two men. On August 17th, Representatives Mc-Dowell, J. Parnell Thomas, and Nixon met in executive session in Room 1400 of New York's Commodore Hotel. Hiss was sworn in and Nixon stated that since the case "at this time" was "dependent upon the question of identity," Chambers had been asked to appear. Hiss said he would "like the record to show" that he had just learned of the death of Harry Dexter White and that "I am not sure that I feel in the best possible mood for testimony." He also vigorously protested a New York *Herald Tribune* story reporting that "the Committee had asked me yesterday if I would submit to a lie detector test."

There was some bickering over "leaks" from the Committee, and then Nixon asked Staff Investigator Louis J. Russell, "Will you bring Mr. Chambers in?" What followed was startling. For though Hiss had repeatedly demanded an opportunity to meet his antagonist face to face, he kept his back turned to the door, not even turning his head as Chambers walked in. In his book *Witness,* Chambers describes how ten years before he, Chambers, a hunted man after his break with the apparatus, had pleaded with Hiss to give up his Communist faith. At that parting of lives and loyalties, Hiss had wept. Now his stony refusal to look at his accuser was perhaps the most damning evidence against

---

Recent experiences with the polygraph machine, however, have indicated its general unreliability and today law enforcement officers concede that its major value is as a psychological device, not as a scientific instrument.

Hiss, for it wordlessly conceded that he did not need to look at Chambers to determine whether he was the "deadbeat" Crosley. Clearly, he *knew*.

And then the comedy began. For Hiss's sole interest seemed to be in the state of Chambers' teeth. He demanded to know the name of the dentist who had worked on the Chambers dentures. He put such stress on this that Nixon was constrained to ask: "Mr. Hiss, do you feel that you would have to have the dentist say just what he did to the teeth before you could tell anything about this man?" Hiss dropped the subject. Nixon and Stripling then took Hiss over the ground of the so-called sublet of his apartment to "George Crosley" in July of 1935. Hiss amplified his previous account. As he told it, the rental had been $75 a month, he had thrown in a six-year-old car as part of the deal, and lent "Crosley" money but had received only a rug in payment. These new details about the car were, at the time, unimportant. Returning to the identification of Chambers, however, Hiss still refused to be categorical. With the Committee's permission, he moved to his own questioning.

HISS: Did you ever go under the name of George Crosley?
CHAMBERS: Not to my knowledge.
HISS: Did you ever sublet an apartment on 29th Street from me?
CHAMBERS: No, I did not. . . .
HISS: Did you ever spend any time with your wife and child in an apartment on 29th Street in Washington when I was not there because I and my family were living on P Street?
CHAMBERS: I most certainly did. . . .
HISS: Would you tell me how you reconcile your negative answers with this affirmative answer?
CHAMBERS: Very easily, Alger. I was a Communist and you were a Communist. . . . As I have testified before, I came to Washington as a Communist functionary. . . . I was connected with the underground group of which Mr. Hiss was a member. Mr. Hiss and I became friends. To the best of my knowledge, Mr. Hiss himself suggested [that I live in the apartment] and I accepted gratefully.

HISS: Mr. Chairman.

NIXON: Just a moment. How long did you stay there?

CHAMBERS: My recollection was about three weeks. It may have been longer. I brought no furniture, I might add.

HISS: Mr. Chairman, I don't need to ask Mr. Whittaker Chambers any more questions. I am now prepared to identify this man as George Crosley. . . .

STRIPLING: You will identify him positively now?

HISS: I will on the basis of what he has just said positively identify him without further questioning as George Crosley.

But the icy calm was now gone. As Chambers repeated his accusation and made his own positive identification, Hiss rose, white-faced with anger, and advanced toward his accuser. "May I say for the record at this point," he said violently, "that I would like to invite Mr. Whittaker Chambers to make those same statements out of the presence of this Committee without their being privileged for suit for libel. I challenge you to do it, and I hope you will do it damned quickly." This was a fatal error, forcing the issue and leading to his trial and imprisonment. But he felt sure that if Chambers possessed documentary proof of espionage, he would have made it known to the Committee. And he was confident that without such proof, Chambers would either run from repeating the accusation where it was not privileged, or be unable to defend a libel action.

Hiss's mistake in judging Chambers and in reading his character was not shared by others who witnessed the unfolding of the Hiss case. After the Hiss indictment, James Wechsler wrote of the first confrontation in the *Progressive:* "There are those who believe that Chambers was in effect imploring Hiss to acknowledge the degree of guilt already ascribed to him—mere association with the Communist ring—so that it would not be necessary to unfold the papers which presumably damaged both men, transforming the case from the level of Communist affiliation to the more desolate plane of espionage. According to this view, Hiss misinterpreted Chambers's initial failure to produce the documents as assurance that he never would; and Chambers was equally confident that Hiss, correctly understanding his gesture, would never sue for libel." The case, then, would have ended inconclusively. But other factors were at work. It was a Presidential election year and issues were scarce. The House Un-American Activities Committee, moreover, was under strong attack, in part to counter the impact on the nation of the Hiss-Chambers case, and its chairman J. Parnell Thomas had been accused by Drew Pearson of accepting kickbacks.

The general political situation was best summed up by Kenneth G. Crawford, then assistant Washington Bureau chief for *Newsweek*, several days after the first confrontation:

The political potential of the spy investigation is dawning slowly on strategists in both parties. They now believe the country is talking about it to the exclusion of almost every other public question. Republicans are a little worried about the bumbling nature of the House Committee, even though it has been strengthened by Nixon and Mundt.... Drew Pearson's exposé of Thomas, made possible by the defection of a former employee with large bundles from Thomas's files, is making the chairman even more of a liability than he used to be.... Some of the Dewey people are talking about this kind of deal: appoint a Senate Foreign Relations Committee to make a detailed study of the influence of Hiss and associates on Roosevelt foreign policy; a Senate Banking subcommittee to follow through on Harry Dexter White's German pastoralization policy, particularly that Communist-packed Treasury mission that went to Germany after the war at White's instigation and under his protection.... Democrats meanwhile are seeing how far out on a shaky limb Truman's "red herring" statements have got him. Some of them advised him to get off the limb after his first press conference statement but they have made no impression on him.

He has now repeated the red herring comment... at two more press conferences. The White House people... are still talking wistfully about a Presidential Commission to study the whole problem of Communists in government with such figures as General Eisenhower, Judge Hand, etc., to give it the necessary stature. I understand that the President himself is beginning to doubt the wisdom of his line—that the Hiss break shook him a little. All the President saw in the thing up to the time Hiss started changing his story was a successful attempt by the Republicans to rob him of the political advantage he thought he had got from the special session of Congress. He still feels more or less that way about it but has wondered out loud to a friend today.... At yesterday's press conference, Truman said no American secret ever was leaked to the Russians.

But the case had moved beyond President Truman's soul-searching. It was now a race between the House Committee and the Administration, between the facts and the cover-up. While House Committee investigators were checking on Hiss's testimony—looking into leases, car sales, etc.—the pro-Hiss forces were seeking to minimize the admissions of the August 17th hearing. It was merely by a normal lapse of memory that Hiss had not immediately recognized Chambers. The serious accusation, that Hiss had been a member of a Communist underground, was still at issue. The cocktail circuit was rife with rumors, all dutifully reported, that Chambers had invented the story of Communist involvement out of malice and for obscure motives. It was necessary, if these theories were to be substantiated, to negate the Chambers account of a meeting in 1939 with Assistant Secretary of State Berle during which he disclosed details of the Soviet apparatus. Perhaps, it was said, Chambers was once a Communist. But if he had told Berle of an underground group in the government, why was nothing done about it? Had he mentioned Hiss at that meeting? Had the meeting actually taken place? Or was the Chambers testimony part of a Republican plot against the New Deal?

The answers to these questions were an important part of any further investigation. And the Committee wanted answers. Before the public confrontation of Hiss and Chambers, the Committee wanted its own corroboration, and it called Isaac Don Levine who, according to Chambers, had been present at the 1939 meeting with Berle, to affirm or deny. Levine had fought the Communists for years (*Newsweek* has described him as the "dean of anti-Communists"), and his liberal and pro-Communist enemies had always been overwhelmed by the solidity of his information. On August 18th, Don Levine laid it on the line.

He told of his meeting with Chambers in June 1939, of the conversations they had, of attempts to get the story to President Roosevelt, and of the meeting on September 3rd with Berle.

"The picture which emerged by midnight was quite appalling," Levine told the Committee, "and I think Mr. Berle was very much shaken by the various names of the Soviet agents that Mr. Chambers disclosed. Mr. Chambers furnished, in addition to the names, descriptions and characterizations of the various persons which served to provide a background and give an authentic and authenticating character both to his narrative and to the answers to the questions which Mr. Berle then propounded. I think it was sometime between midnight and one o'clock when we left [Mr. Berle]. When I got to my hotel, after I took leave from Mr. Chambers, tired as I was, I jotted down all the names that I could recall on a sheet of hotel stationery."

NIXON: Can you tell us whether the name of Alger Hiss was mentioned in that conversation with Mr. Berle?

LEVINE: Both Hiss brothers were mentioned. The name of Alger Hiss and the name of the other Hiss.

NIXON: There is no question that those names were mentioned?

LEVINE: There isn't any question, because I made a record at the time and I am looking at it now.*

Isaac Don Levine's testimony was a blockbuster, demolishing the ugly and carefully disseminated gossip that Chambers had been coached by the Committee and/or the Republican Party. It even jarred those who professed to believe that the Chambers testimony was a sudden aberration, a Johnny-come-lately effort to "get into the anti-Communist act." Yet the doubt persisted in the minds of many, particularly the Washington press corps, which only knew of the Commodore Hotel confrontation from Committee leaks and the planted rumors of the Hiss camp. Even after Hiss had invented "George Crosley," the *Christian Science*

---

* The Levine notes, written on hotel stationery, were not only made available to the Committee but were heavily quoted in a series of articles for *Plain Talk,* which Don Levine was editing at the time of the hearings. He also allowed the press to inspect them.

Monitor continued to work on a story which was to feature a compendium of laudatory statements by prominent people, all defending Hiss's integrity and vouching for his loyalty.*

On a hot, heavy August 25th Alger Hiss and Whittaker Chambers had their public confrontation. It was steamy in the caucus room of the Old House Office Building, but one thousand spectators sat tensely in the wilting heat (another three hundred, held off by Capitol police, waited outside). They knew that this was the moment of crisis, that it was either win or lose for the protagonists in what had become a titanic drama. Hiss surveyed the scene wryly from a small table at one end of the Committee bench, calmly chatting with his lawyer and smiling at friends. At the other end of the bench Chambers sat impassively. Only the Committee members and staff knew that they had finally come up with hard, documented proof that Hiss was lying about his relationship with Chambers—and corollary, though circumstantial, evidence that the former State Department *Wunderkind* was associated with the Communist Party.

It started out quietly and easily. The only ominous note was the quiet assertion by Chairman Thomas that "as a result of this hearing, certainly one of these witnesses will be tried for perjury." This put Hiss on notice, and from that point on he began bickering with the Committee, playing semantic games, arguing over unessential and irrelevant points, and attempting to put the Committee on the defensive by falsely stating that he had been deprived of copies of the transcript of previous hearings—then being forced to concede that they had been furnished to him as promptly as possible. Even the *Manchester Guardian's* Alistair Cooke, whose sympathy for Hiss was abounding, admitted that these petty and pettifogging tactics did not sit well with those who had admired his seemingly frank performance of August 5th. The crowd in the room was disposed to sympathize with Hiss's accusations of bad faith against the Committee, but as these were demolished one by one, the mood changed.

* "I feel entirely convinced," said Mrs. Roosevelt, "that if he had been a Communist I certainly would have caught something to make me suspicious."

In quick order, Hiss identified Chambers as the "George Crosley" he had known until "sometime in 1935." Chambers identified Hiss and said the last time he had seen him was "about 1938." But after some fencing, the Committee got down to the issue which broke the Hiss case wide open: the disposition of an old 1929 Ford which Hiss claimed he sold to "Crosley" in the summer of 1935. It has been said that Hiss was caught unaware by the close questioning he received on this subject from the Committee. The fact is that he knew his original story was punctured, that the Committee had checked auto registrations. Hiss was therefore faced with the need to qualify or deny what he had previously said, without seeming to do so. But he was impaled by the very detailed and graphic account in his earlier testimony, and his tactic was to develop a progressive loss of memory.

The story of the car may seem petty, in view of the later espionage disclosures. But it is significant as an example of proper investigative procedures—and because it forced Hiss's most ardent adherents to concede that at the very least he was hiding something. It is very difficult to boil down the massive detail involved in the car story and requires some recapitulation of earlier testimony. These are the essentials:

In admitting that he knew Chambers, Hiss had been compelled to come up with a legitimate story of the background of this association. He was handicapped by not knowing just how much of the Chambers testimony would be susceptible of proof. To explain Chambers' knowledge of his homes, he had invented the story of having sublet his apartment. But he had improvised just a little too rapidly about the Ford. When the Committee had asked him if he had owned such a car, he had assumed that Chambers must have told the members of its ultimate destination.

In executive session testimony, he had tried to rid himself of this albatross by stating that he had given it to Chambers as part of the sublet arrangement, in May or June of 1935. This required that he acknowledge possession of his new Plymouth as of that date—but Hiss had embroidered this by swearing that the old Ford had stood on the streets "in the snows" for one or two years. During the public confrontation, he retreated from the flat assertion that he had thrown in the car as part of the sublet deal. He may have done it before, during, or after the time that Chambers had occupied the "sublet" apartment. And he wasn't quite sure whether or not he had sold it or merely allowed Chambers the use of it. He was no longer certain that any legal transfer had taken place at the time, though he had previously so testified. Though he had been categorical about having had the Plymouth during the one or two years the Ford had sat in semi-abandonment, he now became vague.

Painstakingly, though sometimes impatiently, clambering over the obstacles Hiss threw in its way, the Committee demonstrated that (1) Hiss had bought his Plymouth in September 1935, months after he testified that he had given, sold, or made available to Chambers the old Ford; (2) it was not until July 1936, long after he insisted he no longer had any association with Chambers, that the Ford had been transferred, and the document with his signature was there to prove it; (3) the sale had been made to one William Rosen, who had given a false address and subsequently took the Fifth Amendment when questioned about the transaction; (4) the transfer, consummated by a reputable motor company in Washington, had been so handled that there would be no record. Caught in the net of his own lies, Hiss tried to explain that he might have given Chambers the car after September, but he could hardly make the Committee or the public believe that he would have presented a car to a man who had "welshed" on the rent and on a number of small debts, had been a "fourflusher" and was by that time repugnant to him. He denied that he had ever said he sold the car to Chambers and sat grimly on the stand as Nixon read pointedly from his August 16th testimony. Yet he continued to argue and was rewarded by the sardonic laughter of the audience which had once applauded him.

His only recourse was to lash out, to counterattack by again challenging Chambers to repeat the Communist accusation where it was not privileged, and to lay the groundwork for the anti-Chambers smears by demanding to know whether his accuser had ever spent time in a mental institution or been convicted of a crime. These questions did not endear him to the Committee. Its members had heard every friendly witness reviled as insane or crooked and spotted Hiss's intent. When questioned as to his motives for raising the insanity issue, Hiss said blandly that it was based on hearsay—someone whom he could not name had told someone else that Chambers had once been committed. Hiss's efforts to deny any other intent except the desire for knowledge further impeached him with Chief Investigator Stripling. For immediately after the first hearing, Hiss and his counsel, William Marbury, had said to Stripling that Chambers was a "psychopathic case—he is crazy"; and then proceeded to pass the word on to friendly reporters.

Hiss's final effort to impress the Committee with his innocence came when he listed a virtual Who's Who in government, then asked the Committee to get the opinions of the dropped names as to his loyalty. But the Committee had its answer for that— and right from Hiss's mouth. How, the witness was asked, could they know? Their testimony would be as worthless, Hébert pointed out, as Hiss's that he had no way of determining whether or not Lee Pressman, Nathan Witt, and the others named as his colleagues in the apparatus were Communists. From that point on, it was all downhill for Hiss. As Samuel Shaffer, *Newsweek*'s Capitol correspondent, remarked, "After the first public hearing, many in the audience pushed their way up to Hiss to shake his hand and congratulate him on his impressive performance. After the public confrontation, he and his lawyer pushed their way out alone."

Clearly, the Committee had scored heavily. Though it had not proved that Hiss was a Communist, it had demonstrated conclusively that he was lying—that there was something murky in his past which he could not admit. Students of Communist subversion and espionage, studying the record, felt without a shadow of a doubt that Hiss and Chambers once were part of the same apparatus. All the telltale marks were there. The Washington press corps was badly shaken. The more ardent Hissophiles still argued that the last word hadn't been said, that an explanation exis'ed. But for the most part correspondents felt a sense of betrayal. They had accepted every word of Hiss's as gospel truth, using him as a stick with which to beat the House Committee on Un-American Activities, and he had let them down. The reaction of the professional liberals was one of utter rage and their attacks at the Committee for proving them wrong verged on the hysterical. Hiss had assassinated his own character; now it was up to them to assassinate the Committee. The Truman Administration kept up its running attack. And behind the scenes, a new strategy was evolved: to minimize the importance of the Chambers disclosures and to rehabilitate Alger Hiss.

Perhaps, it was argued, Hiss had flirted with the Communists in the 1930's and then lied about it in the "Red-baiting, witch-hunting" Cold War era. To admit even a passing acquaintance with a Communist put a man in jeopardy, the Elmer Davises insisted, and Hiss was foolish enough to lie in order to protect his position. He may even have been sentimental enough in the depression years to donate his old and useless car to some Communist Party organizer, but this was no more reprehensible than contributing to a Communist front with noble purposes or sending money to the Spanish Loyalists. This thought was comforting for those who had been shocked by Hiss's performance before the House Committee. It conjured up a picture, romantic and idealistic, of a young man concerned over the world's problems. The next step for the Committee, therefore, was to probe this aspect of the case—and the most logical witness to question was A. A. Berle, who had heard the Chambers story in 1939.

On August 30th, the House Committee called Berle, put him under oath, told him he could smoke if he wished, and asked him to speak his piece. It was a difficult moment for Berle. He was fully aware that anything he might say could hurt the electoral chances of President Truman. As chairman of New York's Liberal Party—though still a Democrat—he was already deeply involved in the 1948 election. On the other hand, he still bore the scars inflicted on him by the Acheson-Hiss group in the State Department during his tenure. And he knew from direct knowledge the laxness of department security procedures and the refusal of the Foreign Service to tighten them. That this dilemma was on his mind is not conjecture. Prior to his testimony he had discussed it fully with some of his colleagues.

"I would like to say," Berle began, "that I am testifying from recollection about something that happened nine years ago. If there are any discrepancies in detail, please lay it to faulty memory and not lack of desire to tell the story." The testimony that followed was long, inaccurate both in detail and in broad outline, and deprecating. Its net effect was to play down the importance of Hiss in the State Department hierarchy, to cast doubt on the Chambers and Levine testimony, and to minimize the seriousness of the case.

Describing the meeting in August 1939, Berle did "not recall that Mr. Levine accompanied Mr. Chambers." Moving on to Chambers' disclosures, Berle said that he had been told of a group of "sympathizers who might be of use to [the Communist Party] later in the United States Government. This was not, as [Chambers] put it, any question of espionage. There was no espionage involved in it. He stated that their hope merely was to get some people who would be sympathetic to their point of view. With that in mind, apparently a study group of some sort had been formed of men who were interested in knowing something about Russia and Russian policy and the general Communist theory of life. . . . He mentioned Alger Hiss, Donald Hiss, Nathan Witt, and Pressman. . . . In one respect, what he told me omitted something that he has told you: He did not make *the direct statement that any of these men were members of the Communist Party*. They were apparently, from what I then gathered, men who were sympathetic to their general point of view." Berle said he considered this a "pretty grave matter" but that Chambers had refused to "bear witness."

Berle was "disturbed" enough by learning of this innocuous "study group" to look into the then position of the two Hiss boys. "According to my recollection, neither of them had any position that amounted to very much in the State Department. . . . Alger Hiss was doing some relatively unimportant work in, I think, the legal department"—he was in fact top assistant to

Assistant Secretary Francis Sayre—"... *but neither was in any position* where he either had access to confidential information or where he had much *to do with policy.*" Nevertheless, he checked with Dean Acheson, who gave the Hiss boys a clean bill of health. So, too, had Supreme Court Justice Felix Frankfurter. He was worried, Berle added, because confidential information handled by the Acheson-Hiss group consistently leaked to columnist Drew Pearson—but this was not "a fatal crime" since other government officials leaked information to the press.

Berle's final remarks, in effect, summed up the views of those who believed that Hiss's only sin had been to show some interest in Communism. (Berle felt constrained at one point to say, "Well, I am not counsel for Mr. Hiss.") "I have had some experience with the men who have been in [the Communist apparatus] and then got out of it. They sometimes tend to exaggerate a little the depths of the experience they had. They have obviously been through a violent emotional experience, and I gather that part of the Communist apparatus is designed to impress the people in it with the all-powerful quality of it, probably exaggerating their own importance.... I should question whether their actual importance, except in a few limited areas in Washington"—which he did not specify—"was as grave as they would like to make out.... I am by no means clear that Hiss would have been taken into the Communist Party unless things had gone along further than they apparently did. *Sympathizer, possibly, but to be taken into the fold, it is a pretty exclusive and secret organization, that Communist Party, and I recall that Chambers did not make any direct statement to me then.*" (All emphasis in Berle testimony added.)

This wrapped up the case. Berle did not inform the Committee that he had taken notes of his 1939 conversation with Chambers, typed them himself, and turned them over to the FBI in 1943. Had the Committee so known, it might have secured copies of those four incriminating pages and allowed Berle, in the lawyer's phrase, to refresh his recollection. Those notes were headed "Underground Espionage Agent" and there was nothing in them about a "study group." In fact, they detailed espionage operations, listed the names of men in key government positions (Sol "sends weekly reports to C.P." from the Treasury), identified underground couriers, told of the theft of Navy secrets in 1937, and indicated that Chambers had understated rather than "exaggerated" in his testimony before the Committee. Of Alger Hiss, the notes stated: "Ass't to Sayre—CP —1937 / Member of Underground Com.—Active." Of Donald Hiss, "Member of C.P. with Pressman and Witt."

Some indication of what may have been going through Berle's mind is suggested in a memorandum sent by the *Christian Science Monitor*'s New York Bureau to the home office:

FROM A THOROUGHLY RELIABLE CONTACT.

ACCORDING TO THIS INFORMANT BERLE HAS SAID PRIVATELY THAT CLASSIFIED MATERIAL WHICH HISS WAS HANDLING WAS REACHING THE RUSSIANS. IT WAS CODED STUFF. BERLE TOOK THE HANDLING OF THIS MATERIAL OUT OF HISS' HANDS AND THE LEAKS STOPPED.

THIS, OF COURSE, IS PARTLY CIRCUMSTANTIAL. AND IT RAISES A NUMBER OF QUESTIONS, THE CHIEF ONE BEING: WHY HAS BERLE NOT TOLD THIS TO THE COMMITTEE?

. . . THIS SEEMS TO ME THE MOST DAMAGING PIECE OF INFORMATION AGAINST HISS I HAVE HEARD. IF CLASSIFIED MATERIAL WITH WHICH HE WAS PERSONALLY CHARGED WAS REACHING THE RUSSIANS, THEN HIS MEMBERSHIP OR NONMEMBERSHIP IN THE COMMUNIST PARTY WOULD APPEAR TO BE MERELY AN ACADEMIC QUESTION.

The memorandum is dated September 2, 1948 ("9/2/48"), just three days after Berle had testified. It should be noted that the Berle testimony followed an appearance by Whittaker Chambers on "Meet the Press" during which he had said, in answer to a question by Washington *Post* reporter Edward Folliard, "Alger Hiss was a Communist and may be now." No immunity protected this accusation, and it threw the gauntlet at Hiss's feet. It took Hiss a month and the impatient prodding of friendly newspapers like the Washington *Post* ("Mr. Hiss himself has created a situation in which he is obliged to put up or shut up") before the threatened libel suit was filed in Baltimore—a period in which Hiss and his lawyers were studying every scrap of testimony taken by the Committee. In this context, what Berle said under oath may have been responsible for the assurance with which Hiss instituted his "daring suit" (to quote Chambers) .

From that point on, the House Committee on Un-American Activities faded into the background. It could probe no further without interfering in a pending litigation. The transcripts of the hearings were forwarded to Attorney General Tom Clark for study and possible action. But no one expected that the Justice Department would do anything more than file them away. President Truman was still describing the hearings as "red herrings" and predicting that the Committee was dead and would not have its mandate renewed. In the newspapers, the Hiss case was receding into the editor's limbo of "no public interest." The Committee believed that it had rested its case, at least partially vindicated, and that the libel suit would result at best in a standoff if Chambers defended himself successfully.

It had no way of knowing that in the law library of William Marbury, Hiss's attorney, the wheels were grinding relentlessly toward a denouement as unexpected as it was dramatic. For with the Justice Department clearly loath to act against him, Hiss had decided to move in for the kill. From the nature of the questioning at the pre-trial sessions in Marbury's office, it became clear to Chambers that "Hiss was determined to destroy me—and my wife—if possible." A sense of self-preservation, and rising anger, impelled Chambers to act. He had carefully skirted the outright charge of espionage on the assumption that Hiss would realize his own danger and not press too hard. But the time for squeamishness, for protecting Hiss, was past. Chambers journeyed to Brooklyn to retrieve a package of papers he had entrusted to his nephew at the time of the break with the apparatus. He was no longer quite certain what was in the package, secreted in an old dumb-waiter shaft, but he remembered vaguely that it included "some papers in Hiss's handwriting."

When he brushed aside the accumulated grime of years and examined the contents, he found typed copies of 47 documents, five rolls of microfilm, four incriminating memoranda in Hiss's handwriting and five in Harry Dexter White's handwriting. "When I saw what I had," Chambers said to this writer later, "I was amazed."

At the next pre-trial hearing, Chambers produced the documents—secret and confidential messages from U. S. ambassadors to the State Department—copied on what would subsequently be proved was Hiss's typewriter. The Justice Department was called in, the papers sealed, and everyone concerned enjoined to keep the matter secret. This was on November 17th. On December 1st, a Justice Department source informed a United Press reporter that the "investigation of the celebrated Alger Hiss-Whittaker Chambers controversy" was being dropped. On the same day, columnist Jerry Kluttz wrote in the Washington *Post* that "some very startling information" had been turned up by the Justice Department.

Nixon was aboard the S. S. *Panama,* en route through the Caribbean to California. But two wireless messages interrupted that leisurely trip. The first, from his administrative assistant William Arnold, informed him that there were serious developments in the case. The second, from newspaperman Bert Andrews, confirmed this and asked if the Committee would reopen its investigation. Nixon wired back, instructing Stripling to advise him on the new evidence and informing Andrews that new hearings would be held if they were "necessary to prevent Justice Department cover-up." Events were moving to a crescendo. Stripling, unable to get confirmation or denial, was successful to a point. Chambers admitted that he had withheld evidence from the Committee, but refused to elaborate. To do so, he said, might put him in contempt of court. The following day, at Nixon's direction, Stripling served Chambers with a subpoena calling for any documentary proof still in his possession. That night, Committee investigators drove with Chambers to his farm. In a scooped-out pumpkin were the five rolls of microfilm.

This hiding place was the source of much gleeful comment from the pro-Hiss forces, and held up as one more indication of Chambers' zany mind. It was not until later that Chambers explained why he had hidden the microfilm there. Hiss investigators had been prowling about his farm, and a scooped-out pumpkin in a patch seemed—and was—the least likely place they might search while he was out of the house. But the case had gone past the stage where jeers could prevent full disclosure. Before the microfilm had been turned over to the Committee, "informed sources" at the Justice Department had let it be known that they were planning to indict Chambers for perjury. The morning after the microfilm had been delivered to the Committee—developed and enlarged to proper size, it gave Stripling a four-foot stack of documents—a federal grand jury was hastily convened in New York, and its first act was to subpoena Chambers.

On December 5th, Nixon was picked up in mid-Caribbean by a Coast Guard plane and flown back to Washington. Operation Whitewash was in full swing, and Nixon moved to block it. On December 6th, he and an angry Committee rushed to New York to question Chambers. They were met at Pennsylvania Station by U. S. Attorney John McGohey who accompanied them to the Commodore Hotel, pleading that the Committee drop out. But none of the members had any faith in the Justice Department's motives. Quickly, the members and McGohey were shouting at each other, pitching accusations, until Stripling threw open the window and said, "We might as well let them hear about it on Fifth Avenue." This ended the curfuffle, but it did not satisfy the Committee that an impartial investigation would be pressed.

On December 7th, the Committee obliterated once and for all the contention that the typed and microfilmed documents were of no importance or that they might have been copied by Hiss in the line of duty and then somehow stolen by Chambers. Former Undersecretary of State Sumner Welles told the Committee that some of the documents were still too secret to release to the public and said that the distribution within the

State Department would have been "extremely restricted," to be "kept under lock and key." He also noted that whatever the contents of the documents, to have delivered them to a foreign power would have broken our most secret codes. Assistant Secretary John Peurifoy went even further. To make verbatim copies of the documents would be "a very unusual procedure." Of the four memoranda in Hiss's handwriting, Peurifoy said, "I would regard anyone making notes of what I have seen here, in personal handwriting, and taking them out of the Department, as violating all security regulations."

HÉBERT: Would there be any reason for an individual to make a memorandum such as you have just looked at, in his own handwriting?

PEURIFOY: No, sir. Not in my judgment.

HÉBERT: You would have to assume that he did it for some ulterior motive?

PEURIFOY: I think that is right. Under the Yardley Act ... a person would be liable to a $10,000 fine, and I think up to ten years' imprisonment, for doing such a thing.

Most damning was the secret testimony of former Assistant Secretary Sayre—not only Hiss's superior but a close personal friend. First he stated that only he, Hiss, and two secretaries of unquestioned loyalty had access to files which were always kept locked, destroying Hiss's alibi that the handwritten memos were prepared as part of his work.

NIXON: Did Mr. Hiss (as he claimed) have as one of his duties the paraphrasing of these documents and bringing them back to you in this way?

SAYRE: The answer is "No."

NIXON: ... Do you agree there was nothing important or nothing wrong with turning this stuff over?

SAYRE: I violently disagree, not only because of the substance of these cables, but because they were in highly confidential codes.... The other point is that some of these cables reveal sources from which information was obtained.

This ended the long debate. It was certain now that Hiss had lied and Chambers had told the truth. Despite the opposition of the Truman Administration and the hostility of the press, the House Committee on Un-American Activities had demonstrated, dramatically and effectively, that Communists in government systematically looted the nation of its secrets. The Communist conspiracy was not a figment of fevered or sick imaginations. The Committee could write Q.E.D. and proclaim its finest hour. The rest was police work, and the FBI, allowed to perform its functions free of the political interference of a political Attorney General, brilliantly gathered together the evidence. On December 15th, Hiss was indicted for perjury involving his denial of passing secret documents to Chambers. ("I hope that nobody anywhere will ever refer to this case as a red herring," Mundt said, but President Truman disappointed him.) On January 21, 1950, after two trials, Alger Hiss was convicted. Dean Acheson refused to turn his back on his most celebrated protégé, but the Supreme Court did. Two years later, before the Senate Internal Security subcommittee, Nathaniel Weyl testified that he had known Hiss in the Communist underground. And even after the courts had closed the case, evidence continued to pour in, corroborating Hiss's guilt.

Between the indictment and the trial, however, the Committee held one more hearing in which it questioned Whittaker Chambers. On December 28, 1948, Nixon, Mundt and Stripling drove out to the Chambers farm in Westminster, Maryland. They were greeted by Mrs. Esther Chambers and led into the living room. There, sitting close to a cheerful fireplace, they asked Chambers to fill in the gaps, to give them the full story of his activities in the Communist underground before he had met Hiss and after. For no explicable reason, this testimony has never been made public. This writer was allowed to study it in 1950, but today the House Committee refuses to repeat this privilege—though the details have appeared in the Chambers autobiography, *Witness*. It is a story of secret meeting places, of Soviet spies in the military establishment, of Hiss and Lee Pressman, of the tangled web of betrayal and espionage, of industrial sabotage. Much of it has been checked out by the FBI and the House Committee. Some of it was repeated in testimony during the Hiss trial.

As a document, it is unique. But it does not figure in the accounts of the Hiss-Chambers case written by the urbane Alistair Cooke, by the badly informed Lord Jowitt, by Alger Hiss, or by the injudicious Fred Cook. These commentators, writing books which were hailed by the pro-Hiss remnants in the press, could not take the time to dig through the records of Soviet espionage—just as they could not be bothered, in their accounts, with such matters as Isaac Don Levine's testimony, the details and significance of the two Hiss cars, the Berle notes, or the more telling evidence.

For them, faith is enough—the kind of faith that led the eminent Morris Ernst to write, after reading Alger Hiss's own account, that he believed the case was a miscarriage of justice, though he had never read the trial transcript. For those who are deliberately blind—who stuff their ears to the testimony of clouds of witnesses and blind their eyes to acres of evidence— the way of convincement is hard. But they can look back and wonder at the words of John Sherman, a member of the Communist apparatus, who was asked by the House Committee on Un-American Activities if he had known Alger Hiss and Whittaker Chambers. He took shelter behind the Fifth Amendment when Chambers was mentioned. But he was forthright in his response about Hiss.

"I would not know him from Adam," Sherman said. He was speaking the exact truth—for he had known Hiss in the underground under the cover name of "Adam."

RALPH DE TOLEDANO

★	
Chapter	**A. THE SAN FRANCISCO RIOTS**
7.	

MOVING *from the Committee's most conspicuous success to its most disputed, and most highly publicized, recent venture: what, actually, are the facts behind the San Francisco riots? On the issues at stake, who was factually correct, who wrong? Did the Committee exceed, as never before, its prerogatives as a Congressional investigating committee looking for the information on which to base wise legislation? What is to be learned from the experience in terms of understanding the nature of the criticism of the Committee, and distinguishing the self-serving criticism of the Communists from that of the liberals?*

The House Committee on Un-American Activities has had its ups and its downs. The Committee has engaged in dull hearings and exciting ones; it has been led by good men and mediocre men; it has conducted fruitful inquiries and inquiries which led to dead ends. But through the flux of the years, one constant has persisted: the Committee has been the focus of unremitting, zealous attack.

A principal opponent of the Committee, of course, has been the Communist Party of the United States. But a considerable non-Communist opposition to HUAC has built up. The attacks upon the Committee from the two quarters have been simultaneous, reaching peaks and valleys together, for reasons that will be discussed in the note succeeding this chapter. In the period since the war, the campaign against the Committee has reached three highs. The first was when HUAC launched its inquiry into Communist infiltration of Hollywood in 1947. The so-called Hollywood Ten were depicted as martyrs victimized by headline-hungry Congressmen; and more thought was given to their tribulations than to the general issues raised by the inquiry, or even to whether the issues should ever have been raised. The Committee's point was that there *were* in the movie industry importantly situated Communists, e.g., Dalton Trumbo (Communist Party Card Number 47187), and Albert Maltz (Number 47196); and that it was the Committee's responsibility to take the measure of their influence. The critics charged either (a) that there really were no Communists in Hollywood of any importance; or (b) that there were Communists in Hollywood but that it made no difference; or (c) that the question whether or not there were Communists in Hollywood was of no concern to the Committee.

The next major assault on the Committee came the following year, in connection with the case of Alger Hiss, which was described in Chapter 6.

A number of years went by before the Committee's critics got hold of a *casus belli* on the scale of the Hollywood and Hiss episodes. And then there was the film *Operation Abolition.* "In the course of this book," says Frank Donner, author of *The Un-Americans,* "it has been urged that HUAC distorts facts, draws crudely strained inferences, and reaches untenable conclusions. But nothing in HUAC's record of hearings and reports matches 'Operation Abolition.'" Donner has thrice been identified under oath as having been a member of the Communist Party during the Roosevelt era. In respect of *Operation Abolition* he speaks for Communists, pro-Communists and certain non-Communists alike.

Here, he says, is the Committee's salient act of infamy.

In view of the widespread belief that here at last, in very plain sight, is the *corpus vile,* exposing the inner corruption of HUAC, it appears wise to go deeply into the matter. From it we will learn a great deal, not merely about the House Committee on Un-American Activities and its activities, but a great deal about its critics and their methods.

What, then, is *Operation Abolition?*

Operation Abolition portrays a student demonstration against the House Committee in San Francisco on May 12, 13 and 14, 1960. It shows student protests outside San Francisco's City Hall; disruptive tactics by identified Communists in the hearing room and, finally, a seriocomic tableau in which city police remove demonstrating students from the premises, spraying them with fire hoses and sliding them down a long marble stairway.

The film describes the demonstration as Communist-inspired, intermittently singling out one or another of the dramatis personae as a "professional Communist agitator." It sums up the episode as a frightening example of how guileless students can be manipulated by Communist agents.

Its purpose is to alert the viewer to the dangers of internal Communism, to maintain that the House Committee on Un-American Activities is doing a needed and often difficult job, and to suggest sinister impulses behind much of the opposition to the Committee.

The liberal community, understandably enough, rushed forward in angry counterattack. *Operation Abolition,* it was charged, was a composite of falsehoods, grossly misrepresenting what had happened in San Francisco.

Among the most vehement of such charges were those leveled by the Washington *Post.* The film, it said, was a "propaganda movie" "mendaciously distorted," nothing less than a "forgery by film," which "warps the truth," a veritable "falsification of facts" by a "curious little film fraud" "elaborately distorted." The *Post* explained:

The film warps the truth in two important respects. First, it suggests as its main thesis that the demonstrations were Communist-inspired and Communist-led. Diligent inquiry has led us to a conviction that this charge is wholly unjustified. It cannot be asserted, of course, that no Communists took part in the demonstrations. But the main body of students who picketed the Committee hearings in protest were inspired only by their own valid and thoroughly creditable indignation at the Committee's conduct; and they were led by fellow students loyal to American ideals and acting in accordance with that loyalty.

Second, the film attempts to represent the rioting which followed the student protest as resulting entirely from student violence and disorder. In point of fact, the San Francisco police acted with altogether needless brutality, turning fire hoses on students whose protests were not flagrantly unruly.

To test the validity of these criticisms, one must reconstruct the events of May 12–14, concentrating on two principal questions: (1) What evidence is there for the charge that Communists manipulated the students? And (2), What evidence is there for the charge that the students (rather than the police) were responsible for the violence which transpired?

Eyewitnesses have affirmed that *Operation Abolition* is a faithful portrayal of the student demonstrations. Mayor George Christopher of San Francisco was one of them. He said: "The pictures I believe speak for themselves: They are true. They are authentic. They tell the real story. . . ." [1]

Unbelievers reply that Christopher was absent during the critical phase of the demonstrations which brought on the violence. Christopher in turn has replied in a telegram:

Mayor's office is directly across the hall from meeting room of Committee. For two days I witnessed all proceedings. There was general disorder, booing, loud shouting, chanting, and derision of the Committee obstructing their processes. I was absent only one and one-half hours during second day at lunchtime but witnessed every other phase and can attest to veracity of film. Police had every reason to evict rioters long before they resorted to this action. Sympathizers who were never present endeavor now to find my short absence as disqualifying me for adequate appraisal. . . . [2]

Reporter Dave Hope of the Oakland *Tribune*, who was on hand during the demonstrations and the violent interlude of the second day, says: "... The film is just too accurate, too revealing. That's why it is so bitterly attacked." [3] Seven ministers who witnessed the proceedings give similar testimony.[4] J. Edgar Hoover, Director of the Federal Bureau of Investigation, having presumably weighed the evidence, wrote:

It is vitally important to set the record straight on the extent to which the Communists were responsible for the conditions which prevailed during the HUAC hearings. It is vitally important that not only the students involved in that incident, but also students throughout the nation whom Communists hope to exploit in similar situations, recognize the Communist tactics which resulted in what experienced West Coast observers familiar with Communist strategy and tactics have termed the most successful Communist coup to occur in the San Francisco area in 25 years.

When the Committee announced its impending hearings in the San Francisco area, Hoover says, identified Communists prepared themselves for action: "It was mandatory for Communists to [do] ... everything possible to disrupt the hearings as part of the over-all aim to destroy the HUAC. ... The first objective of the Party was to fill the scene of the hearings with demonstrators. The second was to incite them to action through the use of mob psychology." [5]

This construction is hotly denied by the students and their partisans. The FBI Director and the House Committee, they charge, go about branding as Communist "anyone who disagrees with them." The Bay Area Student Committee * charged that HUAC relied on "hackneyed innuendoes to the effect that anyone who criticizes the Committee must either be a Communist or is, in some mysterious way, a Communist dupe." [6] In debating the issue with divers liberals, one hears the argument raised to a more sophisticated level. HUAC, they charge, believes the students were Communist dupes because (1) their

---

* Full name, "The Bay Area Student Committee for the Abolition of the House Committee on Un-American Activities"—a group formed in the aftermath of the May demonstrations by some of the students.

actions were objectively beneficial to the Communist Party—
therefore the Communists must have planned it that way; and
(2) this is the sort of thing Communists do—therefore people
who do that sort of thing must do it at the instance of Communists.

Now, while the premise in each of these statements is quite
true, it does not follow that the students were *necessarily* manipulated by Communists. And there are indeed those friends of
the Committee who do not spot the faulty enthymeme—the missing premise upon which the improper conclusion rests. *Some*
critics of the student rioting do, falsely, arrive at conclusions
merely by the test of objective benefit and political style.

But, having noted this fact, opponents of HUAC resort to the
very indiscrimination of which they accuse others. Because *some*
anti-Communists reason loosely, it does not follow that HUAC
or its film does likewise. And if we examine the statements contained in the film, and the typical statements of Committee
members, we find the charge of "Communist dupe" is not aimed
simply at opponents of the Committee, or even at actions suited
to the purposes and techniques of the Communist Party.
Operation Abolition charges the students were Communist
dupes because, in the opinion of those who put the film together, the data indicated, as a matter of *ascertainable fact,* that
this was a Communist enterprise.

2.

What *are* the ascertainable facts? To begin with, massive
demonstrations generally don't just happen. Even under immediate provocation, they must be organized. Someone has to
agitate, inflame latent hostilities, choose issues for emotional
exploitation, arrange meetings, print and distribute literature.
And someone has to handle the human logistics which ensure
that inflamed sentiment issues in specific action at a specific time
and place. The question to be answered, then, is: Who performed these necessary tasks?

Hoover's report, *Communist Target—Youth,* is the source of

the charge that the demonstration was "Communist-inspired and Communist-led." *Operation Abolition* scrupulously follows the report in its narrative, and the second, shorter edition of the film uses verbatim excerpts from Hoover's remarks for its commentary. To test the validity of Hoover's charges, one must examine the evidence marshaled by him, and by others, in their support.

It is an established fact that both the Communists in the San Francisco area and the students were at work to generate protests against the Committee. Defenders of the students say the Communists were simply trailing along in the wake of the non-Communist protest. The critics of the students say the facts were precisely the reverse.

The students claim they were inflamed by an episode of the preceding year, when HUAC had scheduled hearings involving California schoolteachers and, after lengthy controversy, canceled them. It was alleged that HUAC had released the names of the teachers to the press and then, by calling off the inquiry, prevented them from giving their side of the case. This episode is put forward as the sufficient and proximate emotional provocation for the student uprisings. At the organizational level, the work of turning the students out was assertedly performed by a group known as the Student Committee for Civil Liberties, on the University of California campus.[7]

So runs the story as told by the film's critics. What it states about the subjective attitude of the students in question is true enough, but what it omits is far more appropriate to the point under discussion. The matter of the subpoenaed teachers burned brightly in the minds of the students. But *why* did it?

An issue of this sort does not tend to percolate for an entire year, suddenly to boil over into militant activity. The students were angry because they had been subjected to a provocative and misleading account of the Committee's behavior, portraying it as a predator on civil liberties. That version, to be sure, had been advanced by various non-Communist opponents of the Committee in California, in newspaper editorials and denunciatory statements. The total indictment was brought together by Congressman James Roosevelt, in a speech in the House of Representatives on April 25, 1960, just prior to the scheduled hearings in San Francisco, which was widely distributed by the Communist Party. Roosevelt's speech, entitled "The Dragon Slayers," became an important focus for student resentments. On the Tom Duggan television show in Los Angeles, Frank Wilkinson, who has been identified as a Communist under oath, acknowledged meeting with college students on at least one occasion, and added: "Jimmy Roosevelt's speech was handed out to everybody there and every one of the 5,000 who showed up later at City Hall." [8]

It is important to note that the Hoover report, from which the film's commentary is abstracted, does not deny the existence of non-Communist hostility toward HUAC in the Bay Area. Nor does it downgrade the significance of the canceled hearings of the preceding year. Its point is that the Communist Party acted upon these hostile sentiments, and inflamed them to the eutectic point of action. Hoover says:

The . . . cancellation of the proposed 1959 hearings left many of these groups and organizations inactive but intact. As a result, when the May 1960 hearings were announced, it required little effort to reactivate these opposition groups, despite the fact that the current hearings were not to be directed at Communist activity in the education field. After the proposed 1959 hearings had been canceled, the HUAC turned over its files on these individuals to the California Attorney General's office and to the school boards of the teachers involved for any necessary action. But the Communist Party members in the area skillfully planted the idea that the 1960 hearings were still aimed basically at teachers and that the stated objective to inquire into Communist Party activities in the area was merely to cover a planned attack on teachers.[9]

That precisely this misconception was conveyed to the students is evidenced by a news story in *The Daily Californian,* May 2, 1960. Headlined, TEACHERS CALLED BY COMMITTEE, it described a meeting of 22 subpoenaed witnesses: "The group, in talking among themselves, discovered that no officer or spokesman of the Communist Party had been called by the Committee, despite the stated purpose of the Committee." This statement was untrue, but it was nevertheless read and presumably taken as fact by the students of the University of California.

On May 4, the *Californian* drove home the point for the benefit of those to whom it might still be obscure: "It should be further noted that many of the persons subpoenaed are educators and intellectuals. We feel that this is an expression of a desire on the part of the Committee to strike at free thought and academic freedom." The paper urged the students to join in the demonstrations against HUAC.

Word of the proposed sessions, Hoover records, was carried to the University of California campus by Douglas Wachter. As the only student subpoenaed, Wachter was the focal point of student interest in the hearings. He received a most respectful write-up in the *Californian*. "Wachter doesn't know why the Committee subpoenaed him," the paper reported. " 'I think the Committee wanted to subpoena someone on campus in order to tag Cal's political movement as un-American,' he said. 'I don't know why they picked my name. Other people have been involved in actions similar to mine,' the youth said." (A very likely, and unmentioned, reason: the fact that Wachter had been an official delegate to the December 1959 national convention of the Communist Party.[10])

Wachter did not confine himself to winsome interviews at the University of California. He also journeyed to neighboring colleges. Jerry Nims, a student at San Francisco State College, said: "On May 5, 1960, in Tub 2 [a campus snack bar], from 4 to 6 P.M., a meeting was held organizing actions against the HUAC. Leading this meeting was Douglas Wachter, a person who has been identified as a member of the Communist Party and one who is trained in agitation at the student level." Nims added: "At this meeting, demonstrations were planned and methods were chosen which would rally and arouse students against HUAC. Also at this meeting, it was announced that the next day at the noon hour, material attacking HUAC could be obtained at the office of Lacey Spake, teaching assistant. It was also stated that this literature was being produced on a San Francisco

State machine using college paper and other facilities. This propaganda was distributed during the next few days in some of the college classrooms." [11]

Wachter similarly addressed the organizational meeting of the Cal Student Committee for Civil Liberties, and spoke to a rally held by SLATE, a student radical group on the Berkeley campus. *The Daily Californian* reported: "The subpoenaed University student spoke about the various groups in the Bay Area who are working against the Committee through petition campaigns. . . . The subpoenaed student said the Committee is 'a public persecution of those people whom they dislike.' He said that the Committee also encourages the firing of those people subpoenaed." [12]

Wachter, in sum, was both the prime mover in stirring up students and the focus of their interest. One story about him in *The Daily Californian* was revealingly headlined: PICKETING, PROTEST RALLIES BACK SUBPOENAED STUDENT.[13] And back him they did. It was Wachter's appearance at the Thursday morning hearings that touched off some of the loudest outbursts from the students in the hearing room. In the film, they can be heard vigorously applauding his defiance of the Committee.

A subcommittee of the California legislature, which conducted a careful investigation of the entire episode, asks the obvious question: "We wonder how many students and professors would have participated in these preliminary activities and in the demonstrations against the House Committee if *The Daily Californian,* the student newspaper, had printed the truth and announced that Wachter, the Communist Party's delegate to the Seventeenth National Convention of the Communist Party of the United States, had been subpoenaed by the House Committee . . . because he was a Communist Party functionary, an official delegate to a national convention, a student at the university, and the Committee might be interested under its Congressional mandate to find out what he knew about this California arm of the world Communist conspiracy that had over and over again sworn to subvert and destroy us." [14]

Other devices, as suggested by the statement from Nims, were used to arouse emotions in the Bay area. An example is a leaflet distributed by a group known as the "Citizens Committee to Preserve American Freedoms." The pamphlet says: "48 Persons Have Been Subpoenaed: Teachers—Civil Rights Sit-In Pickets—Trade Unionists—A Student—A Defense Attorney—A Radio Commentator—Peace Advocates! Un-American Activities Committee Hearings City Hall—San Francisco—May 12–14." [15] The leaflet contained a condensed version of Congressman Roosevelt's April speech, reproduced from the Communist-lining *National Guardian*. The group distributing it, the San Francisco Chapter of CCPAF, was, according to Hoover, "organized . . . on April 4, 1960, for the specific purpose of opposing the HUAC hearings." [16] The state CCPAF had previously been named by HUAC as a Communist front. "The Communist Party," Hoover says, "furnished funds to the CCPAF to defray the expense of mailing literature during the campaign, and, when the whole affair had ended, [Communist leader] Mickey Lima praised the executive secretary of the CCPAF, Frank Wilkinson [himself an identified Communist] for the role he had played in organizing the demonstrations." [17]

Hoover explains in some detail the activities of the Communist hierarchy in the Bay Area, including Archie Brown, Mickey Lima, Roscoe Practor, Merle Brodsky, and others. "A telephone campaign," Hoover says, "was conducted by Party members to solidify opposition to HUAC and was designed specifically to reach 1,000 people. Merle Brodsky, an active leader in Communist Party affairs in California for more than 20 years, boasted that he was calling everyone he had ever known, enlisting support for the demonstrations." [18] One identified Communist collected signatures for a newspaper advertisement attacking the Committee. The San Francisco chapter of the National Lawyers Guild—a chapter at that time headed by an identified member of the Communist Party—on May 10 issued a statement opposing the hearings. Lawyer Bertram Edises, also identified under oath as a Party member, filed a petition asking that subcommittee Chairman Willis be disqualified. An organization known as the Bay Area Defense Committee, headquartered in the offices of three lawyers identified in sworn testimony as Communists, published an anti-Committee advertisement in the San Francisco *Chronicle* on May 13. The East Bay Community Forum, a group which, according to Hoover, was identified as Communist-controlled by a Party official, held a protest meeting attended by 300 people.[19]

On the campuses, in addition to Wachter, the sons of Vincent Hallinan, Progressive Party Presidential candidate in 1952, and the daughter of Clinton Jencks, of the pro-Communist Mine, Mill and Smelter Workers, served as members of SLATE, one of the principal groups agitating against the Committee. At San Francisco State College, the daughter of identified Communists Vernon and Ruth Bown addressed a student rally on May 9. The California subcommittee, moreover, concluded that Frank Wilkinson "displayed his organizational talents, going back and forth between San Francisco and Los Angeles as well as maintaining constant liaison with the front organizations and the student groups." [20]

When confronted with proof of Communist involvement, critics of the film replied that the Communists had simply tried to tag along, to reap credit for what the students had originated. In view of the crucial role played by Wachter, this possibility seems remote. No doubt the students were acting out their own preconceived distaste for the House Committee. But the pre-existence of their emotions is not at issue: the point is that those emotions were heightened and released under guidance of the Communist Party. And it is noteworthy that, in attempting to show otherwise, defenders of the students find it convenient to drop references to Wachter (who is not even mentioned, for example, in Frank Donner's discussion of the film, which contains only a passing reference to "one student" having been subpoenaed) .[21]

These conclusions are supported by an examination of the second aspect of the film's charge against the students—that the

Communist Party led them in transforming a pacific demonstration into an overt challenge to constituted authority.

Every relevant authority in San Francisco testifies to Communist leadership in this phase of the activities. "Known Communists," says San Francisco Mayor George Christopher, "and I repeat this emphatically, *known Communists* were in the lead of this demonstration." [22] Police Inspector Michael Maguire, in charge of the security forces on the scene, testified that he had seen agitational activities among the students by Archie Brown and Merle Brodsky, two of the Communist functionaries called before the Committee.[23] Police Chief Thomas Cahill testified that his security officers "told me that a number of those who seemed to whip those people in the group into a mob frenzy were individuals who had been hostile and who had testified at the hearing." [24]

Again, critics of the Committee allege the Communists were simply trying to tag along—to cash in on the activities of the students. Instances are cited in which Communists made approaches and were rebuffed.[25] One must hope that some of the students, at least, were impervious to direct blandishments from notorious Party functionaries like Merle Brodsky. But these instances do not answer the charge that Communists, trained in the manipulation of crowds, stationed throughout the rotunda, kept up the rallying cries and the demands which goaded the students into defiance of constituted authority. One identified Communist, Ralph Izard, was questioned in this regard. Staff Director Arens asked him: "Have you been a participant in the incitement of the riotous conduct which has been witnessed here in the course of the last two or three days of our Committee sessions?" Izard's answer: "I stand on the First Amendment, and I stand on my rights not to be a witness against myself." [26]

The testimony of Sheriff Matthew Carberry on this point is particularly valuable. Carberry has certainly shown no animus toward the students and, both in print and in personal conversation, displays notable coolness toward the House Committee on Un-American Activities. (Perhaps in recognition of this, the students have tried to co-opt him as an authority for their total innocence.) "The general temper of the crowd," Carberry testified, "was orderly, except that there were certain individuals—some of whom I can see and remember and can find if I choose to do so—who continued to heckle and who continued, in my opinion, to excite those assembled." [27] Carberry amplified these remarks in a telephone conversation with this writer: "The people stirring these students up, and bringing them to an emotional pitch, were well-known Communists in the San Francisco area." [28]

There is a striking scene in *Operation Abolition* itself in which the students are quite visibly taking their cues from identifiable Communists. The scene took place at the resumption of the hearings after the noon recess on Thursday, May 12. Communists Archie Brown, Ralph Izard and others led the students in a riotous outburst of noise, culminating in the singing of the National Anthem. Students can be seen standing in their chairs, clapping their hands, shouting and singing—all while the Committee was trying to conduct its inquiry.

Some liberals contend that, in this episode, the students began the singing of the National Anthem, and the Communists joined in. The point is beyond proof or refutation, since all the Communists and a number of the students had their mouths wide open throughout the proceedings; it is, moreover, irrelevant, since the episode culminating in the songfest was concededly launched by the Communists.

If we assume, however, that the students *did* begin singing the National Anthem on their own initiative—in a hearing room where a committee of Congress was conducting the business of the United States—the students are thrust into an interesting logical trap. For in insisting that they were not manipulated by the Communists, they also insist they behaved themselves with admirable restraint until they were excluded from the hearing room. Yet here we have students *inside* the hearing room, noisily breaking up the hearing. If the plea of autonomy is valid, what then happens to the plea of student decorum? Something, obviously, has to give.

3.

The question brings us to the second major category in the San Francisco dispute, responsibility for the violence of Friday, May 13. *Operation Abolition* says violence erupted when a student jumped over a police barricade and struck an officer with his own night stick. This statement is taken almost verbatim from Hoover's report. Hoover wrote:

One of the demonstrators provided the spark that touched off the flame of violence. Leaping a barricade that had been erected, he grabbed an officer's night stick and began beating the officer over the head. The mob surged forward as if to storm the doors, and a police inspector ordered the fire hose turned on.[29]

The film's narration is virtually a carbon copy: "One student provides the spark that touches off the violence when he leaps over a barricade, grabs a police officer's night stick, and begins beating the officer over the head. As the mob surges forward to storm the doors, a police inspector orders that the fire hoses be turned on." [30]

Contemporary newspaper reports contain the same story. The San Francisco *News-Call Bulletin* for May 14, 1960, reported:

Judges in upstairs courtrooms were complaining the racket was interfering with due processes of law. Patrolman Ralph Schaumleffel, 33, standing guard, was trampled underfoot as a stampede to the hearing room began. One of the mob . . . wrested the policeman's billy club from his hand and walloped him on the head. Another kicked him in the groin.

And the San Francisco *Examiner* for the same date:

The riot apparently was triggered shortly before 1:30 P.M. when the mob rushed the door of the supervisor's chambers. When all the seats in the chamber were filled, Patrolman Ralph Schaumleffel, on duty at the door, closed it, informing the crowd there were no more seats. The mob then climbed over the barricades and stormed the door, knocking Schaumleffel down.

Dave Hope of the Oakland *Tribune* writes:

> I didn't hear any orders, but I did hear the police ask, even beg, the students to be quiet and to leave the City Hall. All through the morning the police were polite and courteous. Even when the mob's mood turned ugly after the noon recess, and the hoses were brought out, the students were warned repeatedly for a period of at least ten minutes before the water was turned on. That didn't happen until one student grabbed an officer's night stick and slugged him with it.[31]

In other words, the Committee's account conforms to the best information available to it: Hoover's report and the testimony of San Francisco reporters. If, in the confusion of that moment, these authorities were led astray, that would not establish a "distortion" on the part of the Committee. It would simply establish that the best available sources could not record the event in full.

All of these accounts, it develops, were derived from police reports filed the day of the riot.[32] The credibility of these reports has been under severe attack since the acquittal, May 3, 1961, of Robert Meisenbach, the student accused of committing the assault. In the opinion of Meisenbach's attorney, "the verdict knocks *Operation Abolition* in the creek." [33] That view is widely shared, and vocally urged, by other critics of the film. An inspection of the record, however, suggests that the Meisenbach trial establishes, not the innocence of the students, but their essential culpability.

From a reading of the rather extensive press accounts of the trial, it is understandable that the Meisenbach jury did not find the defendant guilty beyond a reasonable doubt. The plaintiff, Patrolman Ralph Schaumleffel, gave contradictory accounts of how and when he was allegedly struck. Two corroborating witnesses, who said they had seen Meisenbach perform the assault, disagreed on a number of important details. In contrast, the defense witnesses presented a smoothly interlocking version of the riot attesting to Meisenbach's innocence.

Let us, therefore, take it as fact that Meisenbach was innocent. Does this establish a "distortion" on the part of *Operation Abolition*? Certainly not on the face of it. The film, after all, does not name Meisenbach as the assailant; it simply says "one student" struck a police officer. The apposite question thus becomes: Was there reason—irrespective of the guilt or innocence of Robert Meisenbach—to believe *someone* struck Patrolman Schaumleffel? Schaumleffel did, after all, suffer a blow on the skull, which sent him to the hospital for treatment. How did this come about? The students say Schaumleffel slipped on the wetted floor, and struck his head in falling. Yet in that seamless skein of defense testimony, curiously enough, no witness was produced who saw Schaumleffel injure himself in this way.[34] Three witnesses, including Schaumleffel, said he was struck by a student wielding a night stick.[35] Granted the corroborating witnesses were so situated that they could not correctly identify the demonstrator in question (one was on the third floor, the other on the fourth).[36] It does not follow that they did not see *somebody* hit Schaumleffel. It would be quite easy, in the confusion of that moment, to mistake the identity of the assailant; it is much less likely that two witnesses would be mistaken about the occurrence of the act as such—the striking of a police officer by a nonuniformed civilian.*

On subsidiary points, the Meisenbach proceedings did show the film to be in error: If a student struck Schaumleffel, he did not, according to Schaumleffel's own testimony, jump a barricade before doing so; and the episode occurred *after,* rather than before, the turning on of the hoses.[37] Critics of the film maintain that discrediting these statements discredits the charge of student provocation, and establishes that the police simply set upon the students without warning. But if it transpires that the students were in fact responsible for the violence,

---

* An interesting point for speculation arises from the defense version of this episode. Meisenbach's attorneys said Schaumleffel lost his night stick when he slipped and fell. Meisenbach testified that he picked the night stick up and threw it away, only to be tackled and beaten by Schaumleffel, wielding a night stick. But if Meisenbach had just thrown the night stick away, how could Schaumleffel have beaten him with it?

the matter of when and how this act occurred, if it did occur, is reduced to the status of subsidiary conjecture.

The principal and controlling question therefore is not: Did the violence result from a particular rush against a particular barricade? It is, rather: Who bears the ultimate responsibility for the violence—the students, or the police? If the students were guilty, then whether Schaumleffel was injured before or after the hosing, and whether his assailant jumped a barricade to get at him, become immaterial.

To determine ultimate responsibility for the violence, which flared shortly after 1 P.M. May 13, we must know something about the students' behavior in the preceding minutes and hours. Were the students behaving in a manner requiring the use of hoses to clear them out of the building? Was their behavior in any sense justified? Were they given warning that they had to leave the premises?

It is generally agreed that the students' performance immediately prior to the hosing was obstreperous and noisy. The controversy hangs on the other two points: whether they had received provocation for the noisemaking, and whether they were given an order to leave City Hall before the hoses were turned on them.

The students plead gross injury on both counts. They were chanting and singing, they maintain, because they had been unfairly excluded from the hearing room, and because Sheriff Matthew Carberry had not fulfilled a "promise" to get them in. These injustices, their defenders allege, combined with the sight of friendly auditors being admitted on the authority of passes issued by the Committee, were too much for anyone to bear.[38] Thus the uproar. As HUAC-slayer Frank Donner puts it: "The film's account of the Friday demonstration completely distorts its cause—the preferential white-card policy."[39]

It is a peculiar view of "peacefulness," I think, which seeks to justify singing and chanting outside a Congressional hearing room on the grounds that the Committee had excluded, however arbitrarily, the noisemakers. But let us discuss the issue on the terms proposed by Mr. Donner.

Were the students noisy simply because the Committee had excluded them from the hearing room? The facts suggest otherwise. If we examine the particulars of the case, we find that considerably fewer students were admitted to the hearing room Friday than were admitted Thursday. It was this reduction in the number of admissions that the students resented, and if their argument is correct, the disturbances should have come after, rather than before it.[40] They should have been considerably noisier on Friday than they were on Thursday. The truth is just the opposite.

The first outburst of noise came Thursday morning, during the testimony of Customs Official Irving Fishman. Richard Arens, Staff Director of the Committee, announced: "I have just been advised by one of our staff members that there is a demonstration going on right around this building against this Committee by people—" At which point Arens was interrupted by a burst of applause from the audience.[41]

Further along in the Thursday morning session, this exchange occurred:

MR. ARENS: Mr. Chairman, I wonder if we could have a little more order. It is very difficult for me to hear the witness, and I am sure it is difficult for him to hear me with the hubbub here.

MR. WILLIS: We cannot hear the witness up here. We must have order. I regret to say that if there will be any more demonstrations I will have to clear the aisles. You must agree to be quiet.[42]

The students, however, agreed to nothing of the sort. During the testimony of Douglas Wachter, there were further outbursts of applause—for the Communists, not for the Committee.[43] In consequence, during the noon recess, Chairman Willis followed through with his threat of clearing the aisles. This touched off the celebrated "open the doors" demonstration, led by Archie Brown, Ralph Izard and other of the subpoenaed witnesses enthusiastically joined by the students, which crescendoed into the singing of the National Anthem.

At this point, Chairman Willis said:

We are now having our hearing room broken up—disturbed. I ask the marshal to eject from the room those people who are leading the crowd right in the midst of our hearings.... This thing was brought about by disorderly conduct this morning. A lot of noise was going on. I announced that one more public display would result in the clearing of the aisles. That was accomplished over the noon recess.[44]

A group of ministers, eyewitnesses to these events, give this account:

For nearly 15 minutes at one point, this lawless crowd of students from the university, together with Party cadres, had the chambers almost in their control. The students, comprising the rear third of the audience, stood up in their seats and yelled, jeered, hissed, and scoffed at the Congressmen. It was almost a complete breakdown of law and order. We witnessed more violations of the law in 15 minutes than we have seen in 15 years.[45]

There is other testimony about events on Thursday, before the alleged "broken promise" was ever made. Thanks to the disturbance being made by the students, municipal courts on the floors above were forced to close down. Sheriff Carberry said: "In my opinion, it appeared that an incipient riot was brewing and there was serious danger to life and property." [46] He also said: "Many could have been arrested Thursday, but police tried valiantly that day to avoid possible provocation to violence." [47] (This despite cries of "Let's break down the doors.") [48]

In short, the students were, if anything, more contumacious on Thursday than they were on Friday. This fact, indeed, is attested to by the students' heartiest admirers. A liberal journal called *The Californian,** in an appendix to a long article on the Meisenbach case, observes: "It is ... an established fact that the students were more disorderly and unruly on May 12

---

* Not to be confused with *The Daily Californian.*

than they were on May 13 and that the events of May 12 came much closer to developing into a student riot than what took place on May 13." [49]

Thus the exclusion of the students on Friday was *not* the cause of their disorderly conduct. The demonstrators were not noisy because they were excluded; they were excluded because they were noisy.

Sheriff Carberry's discussion of the circumstances surrounding his so-called "promise" is similarly instructive. It tells us the students were disorderly at noon, before the alleged bargain was struck, that a municipal judge had protested their behavior, and that certain members of the crowd were agitating for violence. Carberry testified:

> The excitement was reasonably controlled until about 12 o'clock on Friday, at which time I was officially apprised by one of the police inspectors here that Judge Clarence Morris in superior court had officially protested to the police department about the loud noise and misconduct, which was interfering with the order of superior court. I was told a similar protest had been made by the presiding judge of municipal court.
>
> I then proceeded to the rotunda and told all the persons assembled there that we were continuing to co-operate to provide access to the general public within this building and I was going to intercede again with the chairman at noon on that point [this is the statement the students interpreted as a "promise"].
>
> I also told them that they were now subjecting themselves to the possibility of arrest for disturbing the peace, that they were making protests about duress [due process?] of law and they, themselves, were interfering with due process in our superior and municipal courts, and I pointed out to them calmly and plainly the facts regarding the physical occupancy of this building.
>
> One in particular, and I can recall him distinctly, said, "Why don't they adjourn the courts today? We want to get in. Cut out everything else. This is the only thing that is important."
>
> I mention this for one reason only, that this did not reflect the general temper of the crowd, but it did reflect the temper of certain individuals who continued to excite the crowd to, apparently, some act or incident.[50]

What of the second question: Were the hoses simply turned on the students, with no forewarning? The Bay Area Student Committee says: "No order to disperse was given, no warning was offered. Instead, hoses were turned upon the group of seated demonstrators." [51] The police dispute this statement, as does the Oakland *Tribune*'s Dave Hope, an eyewitness to the proceedings. Hope says: "I didn't hear any orders, but I did hear police ask, even beg, the students to be quiet and to leave the City Hall." Hope says that even after the hoses had been produced, the students were warned for a period of ten minutes before the water was turned on. [52]

The police version on this essential point is also supported, curiously enough, by the very episode which supposedly "knocked *Operation Abolition* in the creek"—the trial of Meisenbach. William Mackey reported in the San Francisco *Examiner*, May 4, 1961: "The jurors ... made it plain that their verdict in no way condoned the actions of the demonstrators in failing to leave the City Hall premises in an orderly fashion when directed to by authorities. (Student groups contend that no such order was ever given them by the police.)" *The New York Times* reported, the same day: "Some jurors said afterward that the verdict was not intended to show that they had condoned the continued presence of the rioters after policemen had ordered them to disperse."

In short, the obiter dicta of the Meisenbach jury establish the central point of the police argument: that the students had been ordered to leave, and would not.

It could be, of course, that the students did not hear the order to disperse. The rotunda was, admittedly, a din of noise. Orders shouted in the midst of bedlam might very well have been missed by most of the students. But, in that event, are the students innocent? They were, after all, creating the conditions which both provoked the orders and made them inaudible.

4.

There are other points appropriate to determining the relative blame of the students and the police. On the day following the riot, the San Francisco *Chronicle* reported eight policemen and four students had been injured. These figures are repeated in *Operation Abolition,* and are chalked up by the Bay Area Student Committee as one of the film's "distortions." [53] The Student Committee itself prints an estimate that six policemen were injured, as opposed to five students.[54] Even if we accept the student committee's figures, the casualty ratio hardly suggests "police brutality."

Moreover, testimony is virtually unanimous that the police conducted themselves with exemplary restraint. Even opponents of the film, and of the police, observe that although the crowd was supremely insolent on Thursday, the police took no retaliatory action. "Their forbearance," said Sheriff Carberry (a civil officer with no official connection with the police) , "considering the insults heaped on them, was amazing. They acted only defensively." [55] The San Francisco *News-Call Bulletin* reports: "Understandably police patience wore thin. Demonstrators taunted them mercilessly, shouting 'goons,' 'blackshirts,' 'fascists.' " [56]

It is interesting to note, in passing, that the charge of "police brutality" was launched by the hostile witnesses at the hearings. Testifying Friday afternoon after the hosing, William Mandel gave a histrionic speech calling the Committee "beaters of children and sadists" and said "the son of a friend of mine had his head split by these goons operating under your orders." [57] John Andrew Negro told the Committee, "You are the cause for the heads that are broken, you are the cause for the backs that are broken or any other things that happened to these students." [58] Saul Wachter was absent, said Attorney Bertram Edises, because "his son, Douglas Wachter, was viciously attacked and beaten up, also was deluged with water from a fire hose, and then was carted off to jail." [59] Saul Wachter later delivered a denunciation of the Committee, saying young Douglas had been "choked, his arm was twisted, and he was flung into jail where he was booked, photographed, and it took me four hours to find him." [60]

Former Communist Party member Karl Prussion, who had served as an FBI agent inside the Communist apparatus in California, testified: "I believe that all of those present here yesterday witnessed a technique commonly used by the Communist Party." As a follow-up, he said, the Communists "will hurl invectives; they will accuse the city of San Francisco of police brutality, sadism, denial of democratic rights, and a whole series of false accusations will flow from the Communist press and all their agencies, through infiltrated organizations, in the interest of the Communist Party. They will get well-known people, professors, ministers, and others to sign petitions and protests—all to embarrass American processes."

The prediction proved to be quite accurate. Hoover tells us:

At a Party meeting on the night of May 20, 1960, Archie Brown disclosed how the Party intended to use a follow-up campaign with campus students as the target. He stated that the Party planned to emphasize "police brutality" as a rallying cry to attract the sympathy of student groups. . . . Brown said that the *People's World* had prepared a special supplement about the demonstrations for distribution to all the colleges and universities in the area, as well as for distribution to all waterfront workers. . . . The Party prepared 20,000 leaflets for distribution on campuses in the area. Captioned "From Blackmail to Blackjack," the leaflets stress the theme that, at the HUAC hearings, "students were peacefully defending the most cherished American freedoms," when "fire hoses, clubs and blackjacks" were used against them "without warning and without provocation" to "browbeat and smash the public opposition" to HUAC. These leaflets were distributed by the Party organization without cost for the sole purpose of exploiting the sympathies of students in the area.[61]

The film itself reflects nothing resembling the "police brutality" charged by the Communists and the students. It does show police patiently grappling with the students, with all the violence coming from the demonstrators. This, the opponents of the film allege, is a "distortion." The Bay Area Student Committee says: "According to news members of KPIX-TV, footage which shows unjustified use of police clubs on demonstrators was deleted from the movie." [62]

Yet the San Francisco *News-Call Bulletin,* in a series of articles sentimentally weighted in favor of the student demonstrators, concluded, after viewing all the film footage available: "No movies whatsoever were taken of the key moment of the tumultuous three days the Committee was here: the explosion of the riot. *Nor, importantly, do the full, uncut, unedited clips show any evidence of possible police brutality critics say was deliberately deleted from Operation Abolition."* [63] (Italics added.)

Moreover, officials at the TV station in question deny the student committee's statement. Two interested California citizens, W. E. Schmitt and A. O. Hanks, wrote to KPIX concerning this allegation. They received the following answer from Philip G. Lasky, vice-president of the company that operates KPIX: "Such a statement implies that KPIX actually shot film of a club or clubs being used. No such film shots appear in our files, nor does our photographer recall photographing such action. I've looked into the matter thoroughly, and am confident that there is no foundation for the statement attributed to KPIX news personnel." [64]

5.

Thus, on balance, the evidence sorts itself out clearly in favor of the central allegations made by *Operation Abolition:* That the demonstrations were indeed "Communist-inspired and Communist-led," and that the students, not the police, were responsible for the violence.

Such a determination, however, does not add up to a complete absolution of the film. For it is possible that the film's two broad charges may be correct, but that so many incidental errors have been committed that the film is not a reliable record of the style and tone of the demonstrations.

There are identifiable errors in the film, as follows:

1. The statement that Harry Bridges was escorted from City Hall "moments before the rioting broke out." Bridges was taken from the building *after* the whole episode had blown over, and had no part in it. The Committee has acknowledged this error, correctly noting, however, that its bearing on the film's message is immaterial.

2. A crowd scene filmed on Saturday is identified as having taken place on Thursday. HUAC acknowledges this and one other error of sequence. (Its critics charge upward of a dozen others, but evidence of these has yet to be adduced.)

3. The statement that "one student provides the spark that touches off the violence when he leaps over a barricade, etc." We now know what the Committee did *not* know when *Operation Abolition* was put together, that a barricade was not leaped, and that if a student did strike an officer, that act did not touch off the violence.

These are errors for which HUAC, whatever its sources and whatever its motivation, should be held accountable. But none of them, by any normal assessment, adds up to "distortion." Only one is operationally significant to the meaning of the film —the statement about a student leaping the barricade and touching off the violence. Yet this assertion is clearly not the result of bad faith, but of an unsuccessful attempt to reconstruct the episode in question. As the San Francisco *Chronicle,* one of HUAC's bitterest critics, put it: "The film makers perhaps cannot be blamed for having relied on an official police report, nor can Director J. Edgar Hoover of the FBI, who also hung his hat on it." [65]

The *Chronicle* adds a suggestion which, though offered facetiously, is, in its oblique way, to the point. "But now that the errors are known, it seems the duty of the House Un-American Activities Committee to put out a new, amended version of the film, possibly to be called *Son of Operation Abolition.*" [66] The suggested title notwithstanding, the recommended excision should be acted upon. HUAC should remove from any new prints of the film the portions which are demonstrably in error.

6.

So much for HUAC's errors, and the likelihood of their being "distortions." Now let us see how they match up against the performance of *Operation Abolition*'s critics. And here, as we turn to an examination of the various statements put forward by opponents of the film, we suddenly find ourselves neck-deep, not simply in errors, but in conscious, knowing distortions. The adjectives are used with deliberation, for an exploration of context in the following cases suggests the authors of such misstatements were, more often than not, engaged in a willful falsification of the record.

Let us examine a few case histories:

1. *The Case of the Deleted Film.* I have already noted one of the false statements printed by the Bay Area Student Committee in its pamphlet, *In Search of Truth.* The assertion that films portraying police brutality had been edited out of *Operation Abolition* is repudiated both by the San Francisco *News-Call Bulletin* and by the television station in question.

2. *The Case of William Wheeler* (of the staff of HUAC). On the cover of *In Search of Truth* there appears what is alleged to be an exchange of remarks on a TV show in Los Angeles, August 9, 1960. The exchange, as it appears in this pamphlet, is as follows:

BURTON WHITE (teaching assistant, University of California, Berkeley) : I am basing my discussion on the fact that the film does have inaccuracies, does have distortions.

WHEELER: All right, we have admitted that. Let's go on to another subject.

WHITE: You have admitted that, Mr. Wheeler?

WHEELER: Certainly.[67]

Anyone reading this could only believe that William Wheeler had impeached the authenticity of the Committee's film. But it develops that the student committee is engaging in a virtuoso distortion of its own.

The student committee carefully omits to point out that the exchange in question occurred in the middle of an effort by

Wheeler to establish that the film was *in no way distorted.* White had said that *Operation Abolition* was distorted, and Wheeler was asked if he agreed with the charge. His reply: "I dispute it wholeheartedly." White brought up some points of sequence, which Wheeler described as "minor issues." Wheeler asked White: "Are you basing the whole fact that everything is a lie because these two minor incidents occurred?"

White answered: "No, I am basing my discussion on the fact that the film does have inaccuracies. Does have distortions." [68]

It will be observed, then, that the exchange quoted by the student committee was immediately preceded by Wheeler's statement that he was discussing "minor incidents," not material distortions. The student committee drops this sentence entirely, as it must to argue that Wheeler confessed to "distortions." Moreover, in attempting to rip this episode from its context, the student committee not only had to omit Wheeler's statement, but was forced to drop the first word from White's own remark. The "no" preceding his charge would have suggested he was trying to rebut something Wheeler had said, and thus would have excited curiosity as to what it was.

These clearly are the techniques of conscious misrepresentation—all the more conscious when we reflect that White, who participated in the exchange with Wheeler, is also head of the student committee which published the doctored version of it.

3. *The Case of Matthew Carberry.* Another charge originated by the Bay Area Student Committee, and reiterated faithfully by all critics of *Operation Abolition,* is that Sheriff Matthew Carberry of San Francisco County said "there was no act of physical aggression on the part of the students." This alleged quotation found its way into the *Reporter* magazine, in an article by Paul Jacobs, thence into the Washington *Post,* and from there into liberal newspapers across the country.

On December 6, 1960, Sheriff Carberry issued the following denial: "I did not make that statement. I do not know the author of the article, Paul Jacobs, and have never spoken to him and have never been interviewed by him.

"I was on the scene on Thursday and Friday (May 12 and

13) up to luncheon time when I went for a luncheon conference with the chairman of the Committee, Mr. Willis. The disorders took place during the luncheon and I was in no position to know anything about them." [69]

The two sides of the dispute are thus: (a) Opponents of the film seek to invoke Carberry as an authority for the claim that there was no violence on the part of the students; (b) Carberry answers that, since he was not on the scene when the acts of violence occurred, he is not capable of testifying as an authority one way or the other.

The issue reached a somewhat elliptical resolution when Carberry protested to the *Reporter*. In response, Jacobs produced a quotation from Carberry saying "no acts of physical violence" [70] preceded the use of the fire hoses. As it stands, the quotation seems to support Jacobs' case. But then, backing into a discussion of the context of the remark, Jacobs in effect confirmed Carberry's denial.

"Sheriff Carberry," Jacobs acknowledged, "did make a qualified statement that he had been 'told' by the local police, who are not under his jurisdiction, that the turning on of the fire hose was occasioned by an 'act of violence against a uniformed police officer,' but he also said that he had not seen this act himself." [71]

In this explanation, Jacobs fails to point out that Carberry's "no violence" remarks, in context, referred to Thursday, while the recapitulation of what he was "told" referred to Friday. The remarks in question were: "No acts of physical violence—"

Question: "Well, what kind of acts?"

"Acts of noise and disturbance which occasioned the court's closing their session on Thursday afternoon." [72]

The second statement, which Jacobs so fuzzily paraphrases, was: "The incident of Friday which took place—as I am told because I was not there—was occasioned by an act of violence against a uniformed police officer." [73] In context, then, it is clear that Carberry was saying there was no student violence on Thursday—when no one ever alleged student violence took place.

As for the fact that "he had not seen this act himself," this was precisely the point which Sheriff Carberry sought to make. He has never represented himself as an authority for the fact that violence did occur, and neither the film nor any of its defenders have so attempted to represent him. Jacobs, the student committee, the Washington *Post,* and numerous others have attempted to use him as an authority for the statement that violence did *not* occur. By acknowledging that Carberry did not observe the incident in question, Jacobs confesses that the liberal effort in this instance is a calculated deception.*

4. *The Case of Judge Albert A. Axelrod.* A final episode involving a remark lifted from context concerns Judge Albert Axelrod, who dismissed the charges against all but one of the demonstrators brought before him. The Bay Area Student Committee quotes the judge as saying: "The defendants for the most part are clean-cut American college students who will within the next few years enter into the business and professional worlds, and many of them I am sure will become leaders in their respective fields. I am convinced that they are not engaged in subversive activities nor in spreading subversive propaganda." [74]

That is the entirety of the Axelrod quotation as it appears in the student committee's pamphlet. Anyone reading this as it stands could only conclude that the charges of Communist manipulation of the students must surely be in error. Again, however, we find the film's critics have brazenly ripped words from their context. For Judge Axelrod went on to say, in the words immediately following those quoted by the student committee: "However, they chose the wrong means to accomplish their purpose *and let themselves become victims of those who profit by creating unrest, riots, and the type of conduct*

---

* It is worth noting that, even in lifting Carberry's remark from context, Jacobs got the quotation wrong, substituting "aggression" for "violence." "At the time I listened to the broadcast," he explained, "I thought the sheriff used the word 'aggression'; instead he said 'violence.' I am sorry that this error occurred, but I do not think the difference between 'aggression' and 'violence' changes in any way the significance of the sheriff's answer to Professor Smith's question." Perhaps not, but this is a strange plea from one attempting to inflate inadvertent errors in *Operation Abolition* into malevolent "distortions."

which is outlawed by the penal code section I have quoted." [75]
(Italics added.)

In order to leave no doubt that he was grossly misrepresented, or any concerning the identity of those "who create unrest," Judge Axelrod told the Associated Press: "At no time did I condone their conduct. A single sentence from my decision, quoted out of context, created that false impression." The judge added, "I very definitely agree" with the view of FBI Director J. Edgar Hoover that the City Hall riot on May 13 was "instigated by Communist subversives." He had dismissed the charges against the students, he said, because "a protracted mass trial with 62 defendants and 16 attorneys would not only be costly from a monetary sense but would play directly into the hands of those who create unrest and do everything in their power to upset our democratic processes and way of life."

"While his decision did not use the specific word 'Communist,'" AP concluded, "Judge Axelrod said in an interview there was no question in his mind that the students were made use of by subversives, and 'it makes no difference whether you pronounce it *tomayto* or *tomahto.*'" [76]

5. *The Case of Vernon Bown.* Perhaps the most flagrant and most archly knowing of the student committee's misstatements concerns a man named Vernon Bown. The film refers to Bown as a "professional Communist agitator," and says he was charged with sedition in the state of Kentucky. The student committee offers this comment:

"The truth is that HUAC itself, in its Friday morning hearing, indicated that Vernon Bown is not a member of the Communist Party." The student committee adds, concerning the sedition charge: "The film omits the vital background in the case. Mr. Bown was guarding the home of a Negro family which had been threatened by racists in a Southern state. The house was subsequently bombed by a group of segregationists in an automobile, and Bown was indicted for the bombing." And: "The film did not tell us these charges were thrown out by the courts, and that Bown was never convicted of these 'crimes.'" [77]

It is difficult to imagine a more artful inversion of the record. In every particular, the student committee has distorted the material data about Bown. To begin with, the student committee implies, without saying as much, that HUAC itself had repudiated the identification of Bown as a "professional Communist agitator." In fact the Committee heard considerable evidence that, in an intra-Party squabble, Bown's section had been ousted by state Communist headquarters. The hearing focused on a petition by Bown's section *seeking readmission to the Party.* The meaning of the episode is the opposite of that suggested by the students.[78]

Other parts of the pamphlet's statement on this point are equally false. The sedition case in which Bown was indicted revolved around a man named Carl Braden—who has been identified under oath as a Communist,[79] and who in 1961 went to jail for refusing to answer questions about that identification. Braden and his wife bought a house in a white neighborhood in Louisville, and turned it over to a Negro couple. The house was subsequently bombed. The Bradens, Bown, and four others formed a "committee" to agitate in behalf of the Negroes, and to convince the public that racists had conducted the bombing.

The authorities, however, found a portable radio beneath the house, and concluded it had been used to detonate the bomb. Owner of the radio: Vernon Bown—who refused to affirm or deny whether he had been under the house, or whether he had taken the radio there.[80]

As for the charges being "thrown out by the courts," the action had nothing to do with the merits of the evidence against Bown. The entire case was dropped after the Supreme Court's decision in *Pennsylvania v. Nelson,* which invalidated state sedition laws on principle, and in which neither Bown nor the Bradens figured.

6. *The Case of the Student Directive.* The Bay Area Student Committee says: "The film asserts that a 'directive' was issued by the Students for Civil Liberties (SCL) telling students to 'laugh out loud' at the Committee, and was published on the

front page of the student newspaper *The Daily Californian* at the University of California at Berkeley. The truth is that the newspaper in a legitimate news article, reported an opinion which was expressed in an open meeting at SCL."

The fact of the matter is that *The Daily Californian,* not HUAC, imputed the "directive" to the Student Committee for Civil Liberties. The film says "a student directive" was published "on the front page of the official University of California student newspaper, *The Daily Californian."* The film then quotes, verbatim, what appeared in the *Californian:* "The SCCL plans to picket the hearings today. *It has issued a call* for students to attend the rally and hearings and suggests that people 'laugh out loud in the hearings when things get ridiculous.' " [81] (Italics added.)

7. *The Case of the "Doctored" Sound Track.* The Bay Area Student Committee charges that the film distorts the "open the doors" demonstration when the students pressed for admission, "by the use of a doctored sound track, and the absurd implication that this demonstration inside the hearing room on Thursday set off the demonstrations outside the hearing room on Friday." [82] Yet nowhere has any attempt been made to connect the two demonstrations in any way. Certainly not in the film *Operation Abolition.* As for the "doctored" sound track charge, Hanks and Schmitt observe, after taping the original sound track from the shots in question: "The sound track of the demonstrations in *Operation Abolition* is exactly identical to that on the original newsreel film taken by KRON-TV." [83]

8. *The Case of William Mandel.* The Bay Area Student Committee says: "The film asserts that it presents the true testimony of William Mandel, but it is clear from the film that much of what Mr. Mandel said to the Committee was edited out of the film." [84] This editing, the students say, amounted to a "flagrant attempt to doctor the record." This charge is amplified by a liberal journal called *New University Thought,* which asserts that one of Mandel's answers is tagged to the wrong question.[85] Study of the transcript shows the film's version to be correct, the charges against it false. The sequence goes:

ARENS: Were you a lecturer in a California Labor School in San Francisco in 1947?

MANDEL: Yes sir, I was, and I lectured on Shostakovich's Oratorio, "Song of the Forest." What do you know about that!

ARENS: Were you at that time a member of the Communist Party and a lecturer as a Communist?

At this point Mandel begins a harangue against the Committee, the fourth sentence of which begins: "This question has no purpose other than to harass me." The referent of "this question" is Arens' inquiry, quoted above, as to whether Mandel was a Communist when he lectured at the California Labor School. The film's narrative paraphrases this:

"When asked about his role as a Communist in lecturing before the Communist-conceived California Labor School in San Francisco, William Mandel replies [sound track picks up Mandel]: 'This question has no purpose other than to harass me.' " [86] Comparison with the question asked Mandel proves this paraphrase to be scrupulously accurate, and the student committee's charge of "doctoring the record" to be thoroughly false.

9. *The Case of the Missing "Credits."* The Bay Area Student Committee says: "Note that no credits are given: There has been no one willing to take responsibility for this shamefully distorted film." [87] This statement, both as to "shameful distortion" and as to lack of responsibility, is wrong. The film is an official document of the United States House of Representatives. The entire transcript is printed in House Report No. 2228 (Union Calendar No. 1014, 86th Congress, Second Session, entitled, "The Communist-Led Riots Against the House Committee on Un-American Activities in San Francisco, Calif., May 12–14, 1960.") In this report, Chairman Francis Walter states: "Bearing in mind the apt saying that 'one picture is worth a thousand words,' and that only the film can portray fully the actual occurrence, we have deemed it necessary to submit a print of the film herewith, which is made a part of this record." [88] The report names Washington Video Productions, Inc., as the firm

which condensed the newsreels of the demonstrations into the form of a motion picture.[89]

The student committee also says: "These films were used in *Operation Abolition* without the knowledge or the permission of the owners, KPIX-TV and KRON-TV." [90] The fact of the matter is that material taken under subpoena, and incorporated into official documents, is never subject to permission.[91] And Philip Lasky, vice-president of the company which operates KPIX-TV, says: "When legally taken under compulsion of subpoena, we do not normally concern ourselves with the use made of the material taken." [92]

10. *The Case of the Subpoenaed Teachers.* It is asserted by Congressman James Roosevelt that HUAC itself had generated resentment which exploded in the student riots—by its disgraceful act of subpoenaing, the previous year, more than 100 California schoolteachers in the presence of their pupils and then canceling the hearings at which they might have cleared themselves of suspicion. In his April 25, 1960, speech, Roosevelt had said: "Most of the subpoenas were served on the teachers at school at 9 o'clock in the morning of June 5." [93] He also implied that the Committee released the names—passing off as unimportant the question of whether they were leaked, or merely got out by accident.[94]

The facts in this episode are as follows: "Most" of the teachers were not subpoenaed at 9 o'clock, and were not subpoenaed in their classrooms. HUAC, in fact, had issued instructions that all subpoenas be delivered at 7:30 in the morning. As Rep. Gordon Scherer stated in a House speech, May 5, 1960: "An examination of 101 files shows that ... 97 teachers were actually served at their homes. Only four were served at their schools— and this was done only because of the inability of the serving officers to locate them at their residences." [95]

As to publicizing the names, Arthur F. Corey, Executive Secretary of the California Teachers Association, has said: "Names of teachers subpoenaed have not been published in Southern California and were not announced by the Committee in Northern California." Finally, with respect to cancellation of the hearings, Corey said: "I wish to express the appreciation of the California Teachers Association for the Committee's decision to cancel the hearings scheduled in California." [96]

Such is the pattern of innuendo, phrases torn from context, and outright misstatement, which has been used to discredit *Operation Abolition,* in the course of the campaign against the House Committee on Un-American Activities. We may well speculate on the condition of minds which resort to such techniques to prove their allegations.

M. Stanton Evans

B. THE CAMPAIGN
AGAINST HUAC

The opposition to the House Committee on Un-American Activities has over the years taken many different forms expressing itself in speeches, manifestoes, rallies, advertisements, handbills, riots, petitions, resolutions, demonstrations, films, forums, books, and pamphlets that trace back to sources as various as a former president of Harvard University and the Communist Party. This is not to say that the opposition is completely unorganized; nor that the former president of Harvard is a Communist. The opposition to HUAC can be divided into two groups: the organized, and the unorganized. For thirty years there has been only one organized group that has devoted itself continuously to the abolition of HUAC, and that is the Communist Party. What is the connection between the Communist Party and the more generalized manifestations of opposition to HUAC?

Mr. Evans' close study of the San Francisco riots reveals, on a small scale, the type of problem that faces anyone who tries to extricate, from the tangle of human conduct in the mass, the underlying, motivating forces. On a larger scale—as, for example, in the 1947 campaign against the Committee—the problem fans out with such permutations of motive, propensity, and heedless-ness that it becomes, in fact, insoluble. Consider this abbreviated chronology of relevant events. . . .

—On October 10, 1947, a letter from Communist Party head-quarters to the thirty districts of the Party urged all Communists to support the Civil Rights Congress in its drive to collect a half million signatures for a petition to abolish HUAC in protest against the Hollywood hearings. (The Civil Rights Congress was a Communist front: the Party itself rarely en-gages in major public campaigns under its own name.) A dead-line of December 5 was set. In short order the petitions, protests, resolutions, denunciations, and calls for abolition started rolling in. The dates, and the organizations heard from, were as follows:

—October 25, the Southern California Chapter of Progres-sive Citizens of America.

—October 29, the Greater Newark CIO Council, and the Swarthmore (Penna.) chapter of the American Veterans Com-mittee.

—October 30, the Battle Creek (Mich.) chapter of the Ameri-can Veterans Committee, and the National Council of Jewish Women.

—October 31, fifty faculty members of Dartmouth College as signatories to a letter from the Public Affairs Laboratory.

—November 1, the Congress on Cultural Freedom and Civil Liberties, and the San Antonio (Tex.) section of the National Council of Jewish Women.

—November 2, Philip Murray, president of the CIO.

—November 3, Local 30, Leather Workers Division of the International Fur and Leather Workers Union; the Brooklyn Men's and Women's Divisions of the American Jewish Con-gress; the Missionary Society of Connecticut; the Connecticut Conference of Congregational Christian Churches.

—November 4, Local 2, United Office and Professional Work-ers of America.

—November 6, El Segundo (Calif.) Local 547, Oil Workers International Union; and San Francisco Local 10, International Longshoremen's and Warehousemen's Union.

—November 10, Local 2-157 of the International Woodworkers of America.

—November 12, the Ladies' Auxiliary of the Conference of Studio Unions (Hollywood); and Local 2-46 (Bellingham, Wash.) of the International Woodworkers of America; and Local 231 (Detroit) of the Federation of Teachers.

—November 13, the Conference of Studio Unions.

—November 14, the National Lawyers Guild; the San Francisco chapter of same; the Chicago chapter of the National Council of Jewish Women.

—November 18, Local 1-83 (Pelican, Alaska) of the International Longshoremen's and Warehousemen's union.

—November 19, the Southern California Continuations Committee of the California Legislative Conference; Local 1-62 (Ketchikan, Alaska) of the International Longshoremen's and Warehousemen's Union; Local 2058 of the United Steelworkers of America.

—November 21, the Civil Rights Congress of Michigan.

—November 24, the Passaic (N. J.) section of the National Council of Jewish Women; the Federal Council of Churches of Christ in America.

—November 25, the Washington Committee of the Southern Conference for Human Welfare.

—November 26, the Mount Eden (Bronx, N. Y.) chapter of the American Veterans Committee; two dozen faculty members of the Yale Law School.

—November 30, the American Education Fellowship.

—December 9, the Missoula County High School (Montana).*

We can make out the profile of the opposition by looking hard at this brief calendar. Here are (1) the organized opposition—the Communist Party, and the Communist fronts. And here are (2) the unorganized opposition: excitable and rebellious students; arch humanitarians; doctrinaire advocates of the "open society."

* The intensity of this particular coalescence of opposition began to diminish in December, but it did not subside entirely.

What is the connection between the organized and the unorganized opposition? It should be clear, by the empirical record, that the proximate cause of the 1947 demonstration was the Communist Party's dynamic response to the Hollywood investigations by HUAC. It was the organizational acuity of the Communist Party that furnished the operative impulse for a wide variety of non-Communist opposition (by December 15 the YMCA and YWCA were co-sponsoring an anti-HUAC rally in Norman, Oklahoma). But we cannot wring from the timetable anything more than proximate cause; indeed, we cannot, strictly speaking, deduce even that. The unorganized opposition, maintaining its innocence of Communist manipulation, reasons somewhat as follows: "Of *course* we knew the Communists were waging a campaign against the Committee in 1947, for self-serving reasons. But their reasons are not our reasons, for we do not seek to further the career of the Communist Party. We are anti-Communists. But we have our own opinions concerning the House Committee, opinions independently arrived at. Perhaps the Communist Party is responsible for calling to our attention the sins of HUAC. Does that make HUAC's sins any the less sinful? Maybe we would have come up with a resolution against the Committee in 1947 even if the Communist Party *hadn't* started the ball rolling—who can say for sure? Maybe we wouldn't have. But the fact of the matter is the Committee should be abolished, and every good liberal should join the campaign to that end, and never mind what the Communist Party feels about it."

Here is a denial of any organizational or ideological subordination to the Communist Party, an affirmation of an unimpeachable independence. Here is the admission that the Communist campaign might indeed have been the immediate cause of non-Communist agitation, but a reminder that the ultimate cause for decrying the Committee is the independent, exercised opinions of men of good will.

One must at this point ask: In actual fact, does the unorganized opposition arrive at its opinions independently?

To answer this question we must further subdivide the opposition into two groups. One group, including the excitable students, the arch humanitarians, and the doctrinaire liberals, one might call the Confused Majority. The other group comprises those who endorse the exact philosophical position of John Stuart Mill. They are the strict constructionists of the open society. These one might call the Purist Minority.

The Purist Minority has indeed arrived at its opinion independently, and does, indeed, go about expressing its opposition to such an organization as HUAC, without serious reference of any kind to the Communist Party, or the threat posed by it. Their philosophical position demands attention and discussion. In fact, the grave question of how much coercion there must be in a free society has been the most consistent object of political thought since Aristotle. This volume, in fact, is an attempt to apply to the question of the House Committee the standards that conservatives have derived from this ageless inquiry. The Purist Minority, though influential within liberalism, is no more in control of the movement or of its agitational arm, than the anarchists are in control of the American conservative movement. Suffice it to say that the Purist Minority—the disembodied intellectualists who forsooth see not Communism, nor understand the traditional American way of treating unassimilable minorities, nor know about the problem of subversion—understand only the utopian imperatives of the essay "On Liberty." They amount to the slimmest fraction of the total opposition to the Committee.

This leaves us with the Confused Majority, who also claim a pristine and virginal independence in the making of their opinions. Yet far from basing their arguments squarely and exclusively on the philosophical position best stated by Mill, these opponents of the Committee rest their case primarily on a variety of misapprehensions about the House Committee—that it has never brought forth any legislative proposals; that its proposals have not led to legislation; that it browbeats the witnesses, refuses them counsel, slanders them; that it wastes money, that it exists for the glorification of the Committee members; that it distorts the evidence—and so on. Whence come these

falsehoods upon which the Confused Majority of the unorganized opposition base their "independent" case?

It would appear that a close study of the San Francisco riots,
and especially of the controversy they touched off in the public
press, will reveal that the Communist Party is the origin of
much of the distortion and plain falsehood that passes for "fact"
about the Committee. The standard falsehoods blare forth from
full-page newspaper ads placed by organizations like the National Committee to Abolish the Un-American Activities Committee, the Emergency Civil Liberties Committee, the Citizens
Committee to Preserve American Freedom—all of them
thoroughly within the Communist orbit. Excitable students, goodhearted men, decent clergymen, pick up these
pages. It is a noble and laudable thing to stand up and
defend those who are downtrodden, browbeaten, abused; to
attack an agent of despotism; to fight for liberty, decency and
order: even conservatives have been known to do it. But it is
essential that a man who stands up in public to speak his piece
should have his facts straight, and those men who have, with
good motives, delivered themselves of noble sentiments based
unwittingly on a tissue of distortions cannot hope to serve just
causes. By their innocence, they have become confused and, in
turn, have become the agents of confusion.

A typical example is the reception given to Frank Donner's
book against HUAC, *The Un-Americans*. Here is a volume on
the Committee which is as invidiously anti-HUAC as any
broadcast by Goebbels was invidiously anti-Semitic, but which
was nevertheless hospitably, even enthusiastically welcomed, by
non-Communist liberals. "A brilliant book," wrote Mr. Gore
Vidal ecstatically in the New York *Herald Tribune,* as guest
writer during the absence of columnist Mr. John Crosby. And
not a mention in Mr. Vidal's column of the adamantly pro-
Communist record of Mr. Donner, no reference to the author's
failure even to mention Alger Hiss in the book, nothing about
Mr. Donner's refusal to concede that any problem whatever is
raised by the existence of a hard-core Communist enterprise in
this country, no mention of Mr. Donner's extraordinary failure

to advance even a word of criticism of the Communists who have been summoned before the Committee. . . . Indeed, Mr. Vidal accepted the book as though it had been written by a disinterested person, and so urged it upon his readers. And during the spring of 1961, the academic community's principal teachers on the subject of the House Committee on Un-American Activities, who gave speech after speech, in college after college, often receiving, in gratitude for their contribution to the common misunderstanding, a standing ovation, were Frank Wilkinson and Carl Braden, identified members of the Communist Party.

The argument that Donner's book or Wilkinson's lectures speak for themselves, and that the bias of the authors is irrelevant, is tenable only if one is willing, e.g., to suppose that a pro-Communist *can* write a speech objectively about a committee whose implicit purpose is to repress their activities. The liberal faces the same problem here that members of the American Right face: the latter are often taking positions similar in some respects to those of neo-fascists like Mr. Gerald L. K. Smith. And conservatives would hotly resent the suggestion, based on the fallacy of *post hoc ergo propter hoc* reasoning, or on guilt by ideological association, that they so act because they have been seduced by Mr. Smith, or are secretly sympathetic with his views. Similarly, the liberals who have recently announced their opposition to HUAC are outraged at the suggestion that their resentment was ignited by the propaganda of the Party, or that the temperature of their opposition in the future will depend on the fever of Communist resistance. It is at this point that intelligence is so very much needed, to formulate the relevant questions, e.g.: Does right-winger X convincingly dissociate himself from Smith—enough so to make plain his alertness to Smith's attempt to influence him? Does he peddle Smith's books? Review them hospitably? Participate in common organizational endeavors? By contrast, does the opposition to HUAC denounce the Emergency Civil Liberties Committee? The National Lawyers Guild? Braden and Wilkinson? The myriad

Communist fronts which are the succubi of innocent civil libertarians?

The connection, then, between the Communist Party and the Confused Majority of the unorganized opposition is surely this: the Communist Party and its epigoni manufacture and distribute erroneous information which seriously affects the indictment by many liberals of the Committee. The opposition to the House Committee is made up of three elements: the Communist Party, the Confused Majority, and the Purist Minority. Having identified these distinct groups and discussed their relations with each other, we now ask: How much thunder about the Committee comes in from each group?

The answer can only be in the form of an educated guess: if the Communist Party did not exist, the opposition to HUAC would lose one per cent of its personnel and 90 per cent of its publicity.

For the Communist Party is engaged in a mortal battle with the Committee, and in its desperate struggle for survival, it has systematically defamed its enemy and involved great libertarian principles. Without those cries, the unorganized opposition might or might not have sent a petition around in 1947. Certainly it did not trouble to protest vigorously the Committee's investigations of non-Communist groups.

If there were no Communist Party, there would still be continuous opposition to HUAC, but that opposition would no longer take the form of nationally synchronized expressions of resistance. The Purist Minority would continue its valuable and challenging part of the eternal dialogue on the uses of coercion in a free society—a dialogue maintained principally in the professional journals and the works of serious scholars. The Confused Majority would add a ritual dart for the Committee to its quiverful of weapons, and its opposition to the Committee would become apparent during sporadic practice sessions or whenever a very tempting target presented itself. But another outcry from Alaska to Florida, without the Communist Party in on it? Most unlikely.

ED.

A. THE COMMITTEE'S
PROCEDURES

SUPPOSE *one grants the legitimacy of the Committee's mandate, and even the empirical need for its existence—
what about the prerogatives of the persons against whom it
moves? What is the provenance of the rights of witnesses who
are summoned by Congressional committees to give testimony?
What "rights" do they have, as against those they claim? How
does the Committee actually deal with its witnesses? Do they
forfeit rights which are otherwise acknowledged on the American scene, and which were traditionally enjoyed? How does the
Committee's modus operandi compare with, say, that of the
Royal Commission established by the Government of Canada
to inquire into the spy rings exposed immediately after the
Second World War by Igor Gouzenko? What improvements
might the Committee make in its procedures?*

"The defenders and detractors of the administrative process,"
writes Professor Walter Gellhorn in *Individual Freedom and
Governmental Restraints,** have in the last twenty-five years

* Walter Gellhorn, *Individual Freedom and Governmental Restraints* (Baton
Rouge: LSU Press, 1956).

"all but exchanged roles, and have done so with almost unbelievable abruptness." He refers, of course, to the struggle over judicial review of the *administrative* process: Before World War II, the liberal intelligentsia opposed it, and conservatives favored it. Since the war, however, it is the liberals who have favored it.

Just as striking, if not more so, has been the reversal in attitudes toward *legislative* investigation. Legislative investigations were a well-tried technique under the New Deal. In many fields, including shipping, oil, utilities and tax evasion, Congressional committees, co-operating with the Executive, exposed real or assumed evils in order to develop public support for Administration programs. And those who opposed were sharply criticized by liberal spokesmen. Not so with the anti-Communist investigations of the postwar era. Congressional committees, in particular the House Committee on Un-American Activities, have been vigorously condemned because of their procedures and on the grounds that they engage in "exposure for exposure's sake." Frequently the suggestion has been made that Congress should adopt, in lieu of the investigating committees, the procedures by which the Canadian Royal Commission on Espionage so successfully uncovered Communist activities after the defection of Igor Gouzenko.

Criticism of the committees has, for the most part, been put forward in general terms, without the specificity needed for appraisal. But Professor Robert H. Carr's exhaustive *The House Un-American Activities Committee: 1945–1950* accomplishes in thirty-five pages a detailed, openly hostile exposition of the Committee's procedures during the Hollywood and Bentley-Chambers hearings of 1946–1948. The alleged grievances fall into the following general categories: (1) The lack of system in the use of open and closed hearings, in the choice between the full committee and subcommittees for the conduct of hearings, in the techniques used in the questioning of witnesses, and in the rights accorded to witnesses; (2) the asking of halfhearted and silly questions; (3) the liberties extended to witnesses for irresponsibly naming other persons.

Professor Carr does not give examples of "character assassination"—pleading his "desire not to give any further publicity to the people whose names have been so used." He agrees, moreover, that every person adversely named was permitted "to appear before the Committee and deny the charges, if he wished to do so," and that "the Committee itself subpoenaed a number of these persons, only to have many of them refuse to confirm or deny the charges, on the ground of self-incrimination." Thus Professor Carr himself handles one of his charges, to the extent that he particularizes it.

Professor Carr gives a few illustrations of what he regards as silly questions which, seen in isolation from context and many years later, do seem facetious or pointless. But here we must take into account the character of the witnesses with whom the Committee had to deal, and Professor Carr himself writes of them:

Certainly the witnesses who have tangled with the Un-American Activities Committee knew what they were doing; often they were arrogant, dogmatic, and vituperative. It is hard to find in the record of the hearings much support for a view of them as innocent, grievously wronged citizens who were defending the cause of liberty and democracy against a too-pervasive arm of the state.

Whatever validity there may have been in Professor Carr's primary dissatisfaction with the Committee's procedures in 1946–48 (viz., "lack of system"), his complaint is apparently no longer applicable. There had at one time been misgivings about the Committee's procedures even among persons friendly to its investigations, for example the Committee on the Bill of Rights of the Association of the Bar of the City of New York, composed of a number of important New York lawyers (Lloyd Paul Stryker served as Chairman). That Committee's 1946 report staunchly defended the investigations, but concluded that protection of individual rights required greater procedural regularity, and set forth a proposed code for Congressional committees generally that was adopted without dissent by the Bar Association at a meeting in December 1948.

At about that time the House Committee, responding to this and other criticisms and suggestions, made its own attempt to achieve great procedural consistency. In 1953 it formalized its practices by a written code which, in general, followed the recommendations of the New York Bar Association, although with certain modifications that will be discussed below. This code, the first to be adopted by any full committee of Congress, was revised in 1961 and is phrased as follows:

Committee Rules of Procedure

I—INITIATION OF INVESTIGATION:

No major investigation shall be initiated without approval of a majority of the Committee. Preliminary inquiries, however, may be initiated by the Committee's staff with the approval of the Chairman of the Committee.

II—SUBJECTS OF INVESTIGATION:

The subject of any investigation in connection with which witnesses are summoned or shall otherwise appear shall be announced in an opening statement to the Committee or Subcommittee before the commencement of any hearings; and the information sought to be elicited at the hearings shall be relevant and germane to the subject as so stated.

III—SUBPENAING OF WITNESSES:

A—Subpenas may be issued under the signature of the Chairman of the Committee or any Subcommittee, or by any Member designated by any such Chairman, and may be served by any person designated by any such Chairman or Member.

B—Witnesses shall be subpenaed at a reasonably sufficient time in advance of any hearing, said time to be determined by the Committee or Subcommittee, in order to give the witness an opportunity to prepare for the hearing and to employ counsel, should he so desire.

C—Each subpena shall contain a statement notifying the witness that if he desires a conference with a representative of the Committee prior to the date of the hearing, he may call or write the Director of the Committee.

IV—EXECUTIVE AND PUBLIC HEARINGS:

(1) If the Committee or a Subcommittee believes that the interrogation of a witness in a public hearing might endanger national security, it shall interrogate such witness in an Executive Session for the purpose of determining the necessity or advisability of conducting such interrogation thereafter in a public hearing.[1]

(2) Attendance at Executive Sessions shall be limited to Members of the Committee, its staff, and other persons whose presence is requested, or consented to by the Committee or Subcommittee.

(3) No testimony taken or material presented in an Executive Session, or any summary thereof, shall be made public either in whole or in part, unless authorized by a majority of the Committee or Subcommittee.

V—TESTIMONY UNDER OATH:

All witnesses at public or executive hearings who testify as to matters of fact shall give all testimony under oath or affirmation. Only the Chairman or a Member of the Committee shall be empowered to administer said oath or affirmation.

VI—TRANSCRIPT OF TESTIMONY:

A complete and accurate record shall be kept of all testimony and proceedings at hearings, both in public and in Executive Session.

Any witness or his counsel, at the expense of the witness, may obtain a transcript of any public testimony of the witness from the Director of the Committee.

Any witness or his counsel may also obtain a transcript of any executive testimony of the witness:

(1) When a special release of said testimony prior to public release is authorized by the Chairman of the Committee or the Chairman of any Subcommittee; or

(2) After said testimony has been made public by the Committee.

A witness examined under oath in a hearing upon request shall be given a reasonable opportunity before the transcript is made public to inspect the transcript of his testimony to determine whether it was correctly transcribed. He may be accompanied by his counsel during this inspection.

VII—ADVICE OF COUNSEL:

A—At every hearing, public or executive, every witness shall be accorded the privilege of having counsel of his own choosing.

B—The participation of counsel during the course of any hearing and while the witness is testifying shall be limited to advising said witness as to his legal rights. Counsel shall not be permitted to engage in oral argument with the Committee, but shall confine his activity to the area of legal advice to his client.

VIII—CONDUCT OF COUNSEL:

Counsel for a witness shall conduct himself in a professional, ethical, and proper manner. His failure to do so shall, upon a finding to that effect by a majority of the Committee or Subcommittee before which the witness is appearing, subject such counsel to disciplinary action which may include warning, censure, removal from the hearing room of counsel, or a recommendation of contempt proceedings.[2]

In case of such removal of counsel, the witness shall have a reasonable time to obtain other counsel, said time to be determined by the Committee or Subcommittee. Should the witness deliberately or capriciously fail or refuse to obtain the services of other counsel within such reasonable time, the hearing shall continue and the testimony of such witness shall be heard without benefit of counsel.

IX—STATEMENT BY WITNESS:

A—Any witness desiring to make a prepared or written statement[3] for the record of the proceedings in executive or public sessions shall file a copy of such statement with the counsel of the Committee not less than 48 hours in advance of the hearing at which the statement is to be presented.

B—All such statements or portions thereof so received which are relevant and germane to the subject of the investigation may, upon approval, at the conclusion of the testimony of the witness, by a majority vote of the Committee or Subcommittee members present, be inserted in the official transcript of the proceedings.

X—RIGHTS OF PERSONS AFFECTED BY A HEARING:

A—Where practicable, any person named in a public hearing, or in the released testimony of an executive hearing, as subversive,

Fascist, Communist, or affiliated with one or more subversive-front organizations, who has not been previously so named, shall, within a reasonable time thereafter, be notified by registered letter, return receipt requested, to the address last known to the Committee, of such fact, including:

(1) A statement that he has been so named;

(2) The date and place of said hearing;

(3) The name of the person who so testified;

(4) The name of the subversive, Fascist, Communist, or front organization with which he has been identified; and

(5) A copy of the printed Rules of Procedure of the Committee.

B—Any person, so notified, who believes that his character or reputation has been adversely affected or to whom has been imputed subversive activity, may within 15 days after receipt of said notice:

(1) Communicate with the counsel of the Committee; [4] and/or

(2) Request to appear at his own expense in person before the Committee or any Subcommittee thereof in public session and give testimony, in denial or affirmation, relevant and germane to the subject of the investigation.

C—Any such person testifying under the provisions of B (2) above shall be accorded the same privileges as any other witness appearing before the Committee, and may be questioned concerning any matter relevant and germane to the subject of the investigation.

XI—ADMISSIBILITY OF TESTIMONY:

A witness shall be limited to giving information relevant and germane to the subject under investigation. The Committee or Subcommittee shall rule upon the admissibility of all testimony or information presented by the witness.[5]

XII—RELATIONSHIP OF HUSBAND AND WIFE:

The confidential relationship between husband and wife shall be respected, and for reasons of public policy, one spouse shall not be questioned concerning the activities of the other, except when a majority of the Committee or Subcommittee shall determine otherwise.

XIII—COMMITTEE REPORTS:

A—No Committee reports, publications, or any summary thereof shall be made or released to the public without the approval of the majority of the Committee.

B—No summary of any Committee report or publication and no statement of the contents of such report or publication shall be released by any Member of the Committee or its staff, prior to the official issuance of the report.

XIV—APPOINTMENT OF SUBCOMMITTEES—QUORUM—
    DELEGATION OF AUTHORITY:

The Chairman is authorized and empowered from time to time to appoint Subcommittees composed of three or more Members of the Committee, at least one of whom shall be of the minority political party, and a majority of whom shall constitute a quorum, for the purpose of performing any and all acts which the Committee as a whole is authorized to perform.

XV—DELEGATION OF AUTHORITY TO SUBCOMMITTEES:

In addition to the general authority delegated to Subcommittees under the preceding section, each Subcommittee is delegated authority:

A—To determine by majority vote thereof whether the hearings conducted by it shall be open to the public or shall be in Executive Session. All testimony taken and all documents introduced in evidence in such an Executive Session shall be received and given as full consideration for all purposes as though introduced in Open Session; and

B—To admit to the hearing room whatever public information media it deems advisable or necessary to the dissemination of testimony, provided that the decision of the Subcommittee shall not be in conflict with the rulings of the Speaker of the House of Representatives or the Rules of the House of Representatives.

XVI—PUBLICATION OF NAMES OF SUBPOENAED WITNESSES:

No Member of the Committee or staff shall make public the name of any witness subpoenaed before the Committee or Subcommittee prior to the date of his appearance.

XVII—WITNESS FEES AND TRAVEL ALLOWANCE:

Each witness who has been subpoenaed, upon the completion of his testimony before the Committee, may report to the office of the Director of the Committee, room 226, Old House Office Building, Washington, D.C., and there sign appropriate vouchers for travel allowances and attendance fees upon the Committee. If hearings are held in cities other than Washington, D. C., the witness may contact the Director of the Committee, or his representative, prior to leaving the hearing room.

XVIII—CONTEMPT OF CONGRESS:

No recommendation that a witness be cited for contempt of Congress shall be forwarded to the House of Representatives unless and until the Committee has, upon notice to all its members, met and considered the alleged contempt, and by a majority of those present voted that such recommendation be made.

XIX—DISTRIBUTION OF RULES:

All witnesses appearing before the House Committee on Un-American Activities shall be furnished a printed copy of the Rules of Procedure of the Committee and paragraph 26 of the Rule XI of the House of Representatives.

In a famous article entitled "Hands Off the Investigations," published in 1924 in *The New Republic,* Justice (then Professor) Felix Frankfurter defends the procedures of the Teapot Dome–Daugherty Congressional investigations, and uses language that is in many respects apposite to the investigations conducted by HUAC. One of his points is as follows: "Of course the essential decencies must be observed, namely opportunity for cross-examination must be afforded to those who are investigated or those representing issues under investigation." A better statement would perhaps be: Although persons adversely affected by public testimony do not have a constitutional right to cross-examination, Congressional committees would undoubtedly be more prudent if they were to accord it, as they do not ordinarily do. The best defense of its omission from the Committee's rules is that based on the tactics of certain lawyers who often represent Communists in court trials, which the late Judge Jerome Frank denounced as "outrageous"—"conduct of a kind which no lawyer owes his client, which cannot ever be justified, and which was never employed by those advocates for minorities or for the unpopular, whose courage has made lawyerdom proud." *

It is to be feared that some lawyers in conducting such cross-examinations as the Committee might permit, would behave like the witnesses who have "tangled with the Committee," as described by Professor Carr.

An example is the conduct of Mr. Frank J. Donner, counsel for the United Electrical, Radio, and Machine Workers of America, which was expelled by the CIO for Communist domination. Mr. Donner has frequently appeared as counsel for hostile witnesses before HUAC, and has himself several times appeared as a witness. The following excerpts are taken from his most recent appearance, on March 11, 1959,† and illustrate the problem.

Said Mr. Donner (over a period of an hour) to the Committee: ". . . an appearance [before you] one is hardly likely to forget, since you conduct it like a circus. . . . The purpose of this [hearing] is quite transparent. . . . I am not on a permanent political, supervisory payroll to this Committee. . . . I don't have to spend my life explaining my prior appearances before this Committee and I don't intend to. . . . Just because you want to make a headline. . . . Look, Congressman, my indifference to your smears is practically stupefying. I am delighted not to share your disapproval. . . . If you had any sensitivity of the obligations of this calling you wouldn't snatch me from the counsel table to appear here as a witness. . . . Don't play games with me, Mr. Arens. I told you that [I will] answer you since I testified that I have not been a Communist. . . . I am just imitating you because you shout plenty yourselves . . . I don't want to play games with you. . . ." Etc. etc. etc.

* Judge Jerome Frank in *Sacher v. United States*, 182 F. 2d 416, 454. Cited with approval by Mr. Justice Jackson 343 U.S. 1, 3-4.
† See Hearings, *Problems of Security in Industrial Establishments Holding Defense Contracts, Greater Pittsburgh Area*, Part II.

The purpose of the hearing was to explore the hold of the Communist Party in the UE, of which Mr. Donner is, as counsel, an important official. Hours were spent attempting to elicit from Mr. Donner relevant information. Finally:

MR. ARENS (approximately the tenth attempt to get the question answered) : Have you ever resigned technical membership in the Communist Party? ... I respectfully suggest, Mr. Chairman, the witness be ordered and directed to answer the question or invoke his constitutional privileges.

MR. DONNER: I can't answer that. I don't invoke my constitutional privileges. ... I never resigned and you have no evidence I joined, so there you are.

MR. SCHERER: We have no evidence that you joined?

MR. DONNER: Well, oh—

MR. ARENS: Were Herbert Fuchs and Mortimer Riemer in error when, under oath before this Committee, they swore that while they were in the Communist Party they knew you, sir, as a member of that conspiratorial apparatus?

MR. DONNER: I decline to answer ... because it would serve no legislative purpose and it is purely for the purpose of getting headlines and trying to promote a smear here.

MR. SCHERER: I ask that the transcript of this testimony taken by tape ... be made a part of the records of this Committee because the cold record will not reveal the contemptuous attitude of the ... witness. ...

MR. DONNER: There is something worse, Congressman, than having a contemptuous attitude and that is surrendering your integrity and giving up your manhood. ...

Add to the existing rights of witnesses and their counsels the right to cross-examination, and the problem seriously arises whether hearings would be mechanically possible.

And it should be noted that the unfriendly literature on the Committee has not, since the adoption of the rules, complained of injustices resulting from the withholding of cross-examination. But even if it could be shown that omission of the right to cross-examination has done no harm in practice, it would remain regrettable.

The one perhaps important recommendation of the New York City Bar Association that the Committee failed to adopt stipulated that persons adversely affected by a witness's testimony should have the privilege of cross-examining that witness for a period not to exceed one hour. The Committee's reasoning on the point in question had been that it conducts investigations, not trials, and that the privilege of filing a statement affords adequate protection.

Since adoption of the Code, criticism of the Committee on procedural grounds (apart from the "exposure" criticism) has virtually ceased, if one may judge from the published literature on the matter. (I leave out of account, of course, attacks on the Committee from pro-Communist sources.) Since 1953, indeed, anti-Communist investigations other than Senator McCarthy's have, with one exception, been little criticized on procedural grounds. The exception is Chief Justice Warren's opinion in *Watkins v. United States* (354 U.S. 178), reversing the contempt conviction of a witness because the Committee member who presided at the hearing failed to identify the subject matter with sufficient particularity. The subject matter, the presiding member had said, was Communism in the Chicago labor movement. The Court explicitly doubted that that really was the topic on which Watkins was questioned: "When almost a quarter of the persons on the list [concerning whom the witness was asked] are not labor people," wrote the Chief Justice, "the inference becomes strong that the subject before the Subcommittee was not defined in terms of Communism in labor." Critics of this opinion contend that since over three-quarters of the list *were* labor people, a contrary inference should have been drawn, and Justice Clark, dissenting, suggested that the 25 per cent composed of non-labor people might well have been " 'drops' or other functionaries in the program of co-operation between the union and the Party."

Except for the *Watkins* case, I have been unable to find any condemnation of the Committee for failing to abide by its own Rule II, which requires that the subject of the investigation be announced at the commencement of any hearing.

We turn now to a question that is not strictly procedural, namely "exposure for the sake of exposure," for which the Committee has frequently been criticized. In *Watkins* the Supreme Court said, "We have no doubt that there is no Congressional power to expose for the sake of exposure." This statement, let us note, was what lawyers call "dictum"; that is, something a court gratuitously observes in a decision, not necessary to either the argument or the finding. In the *Watkins* case the Court did *not* reverse Watkins' conviction because he had been required to testify without regard to pending legislation; and although many of the prosecutions growing out of alleged contempt of the Committee have failed, this has never been on the ground that the Committee was engaged in mere exposure.

It is quite true that the Committee has often asserted that exposure is one of its purposes. It is also true, though perhaps beside the point, that the public has over the years derived much valuable information—about the workings of the government, about social and economic problems and various other matters—from Congressional investigations. Should they nevertheless be condemned? Should investigations be strictly limited to prospective legislation? Is it unlawful or wrong for Congressional committees to hold open hearings so that people generally may have information the Committee already has? I do not think so.

Discussions of this subject often begin with a famous passage from Woodrow Wilson's *Congressional Government*. This work, first published in 1885, went through many editions covering the entire period of Wilson's life and represented, presumably, his matured convictions. The celebrated passage reads, in part, as follows:

... Even more important than legislation is the instruction and guidance in political affairs which the people might receive from a body which kept all national concerns suffused in a broad daylight of discussion. ... It is the proper duty of a representative body to look diligently into every affair of government and to talk much about what it sees. ... *The informing function of Congress should be preferred even to its legislative function.* [Emphasis added.]

In the *Watkins* case, to be sure, Chief Justice Warren asserts that Wilson intended the expression "informing function" to apply only to "corruption, maladministration or inefficiency in agencies of Government," and the immediate context of the passage does support the view that Wilson was thinking of maladministration when he described the informing function. Wilson's enthusiasm for Congressional investigations was certainly based, at least in part, on exposures of governmental misconduct during the Grant Administration. We must remember, however, that the affairs of the national government in those days had to do almost exclusively with administration, since social and economic matters were not yet thought to be matters of governmental responsibility. And we must not overlook the phrase "national concerns" and "every affair of government," which suggest that in Wilson's opinion Congress should inform the public upon whatever problems the national government had in hand. Today Communism is clearly such a problem, and Wilson certainly said nothing affirmative about restricting the informing function to maladministration.

Nor is that all. The general impression notwithstanding, Wilson did not coin the expression "informing function." He borrowed it from Walter Bagehot, the great British economist, social philosopher, and political scientist, whose work, *The English Constitution,* Wilson greatly admired. There, Bagehot had written:

... The House of Commons has what may be called an informing function which, though in its present form quite modern, is singularly analogous to a mediaeval function. In old times one office of the House of Commons was to inform the sovereign what was wrong. ... The nation needs it quite as much as the king ever needed it.

And we may reasonably suppose that if Wilson had thought the informing function of Congress should be more limited in scope than that of the House of Commons he would have said so, and that the phrase "what was wrong" would, for him, have covered matters other than governmental maladministration. And, in any case, "what *is* wrong" pretty well describes the subjects of most Congressional investigations, including those of the Committee on Un-American Activities.

What Bagehot referred to as the "modern form" of the House of Commons' "informing function" emerged after the Glorious Revolution of 1688. Nor were espionage and treason outside the scope of such investigations. In 1689, Parliament voted an inquiry to determine "By what means the Intelligence came to be given to their Majesties' Enemies, concerning the several Stations of Winter Guards of their Majesties' Navy." In 1742 the elder Pitt referred to the House of Commons as the "Grand Inquest of the Nation," an expression approved by a British court in 1845. In the last fifty years, however, the House of Commons has pretty much abandoned its "informing function," the task of investigation having been left largely to special tribunals. But whether or not this trend is an improvement in democratic government is, it would seem, open to question.

The most exhaustive and vigorous defense in modern times of the "exposure" type of investigation we owe to Justice (then Senator) Hugo Black's article in *Harper's* magazine (February 1936), "Inside a Senate Investigation." Justice Black begins his article with a quotation from Woodrow Wilson: "If there is nothing to conceal, then why conceal it? . . . [We] believe it a fair presumption that secrecy means impropriety. So, our honest politicians, and our honorable corporation heads owe it to their reputations to bring their activities out in the open." Justice Black defines a Congressional investigation not as an aid to legislation, but "as a study by the government of circumstances that seem to call for study in the public interest." Seem to whom? Justice Black does not say, but judging from the context he can only mean the Congressional committee with jurisdiction over the subject in question. Justice Black writes of exposure as the almost exclusive function of investigations, and treats most sympathetically a number of specific investigations, many of them concerned with social and economic matters as distinguished from government maladministration. And at the end of his article he sums up the benefits of investigations, one of which is that beneficial legislation may result. However, in his view the "most valuable" benefit is that "this power of the probe is one of the most powerful weapons in the hands of the people to restrain the activities of powerful groups who can defy every other power." "The spokesman of these greedy groups," he declares, "never rest in their opposition to exposure and publicity. That is because special privilege thrives in secrecy and darkness and is destroyed by the rays of pitiless publicity."

Not all New Dealers by any means changed their position on Congressional committees when the investigators turned on the Communists. Federal Judge Charles E. Wyzanski, Jr., told the New York Bar Association in 1948:

Congressional investigations are only one, if an extreme example, of our belief that exposure is the surest guard not only against official corruption and bureaucratic waste, inefficiency and rigidity but against private malpractice, divisive movements and anti-social tendencies in the body politic.

General Telford Taylor, in his book on Congressional investigations, *Grand Inquest,** condemns only exposure in "massive and unlimited doses" and exposure "needlessly intrusive, undignified and indecorous."

Decisions of the Supreme Court subsequent to *Watkins* have not repudiated the dictum against "exposure for the sake of exposure." They have, however, by a majority of five to four, construed it narrowly and in a way not likely to hamper HUAC. The majority's reasoning is that a "motive" of mere exposure is irrelevant provided that a "legitimate legislative interest" can be seen to exist.

Wilkinson v. United States, decided February 27, 1961, is illustrative. The Committee was holding a hearing in Atlanta, Georgia, in connection with proposed legislation. According

*Telford Taylor, *Grand Inquest: The Story of Congressional Investigations* (New York: Simon and Schuster, 1955).

to the Committee's information, Wilkinson was a Communist Party member whose assignment was to whip up sentiment against the Committee wherever it held hearings. Some nineteen months earlier, Wilkinson had been subpoenaed; appearing before the Committee now, again refused to answer such questions. The conclusion is difficult to avoid that the Committee's purpose was to identify Wilkinson as a Communist, so that persons in Atlanta whom he might approach in the performance of his task would be aware of that fact. The Supreme Court nevertheless overruled the exposure argument (the vote was 5—4) and held that the Committee "had reasonable ground to suppose that the petitioner was an active Communist Party member, and that as such he possessed information that would substantially aid it in its legislative investigation."

Undoubtedly Wilkinson had information which, if he had been willing to disclose it, would have aided the Committee enormously. But the Committee could hardly have expected that a professional Soviet agent, sent to Atlanta to harass the Committee, would, upon being subpoenaed, make his information available to it.

A better rationale, in the writer's opinion, is that which the precedents provide; namely, that the informing function is in itself a valid function of a legislative body, that such a body is a Grand Inquest to inform the nation "what is wrong," and, in Justice Black's language, to study "circumstances that seem to call for study in the public interest."

A further reason for holding this view of the informing function is found in the public's need to know the factual basis of proposed legislation. Without such knowledge, the public will not provide the support indispensable to the enactment of regulatory legislation—against Communists or any other group. As already noted, the exposure technique was repeatedly used by the New Deal to raise such support, and to treat exposure for that purpose as proper while condemning "mere exposure" is quibbling. We can be sure that a committee of Congress will not take the trouble to expose anything or anybody unless the members conceive the exposure to be of public interest; and, if it is of public interest, why should the public be kept in ignorance? Moreover, the exposure of matters deemed to be of public interest by a committee of Congress is almost certain to have legislative or administrative consequences.

The New Deal era has been well summarized, in this regard, by the late Justice Jackson. Writing in 1950, seventeen years after his coming to Washington, he reminisces: "But always, since I can remember, some group or other is being investigated and castigated here. At various times it has been Bundists and Germans, Japanese, lobbyists, tax evaders, oilmen, utility men, bankers, brokers, labor leaders, Silver Shirts and Fascists. At times, usually after dramatic and publicized exposures members of these groups have been brought to trial for some offense."

Let us consider now the procedures adopted by the Canadian Royal Commission on Espionage, whose successful investigations of subversive activities in Canada attracted much attention and many favorable comparisons with Congressional committees. The following material is drawn from the Commission's report, mostly Section XI, entitled "Law and Procedure."

What was the Commission? According to the report it was:

> ... a primary institution, though of a temporary kind, and ... upon a formal equality with the other institutions of the State such as the Courts, Houses of Parliament and Privy Council.... It is independent in every sense. It is not subject to, or under the control of, the Courts.... The Commission's findings are as authoritative as those of any court, and, as it is the sole judge of its own procedure, and may receive evidence of any kind in its discretion, it is sometimes in a better position than a Court subject to strict rules as to the admissibility of evidence, to ascertain facts.

The Commission on Espionage was created by an Order-in-Council of February 5, 1946, with two justices of the Supreme Court of Canada as its members. The Commission on Espionage was supplied with a staff that included clerks, stenographers, etc. The need for it, as set forth in the Order-in-Council, was as follows:

It has been ascertained that agents of a Foreign Power have been engaged in a concerted effort to obtain from public officials and other persons in positions of trust, secret and confidential information.

The Commission did not let grass grow under its feet. On February 14th it arrested and imprisoned 12 suspects, one of them a British national whose arrest had been consented to on that same day by the British High Commissioner to Canada. The suspects were imprisoned in the barracks of the Mounted Police, not in a regular jail or prison. At the time they were arrested, moreover, no charges were made against any of them, and for a very good reason; namely, that the Commission lacked sufficient evidence to warrant charges. They were imprisoned, that is to say, not for purposes of punishment, since they had been convicted of no crime, nor to assure their presence at trial, since they stood under no accusation. The objective, as the Commission explains in its report, was rather to prevent the suspects from committing crimes in the future, and to make sure that their evidence would be available in the course of the investigation. If the suspects had remained at large, the Commission points out, the "work of the Commission" would have been "hampered."

The suspects' imprisonment, or "detention" (as it was euphemistically characterized by the Commission), was originally incommunicado, although eventually they were permitted limited access to legal counsel. They were, in consequence, continually and readily available to the Commission, which could examine them at length. There was no pretense of avoiding questions whose answers might be self-incriminating, nor did the Commission deem it necessary to warn the suspects that what they said might be used against them. The purpose of such a warning, the Commission dryly observes, is to enable the witness to remain silent if he so chooses; the warning is, therefore, pointless when the examiner proposes to disregard the privilege against self-incrimination. Nor is that all: although the testimony of some of the suspects incriminated other suspects, the latter were not allowed to cross-examine those who implicated them. They were not, in fact, even permitted to be present.

The Commission's way of getting documentary evidence was similarly vigorous. The Mounted Police searched the homes of suspects, and seized whatever evidence of espionage they found. No one bothered about search warrants.

Under these circumstances—indefinite imprisonment, communication with friends and counsel forbidden, no privilege against self-incrimination or right of cross-examination recognized—most of the suspects confessed. Two did not, simply refusing to testify, and as the recalcitrants were already in jail, the only thing the Commission could do about their refusal was to keep them in custody. Enough confessed, however, to satisfy the Commission of the existence of a widespread Communist espionage network, and to inform it about the latter's character.

These procedures were a key feature, and not an insignificant detail, in the work of the Commission; to them the Report largely attributes the success of the investigation. When, for example, several of the suspects who had testified freely were released and "had the opportunity of discussing matters with others and receiving instructions from others," they refused to testify at the criminal trials subsequent to the Commission's investigation. Had they enjoyed the same privileges and rights while before the Commission, they would presumably have withheld their testimony.

What, one may ask, of the Bill of Rights? What of that protection of the individual which is the cornerstone of Anglo-Saxon jurisprudence?

As the Commission puts it: ". . . the disclosure of secret or confidential information to a foreign power is a subject which is not regarded either here or in England as on a level with what may be called ordinary domestic offenses." The Report elaborately expounds this thesis, with many references to and quotations from statutes and judicial opinions, insisting, persuasively, that the traditional Bill of Rights does not apply in Canada to the detection and punishment of espionage. *Salus populi suprema lex,* with the reasonable implications of that principle, are the law in Canada, according to the Royal Commission, and are shown to be so by both argument and practice. The Report demonstrates, moreover, by frequent citation of statute and judicial opinion, that the law of Great Britain is the same.

The Commission relied particularly on Canadian Order-in-Council P.C. 6444, of which Sections 1–3 authorized imprisonment at the pleasure of the Commission, and of which Section 4 authorized the Mounted Police to engage in searches without a warrant. The Order-in-Council, in turn, was authorized by the Inquirers Act, R.S.C. 1927, C. 99, and the Official Secrets Act, 3 Geo. VI, C. 49, of the Statutes of Canada. When we compare the Order-in-Council with these statutes, it becomes apparent that a Royal Commission, in its own opinion at least, amalgamates the powers of an investigatory tribunal with those of law enforcement officers. It is as if a tribunal were created combining the powers of a Congressional committee, the Attorney General, and the Federal Bureau of Investigation, and unchecked by such safeguards as habeas corpus, the privilege against self-incrimination, and similar constitutional limitations, or by the orders of courts. A Royal Commission is, clearly, a formidable body.

To demonstrate the similarity of British law, the Commission refers to the Tribunals of Inquiry Act, 1921, c. 7, and the Official Secrets Act (of Great Britain) 1911, c. 28 and 1920, c. 75, various court decisions, including *Rex v. Halliday* [1917] A.C. 260, and Dicey's treatise, *Law of the Constitution*. In *Rex v. Halliday*, the House of Lords upheld the power of the state to imprison on suspicion in matters of state security—with, however, a forceful dissent by Lord Shaw of Dunfermline, which expresses the view generally held in the United States.

Congressional committees are often accused of "smearing"—that is, of using derogatory reports and statements which injure reputations, and without the safeguards provided by judicial procedure.

The report of the Commission on Espionage does not suggest that investigation by commission will avoid such "smearing." Free from the obligation to follow rules of judicial procedure, and depending on ex parte and in many instances hearsay evidence, the Commission dogmatically found "that the following public officials and other persons in positions of trust or otherwise have communicated, directly or indirectly, secret and confidential information . . . to the agents of a foreign power," and named fourteen individuals. The conduct in question certainly constituted a violation of the Canadian Official Secrets Act. Four persons were named as having served as "media of communication between espionage agents," also a violation of the Official Secrets Act. Three other persons were said not to have taken "any active part in the subversive activities but would have done so if required"—apparently not a crime.

All fourteen of the persons said to have betrayed their trust were subsequently prosecuted. Eight were convicted, six acquitted. Of the four "media of communication," two were tried and acquitted; in one instance the Crown withdrew the prosecution prior to verdict; in the other the Crown did not prosecute at all. Thus in ten cases there was a conflict between the results of judicial and Commission procedure; the same persons were innocent by one standard and guilty by the other. If the thesis is accepted that only judicial procedures can correctly arrive at facts, then it follows that these ten were unjustly smeared. On the other hand, the eminent judges who composed the Commission thought that because they were not bound by the rules of evidence applicable in judicial proceedings they were better able to *arrive* at facts. The Commission justified its procedure at some length. "We were conducting an inquiry, not trying an issue," its Report stated. ". . . After full consideration, we had no hesitation in deciding that all evidence available, direct, hearsay or secondary, should be considered. In fact if this were not done, it was doubtful whether the purposes of the Commission could be achieved." In any event, the reputations of persons who could not be shown in a court of law to have committed any crime suffered severely.

Another criticism of Congressional investigations alleges that the Congressmen bully witnesses. Whatever force there may be to these criticisms, it is clear that the procedures of the Royal Commission would provide no solution. The Commission heard 116 witnesses, received over 1,000 exhibits, and took 6,000 pages of testimony, but made public only selected excerpts from its interrogations. Although we may assume that the justices themselves were never rude, it is certainly conceivable that the lawyers or Mounted Police of the Commission's staff were on occasion rude to some of the suspects. But because the full minutes have never been released, the public has no way of knowing whether indignation is in order. By contrast, the publicity of Congressional investigations provides a major safeguard against oppression, a safeguard not available in investigations such as those conducted by the Royal Commission.

Still another criticism of Congressional investigations is that on the whole they have not been effective, and that, compared with, for example, the Commission, they have not turned up many who could be shown in a court of law to be spies. A possible answer to this criticism is that Congressional committees have not had the legal and other equipment available to the Royal Commission. If they had the Mounted Police, the jails, the powers of indefinite imprisonment in those jails, the right to disregard the plea of self-incrimination and the right to conduct proceedings in secret, making public only such testimony as they pleased, it is quite likely that the committees would serve up more spies; especially as the success of the Royal Commission was based in such large part on confessions.

It is clear that Canadian procedures do not provide a solution for those who believe that HUAC is not sufficiently respectful of individual rights. Those who advocate Canadian procedures apparently do not realize what those procedures actually are; they have, perhaps, been misled by the quiet with which the Royal Commission on Espionage did its work. Presumably they do not know that the quiet can be attributed to the fact that the Commission's inquiries were undertaken in camera, in the barracks of the Mounted Police.

The established procedures of the Royal Commission do not, simply because they were adopted in context of traditional

English legal standards, certify as satisfactory by American standards the procedures of the House Committee on Un-American Activities. We should, rather, ask ourselves whether our own views on safeguarding individual rights, even the right to conspire against the safety of all one's countrymen, are not, in the light of the position and experience of at least one other mature and libertarian society, becoming obsessive, and even idiosyncratic.

In summary, it may be said that while the procedures of the Committee are not perfect from the point of view of the individual, they do afford substantial protection; and further, that even hostile commentators do not appear to have shown any specific injustice resulting from the Committee's principal failure to achieve the ideal; viz., the lack of cross-examination.

C. DICKERMAN WILLIAMS

B. A COMMENT BY A CIVIL
LIBERTARIAN

WHO, *actually, is primarily to blame for the derivative impositions visited upon witnesses before the Committee? To what extent can the witness be protected by a reform of the Committee's procedures, or the Committee's mandate? To what extent by a revision of the public attitude toward those persons who appear before the Committee? Might something sensible be done to clarify the legitimate uses of the First Amendment by witnesses who choose not to co-operate with the Committee? Are there reforms on which conservatives and liberals might jointly agree?*

It may startle some to find a onetime American Civil Liberties Union official contributing a chapter to a book that is friendly to the work of the House Committee on Un-American Activities. However, when I was asked to submit a chapter detailing those reforms of the Committee I would recommend, I felt an obligation to respond. A reformer in a society such as ours must, if he is to fulfill his responsibilities, contribute to the political debate an example of personal responsibility as well as a sense of sobriety. We must always be mindful of the fact that it is the continuing quality rather than the specific subject matter of this debate which is the determining factor in the formation of the climate of opinion in which freedom can flourish.

Congressional inquiries into subversive activities have been condemned for disregarding free expression and concomitant rights guaranteed by the First Amendment. The argument supporting this condemnation is that to ask a man to answer publicly questions about his political activity under compulsion abridges his freedom to hold and express the beliefs which underlie such activity; and further, that the official body doing this perpetrates such an abridgment. The consequence might be that in anticipation of such public exposure, people will be made too fearful to engage in unpopular political activity. The development of such fear, the opponents of the Committee claim, runs counter to the First Amendment.

The press in the broadest sense—newspapers, radio and TV combined—do more to coercively inhibit such expression than is realized. The reporting of a Committee hearing by these media normally seems designed to excite a public fever of recrimination, and it is this that also tends to penalize the witness.

Let us examine this more closely in terms of a specific but typical incident. On February 25, 1953, the House Committee on Un-American Activities opened its hearings on subversive influences in education amidst a flurry of sharp public debate and wide polemic. At the commencement of the hearings, Committee Chairman Harold H. Velde read a statement in which he said:

From time to time, the Committee has investigated Communists and Communist activities within the entertainment, newspaper and labor fields, and also within the professions and the government.

In no instance has the work of the Committee taken on the character of an investigation of entertainment organizations, newspapers, labor unions, the professions, or the government, as such, and it is not now the purpose of this Committee to investigate education or educational institutions as such.

Then the first witness, Robert Gorham Davis, was called. Mr. Davis, then a professor at Smith College, described his experiences in a Communist cell at Harvard fourteen years before. Considering that he was the initial witness in the new line of inquiry, the legal basis and propriety of which were hotly challenged by many people, he made some very interesting points which produced a worth-while give and take between Davis and the Committee members. For instance, as to the disciplined allegiance of Communist teachers to the Party, a problem most pertinent to the inquiry:

CONGRESSMAN JACKSON: . . . Mr. Davis, I am not asking you to enter into the realm of opinion, but out of your experience in the Communist Party during the period of time you were a member—to what extent would you say that one submits himself to the expressed or implied discipline of the Communist Party?

MR. DAVIS: This is often, I believe, a motive for joining because those who join desire certainty. They want a line which will give them a sense of significant action. The Communist always has an answer to everything. The answers aren't always very good, but he does have an answer. This is part, unquestionably for many people, of the psychological satisfaction of being a Communist.

And on the important question of Communist teachers' influence on the classroom:

CHAIRMAN VELDE: I am referring to this: do you think a Communist Party member can have a free and open mind, especially in teaching in a classroom, even though he was given no instruction by the Communist Party as to what he should teach?

MR. DAVIS: It depends on the subject. I should think a teacher of music or mathematics might teach in a way that was quite unaffected by his political theories. In the political sciences, and even in the humanities, I doubt if this can be so; and I, myself, now feel that no one who is genuinely humane could be a defender of what does go on now in the Soviet Union and the Communist countries.

And so Professor Davis' testimony went on for several hours. After being cautioned by the Committee members to give only the names of former Communists of whose identity he was certain, Davis named a few people whom he had known to be members of the Communist Party.

Now, let us see how this was reported the next day:

New York Herald Tribune
PROFESSOR TELLS OF RED CELL AT HARVARD IN '39

Washington, Feb. 25.

A Smith College English professor today named a Harvard physicist, two former Smith College faculty members and ten former Harvard graduate students and faculty assistants as persons known to him as Communists during his two years of membership in a Communist unit at Harvard 14 years ago.

Washington Post
PROFESSOR TELLS ABOUT JOINING COMMUNISTS WHILE AT HARVARD, NAMES 14 FELLOW REDS

Washington, Feb. 25

A Smith College professor told House investigators yesterday that 15 years ago he was a Communist along with 12 other persons from Harvard University and two from Smith College.

Such distorted emphasis of the record of a legislative inquiry helps not a little to create an atmosphere that tends to make of the whole investigation a penalty for past thought and action. And one must admit that this penalty was not imposed by the Congressional Committee alone. The press was the particular villain in this piece.

Most of the reforms suggested to prevent the abuse of Congressional inquiry have been directed to the situation involving a subpoenaed witness about whom the Committee has derogatory information. They have been proposed in the form of codes providing for an adoption of procedural rules including the right to counsel (a practice HUAC has followed since 1953) and the recommendation that counsel should under certain circumstances be allowed to inject himself directly into the hearing. The suggested rules embody such provisions as the right of the witness to be notified in advance of the hearing with particularity about the purpose of such hearing (a practice the Committee usually follows), absolutely the right of the witness to make a statement (a practice the Committee follows, provided, in its judgment, the statement is relevant to the matter at hand), and the right to call witnesses and cross-examine them (a privilege the Committee does not grant).

Provision for the enforcement of these rules, however, has not normally been made. These codes suggest the imposition of self-denying ordinances upon its own behavior by Congress. As such, however, they may be breached or abrogated when Congress so pleases.

These codes assume that the witness who appears before a Congressional committee should be accorded certain procedural rights because of the penalty that may be inflicted on him. This penalty is public exposure of his unpopular views, or unpopular activities. In most instances, the activities of the witness exposed to the public by an open committee hearing are not violations of law but constitute an activity considered by many people as unethical, unpatriotic, or immoral. Under our system of law a man is subject to penalty only when his conduct is in violation of a specifically written statute. Those who argue for reform insist that the punishment of a person through public exposure for other than criminal conduct is in basic violation of the Anglo-Saxon system of law.

The use of the compulsory process—that is, the summoning of a witness under subpoena, compelling him to testify—is essential to the effective performance of a legislative mandate of inquiry. It is very difficult to argue that Congress can conduct inquiries of this type without such power. It is as difficult to establish the intent of the investigators to expose for exposure's sake when a committee is seeking, in open hearing, evidential support of testimony or information already in the possession of the committee. Furthermore, there is no easy answer to the argument that HUAC has the right to make a quantitative analysis, supported by extensive hearings, of the depth of Communist penetration and influence. As a matter of fact, this is a procedure commonly used in the behavioral sciences.

In view of all of this, how are we to justify the right of Congress to subpoena a witness when the ensuing testimony may result in public exposure harmful to him? The answer is simple. It is incumbent upon those who are aware of the propriety and legality of such investigations to help the public to understand what it means to give hostile testimony that does not lead to a citation of contempt of Congress. It does not signify legal guilt. It does not mean an indictment. It simply indicates that a person has testified before a Congressional committee.

If, however, the recommended codes were adopted, they would have the perverse effect of reinforcing the incorrect assumption by the public that an unfriendly witness is actually on trial.

The right to call and cross-examine a witness, etc., is based on a judicial or quasi-judicial procedure in which the test of relevancy is firmly established by pleadings or by a specifically worded indictment. These codes cannot significantly protect a witness in a Congressional inquiry where the test of relevancy is inapplicable, in any precise way, because of the very nature of the inquiry. An inquiry should at times roam over the field, just as a good Ph.D. student will cover the entire area of investigation before salting down his dissertation. As John Stuart Mill said in his essay "On Liberty":

The only way in which a human being can make some approach to knowing the whole of a subject, is by hearing what can be said about it by persons of every variety of opinion, and studying all modes in which it can be looked at by every character of mind. No wise man ever acquired his wisdom in any mode but this; nor is it in the nature of human intellect to become wise in any other manner.*

A legal inquiry of this type, like a scientific investigation, cannot start out with an exact knowledge of the limits of the field it seeks to cover because that is the very thing to be determined in the course of the investigation itself.

The fact that these procedural rights do not apply to a Congressional inquiry was vividly brought home to me several years ago when, as an observer, I attended a hearing conducted by Senator McCarthy and his committee. The Senator confronted the witness before the committee with another who was prepared to testify against him on the basis of direct knowledge. Senator McCarthy further accorded to the main witness the right to question the person who testified derogatorily in a face-to-face session. In this hearing, in other words, the witness was given both the right to confront and to cross-examine the person who testified against him, and these rights were exercised. I recall riding back to town from Capitol Hill in a cab with a journalist deeply committed to civil liberties. The point that he made in the course of our journey was, "What a damn shame to have embarrassed the witness by confronting him with persons who knew something of his background, and then to make a *show* of that!"

Modern rebels apparently seek protection for their reputations along with the thrill of rebelliousness. The rebel of yesteryear did not feel that he was punished by public exposure. As a matter of fact, the old Wobbly of pre-World War I vintage would visibly have enjoyed access to any forum in which he could sound off against the dirty capitalists. He was not Fifth Amendment-conscious. He had made his decision that the rewards of rebelliousness were worth the price of unpopularity. Even though we should always be vigilant in protecting the rights of the dissenter, we must also understand and teach our

* Basil Blackwell: Oxford, 1946, p. 18.

young people that if they decide to rebel they should be honest and strong and open in the expression of their views, and ready to countenance the resulting unpopularity.

The debate on the proceedings of the House Committee on Un-American Activities, as well as other Congressional committees, has not been responsive to some of the more significant abuses. The reason is that the debaters have used the static language of the lawyer in characterizing the rights of a defendant in a judicial or quasi-judicial proceeding, in which the penalty is specific in terms of a fine, or imprisonment, or injunctive restraint. What we have in the Congressional committee procedure could be better described in the language anthropologists use to define a social ceremonial which provides a catharsis of a violent public mood. We avoid the brittleness of a government of laws in the long pull by having a mechanism, in the form of a Congressional committee, to absorb and contain the shock of public indignation. I often wonder whether my liberal friends realize that if we had not had the Congressional committees investigating subversive activities, public indignation would have percolated into the inner core of the legislative process, resulting in even more stringent laws, which could have violated the First Amendment rights of individual citizens.

A good example of this is the recent case of Charles Van Doren, who represented himself on television as knowing spontaneously the answers to extremely difficult questions when in fact he had already been given the answers. The House Committee on Interstate Commerce, under the chairmanship of Congressman Oren Harris, held extensive hearings on the incident and thereby refrigerated the hot debate before it was permitted to change our basic law, which provides that the government be kept out of detailed censorship of the airways. The consequence was that this problem was subjected to a double exposure, first before and then during a consideration of the matter by Congress. The result was a more levelheaded legislative response than we would otherwise have had.

In suggesting the possibility of using the language of the anthropologist to describe ceremonial processes and their cathartic effect, I do not intend to support the inference of a belief in the relativism of values that is commonly drawn when such language is used, but rather seek to point out the utility of characterizing this diffuse process of inquiry in other than legal terms in order to promote reform.

I would suggest two reforms which I think would be significantly responsive to the abuse of Congressional inquiry, and to HUAC in particular.

I do not think that we could ever effectively argue that Congress does not have the right to ask a question concerning the political activity of a witness, in instances where it might be shown that such political activity may be related to a conspiracy to overthrow our government. Surely such activity is a matter about which Congress has the right to legislate. Neither do I think any right to anonymity, as a concomitant to First Amendment rights, can prevail over the power of Congress to investigate in an area in which it can legislate. However, because of the extremely broad language of the mandate to investigate un-American propaganda given by the Congress to HUAC, a witness appearing before it may not be able to decide clearly whether the Committee has the power to ask a particular question, much as he may doubt the point. Persistence in refusing to answer a question may subject him to citation for contempt by Congress, in the absence of any line of legal reasoning which would lead to a test of the relevancy of the disputed question to the mandated function of the Committee. To avoid the penal consequences of such citation he is placed in unreasonable jeopardy; he must answer at his peril.

The general rule in these matters is that the significant difference between a free society and an authoritarian society lies in the ability of a citizen of the former to predict the legal consequences of his conduct. Thus we have a very important and significant constitutional rule providing that due process dictates that criminal statutes should be clearly and definitely and specifically worded so that a man knows plainly what the law is and whether he is about to break it. The witness does not have a basis for this kind of predictability when he confronts a question which he doubts the Committee has the authority to put to him. This is the principal point made by the Supreme Court in *Watkins v. United States.*

Senator Kenneth Keating has proposed legislation the effect of which is to relieve the witness of the necessity to answer a question unless he is instructed to do so by court order. A court hearing on the application of the Committee would enable the witness to give his reasons for refusing to answer a question or questions put to him, and get an answer on the validity of his objections from the Court. Only after the Court rules that a witness must testify—because of the Committee's power to ask the question—can he be held in contempt for refusing to answer. This is a reform which should be supported by conservatives and liberals alike.

The case for this reform was articulately made by Senator Keating on June 13, 1961, when he introduced his bill:

My bill would expedite the hearing and disposition of such cases, avoid the necessity of criminal charges against witnesses whose refusal to answer is justified, and aid the committees of Congress in obtaining information they should have at the time it is required.

Under the present law, if a witness refuses to appear or to testify before an investigating committee, the particular subcommittee must make a report to the full committee, the full committee must then report the matter to the Senate or House. The legislative body must then resolve to cite the witness for contempt, after which the President of the Senate or the Speaker of the House, as the case may be, must refer the matter to a U. S. attorney, who in turn must present the case as a criminal matter to a federal grand jury. If an indictment is returned, a full-scale trial in a federal district court must follow. Finally, months, or sometimes even years later, there may be a conviction and punishment. Meanwhile, in most instances, the original investigation has been closed without ever having obtained the testimony for which the witness was originally called.

My proposal would greatly improve the complicated and time-consuming procedures under the present law by authorizing immediate resort to the courts for aid in requiring the attendance and testimony of a reluctant witness. Under the provisions of the bill, when a witness refuses to testify before a Congressional committee, he could be required to appear that very same day in the district court in whose jurisdiction the investigation is being conducted. Upon his appearance before the court, the witness would be subject to judicial jurisdiction, and a further refusal to testify in accordance with the order of the court would be punishable as a contempt of court. This procedure should bring home to a witness that he could immediately be punished for contempt if he decides, without justification, not to testify before a committee of Congress. At the same time, if the witness is justified in refusing to testify, his vindication will be prompt and he will be spared the opprobrium of a criminal prosecution.

The second reform that I would recommend is a change of the language in the House Committee on Un-American Activities' mandate. The language describing its function should be tightened to confine the scope of its investigations to subversive activity. References to "un-American" propaganda should be excluded altogether.

The legislation under which the House Committee on Un-American Activities operates is Public Law 601, 79th Congress (1946); 60 Stat. 812. It provides the powers and duties of the Committee as follows:

The Committee on Un-American Activities, as a whole or by subcommittee, is authorized to make from time to time investigations of (i) the extent, character, and objects of un-American propaganda activities in the United States, (ii) the diffusion within the United States of subversive and un-American propaganda that is instigated from foreign countries or of a domestic origin and attacks the principle of the form of government as guaranteed by our Constitution, and (iii) all other questions in relation thereto that would aid Congress in any necessary remedial legislation.

My recommendation would exclude the language in (i) "the extent, character, and objects of un-American propaganda activities in the United States."

Supporters of HUAC should recognize that this language in the mandate is too broad and suggests problems involving the intrusion of government into the area of human activity sanctified by the First Amendment. And since HUAC has not in fact conducted its investigations in the constitutionally trouble-some areas of propaganda but, on the whole, has confined them to subversive activity about which the Congress can legislate, its supporters should be among the first to propose such a change.

Let us recognize once and for all that it is possible to fight Communism with all the vigor and strength necessary for its defeat by the use of weapons that are consistent with the Constitution.

Lastly, there is no reform that can be more effective than the maintenance of high standards by HUAC in its investigative work. Much of the abuse over the past has resulted from the fact that it has been, occasionally, sloppy and incomplete. Individuals who are harmed by Congressional inquiry are, in the main, harmed by efforts of the Committee to make up for the insufficiency and incompleteness of evidence or information in its possession. There has been a tendency toward the mechanical repetition of established lines of inquiry, no matter what new material may come before the Committee. The Committee should keep in mind that its job is to investigate Communist subversion in its varied and ever-changing forms.

The most significant reform that could be proposed is that of maintaining a sense of high responsibility at all times and using the knife of the surgeon rather than the cleaver of the butcher.

IRVING FERMAN

HUAC AND LEGISLATION

WHAT *response should a pluralistic society make to
the threats of a political enemy that deals in subterfuge, evasion,
deceit, trickery? Is it enough, as it is so often contended, simply
to apply the criminal codes already on the books? Or does the
Communist movement constitute a special threat that must be
met with special laws? How has Congress expressed itself concerning the Communist threat? Has Congress enacted such
special laws? Has the Supreme Court found them to be constitutional? What portion of such legislation has derived from
the investigatory work and legislative proposals of HUAC?
What portion of HUAC's proposals has become law? What proposals are still pending?*

William Z. Foster, for many years the Chairman of the Communist Party, gave us in 1932 rather more concrete details than
we normally get from Communist theorists about the projected
plan for the United States.

Under the dictatorship [he wrote] all the capitalist parties—
Republican, Democratic, Progressive, Socialist, etc.—will be liqui-
dated, the Communist Party functioning alone as the party of the

toiling masses. Likewise will be dissolved all other organizations that are political props of the bourgeois rule, including chambers of commerce, employers' associations, Rotary clubs, American Legion, YMCA, and such fraternal orders as the Masons, Odd Fellows, Elks, Knights of Columbus, etc.*

And how will this Utopia be realized? Lenin prescribed the road:

It is necessary to agree to any and every sacrifice, and even—if need be—to resort to all sorts of devices, maneuvers, and illegal methods, to evasion and subterfuge.†

What is the appropriate response of a self-governing, pluralistic society? There are those who believe we need do nothing very much beyond strictly enforcing the criminal code. There are others who feel we need special legislation especially adapted to inhibit a force or a scare of revolution which was not known by those who drafted our Constitution.

Mrs. Eleanor Roosevelt is one of the more prominent spokesmen for the former view. She wrote recently in "My Day,"

Does the [American Legion] really believe we are in danger of becoming Communists in this country? If it does, it has far less faith in the American people than many of the people and organizations whom it attacks.

No one who has ever been in a country where freedom exists, and has known the feel of it, ever will be tempted to accept the material benefits offered by Communism as a substitute for freedom.

One can read only with stupefaction Mrs. Roosevelt's words, "No one . . ." Apparently she disbelieves even the outright admissions of the hundreds of men who chose Communism in preference to freedom, many of them associated with her husband's Administration. One wonders also, in passing, at the tacit assumption that Communism offers greater material benefits than a free society; Mrs. Roosevelt's statement makes it appear

* William Z. Foster, *Toward Soviet America* (New York: Coward-McCann), p. 275.

† V. I. Lenin, *Selected Works* (New York: International Publishers, 1943), Volume X, p. 95.

that people fall under Communist regimes only by "becoming Communists," i.e., voluntarily choosing to give up freedom and "accept the material benefits offered by Communism." The conspiratorial and coercive nature of Communist ascendancy, in every place where it has occurred, Mrs. Roosevelt and many categorical critics of anti-Communist legislation tend to ignore.

The other type of response, resting on Edmund Burke's adage "Early and provident fear is the mother of safety," recognizes the Communist network in the United States as part of a world-wide apparatus which seeks to impose on this country a totalitarian dictatorship if need be by treachery and by force and violence. It holds that the Communist Party is a criminal conspiracy, not a political contender for majority approval. It favors continuing investigation and the evolution of effective protective legislation. This has been, for over twenty years, the view of the Congress of the United States.

The Supreme Court, looking back, said in 1959:

> That Congress has wide power to legislate in the field of Communist activity in this country, and to conduct appropriate investigations in aid thereof, is hardly debatable. The existence of such power has never been questioned by this Court, and it is sufficient to say, without particularization, that Congress has enacted or considered in this field a wide range of legislative measures, not a few of which have stemmed from recommendations of the very committee whose actions have been drawn in question here [HUAC]. In the last analysis this power rests on the right of self-preservation. . . .*

It is not an easy area in which to legislate, for the lawmakers must accommodate the exigencies of self-preservation and the values of the Constitution. Through the years, the task has been impeded by strong political crosscurrents, occasional judicial setbacks, and recurrent periods of apathy resulting from the deceptive techniques of an adversary who has worked day and night to drain from the American people and their elected representatives all sense of danger and urgency. "The mills of the Gods [that] grind slow" have nothing on Congress—which has,

* *Barenblatt v. United States*, 360 U. S. 109, 127.

in some instances, dawdled for years over the recommendations of its own investigating committees.

The wheels of the courts seem to turn even more slowly. The constitutionality of the party membership clause of the Smith Act * of 1940 was decided for the first time by the Supreme Court in 1961, in a case which had been in the courts for six and one-half years. In another case, proceedings to compel the Communist Party to register itself, its officers and members under the Subversive Activities Control Act of 1960 † were started by the Attorney General on November 22, 1950. In its peripatetic career, this case went before the Subversive Activities Control Board three times, the U. S. District Court once, the U. S. Court of Appeals four times, and the Supreme Court three times. Ten and one-half years had elapsed, during all of which time the Communist Party was contumaciously flouting the will of Congress. The Supreme Court, on June 5, 1961,‡ at the end of a 112-page majority opinion, arrived at the long-awaited conclusion: "The Constitution does not prohibit the requirement that the Communist Party register with the Attorney General as a Communist-action organization pursuant to §7." **

---

* "Whoever organizes or helps or attempts to organize any society, group, or assembly of persons who teach, advocate, or encourage the overthrow or destruction of any such government by force or violence; *or becomes or is a member of,* or affiliates with, any *such society, group,* or *assembly of persons, knowing the purposes thereof*...shall be fined, etc.

† The act in question, sometimes called the McCarran (Internal Security) Act, requires officials of organizations determined, upon due process, to be *"Communist-action"* or *"Communist front"* organizations to register with the Department of Justice as agents of a foreign power, and to label their material as emanating from a Communist organization.

‡ *Communist Party of the United States v. Subversive Activities Control Board,* 367 U.S. 1.

** If Chief Justice Earl Warren had had his way, this issue would have remained undecided until the indefinite future. In his dissenting opinion he favored remanding the case "to the Board for reconsideration," even though the Board had thrice considered the case and handed down three reports, all reaching the same conclusion. "The resolution of the difficult constitutional issues presented by this case would certainly be postponed and perhaps made totally unnecessary," if the case were remanded, said the Chief Justice, as though an indefinite postponement were desirable. He wrote: "In my view, the Court today strays from the well-trod path of our prior decisions by reaching out to decide constitutional issues prematurely." None of the other justices thought the case should be sent back to the Board again.

The Court declined to decide other issues that had been raised concerning the practical application of this and other sections of the Act, terming the questions "premature." It is a practice of the Court to refrain from adjudicating issues not unavoidably presented by the facts of a particular case. Further years of litigation, it would seem, are in the offing before Congress will know the full extent to which the law it passed in 1950 can effectuate its purpose. This purpose is not a trivial one. The Supreme Court summarized the law's purpose as designed "to prevent the world-wide Communist conspiracy from accomplishing its purpose in this country," and "to bring foreign-dominated organizations out into the open where the public can evaluate their activities informedly against the revealed background of their character, nature, and connections."

There have been, then, costly discouragements; but in spite of them, there has gradually developed a substantial body of statutory law and judicial decision to interpose against the Communist threat. Much, as will be seen, remains to be done to implement the preliminary work in which HUAC has patiently persevered down through the years. Yet the record is already rich in accomplishment.

Laws Enacted by Congress
in Consequence of HUAC's Investigations and Recommendations

It is widely believed that HUAC has done little or nothing in the field of legislation and has not fulfilled its primary duty of recommending laws in the area of its jurisdiction.

The Congressmen, Republicans and Democrats, who year after year renew HUAC's mandate by overwhelming vote, are, most of them, aware that much legislation in the field of national security which comes out of other committees is actually based on the work of HUAC. It is not surprising, under the circumstances, that when Congressman James Roosevelt made a vitriolic attack on HUAC in February 1961, charging it with, among other crimes, a negligible record of contributions to antisubversive legislation, and urging that 80 per cent of its operating funds be cut off, his recommendations were greeted with acid disfavor by the members of his own party who control the House. On March 1, 1961, the day the appropriation came to a vote, HUAC's chairman, Congressman Francis E. Walter, a Democrat from Pennsylvania, spoke to the House in answer to Mr. Roosevelt: "I was staggered—and this after twenty-seven years' service in this House," he said, "by the extent to which [Mr. Roosevelt's assault] was based on fuzzy reasoning, distortions, falsehoods and what, at best, could be described as a total failure to comprehend, even remotely, the nature of Communism." When the roll was called, Mr. Roosevelt's effort was defeated by a vote of 412 to 6.

In the years 1941 to 1960, HUAC made 129 legislative recommendations to Congress. Of these, 33 were repetitions of recommendations HUAC itself had made, and 96 were separate, distinct and new. Thirty-five of these recommendations were passed by both the House and the Senate. They are today a part of the law of the land.*

When the last Congress (the 86th) adjourned at the end of 1960, eight more bills embodying recommendations made by HUAC had been passed through the House, although the Senate had not acted on them. In the present Congress (the 87th), legislation on more than 30 separate matters involving HUAC recommendations is pending.

Research also reveals that the Executive branch of the government had implemented 13 recommendations by HUAC which covered executive policy matters rather than legislation. Among these are the President's Executive Order 10450, in 1953, which established a revised security program for the federal departments and agencies; the President's Executive Order 10491, in 1953, directing that a government employee's refusal to testify before a Congressional committee regarding charges of alleged disloyalty or other misconduct be taken into consideration in determining whether such employee is a security risk; the Attorney General's Order 51-54, in 1954, establishing in the De-

---

* These statistics are corroborated by the Legislative Reference Service of the Library of Congress.

partment of Justice an Internal Security Division, headed by an Assistant Attorney General, to have charge of matters affecting the internal security of the United States, including the prosecution of cases involving subversion; the Industrial Personnel Security Review Regulation issued by the Secretary of Defense in 1955, prescribing standards for determining eligibility of contractors and contractor employees for access to classified defense information, and establishing procedures for denial or suspension of clearance; the Attorney General's ruling in 1957 strengthening the procedure for detention of aliens pending deportation; and the President's Executive Order 10865, in 1960, authorizing the Secretary of State, the Secretary of Defense, the Atomic Energy Commission, the National Aeronautics and Space Administration, and the Federal Aviation Agency to prescribe safeguards to protect classified information released to industry in connection with contracts.

Basic legislative enactments are the Smith Act of 1940, the Internal Security Act of 1950 (of which the Subversive Activities Control Act comprises Title I), various provisions of the Immigration and Nationality Act of 1952 (the Walter-McCarran Immigration Act), and the Communist Control Act of 1954[*] and the Espionage and Sabotage Act of 1954.[†]

Others—some more particularized, some more peripheral—touch widely within the variegated, mobile spectrum of national security. By subject matter, investigations and recommendations of HUAC have produced legislation on the following subjects:

> Membership in, and conspiracies to abet, foreign-directed organizations seeking to overthrow the Government of the United States by force or violence.

[*] This act states that the Communist Party, as an agent of a foreign power, "should be outlawed," and clarifies the enforcement provisions of the Internal Security Act by declaring that anyone who joins the Party with knowledge of its objectives will be subject to punishment, and by listing 14 specific activities which juries should consider in determining whether a defendant is a Party member.

[†] This act declares, in part, that anyone who acts with intent to injure the United States or, in time of war, acts with intent to aid the enemy, "shall be punished by death or by imprisonment for any term of years or for life."

Political organizations which are dominated by a foreign power.

Distribution of totalitarian propaganda emanating from foreign sources.

Withholding of veterans' benefits for study or training in educational institutions listed by the Attorney General as subversive.

Refusal of foreign countries to accept deportees.

Revocation of naturalization for fraud.

Revocation of naturalization for contempt of Congress in refusing to testify concerning subversive activities.

Cancellation of passports fraudulently obtained.

Employment of members of Communist or Communist front organizations in defense facilities or government service.

Exclusion and deportation of alien criminals and subversives.

Restriction of tax-exemption of Communist organizations and fronts posing as educational or charitable institutions.

Regulation of mailing privileges of Communist organizations.

Mandatory continuance of study of administration of immigration laws and effect on national security.

Detention of undeportable alien Communists.

Exposure of Communist organizations and fronts.

Statute of limitations in espionage cases.

Mandatory continuance of study of laws relating to espionage, sabotage, and protection of national security.

Members or former members of the Communist Party serving as labor union officials.

Penalties for espionage in peacetime as well as wartime.

Authorizing, in appropriate cases, immunity from prosecution for witnesses before Congressional committees, to facilitate obtaining of information otherwise denied by a Fifth Amendment (self-incrimination) plea.

Emergency powers of the Executive branch in matters dealing with national security.

Registration of agents of foreign principals, including agents of domestic organizations subsidized by a foreign government or political party, engaged in disseminating propaganda in the United States.

Registration of persons who have received training in espionage, counterespionage, or sabotage tactics of a foreign government.

Increase of penalties for seditious conspiracy.

A single thread runs through all this legislation. "Security against foreign danger is one of the primitive objects of civil society," James Madison wrote. "It is an avowed and essential object of the American Union. The powers requisite for attaining it must be effectually confided to the federal councils." In our generation, the elected representatives of the nation in Congress, after detailed investigation, perceived such danger. In Section 2 of the Subversive Activities Control Act they spelled it out unequivocally.

This Section is an example of legislative perspicuity which puts the Congress of the United States far ahead of other parliamentary bodies of the world in creative anti-Communist legislation. In this Section 2, the United States Congress, fortified by the findings of its investigative committees, wrote into law legislation based on critical conclusions, the first of which is:

There exists a world Communist movement which, in its origins, its development, and its present practice, is a world-wide revolutionary movement whose purpose it is, by treachery, deceit, infiltration into other groups (governmental and otherwise), espionage, sabotage, terrorism, and any other means deemed necessary, to establish a Communist totalitarian dictatorship in the countries throughout the world through the medium of a world-wide Communist organization.

The characteristics of a "totalitarian dictatorship," as set forth in subsections (2) and (3), are the existence of a single, dictatorial political party substantially identified with the government of the country in which it exists, the suppression of all opposition to the party in power, the subordination of the rights of the individual to the state, and the denial of fundamental rights and liberties characteristic of a representative form of government. Subsection (4) finds that the direction and control of the "world Communist movement" is vested in and exercised by the Communist dictatorship of a foreign country; and subsection (5), that the Communist dictatorship of this foreign country, in furthering the purposes of the world Communist movement, establishes and utilizes in various countries action organizations which are not free and independent organizations, but are controlled, directed, and subject to the discipline of the Communist dictatorship of the same foreign country. Subsection (6) sets forth that:

The Communist action organizations so established and utilized in various countries, acting under such control, direction, and discipline, endeavor to carry out the objectives of the world Communist movement by bringing about the overthrow of existing governments by any available means, including force if necessary, and setting up totalitarian dictatorships which will be subservient to the most powerful existing Communist totalitarian dictatorship. Although such organizations usually designate themselves as political parties, they are in fact constituent elements of the world-wide Communist movement and promote the objectives of such movement by conspiratorial and coercive tactics, instead of through the democratic processes of a free elective system or through the freedom-preserving means employed by a political party which operates as an agency by which people govern themselves.

In subsection (7) it is found that the Communist organizations thus described are organized on a secret, conspiratorial basis and operate to a substantial extent through Communist front organizations, in most instances created or used so as to conceal their true character and purpose, with the result that the "fronts" are able to obtain support from persons who would not extend their support if they knew the nature of the organizations with which they dealt. Congress makes other findings: that the most powerful existing Communist dictatorship has caused the establishment in numerous foreign countries of Communist totalitarian dictatorships, and threatens to establish such dictatorships in still other countries (10); that Communist agents have devised espionage and sabotage tactics successfully carried out in evasion of existing law (11); that the Communist network in the United States is inspired and controlled in large part by foreign agents who are sent in under various guises (12); that international travel is a prerequisite for the carrying on of activities in furtherance of the Communist movement's purposes (8); that Communists have infiltrated the United States by procuring naturalization for disloyal aliens (14); that under our present immigration laws, many deportable aliens of the subversive, criminal or immoral classes are free to roam the country without supervision or control (13). Subsection (9) finds that in the United States individuals who knowingly participate in the world Communist movement in effect transfer their allegiance to the foreign country in which is vested the direction and control of the world Communist movement. Finally in §2 (15), Congress concludes that:

> The Communist movement in the United States is an organiza-
> tion numbering thousands of adherents, rigidly and ruthlessly
> disciplined. *Awaiting and seeking to advance* a moment when the
> United States may be so far extended by foreign engagements, so far
> divided in counsel, or so far in industrial or financial straits, that
> overthrow of the Government of the United States by force and
> violence may seem possible of achievement, it seeks converts far and
> wide by an extensive system of schooling and indoctrination. Such
> preparations by Communist organizations in other countries have
> aided in supplanting existing governments. The Communist or-
> ganization in the United States, pursuing its stated objectives, the
> recent successes of Communist methods in other countries, and the
> nature and control of the world Communist movement itself, pre-
> sent a clear and present danger to the security of the United States
> and to the existence of free American institutions, and make it
> necessary that Congress, in order to provide for the common de-
> fense, to preserve the sovereignty of the United States as an inde-
> pendent nation, and to guarantee to each State a republican form
> of government, enact appropriate legislation recognizing the exist-
> ence of such world-wide conspiracy and designed to prevent it from
> accomplishing its purpose in the United States. [Emphasis added.]

These findings were adopted by a more than two-thirds vote in both the Senate and the House of Representatives. Eventually they came under the scrutiny of the Supreme Court. On June 5, 1961, the Court, speaking through Mr. Justice Felix Frankfurter in the case of *Communist Party of the U.S.A. v. Subversive Activities Control Board,* said of them: "It is not for the courts to re-examine the validity of these legislative findings and reject them. *They are the product of extensive investigation by Committees of Congress* over more than a decade and a half. We certainly cannot dismiss them as unfounded or irrational imaginings." (Emphasis added.) In a supporting footnote, the Court cited a long list of committee reports, chiefly by HUAC.

Mr. Justice William O. Douglas, whose judicial opinions have almost uniformly been unfavorable to the efforts of government agencies to unmask Communists, was one of the dissenters; but it is noteworthy that his dissent was on the ground that the registration requirement in the Act conflicted with the Fifth Amendment bar against self-incrimination. As to the factual underpinnings of the case, he did not dissent. Indeed, it is comforting to know that Mr. Justice Douglas, whose opinions in the past have been so often and so gleefully reprinted and quoted by the detractors of HUAC, appears to have arrived, at some unspecified time, at a conclusion that "the Communist Party of the United States is 'a disciplined organization' operating in this nation 'under Soviet Union control' to install 'a Soviet style dictatorship in the United States.' Those findings are based, I think, on facts; and I would not disturb them."

The foes of HUAC, who rake through judicial opinions in search of succor, are unlikely to cull this sentence from the writings of Mr. Justice Douglas; for, whether intended to do so or not, it largely vindicates the hard and patient work of HUAC down through the years.

Not all of the legislative enactments listed above have been fully effective in application. Many need tightening or supplementation, as is true of most statutory incursions into a broad field. The Communist is infinitely ingenious in opportunizing on freedoms he seeks to destroy. The Communists maintain a legal corps which indefatigably distends loopholes and prolongs delays. A committee of the American Bar Association set up to study this process found "a far-flung program to obstruct the administration of the courts," and to bring into disrepute, if possible, all law enforcement agencies. This legal program is the more insidious, of course, because it is carried on under a cloak of seeming conformance with the laws and customs of the land. Mao Tse-tung learned this years ago during his instruction in Moscow on the arts of subversion. "The tactic of the revolution led by the Communist Party," he wrote, "is always to take advantage of situations permitted by public laws and social customs." To the apparatus in the United States and its lawyers, this is elementary.

Nevertheless, much of the legislation is doing its work successfully, and several strengthening amendments proposed by HUAC are under consideration in Congress. In spite of deep divisions within the Supreme Court, the constitutional challenges have, on the whole, failed. The "advocacy" and "organizing" clauses of the Smith Act were held constitutional in the *Dennis* case in 1951, although subsequently, in the *Yates* case in 1957, the Court gave them a narrow interpretation which caused some convictions to be overturned and made other prosecutions more difficult. The "membership" clause has been upheld in the *Scales* case in 1961. The Communist Control Act, which declared that the Communist Party is not in fact a political party but an instrument of a conspiracy to overthrow the government, and should therefore be outlawed, has come before the Supreme Court only once, in *Communist Party v. Catherwood,* decided in 1961. It involved a tax situation to which the Court ruled the Act was not intended to apply, so there was no adjudication as to other aspects of its application.*

---

* The 1954 Communist Control Act is something of a hodgepodge, and thus far there have been no successful prosecutions under it, though one case (against the International Mine, Mill and Smelter Workers Union) is pending. The Act begins by saying that the Communist Party *ought to be* outlawed, and proceeds to deprive the Party of all its rights, privileges, and immunities as a legal body. Another provision of the Act requires Communist-infiltrated (as distinguished from Communist-dominated) organizations also to register with the Subversive Activities Control Board, set up under the Internal Security Act of 1950. The principal difficulty in applying the provision in the act (Section III) depriving the Communist Party of its legal rights, is that to do so could result in immunizing the Party from the provisions of the preceding Internal Security Act, since the Party might successfully maintain that an organization without legal rights, can have no legal obligations. Though the law has not been tested, it appears to deny to the Communist Party the right to run candidates for national office, or even to seek to influence political elections.

The Subversive Activities Control Act has been upheld as to its requirement of registration but, as has been mentioned, many questions remain unsettled. Some of the other measures entail administrative or legal problems which are still extant. These situations come within HUAC's legislative oversight function, to oversee the administration of laws with a view toward remedial legislation where necessary. This is a normal process, and an unceasing one in the interest of sound government.

Unfinished Business:
HUAC's Legislative Recommendations Pending in Congress

It will never be known how many of the Senators and Congressmen who voted for the Smith Act in 1940 were surprised, if not astounded, to read in their newspapers in 1957 that when they used the term "organize" in that statute, to condemn persons who organize groups to bring about the destruction of the government by force and violence, they meant to refer to an initial organization of the Communist Party, but not to continuing acts of organization or recruitment. In the opinion of the Court, the organization of the Communist Party took place in 1945, when the Communist Political Association was disbanded and reconstituted as the Communist Party of the United States. The indictment, in 1951, was therefore barred by the three-year statute of limitations. For that is what a majority of the Supreme Court decided in the *Yates* case, in which 14 known Communists had been convicted by a jury. The trial judge had instructed the jury that the term "organize" included such activities "as the recruiting of new members and the forming of new units, and the regrouping or expansion of existing clubs, classes, and other units. . . ." This, said the Supreme Court, was not what Congress had intended; so the prosecution was barred by the three-year statute of limitations. Seven similar cases were then reversed by obedient courts of appeal, other prosecutions abandoned, and numerous Communist conspirators walked away free.

The wheels of Congress soon began to turn, to overcome the *Yates* decision. An amendment to the Smith Act, to make it clear that the lawmakers mean exactly the kind of "organizing" the trial judge had described to the jury, was passed in the House in both the 85th and 86th Congresses; but a lethargic Senate failed to act on it, in spite of the expressed concern of the Department of Justice. In the 87th Congress, this corrective legislation is again pending, and HUAC's recommendation is buttressed by a report by the House Committee on the Judiciary, which bluntly states that the Supreme Court's ruling in the *Yates* case had a "deleterious effect upon the Government's efforts to combat the Communist conspiracy in this country."

Congress is frequently learning from the Supreme Court what were its intentions on this point or that. Steve Nelson, an acknowledged Communist, was convicted by the State of Pennsylvania under the Pennsylvania Sedition Act, in a trial which probed deep pools of treachery. The case was eventually appealed to the Supreme Court—which ruled, upholding what had theretofore appeared to be an eccentric finding of the Pennsylvania Court, that in passing the Smith Act, Congress had meant to occupy "the field of sedition" to the exclusion of the states, and that thereafter no state sedition law was enforceable. HUAC, rejecting the implicit assumption that Congress, relying on its own vigilance, had dismissed as superfluous, and hence unlawful, all of the states' precautions against acts of subversion against their own governments, thereupon recommended legislation to prohibit any act of Congress from being construed as indicating an intent on the part of Congress to exclude all state laws on the same subject matter, unless such act contains an express provision to that effect, or unless there is a direct conflict between such act and a state law so that the two cannot stand consistently together; and the proposed bill expressly provided that the federal laws covering sedition or subversion should not prevent the enforcement of similar state laws. A Democratic House passed that bill in the 86th Congress, but it received no action in the Senate. HUAC is urging this legislation in the 87th Congress.

In the last Congress, the House of Representatives also passed bills (again without getting action from the Senate) designed to:

1. Plug loopholes which have enabled the Communists to devise techniques to nullify enforcement of the Foreign Agents Registration Act. The bill required registration of domestic organizations disseminating propaganda, when directed or financed by a foreign country or foreign political party; and it established a Comptroller of Foreign Propaganda in the Bureau of Customs to maintain liaison with appropriate committees of Congress and advise them with respect to identification and labeling of Communist and other foreign propaganda. It is estimated that about fourteen million bulk packages of Communist foreign propaganda are poured into the United States in a year, as part of a subtle masquerade. This law's purpose is not to censor it, but to put the public on notice as to its source. (H.R. 12753)

2. Counter the Communist technique of avoiding or delaying registration of action or front organizations by the subterfuge of changing their names or formal, technical structure. (H.R. 8429)

3. Deny passports to Communists and, under certain circumstances, to those who have been Communists in recent years. (H.R. 9060)

4. Tighten the procedure for judicial review of deportation orders, to prevent the indefinite postponement of deportation by a multiplicity of court proceedings. (H.R. 2807)

5. Authorize the Secretary of Defense to prescribe uniform standards and criteria for eligibility for access to classified information in connection with defense contracts. (H.R. 8121)

These measures have been reintroduced. The last has been broadened to repose the authority in the President and extend it to all government agencies concerned with national security. The bill on passports has been reworded to preclude the issuance of passports to persons who wish to travel abroad to engage in activities to further the aims of the Communist movement, or in activities which would violate the laws of the United States or be prejudicial to the orderly conduct of foreign relations. Communist agents going abroad as couriers and to receive firsthand instructions from foreign masters in the movement are now creating a visible problem. HUAC is emphasizing that the lack of adequate legislative authority to deny passports to such persons is "a glaring weakness in our national security program."

In addition, other pieces of legislation growing out of investigations and hearings by HUAC, but not previously voted upon by either House, are pending in the present Congress. They were drafted to accomplish these purposes:

1. Make it a misdemeanor for any person to misbehave before Congress or Congressional committees so as to obstruct these bodies in the performance of their duties. This could provide a penalty for such conduct as occurred in San Francisco in May 1960.

2. Prohibit Communist lawyers from practicing before executive departments or Congressional committees. Experience has shown that these lawyers do not observe the indispensable canons of ethics, and connive at disruption and disorder.

3. Define the terms "advocate," "teach," "duty," "necessity," "force," and "violence," as used in the Smith Act, in a manner which will prevent judicial interpretations at variance with the intent of Congress.

4. Protect the security of confidential government files by reasonable rules governing their forced disclosure in court proceedings. This is to thwart Communist attempts, for example, to obtain names of FBI informants and other information, the disclosure of which can be ruinous to the work of the government's intelligence agencies in detecting crime and subversion, when the disclosure is unnecessary in the case at hand and would jeopardize the national security. The bill would improve a similar measure passed hurriedly in 1957 to overcome the Supreme Court decision in the *Jencks* case, in

which the Communists' legal corps had snatched up a new tool with which to obstruct the government's antisubversion machinery.

5. Permit, when authorized by the Attorney General and under safeguards to prevent abuse, the interception and restricted disclosure of wire and radio communications by the FBI and the security investigative agencies of the Army, Navy, and Air Force, in the detection of offenses against the security of the United States.

6. Prohibit unauthorized disclosure of "top secret," "atomic top secret," "secret," or "atomic secret" information (affecting national defense in such degrees that disclosure could result in serious damage to the nation), by any person who has obtained it. This bill would reach situations not covered by espionage statutes but which can involve disastrous consequences.

7. Make it an offense to use a false name or display a false social security card to obtain employment in defense facilities.

8. Extend from 10 to 15 years the statute of limitations for treason, espionage, sabotage, sedition and subversion.

9. Prohibit persons who refuse to answer under oath questions relating to Communist or other subversive activities from being employed on merchant vessels of the United States or within waterfront facilities such as piers, docks, etc.

10. Authorize the President to institute measures to bar from defense facilities persons as to whom there is reasonable ground to believe they may engage in sabotage, espionage, or other subversive acts. Notice of charges and opportunity to defend are provided for. This would plug some present loopholes. The bill is prompted by the vital importance of the industrial plant in modern warfare and the urgency of preventive vigilance.

11. Require the removal of any federal officer or employee who refuses to answer under oath questions as to Communist membership or activities.

12. Prohibit a representative of a labor union from insti-

gating or following a course of action, the effect of which is to impede, obstruct, or interfere with the free movement of defense materials in foreign commerce during war or a national emergency. (The presence of Harry Bridges as a commanding figure on the waterfronts of the Pacific Coast and Hawaii may not be without relevance to this measure.)

13. Prescribe eligibility for legal practice before administrative agencies.

14. Permit the head of a government department or agency, in his discretion when deemed necessary in the interest of national security, to suspend without pay any civilian officer or employee. Provision is made for subsequent hearing, and for termination of employment when it is determined advisable in the interest of national security. Review by the Civil Service Commission is provided for.

15. Prohibit the licensing of persons as station operators of communication facilities who refuse to answer under oath questions as to Communist membership or activities.

16. Require persons who register under the Federal Regulation of Lobbying Act to divulge Communist Party membership and to state whether they are employed by an organization which has been determined under existing law to be a Communist front or other subversive group.

17. Require a prospective federal grand or petit juror to affirm that he does not advocate, nor is a member of an organization which advocates, destruction of the government by force or violence; and provide penalties for making false statements in qualifying to serve as a juror.

18. Extend the espionage laws to acts committed against the United States anywhere in the world. At present they apply only in the United States, within the admiralty and maritime jurisdiction of the United States, and on the high seas. Yet American military and civilian personnel are distributed widely about the globe; and espionage knows no geographical boundaries.

19. Provide that statements or confessions shall not be inadmissible solely because of delay in the arraignment of an

arrested person, although the delay shall be considered as an element in determining whether the statement or confession was voluntary.

20. Permit immigration officers to be detailed to foreign countries to perform certain functions in issuance of visas.

21. Tighten the immigration laws to prohibit the issuance of visas to persons of a foreign state which refuses to accept deportees.

22. Permit the detention and supervision of certain aliens under order of deportation.

23. Require the Attorney General to report annually to Congress waivers in the administration of the immigration laws.

24. Eliminate from inclusion in the "Central Index of Aliens" the names of aliens who have entered under a provision of law permitting their entry without visas or other travel documents.

25. Cancel naturalization procured by concealment or willful misrepresentation; and provide that refusal to testify concerning subversive activities within ten years after naturalization, resulting in conviction for contempt, shall be ground for revoking naturalization.

26. Provide for forfeiture of American citizenship by a person who accepts or performs the duties of any office, post or employment under a foreign state which is Communist-dominated or Communist-occupied, without the specific consent of the Government of the United States.*

HUAC has recommended this varied legislation in its report to Congress at the end of 1960 and in an omnibus bill introduced in the present Congress by Chairman Walter, a Democrat, and Congressman Scherer, the ranking Republican member. Addressing the House on March 1, 1961, Mr. Scherer said:

"The Committee on Un-American Activities is asking this

---

* Currently being considered by HUAC is a bill (passed by the Senate in the spring of 1960 without opposition) calling for the establishment of a so-called Freedom Academy to train students in the critical science of political warfare.

House to pass this omnibus bill. As an example, among other things, it will enable us to deal effectively with Communist security risks, potential espionage agents, and saboteurs in defense plants, on our waterfront facilities, in our merchant marine, and in our communication system."

In addition, some of the specific items have been introduced as single bills, and under the Rules of the House have been referred to other committees for processing. Thus, the Committee on the Judiciary has specific jurisdiction over amendments to the Judicial Code, so that any bill dealing with that subject alone is, as a matter of course, referred to it; similarly, the Committees on Education and Labor, Interstate and Foreign Commerce, Merchant Marine and Fisheries, and Post Office and Civil Service at times are called to process bills urged by HUAC. This does not render superfluous the activities of HUAC. For each of these committees to set up subcommittees with staffs of trained experts to investigate the specialized subject of Communist penetration would be inefficient and costly. All committees draw on the work and experience of HUAC and its staff when touching upon problems that relate to subversion. By the same token, individual Congressmen rely heavily on HUAC. The Committee receives each year an average of two thousand requests for information from members of Congress. HUAC has no author's pride. Its concern is with the ultimate enactment of its recommendations into law, not with the formal question of which committee formally sponsors a bill.

The Americans for Democratic Action recently resolved:

We urge that Congressional investigations be limited to obtaining information leading toward legislative action. We urge that the Un-American Activities Committee of the House of Representatives be discontinued.*

The confusions embodied in this resolution are characteristic of the wider confusions in many quarters about the work of HUAC. ADA is not here saying that HUAC's investigations do

* Incorporated in a statement of Americans for Democratic Action, annual convention, May 19, 1960.

not lead to legislative action—that would be too blatant a historical misrepresentation. Yet the juxtaposition of the two sentences can only induce such a conclusion in the unwary reader.

In fact, HUAC's critics expend much energy in suggesting that the Committee's investigations do not lead to legislation, and as much energy again agitating and lobbying to defeat every piece of legislation HUAC proposes. It is for the individual citizen to decide for himself whether to endorse, or oppose, any given legislative proposal of the House Committee on Un-American Activities. It is to go a drastic step further to suggest that a committee which makes such proposals, for the elected representatives of the people to accept or reject according to their lights, should not even exist.

GEORGE N. CROCKER

Chapter 10.

A RECORD OF THE
COMMITTEE'S WORK

DURING *the years 1945–1960, the Committee issued more than 475 publications, including verbatim transcripts of public hearings, selected executive hearings, reports resulting from its hearings and investigations, consultations with experts on Communist subversion, and compilations of legislative recommendations. The present chapter lists the publications of the Committee, and a brief description of the subject, or subjects, deemed by the editor to be of salient interest. Some of the publications are listed out of chronological order. This usually occurs with respect to executive hearings, which are held up until the full Committee votes to release them. The supply of those publications issued before 1959 is virtually exhausted, but the entire list can be consulted at the Committee's offices, or at larger libraries.*

1945—79th Congress, First Session

HEARINGS

Investigation of Un-American Propaganda Activities in the United States (Office of Price Administration), June 20, 21, 27, 1945; 88 pp., with exhibits.—Includes statements by Chester Bowles, D. B. Stetler, Zenas L. Potter, Damier R. Woolley, George V. McDavitt. Topic: infiltration of the OPA and the Office of War Information, primarily involving a radio script writer, Tex Weiner.

Investigation of Un-American Propaganda Activities in the United States (Communist Party), September 26, 27; October 17–19, 1945. 175 pp.—

Includes testimony by Earl Browder, Jacob Stachel, William Z. Foster. Topic: current Communist Party policy. Also includes Foster's "Syndicalism," a pamphlet detailing the premises on which the CPUS was to conduct its future activities.

1946—79th Congress, Second Session

HEARINGS

Investigation of Un-American Propaganda Activities in the United States (Gerald L. K. Smith), January 30, 1946; 60 pp., with exhibits.—Topic: the America First Party, the magazine *The Cross and the Flag,* Gerald L. K. Smith, the magazine's editor, and the activities of the America First's leadership.

Investigation of Un-American Propaganda Activities in the United States (Executive Board, Joint Anti-Fascist Refugee Committee), April 4, 1946; 105 pp.—Includes testimony by the 17 members of the organization's executive board (all the latter were cited for contempt when they refused to turn over to the Committee the organization's records).

Investigation of Un-American Propaganda Activities in the United States (Louis F. Budenz), November 22, 1946; 75 pp., with exhibits.—Includes testimony by Louis F. Budenz, former editor of the *Daily Worker,* concerning his experiences in the CPUS, his associates (whom he identified), and his ultimate disillusionment.

REPORTS

House Report No. 1829—Proceedings Against Dr. Edward K. Barsky and Others, March 28, 1946; 4 pp.—Includes the Committee's citation of Barsky, Chairman of the Joint Anti-Fascist Refugee Committee, for contempt (refusal, on First Amendment grounds, to produce the organization's records). (Conviction affirmed, 167 F. 2d 241 (1948).)

House Report No. 1936—Proceedings Against the Joint Anti-Fascist Refugee Committee, April 16, 1946; 3 pp.—A series of citations for contempt (refusal to produce the records requested, failure to answer questions on First Amendment grounds). (All 17 persons * were convicted, and convictions upheld.)

House Report No. 1996—Sources of Financial Aid for Subversive and Un-American Propaganda, May 10, 1946; 5 pp.—Inquiry into the money-raising techniques of the Joint Anti-Fascist Refugee Committee, the Na-

---

* Helen R. Bryan (183 F. 2nd 996 (1949)), Ernestine G. Fleischman (*ibid.*), Jacob Auslander (167 F. 2d (1948)), Lyman R. Bradley (*ibid.*), Marjorie Chodorov (*ibid.*), Howard Fast (*ibid.*), Harry M. Justiz (*ibid.*), Mrs. Samuel Kamsley (*ibid.*), Ruth Leider (*ibid.*), James Lustig (*ibid.*), Manuel Magana (*ibid.*), Louis Miller (*ibid.*), Charlotte Stern (*ibid.*), Leverett Gleason (not reported), Herman Shumlin (not reported), Jesse Tolmach (not reported), Mrs. Bobbie Weinstein (not reported).

tional Council of American-Soviet Friendship, Inc., Friends of Democracy, Inc., *The Protestant*, the Society for the Prevention of World War III, and similar organizations (all enjoyed tax-exempt status).

Investigation of Un-American Propaganda Activities in the United States —Citations by Official Federal Government or State or Municipal Agencies or Reliable Private Organizations Regarding the Character of Organizations Named, May 29, 1946; 42 pp.—The Committee's first venture into the area later occupied by the Guide to Subversive Organizations and Publications of May 14, 1951, revised January 2, 1957. The purpose: to provide an authoritative list of all organizations that had been cited as subversive by the Attorney General, and all organizations and publications so cited by the Committee, and other official committees, federal, state, and local.

House Report No. 2233—Annual Report of the House Committee on Un-American Activities, June 7, 1946; 73 pp., with exhibits.—Reviews the Committee's activities from its establishment as a permanent committee (1945) to date, and embodies the conclusions arrived at by the Committee on the basis of its hearings and investigations.

House Report No. 2354—Proceedings Against Corliss G. Lamont, June 12, 1946; 4 pp.—The citation of Lamont for contempt (refusal, in his capacity as Chairman of the National Council of American-Soviet Friendship, Inc., to produce the organization's records). (No action by Grand Jury.)

House Report No. 2707—Proceedings Against George Marshall, July 31, 1946; 4 pp.—The citation of Marshall, Chairman of the National Federation for Constitutional Liberties, for contempt (refusal, on First Amendment grounds, to produce the organization's records). (Convicted, affirmed, 176 F. 2d 473 (1949).)

House Report No. 2708—Proceedings Against Richard Morford, July 31, 1946; 4 pp.—The citation of Morford, Director of the National Council of American-Soviet Friendship, Inc., for contempt (noncompliance, on First Amendment grounds, with the Committee's request for the organization's records). (Convicted, affirmed, 184 F. 2d 864 (1950).)

House Report No. 2742—Annual Report of the House Committee on Un-American Activities, January 2, 1947; 18 pp.—Reviews the Committee's activities during the six months following its latest previous report, and includes a report by J. Edgar Hoover, testimony by William Z. Foster, a critique of the CPUS and the Communist International, a summary of reports and hearings during 1946, and recommendations for legislation.

1947—80th Congress, First Session

HEARINGS

Hearings on Gerhart Eisler: Investigation of Un-American Propaganda Activities in the United States, February 6, 1947; 83 pp., with appendix and exhibits.—Includes testimony establishing that Eisler was "an important international Communist and responsible representative for the Communist International," sufficiently powerful to discipline William Z. Foster, Chairman of the CPUS. ,

Hearings Regarding Communism in Labor Unions in the United States, February 27; July 23–25, 1947; 231 pp., with appendix.—An inquiry into Communist goals with respect to organized labor. (The hearings resulted in expulsion proceedings against individual unions in several labor union federations.)

Investigation of Un-American Propaganda Activities in the United States (Regarding Leon Josephson and Samuel Liptzen), March 5, 21, 1947; 86 pp.—Includes evidence showing that Josephson, who refused to be sworn, had become a member-at-large of the Communist Party in 1926, and Liptzen's admission that he himself was a Communist at the time of the hearing.

Investigation of Un-American Propaganda Activities in the United States —Hearings on H.R. 1884 and H.R. 2122, bills to curb or outlaw the Communist Party of the United States, March 24–28, 1947; 340 pp.—Includes testimony on Communist subversion by leaders of various groups and organizations, among others William Green, President of the American Federation of Labor, Mrs. Julius Y. Talmadge, President General of the Daughters of the American Revolution, and Eugene Dennis, General Secretary of the Communist Party.

Investigation of Un-American Propaganda Activities in the United States —Hearings on H.R. 1884 and H.R. 2122, bills to curb or outlaw the Communist Party of the United States—Part I, Testimony of Hon. William C. Bullitt, March 24, 1947; 31 pp.—Includes testimony by Bullitt, who had been the first ambassador of the U. S. to the Soviet Union; on Russia, international Communism, and U. S. foreign policy.

Investigation of Un-American Propaganda Activities in the United States —Hearings on H.R. 1884 and H.R. 2122, bills to curb or outlaw the Communist Party of the United States—Part II, Testimony of J. Edgar Hoover, March 26, 1947; 17 pp.—Includes testimony by Hoover, Director of the Federal Bureau of Investigation, concerning the nature of Soviet espionage throughout the world, Communist activities in the United States, and the role of the FBI in combating Communist infiltration.

Investigation of Un-American Propaganda Activities in the United States (Regarding Eugene Dennis), April 9, 1947; 15 pp.—Includes testimony concerning the Communist activities of Eugene Dennis, who refused to appear. (Dennis was subsequently cited for contempt for non-appearance.)

Testimony of Walter S. Steele Regarding Communist Activities in the United States—Hearings on H.R. 1884 and H.R. 2122, bills to curb or outlaw the Communist Party in the United States, July 21, 1947; 176 pp., with appendix.—Includes testimony by Steele, Chairman of the National Security Committee of the American Coalition of Patriotic, Civic, and

Fraternal Societies, listing persons, publications, and organizations he and his associates regarded as subversive, and detailing relevant subversive activities.

Testimony of Victor A. Kravchenko—Hearings on H.R. 1884 and H.R. 2122, bills to curb or outlaw the Communist Party of the United States, July 22, 1947; 30 pp.—Testimony by Kravchenko, a former high-ranking Soviet official, concerning his activities in the CPUSSR, and the scope of international Communist operations. (Kravchenko presented a summary of his best-selling book, *I Chose Freedom.*)

Hearings Regarding Hanns Eisler, September 24–26, 1947; 209 pp., with appendix.—Includes testimony showing that Eisler (Gerhart Eisler's brother), a musician highly regarded by the Communists and author of numerous Party songs, had been admitted to the United States in violation of U. S. immigration laws, and with the assistance of "certain individuals in the highest circles of the Government."

Hearings Regarding Communist Infiltration of the Motion-Picture Industry, October 20–24, 27–30, 1947; 549 pp., with appendix.—Includes testimony by Adolphe Menjou, Robert Taylor, Walt Disney, Gary Cooper, Ronald Reagan, Robert Montgomery, and others concerning patterns of infiltration of the motion-picture industry. (These hearings led to the conviction of the screenwriters who came to be known as the "Hollywood Ten.")

REPORTS

House Report No. 209—The Communist Party of the United States as an Agent of a Foreign Power, April 1, 1947; 56 pp.—Includes a brief history of the CPUS and the Communist International, based upon typical Party documents and directives; lists American agents of Moscow; contains evidence showing that the CPUS and the Communist International follow parallel policies.

House Report No. 271—American Youth for Democracy, April 17, 1947; 20 pp.—An account of the organization's origin, the history, and record of Communist loyalties, with special attention to the organization's leaders, their activities, and their methods of establishing contact and co-operative relations with unsuspecting organizations of an innocent character.

House Report No. 592—Southern Conference for Human Welfare, June 16, 1947; 17 pp.—Includes evidence of Communist manipulation of the organization, lists the latter's officers, and points up the close parallel between its foreign policy proposals and those of Eugene Dennis.

House Report No. 1115—The Civil Rights Congress as a Front Organization, September 2, 1947; 47 pp., with appendix.—An account of the origin, the influence, and the purpose of the subject organization, its interlocking relations with Communist front organizations, and its activities and key personnel, among whom were Dr. Harry F. Ward, George Marshall, Ira Latimer, and Vincent Sheean.

House Report No. 43—Proceedings Against Gerhart Eisler, February 18, 1947; 4 pp.—The citation of Eisler for contempt (refusal to be sworn). (Convicted, affirmed, 170 F. 2d 273 (1948).)

House Report No. 281—Proceedings Against Leon Josephson, April 22, 1947; 6 pp.—Includes the Committee's citation of Josephson for contempt (refusal to be sworn). (Convicted, affirmed, 165 F. 2d 82 (1947).) A second citation was dismissed on a motion by the government.

House Report No. 289—Proceedings Against Eugene Dennis, also known as Francis Waldron, April 22, 1947; 2 pp.—Includes the Committee's citation of Dennis for contempt (refusal to appear). (Convicted, affirmed, 171 F. 2d 986 (1948).)

A series of reports (House Reports Nos. 1128-1137) on contempt proceedings against the "Hollywood Ten" (refusal to answer questions on First Amendment grounds), all dated November 24, 1947. (Each of the Ten * was convicted.)

Decision of the U. S. Circuit Court of Appeals for the Second Circuit in re United States v. Leon Josephson (includes both the majority and minority opinions), December 19, 1947; 20 pp.—This decision upheld the contempt proceedings against Josephson, who was convicted.

1948—80th Congress, Second Session

HEARINGS †

Hearings on H.R. 4422 and H.R. 4581, proposed legislation to curb and control the Communist Party of the United States, February 5, 6, 9–11, 19, 20, 1948; 500 pp.—Includes hearings pursuant to those of 1947 on H.R. 1884 and H.R. 2122, with testimony by James Burnham, John Foster Dulles, Hon. Karl E. Mundt, Ferenc Nagy, Raymond Moley, Eugene Lyons, and others.

Investigation of Dr. Edward U. Condon, March 5, 9, 10, 1948; 93 pp.—Includes testimony by John L. Towne, Adrian S. Fisher, and others concerning Condon, Director of the National Bureau of Standards, whom a member of the Committee characterized as "one of the weakest links in our atomic security."

---

* Albert Maltz (not reported), Dalton Trumbo (convicted, affirmed, 176 F. 2d 39 (1949)), Samuel Ornitz (not reported), Robert Adrian Scott (not reported), John Howard Lawson (convicted, affirmed, 176 F. 2d 39 (1949)), Edward Dmytryk (not reported), Lester Cole (not reported), Alvah Bessie (not reported), Herbert Biberman (not reported), Ring Lardner, Jr. (not reported).

† The Committee issued no annual report for 1947. See annual report for 1948 for a review of 1947.

Hearings Regarding Communist Espionage in the United States Government, July 31; August 3–5, 7, 9–13, 16–18, 20, 24–27, 30; September 8, 9, 1948; 877 pp., with index.—Includes testimony by Whittaker Chambers, Alger Hiss, Elizabeth Bentley, and others, concerning the influence of J. Peters in the Communist underground and activities of Alger Hiss; also testimony by Victor Perlo, Soloman Adler, Lee Pressman, and Lauchlin Currie, concerning the extent of Communist infiltration within the Federal Government.

Hearings Regarding Communist Espionage in the United States Government—Part II, December 7–10, 14, 1948; 95 pp., with index.—Includes testimony by Isaac Don Levine, Sumner Welles, John Peurifoy, Nathan L. Levine, Marion Bachrach, and others, pursuant to Whittaker Chambers' disclosure of the so-called "pumpkin papers."

Excerpts from Hearings Regarding Investigation of Communist Activities in Connection With the Atom Bomb, September 9, 14, 16, 1948; 79 pp.—Includes testimony by Clarence Hiskey, Martin Kamen, and John Hitchcock Chapin, concerning the transmission of atomic secrets to Russia by persons affiliated with U. S. government atomic operations. Hiskey refused to testify.*

REPORTS

Report to the Full Committee of the Special Subcommittee on National Security (Report on Dr. Edward U. Condon), March 18, 1948; 7 pp.—Includes the Committee's recommendation that Condon be removed from his position as Director of the Bureau of Standards, a critical federal agency for research in physics, mathematics, chemicals, and engineering.

Decision of the U. S. Court of Appeals for the District of Columbia in re Edward Barsky et al., Appellants v. United States of America, Appellee *(majority and dissenting opinions), March 24, 1948; 23 pp.*—The decision affirming the conviction of the Board of Directors of the Joint Anti-Fascist Refugee Committee.

Report of the Subcommittee on Legislation of the Committee on Un-American Activities on Proposed Legislation to Control Subversive Communist Activities in the United States, April 10, 1948; 7 pp.—Explains the need for further legislation in view of the inadequacy of the existing statutes, and gives ten recommendations for such legislation.

House Report No. 1844—Protecting the United States Against Un-American and Subversive Activities (Report on H.R. 5852), April 30, 1948; 14 pp.—Argues that Communist activities cannot be curbed solely by existing legislation, recommends that Communist organizations be required to

---

* Here, as elsewhere in the present listing, "refused to testify" means that the witness appeared, answered at least some questions, but invoked constitutional rights under the First or Fifth Amendments when questioned about Communist activities or associations.

register and submit annual reports, and that Communists be refused passports. Further recommendations deal with tax exemptions for Communist organizations, the role of judicial review, and penalties for subversion.

Report on the Communist Party of the United States as an Advocate of Overthrow of the Government by Force and Violence, May 10, 1948; 160 pp.—Includes documents tracing the history of the Communist International, and the Lenin School in Moscow; of Communist legal machinations within the U. S.; and of the use of force and violence by various foreign Communist Parties. Several pages are devoted to each of the national Parties. Also includes definitions of terms used by Communists, and the text of the Smith Act.

100 Things You Should Know About Communism in the United States, June 18, 1948; 29 pp.—Sets forth the basic facts about Communist subversion in a series of questions and answers.

Interim Report on Hearings Regarding Communist Espionage in the United States Government, August 28, 1948; 15 pp.—Focuses attention on the major accomplishments of the Committees' hearings to date, summarizing the Silvermaster, Perlo, and Ware-Abt-Witt groups, involving U. S. government personnel.

Report on Soviet Espionage Activities in Connection with the Atom Bomb, September 28, 1948; 23 pp.—Includes accounts of the Chapin-Hiskey case, the Scientist X Case, the Kamen case, with special attention to the interlocking associations with Communists brought to light in each case.

Index II to Publications of the Special Committee on Un-American Activities (Dies Committee), and the Committee on Un-American Activities (1942–1947 inclusive)—Supplement to 1942 index, October 21, 1948; 221 pp., with key.—Lists, for the first time following the war, all Committee witnesses and all individuals mentioned in Committee testimony, with page references. Predecessor of the Cumulative Indices of 1955 and 1961.

100 Things You Should Know About Communism and Religion, November 20, 1948; 16 pp.—Sets forth further facts about Communist subversion in a series of questions and answers.

100 Things You Should Know About Communism and Education, December 7, 1948; 19 pp.—Sets forth further facts about Communist subversion in a series of questions and answers.

100 Things You Should Know About Communism and Labor, December 24, 1948; 21 pp.—Sets forth further facts about Communist subversion in a series of questions and answers.

100 Things You Should Know About Communism and Government, December 31, 1948; 18 pp.—Sets forth further facts about Communist subversion in a series of questions and answers.

Citations by Official Government Agencies of Organizations and Publications Found to be Communist or Communist Fronts, December 18, 1948;

144 pp.—A follow-up of the Committee publication of May 29, 1946, with revisions, but confined to federal agencies.

Soviet Espionage Within the United States Government (Second Report), December 31, 1948; 129 pp., with appendix and exhibits.—Supplements the Committee Report of August 28, 1948, summarizing the information supplied to the Committee by Whittaker Chambers, with special attention to how Chambers acquired it, its significance, and its bearing on the scope of the conspiracy in which Chambers and Alger Hiss participated.

Report of the Committee on Un-American Activities to the United States House of Representatives (Annual Report), December 31, 1948; 25 pp.—A synopsis of the Committee's activities and findings during 1947–1948 (no report had been issued for 1947). Reviews the hearings on labor unions, legal espionage, infiltration of the government, atomic espionage, and the J. Peters apparatus, and includes an eight-point Committee program against Communism, together with its recommendations for new legislation.

1949—81st Congress, First Session

HEARINGS

Documentary Testimony of General Izydor Modelski, Former Military Attaché of the Polish Embassy, Washington, D. C., March 31; April 1, 1949; 100 pp., with appendix, exhibits, and index.—Includes testimony by Modelski concerning current Soviet espionage, especially a spy ring operating, with assistance from the Russian embassy, from the Polish embassy as a base. Modelski named the ring's leaders.

Hearings on Soviet Espionage Activities in Connection with Jet Propulsion and Aircraft, June 6, 1949; 27 pp.—An account of attempts by the Soviet espionage agent Andrei V. Schevchenko to obtain secret information regarding aeronautical development at the Bell Aircraft Corporation and the Westinghouse Corporation during World War II.

Hearings Regarding Steve Nelson (including foreword), June 8, 1949; 25 pp., with appendix and exhibits.—An account of the activities of the Communist cell that Steve Nelson organized in the wartime atomic project at the radiation laboratory of the University of California, Berkeley. The cell included Joseph W. Weinberg, Giovanni Rossi Lomanitz, Bernadette Doyle, and others.

Hearings Regarding Toma Babin, May 27; July 6, 1949; 24 pp., with exhibits.—Further hearings regarding Soviet espionage (it transpired that Babin, attached to the Yugoslav consulate in New York, lied under oath.)

Testimony of Paul Crouch, May 6, 1949; 38 pp., with appendix and exhibits.—Includes testimony concerning Communist espionage activities, especially in the armed forces, by Crouch, who had belonged to the CPUS from 1925 until 1942.

Testimony of Philip O. Keeney and Mary Jane Keeney and Statement Regarding Their Background, May 24, 25; June 9, 1949; 61 pp., with appendix and exhibits.—Includes testimony by the Keeneys, two former U. S. government employees, who had associated with numerous persons connected with espionage rings. (Mrs. Keeney denied having belonged to the Party; Mr. Keeney objected to questions regarding his associations.)

Hearings Regarding Communist Infiltration of Radiation Laboratory and Atomic Bomb Project at the University of California, Berkeley, California—Volume I (including foreword), April 22, 26; May 25; June 10, 14, 1949; 102 pp.—Includes testimony by Steve Nelson, Joseph Weinberg, Frank and Jacquenette Oppenheimer, David Joseph Bohm, and others. (Bohm, an assistant professor at Princeton University, refused to testify regarding his alleged present Party membership, but both the Oppenheimers admitted they had belonged to the Party.)

Hearings Regarding Clarence Hiskey and Paul Crouch, May 24, 1949; 41 pp., with appendix and exhibits.—Includes testimony by both Clarence Hiskey and Paul Crouch, who named Hiskey as a member of the Communist Party. Hiskey, on the grounds of self-incrimination, refused to confirm or deny the charge.

Hearings Regarding Communist Infiltration of Minority Groups—Part I, July 13, 14, 18, 1949; 70 pp., with appendix.—Includes testimony by Jackie Robinson, Rabbi Benjamin Schultz, Manning Johnson, and others, bearing upon certain statements by singer Paul Robeson concerning the political leanings of American Negroes.

Hearings Regarding Communist Infiltration of Minority Groups—Part II (Testimony of Manning Johnson), July 14, 1949; 42 pp., with appendix and exhibits.—Includes testimony by Manning Johnson, ex-member of the National Committee of the CPUS and of its Negro Commission, concerning especially the Party's money-raising and organization techniques.

Hearings Regarding Communist Infiltration of Labor Unions—Part I (Local 601, United Electrical, Radio, and Machine Workers of America, CIO, Pittsburgh, Pa.), August 9–11, 1949; 140 pp., with appendix and exhibits.—Includes testimony by Charles Edward Copeland and Joseph Zack Kornfeder, both ex-members of the CPUS, concerning Communist influence in their union, and by several workers who stated that they had been approached about becoming Party members, naming the men who had solicited them. (The union was expelled from the CIO after the testimony in these hearings had become known.)

Hearings Regarding Communism in the District of Columbia—Part I, June 28, 29; July 6, 12, 28, 1949; 91 pp., with foreword.—Includes testimony concerning extra-governmental Communist operations in Washington, D. C., and the methods used by agents outside the government to communicate information to agents inside it. One of the operations in question was the Washington Co-operative Bookshop, which shortly thereafter ceased to exist.

Hearings Regarding Communist Infiltration of Radiation Laboratory and Atomic Bomb Project at the University of California, Berkeley, California—Volume II (Identification of Scientist X), August 26, 1949; July 1, September 10, 1948; August 14, September 14, 27, 1949; 35 pp.—Includes testimony by Ken Max Manfred and Irving David Fox, both of whom invoked the Fifth Amendment when asked questions about their party affiliations, and others. Scientist X, the hearings revealed, was Joseph Weinberg.

Hearings Regarding Communist Infiltration of Labor Unions—Part II (Security Measures Relating to Officials of the UERMWA-CIO), December 5, 6, 1949; 42 pp.—Testimony by Julius Emspak, General Secretary of the United Electrical, Radio, and Machine Workers of America, James J. Matles, and others. Both Emspak and Matles refused to testify as to whether they were Communist Party members.

Testimony of James Sterling Murray and Edward Tiers Manning (Regarding Clarence Hiskey and Arthur Adams), August 14; October 5, 1949; 22 pp.—Includes mostly testimony by Manning concerning Communist activities on the part of Hiskey and Adams, and concerning John Chapin's affiliations.

REPORTS

Spotlight on Spies, March 23, 1949; 17 pp.—An account of how the Soviet espionage system operates in the U. S., set forth in a series of questions and answers, with special attention to the kind of information spies try to obtain, and to how successful they have been in the past. Other topics covered: how agents are recruited and trained, the functions of couriers, and the use of microfilm.

House Report No. 1954—Review of the Scientific and Cultural Conference for World Peace, Arranged by the National Council of the Arts, Sciences, and Professions, held in New York City, March 25-27, 1949; 61 pp.—Sets forth information concerning the World ("Waldorf") Peace Conference, its sponsors, and its financial supporters. Includes also lists of board members of Communist publications, Communist organizations, and Communist fronts.

House Report No. 1951—Report on the American Slav Congress and Associated Organizations, June 26, 1949; 151 pp., with appendix, exhibits, and index.—An historical account of the American Slav Congress, its activities, its leaders' Communist affiliations, its supporting organizations and publications, its collaboration with the embassies of various Communist governments, and its affiliation with the All-Slav Congress in Moscow.

House Report No. 1952—Report on Atomic Espionage (Nelson-Weinberg and Hiskey-Adams Cases), September 29, 1949; 15 pp.—Reviews the cases, and recommends perjury proceedings against Weinberg.

House Report No. 1953—Report on the Congress of American Women, October 23, 1949; 114 pp., with appendix and exhibits.—Traces affiliations between the Congress of American Women and International Democratic Federation, and its history of subordination to Soviet control from its beginnings, including its activities in connection with the Soviet "peace" campaign. Among the Congress's leaders were: Susan B. Anthony II, Elizabeth Gurley Flynn, Muriel Draper, Gene Weltfish, and Anna Pauker.

House Report No. 1950—Annual Report for the Year 1949, March 15, 1950; 75 pp., with appendices.—An account of the year's hearings and investigations, together with the Committee's findings and nine recommendations for future legislation. Also lists the statutes of several states with respect to subversive groups.

1950—81st Congress, Second Session

HEARINGS

Hearings Regarding Communist Espionage, November 8, December 2, 1949; February 27, March 1, 1950; 70 pp.—Includes testimony by Max Bedacht, who had belonged to the CPUS from its earliest days, concerning his experiences as a party member (he named numerous associates), and by Dr. William Gregory Burtan (he and Nicholas Dozenberg had been involved in counterfeiting operations in the 1930's), John Loomis Sherman, and Maxim Lieber.

Hearings Regarding Shipment of Atomic Material to the Soviet Union During World War II, December 5, 7, 1949; January 23–26; March 2, 3, 7, 1950; 293 pp.—Includes testimony by George Racey Jordan, Henry A. Wallace, Victor Kravchenko, and others, warranting the conclusion that the Soviets had shipped from the United States (from Great Falls, Montana), not only secret documents, but also large quantities of uranium nitrate, uranium oxide, and diagrams of projected American ships and weapons.

Exposé of the Communist Party of Western Pennsylvania, Based on the Testimony of Matthew Cvetic (Undercover Agent), February 21–23; March 13, 14, 24, 1950; 157 pp.—Includes testimony by Cvetic concerning the Communist Party's influence in the Progressive Party, naming numerous persons, many of them employees of industrial plants in Pittsburgh, whom he had known within the Party.

Hearings Regarding Communist Activities in the Territory of Hawaii—Part I, April 10–12, 1950; 182 pp.—Includes testimony concerning the Communist Party of Hawaii, its status as a subdivision of District 13 of the CPUS, its nominal chairmanship by Charles K. Fujimoto, and its actual day-to-day leadership by Jack Hall, Regional Director of the ILWU—an appointee of Harry Bridges.

Hearings Regarding Communist Activities in the Territory of Hawaii—Part II, April 13–15, 1950; 158 pp.—Includes testimony by numerous witnesses who had joined the Communist Party hoping to serve the cause of organized labor, and had subsequently become disillusioned. The Communists currently active in the islands, the testimony shows, had for the most part come from the mainland.

Hearings Regarding Communism in the United States Government— Part I, April 20, 21, 29; May 4–6, 1950; July 30, August 7, 1948; June 8, 1950; 241 pp.—Includes testimony by Merwin and Elizabeth Todd, Kenneth McConnell, Soloman Adler, William W. Remington, William and Margaret Hinckley, Elizabeth T. Bentley, and others. Miss Bentley alleged that Remington was a Communist; he subsequently resigned his job as economist in the Commerce Department and was tried for perjury, and was convicted.

Hearings Regarding Communist Activities in the Territory of Hawaii— Part III, April 17–19, 1950; 171 pp., with appendix, exhibits and an index to all three parts.—Includes testimony concerning Communist infiltration of the local precinct organizations of the Democratic Party of Hawaii, and the formation of the Territorial CIO Political Action Committee with a view to endorsing, and so giving added strength to, candidates who were rank-and-file members of the ILWU.

Hearings on Legislation to Outlaw Certain Un-American and Subversive Activities, March 21–23, 28, 1950; 253 pp.—Includes testimony by the leaders of certain national organizations, among them Benjamin C. Sigal of Americans for Democratic Action, Arthur Garfield Hays of the American Civil Liberties Union, Thomas I. Emerson of the Progressive Party, Harry C. Lamberton of the National Lawyers Guild, Norman Thomas of the Socialist Party, Clarence Mitchell of the National Association for the Advancement of Colored People, and Omar B. Ketchum of Veterans of Foreign Wars.

Exposé of the Communist Party of Western Pennsylvania—Part II, Based on the Testimony of Matthew Cvetic (Undercover Agent), March 24, 25, 1950; 277 pp., with appendix, exhibits, and index to both parts.—Includes testimony by Cvetic concerning CPUS precautions against antisubversive activity, which included destruction of all lists, records, and Party membership cards, and also concerning the Party's ability to exercise influence out of all proportion to its numbers.

Testimony of Philip A. Bart (General Manager of Freedom of the Press, publishers of the Daily Worker, *official organ of the Communist Party) and Marcel Scherer (Co-ordinator, New York Labor Conference for Peace, and formerly District Representative of District 4, United Electrical, Radio, and Machine Workers of America, CIO), June 26, 1950; 21 pp.*—Both Bart and Scherer invoked the Fifth Amendment when questioned about their Communist activities. The questions put to Scherer mostly concerned his efforts to organize workers.

Hearings Regarding Communist Activities in the Cincinnati, Ohio, Area —Part I, July 12–15; August 8, 1950; 172 pp., with index.—Includes testimony of John and Martha Edmiston, both undercover members of the Communist Party of the State of Ohio, outlining the activities of the Party among workers. Also testimony by Victor Decavitch, former District President of the UE and a former Communist.

Hearings Regarding Communist Infiltration of Minority Groups—Part III (Testimony of "Josh White"), September 1, 1950; 6 pp.—Includes testimony by White (who requested to testify) concerning how he had been duped into performing for Communist fronts. White went on to say that the grievances the Communists exploit for their partisan purposes are genuine grievances all the same.

Hearings Regarding Communism in the United States Government— Part II, August 28, 31; September 1, 15, 1950; 163 pp., with appendix and index.—Includes the record of appearances by Lee Pressman, Abraham George Silverman, Nathan Witt, Charles Kramer, John J. Abt, and Max Lowenthal, all former U. S. government employees. Each refused either to affirm or deny Communist Party membership.

Exposé of the Communist Party of Western Pennsylvania—Part III, Based upon the Testimony of Matthew Cvetic and Documents of the Communist Party of Pennsylvania, June 22; September 28; October 13, 21, 1950; 160 pp., with exhibits.—Includes the final testimony concerning the operations and the effectiveness of the Party in the area in question, and concerning the accomplishments there of Communist front organizations, especially the Civil Rights Congress, whose main purpose was to defend the "Communist Party leadership."

Hearings Regarding Communism in the District of Columbia—Part II, December 6, 11–13, 1950; 128 pp.—Includes testimony by eleven witnesses, of whom six admitted they were former members of the Communist Party, and five refused to answer questions on grounds of self-incrimination. Witness Henry Thomas named more than 30 persons whom he knew to be Party members, and witness Thomas G. Sampler, 27.

Testimony of Edward G. Robinson, October 27; December 21, 1950; 45 pp., with foreword.—Includes a statement by Robinson in which he refuted charges against him that had appeared in a book entitled *Red Channels,* and includes lists of his contributions to various organizations. Robinson denied he had belonged to the Communist Party.

American Aspects of the Assassination of Leon Trotsky, July 26; August 30; October 18, 19; December 4, 1950; 71 pp., with foreword.—Includes testimony concerning the plans and events that led up to the assassination, and the unsuccessful attempt to obtain the assassin's release from a Mexican prison. Includes also a statement by Louis Budenz, in which he charged that the CPUS was implicated in the affair, and which led to the summoning of further witnesses.

Hearings Regarding Communist Infiltration of Radiation Laboratory and Atomic Bomb Project at the University of California, Berkeley, California—Volume III, December 20-22, 1950; 95 pp.—Includes testimony by Dr. David Hawkins, Dr. Kenneth Ownsworth May, Alexander Plaisted Saxton, and Mary Bernadette Doyle. Hawkins and May, both former members of the Communist Party, listed their associates, the other two refused to answer the questions put to them concerning alleged Communist activities.

Hearings Regarding Communist Infiltration of Labor Unions—Part III, August 29, 30, 1950; 25 pp.—Includes the record of appearances by Alex Leith, a free-lance writer who had been employed by the UE to write radio sketches in connection with a strike, and Henry W. Fiering, who had been a United Electrical Workers organizer. Both refused to testify.

Testimony of Hazel Scott Powell, September 22, 1950; 15 pp.—Includes testimony by Hazel Scott (Mrs. Adam Clayton) Powell, and a statement by her denying accusations against her in *Red Channels*.

REPORTS

House Report No. 2986—Report on Hawaii Civil Liberties Committee, a Communist Front, June 23, 1950; 55 pp., with appendix and exhibits.—An account of the formation of the Hawaii Civil Liberties Committee, in 1947, on behalf of Dr. John Reinecke and his wife Aiko, both of whom had been discharged from teaching jobs, and of HCLC's effectiveness as a sounding board for Hawaiian Communists.

Index III to Publications of the Committee on Un-American Activities, June 28, 1950; 108 pp., with key—A revised edition of Index II, October 21, 1948.

The Communist "Peace Petition" Campaign (Interim Statement), July 13, 1950; 3 pp.—Analyzes the CPUS "peace petition," and the drive on its behalf in the United States.

A series of reports (House Report Nos. 2847–2849) on citations for contempt (refusal to answer questions on Fifth Amendment grounds), all dated August 10, 1950. (Conviction reversed in all three cases). *

A series of reports (House Reports Nos. 2855–2858) on citations for contempt (refusal to answer questions on Fifth Amendment grounds), all dated August 11, 1950.†

A series of Reports (House Reports Nos. 2859–2897) on Committee citations for contempt (refusal to answer questions on Fifth Amendment

---

* Julius Emspak (349 U.S. 190 (1955)), Steve Nelson (103 F. 2d 215 (1952)), Philip Bart (349 U.S. 219 (1955)).

† James J. Matles acquitted (not reported), Thomas J. Fitzpatrick acquitted (96 F. Supp. 491 (1951)), Thomas Quinn convicted, reversed (394 U.S. 155 (1955)), Frank Panzino acquitted (not reported).

grounds at the Honolulu hearings, *April, 1950*), all dated *August 11, 1950*. (*All the persons cited* were acquitted.*)

A series of Reports (House Reports Nos. 2898–2907) on Committee citations for contempt (refusal to answer questions on Fifth Amendment grounds), all dated August 11, 1950. (All of the persons cited † were acquitted.)

House Report No. 2980—Protection of the United States Against Un-American and Subversive Activities, Report to Accompany H.R. 9490, Internal Security Act of 1950, August 22, 1950; 13 pp.—Sets forth the essence of the Internal Security Act, with 14 points regarding the control of Communist activities within the U. S.

House Report No. 3123—Report on the National Lawyers Guild, Legal Bulwark of the Communist Party, September 17, 1950; 50 pp., with appendix.—Sets forth the basic facts about the National Lawyers Guild, its history, activities, and leaders. The appendix collates statements of the Guild with those of the Communist Party.

Conference Report No. 3112—Internal Security Act of 1950, September 19, 1950; 68 pp.—Includes the text of the Internal Security Act of 1950, some of whose provisions are: (1) All members of Communist-action and Communist front organizations are required to register; (2) knowing participation in a conspiracy to establish a totalitarian dictatorship is unlawful in the U. S.; (3) a Subversive Activities Control Board shall be established, and shall have the power to determine what persons or organizations are subject to the other provisions of the Internal Security Act. The Act was upheld by the Supreme Court, June 5, 1961.

Report on the Honolulu Record, October 1, 1950; 38 pp., with appendix and exhibits.—Establishes that beginning with its first issue, in August, 1948, the *Record* had continuously adhered to the Communist Party line, and that the *Record* is a Communist front.

House Report No. 3248—The National Committee to Defeat the Mundt Bill, a Communist Lobby, December 7, 1950; 15 pp.—Proves that the committee was a propaganda adjunct of the Communist Party.

* Ralph Tokunaga, Charles Fujimoto, Dwight James Freeman, Esther Bristow, Rachel Saiki, John Reinecke, Ernest Arena, Koichi Imori, Denichi Kimoto, Pearl Freeman, Marshall McEuen, Ruth Ozaki, Stephen Murin, Jack Hall, Frank Silva, Jack Kawano, John Akana, Yukio Abe, Yasuki Arakaki, Edward Hong, Kameo Ichimura, Douglas Inouye, Levi Kealoha, Adele Kensinger, Benjamin Kaahawinui, Frank Kalua, Yoshita Marumo, Robert Murasaki, Robert McElrath, Julian Napunoa, Tadashi Ogawa (also known as Castner Ogawa), Hideo Okada, Wilfred Oka, Jeanette Nakama Rohrbough, Mitsuo Shimizu, Frank Takahashi, Shigeo Takemoto, Ralph Vossbrink, Thomas Yagi.

† Giovanni Rossi Lomanitz, David Joseph Bohm, Irving David Fox, Clarence Hiskey, Frank Hashmall, Talmadge Raley, Esther Tice, Marcel Scherer, Mrs. Louise Berman, Pasquale Leonard James Branca.

100 Things You Should Know About Communism Series: —in the U.S.A.; —and Religion; —and Education; —and Labor; —and Government; and Spotlight on Spies, December 1, 1950; 126 pp.—Reprints, with revisions, of the 1948 and 1949 publications.

House Report No. 3249—Annual Report for the Year 1950, January 2, 1951; 43 pp.—An account of the Committee's work during the year, including each of its contempt citations, each of its hearings and investigations, and each of its legislative recommendations, together with a survey of its major accomplishments during the preceding three years, and a description of Committee's files.

1951—82nd Congress, First Session

HEARINGS

Hearings Regarding Communist Activities in the Territory of Hawaii— Part IV (Testimony of Jack Kawano), July 6, 1951; 53 pp.—Includes testimony by Kawano, who as a result of the Honolulu hearings had been indicted in 1950 (along with 38 others), and had subsequently renounced his membership of 12 years' standing in the Communist Party.

Communist Infiltration of the Hollywood Motion-Picture Industry— Part I, March 8, 21; April 10–13, 1951; 247 pp.—Includes testimony by the former Communist Richard Collins, and others, showing that four Communist front organizations, all operating in California, had received approximately $1,000,000 from persons connected with the motion-picture industry.

Communist Infiltration of the Hollywood Motion-Picture Industry— Part II, April 17, 23–25; May 16–18, 1951; 229 pp.—Includes testimony by former Communist Edward Dmytryk and others, many of whom minimized the Communists' influence in the motion-picture industry.

Communist Infiltration of the Hollywood Motion-Picture Industry—Part III, May 22–25; June 25, 26, 1951; 205 pp.—Includes testimony by Budd Schulberg, José Ferrer, Robert Rossen, J. Edward Bromberg, and Frank Wright Tuttle. Topic: Communist methods of inducing writers to follow the party line.

Hearings Relating to Communist Activities in the Defense Area of Baltimore—Part I (Based on the Testimony of Mary Stalcup Markward), June 19–21, 26–28; July 11, 13, 1951; 164 pp.—Includes testimony by an undercover agent for the FBI, Mrs. Markward, concerning for the most part Communist infiltration of the Bethlehem Steel Corporation's steel-processing plant at Sparrows Point, and concerning the steel industry in general as a prime target for Communist infiltration.

Hearings Relating to Communist Activities in the Defense Area of Baltimore—Part II (Maryland Committee for Peace and Baltimore County

Committee for Peace), June 28; July 10, 12, 1951; 49 pp.—Includes testimony showing how "peace committees" function, with well-known non-Communists as nominal leaders, but with actual direction in the hands of Communists.

Hearings Relating to Communist Activities in the Defense Area of Baltimore—Part III, June 19, 20, 26–28; July 10–13, 1951; 176 pp.—Includes testimony concerning heavy industry and labor unions in the Baltimore area: out of a total of some 500 known Communists in Baltimore more than 300 had worked in defense industries during World War II.

Hearings on American Aspects of the Richard Sorge Spy Case (Based on the Testimony of Mitsusada Yoshikawa and Maj. Gen. Charles A. Willoughby), August 9, 22, 23, 1951; 122 pp.—Includes testimony on the activities of the famous Sorge Spy ring during the 1930's and the early 1940's. Yoshikawa had helped to expose the ring and get Sorge arrested. General Willoughby had been in charge of military intelligence in the Far East over a long period.

Exposé of Communist Activities in the State of Massachusetts (Based on the Testimony of Herbert A. Philbrick), July 23, 24; October 10, 11, 1951; 156 pp., with foreword, appendix, and exhibits.—Includes testimony by Philbrick concerning Communist concentration on key industries, and Communist methods of recruitment and colonization. Philbrick named his associates in the Communist movement, among them a teacher at Massachusetts Institute of Technology, Dirk Struik. Struik denied Philbrick's statement about him.

Communist Infiltration of the Hollywood Motion-Picture Industry—Part IV, September 17–19, 1951; 223 pp.—Includes testimony by Harold J. Ashe, Charles Daggett, Henry Blankfort, Philip Edward Stevenson, Georgia Backus Alexander, Martin Berkeley (Ashe, Daggett, and Berkeley were former Communists), and others.

Communist Infiltration of the Hollywood Motion-Picture Industry—Part V, September 20, 21, 24, 25, 1951; 243 pp.—Includes testimony by, variously, persons who admitted they had belonged to the CPUS, and persons whom others had named to the Committee as Communists. Most of the witnesses were screenwriters.

Hearings Regarding Communist Activities Among Farm Groups, February 28; March 9, 1951; 40 pp.—Includes testimony by Lement U. Harris, Secretary of the Farmers National Committee of the CPUS. Harris refused to answer questions concerning his membership and activities in the CPUS.

Communist Tactics Among Veteran's Groups (Testimony of John T. Pace), June 13, 1951; 39 pp.—Includes testimony by Pace, who as a Communist had sought to penetrate veterans' organizations with a view to using them for Party purposes, including, ultimately, armed revolution.

Testimony of Oliver Edmund Clubb, March 14; August 20, 23, 1951; 87 pp.—Includes testimony by Clubb, a Foreign Service officer, to whom the

Committee's attention had first been directed by Whittaker Chambers. Clubb, who had belonged to the Institute of Pacific Relations and had held important diplomatic posts in China, denied he had ever been a Communist.

Communist Infiltration of the Hollywood Motion-Picture Industry— Part VI, May 10; September 10–12, 1951; 73 pp.—Includes the last of the 1951 hearings on Communist influence in Hollywood, bringing to more than 90 the number of witnesses heard, and to more than 300 the number of motion-picture industry personnel who had been named as past or present members of the CPUS.

REPORTS

Statement on the March of Treason, A Study of the American "Peace" Crusade, February 19, 1951; 2 pp.—Describes the various organizations that had participated in the Crusade, with special attention to the incidence among their leaders of persons who had been named as members of the CPUS.

House Report No. 378—The Communist "Peace" Offensive, a Campaign to Disarm and Defeat the United States, April 1, 1951; 166 pp., with appendices.—Sets forth the basic facts about "peace" conferences and "peace" movements and campaigns, especially those aimed at youth and at scientists, with special attention to Communist techniques for gaining sympathy and support from persons whose objective is simply to prevent war. Includes lists of persons who had participated in various "peace" organizations that had served Communist purposes.

Guide to Subversive Organizations and Publications (and appendix), Revised, May 14, 1951; 166 pp.—Lists the organizations and publications which either the Attorney General or a Congressional investigating committee had, to date, designated as subversive or as Communist fronts.

100 Things You Should Know About Communism Series: —in the U.S.A.; —and Religion; —and Education; —and Labor; —and Government; and Spotlight on Spies. May 14, 1951; 126 pp.—A revised edition of the 1948, 1949, and 1950 publications bearing these titles.

House Report No. 1229—The Shameful Years, Thirty Years of Soviet Espionage in the United States, December 30, 1951; 70 pp., with introduction and foreword.—A concise history of espionage within the U. S. over the preceding 30 years, in two parts, which deal respectively with pre-World War II espionage and espionage during and after World War II. Sets forth the basic facts concerning each spy case, and each apparatus, beginning with Ludwig Martens in 1921 and including Klaus Fuchs, Morton Sobell, David Greenglass, and Julius and Ethel Rosenberg.

House Report No. 2431—Annual Report for the Year 1951, February 17, 1952; 30 pp., with foreword.—An account of the Committee's activities during the year, summarizing each set of hearings, listing the publications released, and setting forth the conclusions arrived at on the basis of the information obtained, together with recommendations for future legislation.

1952—82nd Congress, Second Session

The Role of the Communist Press in the Communist Conspiracy, January 9, 10, 15–17, 1952; 179 pp., with foreword.—Includes testimony by John Carter Vincent, Morris L. Appleman, Elizabeth Bentley, Louis Budenz, and Max and Grace Granich. The Granichs, the hearings showed, had organized the Inter-Continent News Service in New York City upon assignment for that purpose by the CPUS; the ICNS had received Moscow directives; and ICNS cable tolls were paid for by the People's Commissariat of Communications of the Soviet Union.

Communist Infiltration of Hollywood Motion-Picture Industry—Part VII, January 24, 28; February 5; March 20; April 10, 30, 1952; 127 pp.—Includes testimony by Melvin Levy, Michael Seymour Blankfort, and Elia Kazan, all former Communists, concerning their experiences as Party members. Also testimony by M. William Pomerance, George Bassman, Hyman Soloman Kraft, and Edward G. Robinson.

Communist Activities Among Professional Groups in the Los Angeles Area—Part I, January 21–26; April 9, 1952; 272 pp.—Includes testimony concerning Communist influence in the legal, medical, and newspaper professions in the area in question. Most of the lawyers identified as Party members, the hearings showed, were also members of the National Lawyers Guild.

Communism in the Detroit Area—Part I, February 25–29, 1952; 247 pp.—Includes testimony showing that more than 600 persons in and around Detroit had been members of the Communist Party, and that many of them had been active on university campuses in Michigan.

Communism in the Detroit Area—Part II, March 10–12; April 29, 30, 1952; 312 pp., with index for both parts.—Includes testimony concerning the Civil Rights Congress; the American Committee for the Protection of the Foreign Born; the Michigan Committee for Peace; the Labor Committee for Peace; the National Negro Labor Council, and other Communist fronts. Also testimony concerning Communist efforts to colonize Local 600 of the United Auto Workers Union.

Communist Activities Among Youth Groups (Based on Testimony of Harvey M. Matusow), February 6, 7, 1952; 70 pp.—Includes testimony by Matusow concerning his experiences as a Party member and his role in the dissemination of Communist literature at a Communist-run camp for youth in upstate New York, and on the general topic of Communist infiltration of the entertainment industry. Matusow, who named his associates in the Party, stressed the low state of morality among Communist youth.

Methods of Communist Infiltration in the United States Government, May 6; June 10, 23, 1952; 107 pp.—Includes the record of appearances by Ruth Rifkin, Irving Kaplan, and Allan Rosenberg, all of whom refused to testify on Fifth Amendment grounds. Also testimony, pursuant to leads supplied by Whittaker Chambers and Elizabeth Bentley, concerning Communist infiltration of the Office of Strategic Services (OSS), and of other government agencies.

Communist Infiltration of the Hollywood Motion-Picture Industry— Part VIII, May 19–21, 1952; 96 pp.—Includes testimony by Clifford Odets, Isobel Lennart, Stanley Roberts, who admitted that they had been Party members and testified concerning their activities and associates in the Party, and the record of an appearance by Lillian Hellman, who invoked the Fifth Amendment.

Communist Activities Among Professional Groups in the Los Angeles Area—Part II, May 22; July 8, 1952; 45 pp.—Includes testimony by Alice K. Bennett and Urcel Daniel, both former Communists, concerning their efforts to infiltrate the newspaper industry for the CPUS, and the record of an appearance by Tom O'Connor, managing editor of the *Daily Compass* at the time of the hearing, who refused to testify.

Testimony of Lynne L. Prout, February 14, 1952; 23 pp.—Includes testimony by Prout concerning his activities as a Communist in the 1930's. Prout had joined the Party at (what was then) the Oklahoma Agricultural and Mechanical College, and had subsequently had jobs on several newspapers and in various government agencies.

Communist Activities in the Chicago Area—Part I (United Electrical, Radio, and Machine Workers of America; and Farm Equipment Workers Council, UERMWA), September 2, 3, 1952; 131 pp.—Includes testimony by Irving Krane, Lee Lundgren, Alcide T. Kratz, John Edward Cooke, Donald O. Spencer, all former Communists, and others. These hearings were interrupted repeatedly by demonstrations, described as "uncontrollable," led by Dick Criley, an identified Communist, and Sidney Ordower, a leader of the Progressive Party.

Communist Activities in the Chicago Area—Part II (Local 347, United Packinghouse Workers of America, CIO), September 4, 5, 1952; 79 pp.—Includes testimony bearing upon pressure exerted by Local 347 of the United Packinghouse Workers on the State Department, with reference to the issuance of passports to Communists. Also testimony concerning recruitment of Party members through union locals, and the activities of Communist cells at the University of Chicago and Roosevelt College.

Testimony of Dr. Edward U. Condon, September 5, 1952; 64 pp.—Includes testimony by Dr. Condon, whom the Committee had invited to answer the Committee's charges against him, which he refused to do. The

Committee then subpoenaed him, but Condon merely reiterated his lack of knowledge of the espionage activities of his associates and appointees, and denied he had ever been a Communist. (See hearings of March 10, 1948, and report of March 18, 1948.)

Communist Activities Among Professional Groups in the Los Angeles Area—Part III, September 30; October 1, 2, 1952; 208 pp.—Includes testimony by Pauline Epstein, Richard L. Rykoff, Aubrey Finn, Victor E. Kaplan, Seymour Mandel, Paul Marion, and others, most of whom had been identified by other witnesses as members of the Communist Party. Marion admitted that he had been a member, and identified his associates.

Communist Activities Among Professional Groups in the Los Angeles Area—Part IV, October 3, 6, 7, 1952; 138 pp.—Includes the final testimony on infiltration of the professions in the L. A. area, most of it testimony by persons whom other witnesses had named as Communists, including Dr. Joseph Hittelman, Dr. Harold Koppelman, Dr. S. Sidney Druckman, Eugene R. Stone, and William Wolff.

Communist Infiltration of the Hollywood Motion-Picture Industry—Part IX, August 19; September 29, 1952; 33 pp.—Includes testimony by Bernard C. Schoenfeld and Roy Huggins concerning their recruitment by the Communist Party, and their subsequent disillusionment and withdrawal. Each named his associates.

Testimony of Gen. Walter Bedell Smith, October 13, 1952; 15 pp.—Includes testimony by the then Director of the Central Intelligence Agency, concerning his agency's screening procedures, and possible loopholes by means of which the Communists might infiltrate it.

Communist Activities in the Philadelphia Area, October 13–16, 1952; 171 pp., with exhibits.—Includes testimony by Thomas Delaney and Samuel DiMaria, both former Communists, and others, concerning Communist infiltration tactics in the basic industries and unions in the Philadelphia area. The witnesses named as Communists, among others, Philip Bart and Russell Nixon.

Communist Infiltration of the Hollywood Motion-Picture Industry—Part X, November 12, 13, 1952; 46 pp.—Includes testimony by Abram S. Burrows, who had been named as a Communist, but denied the charge, and the record of an appearance by Karan Morley, who invoked the Fifth Amendment when questioned regarding her alleged Communist affiliations.

REPORTS

House Report No. 1293—Proceedings Against Sidney Buchman, February 5, 1952; 10 pp.—Includes the Committee's citation of Buchman for contempt (refusal to appear). (Buchman was convicted.)

House Report No. 1661—Review of the Methodist Federation for Social Action, Formerly the Methodist Federation for Social Service, February 17, 1952; 87 pp., with appendix and exhibits.—An account of the Federation's activities and policies, based on their own documents, letters, articles, and statements by their officials, and on articles about them that had appeared in the press.

Index IV to Publications of the Committee on Un-American Activities, April 25, 1952; 639 pp., with key.—A revised edition of the October 21, 1948, and June 28, 1950, indices.

House Report No. 2353—Proceedings Against Arthur McPhaul, June 30, 1952; 8 pp.—The citation of McPhaul for contempt (refusal to produce the records of the Civil Rights Congress, refusal to answer questions, on Fifth Amendment grounds). (Convicted, affirmed, 364 U.S. 372 (1960).)

House Report No. 2354—Proceedings Against Saul Grossman, June 30, 1952; 9 pp.—The citation of Grossman for contempt (refusal to produce the records of the Michigan Committee for Protection of the Foreign Born, on Fifth Amendment grounds). (Convicted, reversed, 229 F. 2d 774 (1956).)

House Report No. 2406—Salary Increase for Members of the Subversive Activities Control Board, July 1, 1952; 2 pp.—A recommendation that the salaries of members of the Subversive Activities Control Board be increased to levels comparable to those obtained by employees in other agencies of similar character.

House Report No. 2516—Annual Report for the year 1952, December 28, 1952; 89 pp.—An account of the Committee's activities during the year, summarizing each set of hearings and each investigation, listing all persons named as members of the Communist Party and the persons naming them, and setting forth the Committee's recommendations for future legislation from 1947 to date.

1953—83rd Congress, First Session

Communist Methods of Infiltration (Education), February 25–27, 1953; 123 pp., with index.—Includes testimony by present or former educators, among them Robert Gorham Davis of Smith College, who admitted he had been a Communist, stated his reasons both for joining the Party and for his subsequent disillusionment.

Communist Methods of Infiltration (Education)—Part II, March 12, 13, 17, 18; April 14, 16, 1953; 140 pp.—Includes testimony by Wendell Hinkle Furry of Harvard University, Abraham Glasser, who openly expressed contempt for the Committee and its function. Also testimony concerning a Communist cell at Yale University in 1947, whose members included Byron Thorwell Darling, Paul Zilsel, Daniel Fine, Theodore S. Polumbaum, Arthur L. Levy, and Harold T. Woerner, Jr.

Investigation of Communist Activities in the Los Angeles Area—Part I, March 23–25, 1953; 171 pp., with index.—Includes testimony, pursuant to previous Committee inquiries concerning Communist penetration of the motion-picture industry and the professions in and about Los Angeles, by, among others, the screenwriter David A. Lang, a former Communist, who attempted to explain the attraction of the Communist Party for intellectuals.

Investigation of Communist Activities in the Los Angeles Area—Part II, March 26–28, 1953; 172 pp., with index.—Includes testimony by LeRoy Herndon, Jr., a professor at Glendale College, California, and a former Communist, and others. Herndon, when questioned about Communist efforts to control the Teachers Union, testified to the concerted action of Communist members within the union, and the increased influence they exercise. Herndon also answered questions about academic freedom, and its meaning to Communists.

Investigation of Communist Activities in the Los Angeles Area—Part III, March 30, 31, 1953; 102 pp., with index.—Includes testimony regarding Communist activities in and around Los Angeles by Abraham Minkus, Dwight Hauser, David Robison, Libby Burke, George B. Rossini, Naomi Robeson, Roy Erwin, and others.

Investigation of Communist Activities in the Los Angeles Area—Part IV, April 7, 8, 1953; 128 pp., with index.—Includes testimony regarding Communist activities in and around Los Angeles by Harry Shepro, Sam Albert, Murray Wagner, Gertrude Purcell, Frank Tarloff, Ned Young, and others.

Investigation of Communist Activities in the Los Angeles Area—Part V, December 2, 1952; February 17; March 12, 27; April 7, 13, 1953; 129 pp., with index.—Includes testimony regarding Communist activities in and around Los Angeles by Charles H. Garrigues, Stanley Rubin, Leopold Lawrence Atlas, Paul Benedict Radin, and others.

Communist Methods of Infiltration (Education)—Part III, April 21, 22, 1953; 95 pp., with index.—Includes testimony by Leo M. Hurvich, Theodore S. Polumbaum, William T. Martin, Paul Rudolph Zilsel, Isadore Amdur, and Max Weitzman, some of whom had been named as former members of a Communist cell at Yale. All of them invoked the Fifth Amendment when asked to affirm or deny the statements that had been made about them.

Communist Methods of Infiltration (Education)—Part IV, April 23, 27, 1953; 75 pp., with index.—An account of efforts by Communist teachers and students to infiltrate the educational system. These efforts were concentrated not on the classroom, but on extracurricular activities, especially semiclandestine Marxist study groups. Participation in these groups, the hearings showed, often led to membership in the Communist Party.

Investigation of Communist Activities in the New York City Area—Part I, May 4, 1953; 84 pp., with index.—Includes testimony from a number of former Communists concerning infiltration of the entertainment industry, education, organized labor, government, and religion. Among the witnesses were Artie Shaw and Mrs. Dorothy K. Funn, a former Communist.

Investigation of Communist Activities in the New York City Area—Part II, May 5, 1953; 106 pp., with index.—Includes testimony by David and Mildred Flacks, Julius and Florence Jacobs, and the record of an appearance by Cedric Henning Belfrage, editor of the *National Guardian,* whom Elizabeth Bentley had named as a Communist spy. Belfrage invoked the Fifth Amendment.

Investigation of Communist Activities in the New York City Area—Part III, May 6, 1953; 83 pp., with index.—Includes the record of appearances by Lionel Stander, Jay Gorney, and Irving Charles Velson, all of whom invoked the Fifth Amendment, and of Robert Gladnick, who answered questions about his experiences as a Party member, and named his associates.

Investigation of Communist Activities in the New York Area—Part IV, May 7, 1953; 75 pp.—Includes testimony by Lee S. Sabinson, Zachary Schwartz, and Robert Rossen. Rossen had invoked the Fifth Amendment in the 1951 Hollywood hearings, but on this occasion answered questions concerning his Party activities.

Communist Methods of Infiltration (Education)—Part V, April 29; May 19, 26–28, 1953; 83 pp., with appendix and index.—Includes testimony by Harold T. Woerner, Jr., William T. Parry, Marcus Singer, and Abe Gelbart, a philosophy professor at the University of Buffalo, invoked the Fifth Amendment when asked whether he was a Communist during student days at Harvard. Singer, who had been a Communist at Harvard, testified concerning his activities in the Party.

Communist Methods of Infiltration (Government-Labor)—Part I, April 17; May 14; June 9, 1953; 99 pp., with index.—Includes the record of an appearance by Russell Arthur Nixon, Legislative Representative of the United Electrical, Radio, and Machine Workers of America, who had been named as a Communist (a member of the same group as Harry Dexter White and William Ludwig Ullmann) by Mrs. Dorothy Funn, Elizabeth Bentley, and others. Nixon, invoking the Fifth Amendment, refused to answer the Committee's questions.

Franciszek Jarecki—Flight to Freedom, July 1, 1953; 18 pp.—Includes information concerning anti-American propaganda in Poland; based upon revelations by a Polish jet pilot who had defected by flying a Polish jet to Denmark.

Soviet Schedule for War, 1955, May 13, 14, 1953; 31 pp.—Includes testimony by Col. Jan Bukar, a former Slovakian army officer, concerning the Frunze Military School in Moscow. The cadets, he related, engage in hypothetical warfare against America, England, Turkey, Germany, and Japan, and are taught techniques for communizing capitalist nations. Bukar stressed seizure of the Ministry of the Interior, the Ministry of the Army, and industrial plants as high-priority objectives for that purpose.

Investigation of Communist Activities in the Columbus, Ohio, Area, June 17, 18, 1953; 102 pp., with appendix and index.—Includes testimony by Bryon Thornwell Darling, Flora Webster, Dr. Bella Dodd, and others. Mrs. Dodd, a former member of the CPUS National Committee, answered questions about Communist techniques of colonization and the Communist mentality. Darling, who had been named as having been a Communist at Yale, had organized a Communist cell while teaching at Michigan State University.

Communist Methods of Infiltration (Education)—Part VI, June 22, 24, 29; July 1, 1953; 94 pp., with index.—Testimony of Harry J. Marks, George F. Markham, Louis Harap, and George Beach Mayberry. Marks and Mayberry, who had been Communists at Harvard, told of their experiences in the Party. Markham and Harap, who had been named as Communists, refused to answer questions on Fifth Amendment grounds.

Testimony of Stephen H. Fritchman, September 12, 1951; 13 pp., with index.—Includes the record of an appearance by Fritchman, a Unitarian minister who had been named as a Communist. Fritchman refused to answer any questions about his alleged Communist Party membership and activities, on Fifth Amendment grounds.

Communist Methods of Infiltration (Government-Labor)—Part II, July 20, 1953; 14 pp., with index.—Includes the record of appearances by I. Philip Sipser, William Greenstein, and Charles Klare. Sipser and Greenstein, both lawyers, refused on Fifth Amendment grounds either to affirm or deny allegations regarding their Communist activities. Klare, an office secretary of the Brewery Workers Joint Board in New York City, also invoked the Fifth Amendment.

Investigation of Communist Activities in the New York Area—Part V, July 6, 1953; 65 pp.—Includes the record of appearances by William Michelson, Carl Andren, David Livingston, Arthur Osman, Jack Paley, Peter Stein, Herbert A. Philbrick, and Archibald Roosevelt, all of whom except Philbrick and Roosevelt invoked the Fifth Amendment. The latter two gave information about Communist infiltration of churches.

Investigation of Communist Activities in the New York City Area— Part VI, July 7, 1953; 108 pp.—Includes testimony by Joseph Zack Kornfeder and Leonard Patterson, both former Communists, by Vladimir Petrov, who gave information about the Soviet concentration camp in which he had spent six years, and about the techniques used in the Soviet campaign of "Godlessness"; and Benjamin Gitlow, ex-member of the Presidium of the Communist International, who gave information about Communist goals and methods of the infiltration of religious organizations.

Investigation of Communist Activities in the New York City Area— Part VII (Based on the Testimony of Manning Johnson), July 8, 1953; 54 pp., with exhibits.—Includes testimony by Johnson, a former Communist, concerning Communist subversion of churches, and how the latter are used to further the Party's purposes.

Investigation of Communist Activities in the New York City Area— Part VIII (Based on the Testimony of Manning Johnson), July 13, 14, 1953; 97 pp., with exhibits and index to Parts V through VIII.—Includes the final testimony on Communist activities in and about New York City, especially the infiltration of religious groups. One of the exhibits is a sacrilegious drawing of Christ disseminated by Rev. Claude C. Williams.

Investigation of Communist Activities in the Los Angeles Area—Part VI, March 21, 1951; June 2, 1953; 61 pp., with index.—Includes testimony by Larry Parks, Charlotte Darling Adams, Roland William Kibbee, Babbette Lang, and Lee J. Cobb, all former Communists, concerning the Party's recruiting techniques.

Investigation of Communist Activities in the Albany, N. Y., Area—Part I, July 13, 14, 1953; 110 pp., with index.—Includes testimony by former Communists Patrick Walsh, Nicholas Campas, Jack Davis, and others. Walsh, a Canadian, gave the Committee its first information about Communist leadership and direction of the Canadian Seamen's Union strike of 1949. Campas and Davis answered questions about their own Communist activities and associates in the Albany area.

Investigation of Communist Activities in the Albany, N. Y., Area— Part II, July 15, 16, 1953; 83 pp., with index.—Includes testimony from John Mills Davis, Samuel Evans, and others regarding Communist activities in and about Albany.

Investigation of Communist Activities in the Los Angeles Area—Part VII, September 4, 1953; 22 pp., with index.—Includes testimony by Lucille Desiree Ball Arnaz, her mother Desiree E. Ball, and her brother Fred Henry Ball, all of whom stated that they had never belonged to the Communist Party, and had signed affidavits that they would vote for Communist Party candidates only as a favor to Miss Ball's grandfather.

Testimony of Dr. Marek Stanislaw Korowicz, September 24, 1953; 24 pp., with index.—Includes testimony by Dr. Korowicz, who only a few days earlier had withdrawn as alternate Polish Delegate to the United Nations, concerning his delegation's subordination to the Soviet delegation, and concerning living conditions in a Sovietized country.

Hearings Regarding Jack R. McMichael, July 30, 31, 1953; 273 pp., with exhibits and index.—Includes testimony by McMichael, pastor of the Methodist church in Upper Lake, California, whom Manning Johnson, Leonard Patterson, and Martha and John Edmiston had named as a Communist. McMichael denied the allegation and when confronted by Johnson, also denied having known him.

Investigation of Communist Activities in the Philadelphia Area—Part I, November 16, 1953; 59 pp., with index.—Includes testimony by 19 witnesses from in and around Philadelphia, mostly teachers, who had been named as Party members. The majority denied that they were then members of the Party, but refused to answer questions about their alleged Communist activities prior to signing the loyalty oath, required by Pennsylvania law, in early 1952.

Investigation of Communist Activities in the Philadelphia Area—Part II, November 17, 18, 1953; 178 pp., with index.—Includes testimony by Mrs. Dorothy Funn, David Perloff, Benjamin David Anton, and others. Mrs. Funn gave information concerning her attempts to infiltrate school groups. (See description for Part I.)

Communist Methods of Infiltration (Government-Labor)—Part III (Based on the testimony of James McNamara), September 15, 1953; 28 pp., with index.—Includes testimony regarding McNamara, Commissioner for the Federal Mediation and Conciliation Service in Cincinnati, whom Jack Davis and Nicholas Campas had named as a Communist. Shortly after the Committee subpoenaed him, he resigned his post as commissioner, and admitted that he had been a Communist in the late 1930's.

Investigation of Communist Activities in the San Francisco Area—Part I, December 1, 1953; 103 pp., with exhibits and index.—Includes testimony by Lou Rosser and the record of an appearance by Donald Niven Wheeler, whom Elizabeth Bentley had named as a Communist. Rosser, a Negro, stated that he had joined the Party in the 1930's, but had in due course concluded that the Communists were not concerned with improving the lot of the American Negro.

Investigation of Communist Activities in the San Francisco Area—Part II, December 2, 1953; 107 pp., with exhibits and index.—Includes the record of an appearance by Roy Hudson, Dixon P. Hill, Eugene Eagle, and others. Hudson, who had been a member of the National Committee and the Political Bureau of the CPUS, refused to testify. Hill admitted he had belonged to the Party.

Investigation of Communist Activities in the San Francisco Area—Part III, December 3, 1953; 81 pp., with one exhibit and index.—Includes testimony by Charles David Blodgett, Lloyd Lehman, Mary Pieper, Robert E. Treuhaft, and John Delgado. Blodgett, who had organized a Young Communist League group during student days at Carleton College, answered questions about his own recruitment by the Party, and about the Communist strategy of recruiting members from all levels of intelligence and income.

Investigation of Communist Activities in the San Francisco Area—Part IV, December 4, 1953; 70 pp., with index.—Includes the record of an appearance by each of 14 witnesses, all of whom had been named as former Party members. All but one, William Donald Ames, refused to answer questions about their alleged Communist affiliation. Ames gave information about his own activities in local groups and organizations.

Investigation of Communist Activities in the San Francisco Area—Part V, December 5, 1953; 78 pp., with one exhibit and index.—Includes the record of an appearance by Harrison George, and testimony by James Kendall, and others. George, sometime brother-in-law of Earl Browder, a former member of the CPUS's Central and National committees, and editor of the *People's Daily World* from 1938 to 1944, refused to testify. Kendall answered questions concerning his Communist activities in shipping unions.

Investigation of Communist Activities in the Los Angeles Area—Part VIII, November 23, 1953; 57 pp., with index.—Includes testimony by Max N. Benoff and Milton Merlin, mainly about Communist infiltration among screen and radio writers. The hearings concluded the Committee's inquiry into Communist activities in and about Los Angeles.

Communist Methods of Infiltration (Education)—Part VII, May 15, 1953; 24 pp., with index.—Includes testimony by Ballis Edwin Blaisdell, research chemist in the pioneering research laboratory in the textile fiber department of the Du Pont Company, concerning his Party membership.

Testimony of Bishop G. Bromley Oxnam, July 21, 1953; 265 pp., with exhibits and index.—Includes testimony by Bishop Oxnam, who appeared at his own request, concerning his alleged Communist affiliations, which he denied. Contains 42 exhibits.

REPORTS

Index V to Publications of the Committee on Un-American Activities, January 19, 1953; 779 pp., with key.—A revised edition of the indices of October 21, 1948; June 28, 1950; and April 25, 1952.

House Report No. 1694—Organized Communism in the United States, August 19, 1953; 150 pp., with index.—A brief history of Communist activities in the United States from 1919 to date, with special attention to shifts in the Party line over the years, the platforms and constitutions by the Party, and the procedures by which it is controlled from the Kremlin.

House Report No. 1192—Annual Report for the Year 1953, February 6, 1954; 195 pp., with appendix.—An account of the Committee's activities during the year, with a summary of each hearing, sections on the Committee's files and reference service, its rules of procedure (it was the first House committee to print rules), its recommendations for future legislation, and lists of all persons named as Communists and of the persons who named them.

1954—83rd Congress, Second Session

HEARINGS

Communist Methods of Infiltration (Entertainment)—Part I, January 13, 18, 1954; 48 pp., with index.—Includes testimony by Allan E. Sloane, a radio and screen writer, and the record of an appearance by Howard Bay, a stage designer. Sloane appeared at his own request and gave an account of his experiences as a Party member. Bay refused to testify.

Investigation of Communist Activities in the Philadelphia Area—Parts III–IV. (Part III: February 16, 1954; Part IV: February 17, 1954.) 111 pp. total, each part with index.—Includes testimony, or records of appearances, by 18 witnesses who had been named as present or past members of the Communist Party, with regard to the hiring of schoolteachers in Philadelphia. Mrs. Goldie E. Watson, Jr., and Dr. Wilbur Lee Mahaney, Jr., were cited for contempt. (Mahaney later purged himself, and proceedings against him were dropped.)

Communist Methods of Infiltration (Education)—Part VIII, April 21; June 8, 1953; April 12, 1954; 40 pp., with index.—Includes the record of appearances by Lawrence Baker Arguimbau, Francis X. T. Crowley, and Bernhard Deutch, all of whom refused to testify regarding their alleged Communist Party affiliations. Each was cited for contempt.

Investigation of Communist Activities in the Baltimore Area—Parts I–III (Part I: March 18, 1954; Part II: March 25, 1954; Part III: March 25, 26, 1954); 109 pp. total, each part with index.—Includes testimony by Joseph Nowak and John Hutchison, both clergymen who had recently completed their education, and both of whom, according to earlier testimony by former Communists Louis Patterson and Earl C. Reno, had offered their services to the Party. Nowak admitted the allegation; Hutchison denied it.

Investigation of Communist Activities in the Chicago Area—Parts I–III (Part I: March 15, 1954; Part II: March 16, 1954; Part III: April 29, 1954); 131 pp. total, each part with index.—Includes testimony by John T. Watkins and the record of an appearance by Abe Feinglass, both officials of the Farm Equipment Workers of the United Electrical Workers Union, and both of whom Walter E. Rumsey had named as Communists. Watkins denied the allegation, Feinglass invoked the Fifth Amendment (Part II). Also testimony concerning Communist infiltration of farmer organizations.

Investigation of Communist Activities in the Albany, N. Y., Area—Parts III–VI (Part III: April 7, 1954; Part IV: April 8, 1954, morning; Part V: April 8, 1954, afternoon; Part VI: April 9, 1954); 168 pp. total, each part with index.—Includes testimony by former Communists John Edward Marqusee, Joseph Klein, and Jack Davis, and by John Patrick Charles and Emmanuel Ross Richardson, both FBI undercover agents, and others, concerning Communist activities in defense industries and education in and around the Albany area.

Communism in the District of Columbia—Maryland Area (Testimony of Mary Stalcup Markward), June 11, 1951; 48 pp., with index.—Includes tes-

---

* Beginning with Parts III and IV of the Philadelphia hearings, the Committee adopted the practice of binding successive parts of area hearings together. They are thus catalogued here, at the expense of strict chronological order.

timony by Mrs. Markward, an FBI undercover agent, who answered questions regarding the inner workings of the Party in the District of Columbia from 1943 to 1949. Also the record of appearances by 11 other persons, all of whom had been named as Party members, and all of whom invoked the Fifth Amendment.

Investigation of Communist Activities in the State of California—Parts I–X (Part I: February 24, 1954; Part II: February 1; March 1; April 12, 1954; Part III: April 12, 14, 23, 1954; Part IV: April 19, 1954, morning; Part V: April 19, 1954, afternoon; Part VI: April 20, 1954, morning; Part VII: April 20, 1954, afternoon; Part VIII: April 21, 1954, morning; Part IX: April 21, 1954, afternoon; Part X: September 11, 1953; April 22, 1954); 473 pp. total, each part with index.—Dealing primarily with Communist activities in the San Diego area. Includes testimony by Carol Bayme, Philip and Mildred Berman, John Dunkel, Gladys Gatlin, Oliver "Red" Hagen, John Lang, Irving Ravetch, Artie Sykes, Daniel Pomeroy Taylor, Stephen Wereb, and others, concerning Communist activities in and around San Diego.

Investigation of Communist Activities in the State of Michigan—Parts I–V (Part I, Education: April 30; May 3, 4, 1954; Part II, Labor: April 28, 29, 1954; Part III, Labor: May 4, 1954; Part IV, Labor: May 5, 1954; Part V, Labor: May 7, 1954); 337 pp. total, each part with index.—Analyzes Party directives and activities and the areas of concentration of Communist efforts in Michigan. One of the directives dealt with a campaign against NATO, and increasing friendship with the Soviet Union and trade with the "People's Democracies."

Investigation of Communist Activities in the State of Michigan—Parts VI–VII (Lansing): (Part VI: May 10, 1954; Part VII: June 8, 1953; May 11, 1954); 157 pp. total, each part with index.—Includes testimony by, among others, Mark Nickerson, Horace Chandler Davis, Richard Fox, John C. Houston, and Harold L. Shapiro, concerning the character and intensity of Communist activities in Michigan.

Investigation of Communist Activities in the State of Michigan—Parts VIII–X (Flint): (Part VIII: April 30, May 12, 1954; Part IX: May 13, 1954; Part X: May 14, 1954); 264 pp. total, each part with index.—Includes testimony concerning colonization of heavy industries, by e.g., putting educated Communists into those industries as "workers," so that they can influence the opinions of their fellow workers.

Communist Methods of Infiltration (Education)—Part IX, June 28, 29, 1954; 84 pp., with index.—Includes testimony by Francis X. T. Crowley, Robert H. Silk, Norman Cazden, and Lester Beberfall and Jack Alexander Lucas, and the record of an appearance by Lloyd Barenblatt. Crowley had previously been cited for contempt, purged himself, and named Barenblatt as a Communist. Barenblatt refused to testify on impertinency and First Amendment grounds.

Communist Activities Among Youth Groups (Based on the Testimony of Harvey M. Matusow)—Part II, July 12, 1954; 9 pp., with index.—Reviews Matusow's testimony of February 6, 7, 1952, pursuant to a published report that Matusow had told Bishop G. Bromley Oxnam he had lied about Oxnam and Communism. Matusow repudiated the report.

Investigation of Communist Influence in the Field of Publications (March of Labor), *July 8, 15, 1954; 52 pp., with index.*—Includes the record of an appearance by Leonard (Len) H. DeCaux, formerly editor of *March of Labor*. DeCaux invoked the Fifth Amendment on questions pertaining to the Communist Party.

Hearings Regarding Communism in the District of Columbia—Part III, July 14, 15, 1954; 70 pp., with index.—Includes the record of appearances by Samuel R. Pearlman, Sammie Abdullah Abbott, Alexander Sherman, and others, pursuant to testimony by Mrs. Markward. In all, 12 witnesses refused to testify regarding their alleged Communist activities.

Investigation of Communist Activities in the Pacific Northwest Area— Part I, October 3, 1952; March 16; May 28; June 2, 9, 1954; 85 pp., with index.—Includes testimony by Eugene Kenneth McClaskey, Howard Costigan, Leonard Basil Wildman, and others. Costigan, a former Communist who had held numerous jobs, answered questions concerning Communist operations and objectives in the subject area.

Investigation of Communist Activities in the Pacific Northwest Area (Seattle)—Parts II–III, Testimony of Barbara Hartle (Part II: June 14, 15, 1954; Part III: June 16–19, 1954); 182 pp. total, each part with index.— Includes testimony by Barbara Hartle, who had been a member of the Party for 21 years, and had broken when she learned that it deemed her expendable. Still under sentence for violating the Smith Act, she answered questions regarding the Communists' recruitment of new members, especially through Communist front organizations.

Investigation of Communist Activities in the Pacific Northwest Area— Parts IV–VIII (Seattle): (Part IV: June 14, 15, 1954; Part V: June 16, 1954; Part VI: June 17, 1954; Part VII: June 18, 1954; Part VIII: June 19, 1954) ; 369 pp. total, each part with index.—Includes testimony by 49 witnesses, pursuant to the testimony of Mrs. Hartle. Eugene Dennett, who had previously invoked the Fifth Amendment, answered questions regarding his Communist activities among both organized and unorganized workers in the Pacific Northwest.

Investigation of Communist Activities in the Pacific Northwest Area— Parts IX–X (Portland): (Part IX: June 18, 1954; Part X: June 19, 1954); 119 pp. total, each part with index.—Includes testimony by Homer LeRoy Owen, Barbara Hartle, Robert Wisehart Canon, and others. Fourteen other persons, all of whom had been named as Party members, appeared and refused to testify.

Investigation of Communist Activities in the Pacific Northwest Area—Part XI (Appendix), June 14–19, 1954; 55 pp., with index.—An appendix to Parts I through X of the Pacific Northwest hearings, containing primarily, communications between the Committee and witnesses.

Investigation of Communist Activities in the Philadelphia Area—Part V, July 30, 1954; 25 pp., with index.—Includes testimony by Dr. Wilbur Lee Mahaney, Jr., who had previously been cited for contempt. Reversing his former position (Philadelphia Area, February 16, 17, 1954), he answered all questions put to him about his membership in the Communist Party. The contempt proceedings pending against him were subsequently dropped.

Investigation of Communist Activities in the Dayton, Ohio, Area—Parts I–III (Part I: September 13, 1954; Part II: September 14, 1954; Part III: September 15, 1954); 220 pp. total, each part with index.—Includes testimony by Arthur Paul Strunk, who had been an FBI undercover agent (Financial Secretary of the Dayton Communist Party), concerning the Party's program of activities in the area since 1945. Strunk also named as a Communist former Congressman Hugh DeLacy, who invoked the Fifth Amendment when questioned about Strunk's allegation.

Investigation of Communist Activities in the State of California—Part XI, September 17, 1954; 54 pp., with index.—Includes testimony by Lynn Akerstein, John Carpadakis, Lura Stevenson Elston, and others, concerning Communist activities in and around San Diego. Mrs. Akerstein, a Party member from 1946 to 1950, told of her activities on behalf of the Independent Progressive Party, and in the canning industry.

Investigation of Communist Activities in the Dayton, Ohio, Area—Part IV, November 17–19, 1954; 20 pp., with index.—Includes the record of an appearance by Norton Anthony Russell, Robert A. Harrison, and Miss Irene Jacobs, all of whom had been named as Party members by Arthur Paul Strunk. All refused to affirm or deny Strunk's charges, Russell invoking the First Amendment; Harrison and Miss Jacobs invoking the Fifth Amendment.

Investigation of Communist Activities in the State of Michigan—Part XI, November 17, 1954; 136 pp., with index.—Includes testimony by Robert Alan Carter, Regional Director for the UAW-CIO in and around Flint, who stated *inter alia* that his union could bar persons from membership only for failure to pay dues. Also the record of appearances by James Andrew Lewis Coleman and Molly Baumkel, who refused to testify.

Investigation of Communist Activities in the State of Michigan—Part XII, November 18, 19, 1954; 77 pp., with index.—Includes the record of appearances by nine persons, all of whom had been named in testimony before the Committee as having been involved in Communist activities either at the University of Michigan, Michigan State University, or in labor unions in Michigan. All of the nine invoked the Fifth Amendment.

Communist Methods of Infiltration (Entertainment)—Part II, December 14, 1954; 29 pp., with index.—Includes testimony by Nicholas Bela, a Hollywood actor, writer, and director, who answered questions about his recruitment into the Communist Party, and about Communist techniques for directing ostensibly harmless and even idealistic non-Communist groups in the entertainment field into channels of activity useful to the Party.

Communist Methods of Infiltration (Government-Labor)—Part IV, January 13; December 15, 1954; 15 pp., with index.—Includes the record of an appearance by Arthur O'Hare, on leave from the Ingersoll-Rand Corporation to serve as Business Agent for Local 451 of the United Electrical Workers. O'Hare refused to affirm or deny the allegation that he was a member of the Communist Party.

Investigation of Communist Activities in the State of Florida—Parts I–II (Part I: November 29, 30, 1954; Part II: December 1, 1954); 176 pp. total, each part with index.—Includes testimony by Edwin E. Waller, Ralph V. Long, Raul Vidal, José D. Tomargo, Jr., Louis J. Popps, Hilda Shlafrock, James Mimmo and others, concerning Communist activities and infiltration in and around Miami and, generally, in the southeastern part of the U. S.

REPORTS

A series of Reports (House Report Nos. 1578–1586) of contempt citations * *(refusal to answer questions on First and/or Fifth Amendment grounds), all dated May 11, 1954.*†

A series of Reports (House Report Nos. 2455-2471) of contempt citations (refusal to answer questions on First and/or Fifth Amendment grounds), all dated July 23, 1954.‡

* The record of contempt proceedings here is complete through July 1, 1961. The usual period from the date of a citation to assignment of a number to that citation is two months. In all cases in which decisions had been rendered but the citations had not yet been published, only the date of the decision appears.

† Bernhard Deutch (pertinency, convicted, reversed Supreme Court, 267 U.S. 456), John Watkins (pertinency, convicted, reversed, 354 U.S. 178 (1957)), Wilbur Lee Mahaney, Jr. (subsequently purged himself of contempt, proceedings dropped), Goldie E. Watson (1st A., convicted, reversed, 280 F. 2d 689 (1960)), Lawrence Baker Arguimbau (1st A. and pertinency, convicted), Marcus Singer (1st and 5th A. and pertinency, convicted, reversed, 246 F. 2d 535 (1957)), Ole Fagerhaugh (5th A., convicted, reversed 232 F. 2d 803 (1956)), Barrows Dunham (5th A., acquitted), Francis X. T. Crowley (subsequently purged himself of contempt, proceedings dropped).

‡ Bolza Baxter (5th A. refusal to produce papers, acquitted, not reported), Horace Chandler Davis (1st A. and pertinency, convicted, not reported), Lloyd Barenblatt (1st A. and pertinency, convicted, affirmed, 360 U.S. 109 (1959)), Richard E. Adams (5th A., subsequently purged himself of contempt, proceedings dropped), George Tony Starkovich (5th A., convicted, reversed, 231 F. 2d 411 (1956)), Thomas G. Moore (5th A., convicted, not reported), John Rogers MacKenzie (5th A., convicted, reversed, 355 U.S. 7 (1957)), Donald M.

House Report No. 2472—In the Matter of Francis X. T. Crowley, July 23, 1954; 2 pp.—Includes a Committee statement to the effect that Crowley appeared before it subsequent to the contempt charges brought against him, and purged himself, and contains recommendation that the proceedings against him be dropped.

House Report No. 2651, Part I—Subversive Activities Control Act Amendments of 1954, Report to Accompany H.R. 9838, August 9, 1954; 27 pp.— Argues that the Subversive Activities Control Board should establish a third category of subversive organizations in addition to "Communist-action organizations" and "Communist front organizations," namely, "Communist-infiltrated organizations," all three categories to be subject to the restrictions listed in the report. Amendments to this effect were incorporated in the Communist Control Act of 1954.

House Report No. 2651, Part II—Subversive Activities Control Act Amendments of 1954, Minority Views, August 10, 1954; 5 pp.—Sets forth the view of Congressmen Walter, Doyle, and Frazier, all of them members of the Committee, on the amendments recommended in House Report No. 2651. The amendments, they argue, would be unfair to "organizations whose leadership remains the same, if those leaders have genuinely broken with Communism."

Colonization of America's Basic Industries by the Communist Party of the U.S.A., September 3, 1954; 18 pp.—Examines Communist techniques for channeling college-educated Party members into laborers' jobs in the nation's basic industries, where they speedily rise to important posts, both in their plants and their unions. This, it argues, enables them to influence their fellow workers, to affect the policies of their unions, and recruit new members for the Party.

This is Your House Committee on Un-American Activities, September 19, 1954; 50 pp., with appendix.—Describes the organization and functions of the Committee: how and why it was set up, its early history, the legislation for which it has been responsible, its legislative recommendations, and its procedures for initiating and conducting an investigation. The appendix reproduces the Committee's Rules of Procedure.

*A series of unnumbered, typewritten Reports** of contempt citations*

Wollam (5th A., convicted, reversed, 355 U.S. 7 (1957)), Herbert Simpson (5th A., convicted, reversed, 355 U.S. 7 (1957)), Mrs. Millie Markison (5th A., acquitted, not reported), Benjamin F. Kocel (5th A., no action taken by Grand Jury), Paul Ross Baker (5th A., no action taken by Grand Jury), Curtis Davis (5th A., no action taken by Grand Jury), Evelyn Gladstone (5th A., no action taken by Grand Jury), Marvin Engel (5th A., no action taken by Grand Jury), Martin Trachtenberg (5th A., no action taken by Grand Jury), Carl Harvey Jackins (5th A., convicted, reversed, 231 F. 2d 405 (1956)).

* None of the cases was assigned a House Report number, Congress having adjourned. In Congress's absence, the Committee compiles the proceedings, and they are signed by the Speaker of the House of Representatives.

*(refusal to answer questions on First Amendment grounds), all of them on December 6, 1954.**

Preliminary Report on Neo-Fascist and Hate Groups, December 17, 1954; 32 pp., with exhibits and index.—Summarizes and interprets the history of domestic fascism in the U. S., discusses fascism as a contemporary problem, and shows that the National Renaissance Party is the most important present-day American fascist organization. Also includes information regarding the National Renaissance leaders, including James H. Madole, Elizabeth Dilling, Lyrl Van Hyning, and Conde McGinley, editor of the anti-Semitic *Common Sense*.

Report on the March of Labor, *December 22, 1954; 26 pp., with index.*— An account of the history of *March of Labor*, nominally a magazine for trade unionists as such, but actually, it is shown, Communist-supported. Attention is fixed upon the affiliations of its contributors, its stockholders, and its editor.

The American Negro in the Communist Party, December 22, 1954; 16 pp., with index.—An account of the Negro Commission of the Communist Party, and the major Negro Communist front organizations and publications. The Communists, it is argued, exploit the Negro's grievances in the short term and for their own purposes, but then fail to follow through and support him in the long term.

House Report No. 57—Annual Report for the Year 1954, January 26, 1955; 27 pp., with index.—An account of the year's activities, including all hearings and investigations, all publications issued, and all the Committee's recommendations for future legislation.

1955—84th Congress, First Session

HEARINGS

Investigation of Communist Activities in the New York Area—Part I (Testimony of Jean Muir), June 15, 1953; 18 pp., with index.—Includes testimony by Miss Muir, a television actress (*The Aldrich Family*) concerning the methods the Communists used to persuade her to join several Communist front organizations, and concerning Communist infiltration of the entertainment industry.

Investigation of Communist Activities in the Fort Wayne, Ind., Area, February 28; March 1; April 25, 1955; 199 pp., with index.—Includes the record of appearances by John Thomas Gojack, David Mates, Julia Jacobs, and others, all but one of whom invoked the Fifth Amendment when questioned about their alleged Communist activities. Some of the questions

* Lee Lorch (acquainted on the basis of the Watkins decision, not reported), Robert M. Metcalf (acquitted, not reported), Norton A. Russell (convicted, affirmed, 280 F. 2d 688 (1960). Cert. granted June 19, 1961.)

concerned alleged misappropriation of members' dues in various unions for Communist purposes.

Investigation of Communist Activities in New York—Part II (Youth Organizations), March 16, 1955; 26 pp., with index.—Includes testimony by Leon Wofsy, Joseph Bucholt, Robert Fogel, Ernest Parent, and Sam Engler, all connected with the Communist-dominated Labor Youth League.

Investigation of Communist Activities in the Seattle, Washington, Area—Parts I–III (Part I: March 17, 18, 1955; Part II: March 18, 19, 1955; Part III: June 1, 2, 1955); 356 pp. total, with index to all parts in Part III.—Includes testimony by several former Communists pursuant to the hearings begun in 1954 concerning Communist activities in the Pacific Northwest area. One of the witnesses was Eugene Dennett, who told of the Party's infiltration of such organizations as the politically powerful Washington Pension Union.

Investigation of Communist Activities in the Milwaukee, Wisconsin, Area—Parts I–II (Part I: March 28, 29, 1955; Part II: March 29, 30; May 3, 1955); 213 pp. total, with index to both parts in Part II.—Includes testimony by government undercover agents James Eggleston and Michael Ondrejka concerning CPUS recruiting methods, and techniques of infiltration into youth groups, community organizations in general, and defense industries.

Investigation of Communist Activities in the New York Area—Parts III–IV (Part III: May 3, 4, 1955; Part IV: May 5, 6, 1955); 170 pp. total, with index to both parts in Part IV.—Includes testimony by Mrs. Mildred Blauvelt, a government undercover agent, who named more than 500 persons as members of the Communist Party, and answered questions about Communist activities in neighborhood groups in and around New York.

Investigation of Communist Activities in the Newark, N. J., Area—Parts I–II (Part I: May 16, 17, 1955; Part II: May 18, 19; July 13, 1955); 335 pp. total, with index to both parts in Part II.—Investigation of Communist influence in labor, education, and professional groups. Includes testimony by an unnamed undercover agent who listed 75 persons who were Party members during the period 1942–1951; by Ernst S. Pollock, Anthony DeAquino, Julius Kolovetz, all former Party members, and others.

Investigation of Communist Activities in the New York Area—Part V, July 25, 28, 29; August 1, 1955; 90 pp., with index.—Includes testimony by Army Private Stanley A. Wechkin concerning six summer camps, and the techniques of indoctrination by which many persons who attended the camps were led to become Party members.

Investigation of Communist Activities in the Ohio Area (Testimony of Keve Bray), July 13, 1955; 16 pp., with index.—Includes testimony by Bray concerning the disputed question of his alleged membership in the CPUS.

Investigation of Communist Activities in the Los Angeles, California, Area—Parts I–IV (Part I: June 27, 28, 1955; Part II: June 29, 1955; Part III:

June 30, 1955; Part IV: July 1, 2, 1955); 468 pp. total, with index to all four parts in Part IV.—Includes testimony by William Ward Kimple, a government undercover agent, who named more than 1,000 persons he had known as members of the Communist Party. Also testimony concerning the activities of George Hugh Hardyman and his bilingual newspaper, *Korean Independence.*

Investigation of Communist Activities in the San Diego, California, Area, July 5, 6, 1955; 134 pp., with index.—Includes testimony by Anita Bell Schneider, an FBI undercover agent, concerning the Southern California Peace Crusade and its dissemination of Soviet propaganda.

Investigation of Communist Activities (The Committee to Secure Justice in the Rosenberg Case, and Affiliates)—Parts I–II (Part I: August 2, 3, 1955; Part II: August 4, 5, 1955); 214 pp. total, with index to both parts in Part II.—Includes testimony showing that the Committee to Secure Justice, etc., was controlled by the Communist Party. The National Committee collected $300,000 in contributions, and when it failed to win tax-exemption privileges, it attempted to avoid paying its taxes. Several of the Committee directors were Communists.

Investigation of Communist Activities in the New York Area—Parts VI–VIII (Entertainment) ; (Part VI: August 15, 16, 1955; Part VII: August 17, 18, 1955; Part VIII: October 14, 1955) ; 247 pp. total, with index to Parts VI and VII in Part VII; index to Part VIII in Part VIII.—Includes testimony showing how the Communists exploited the talents and financial resources of pro-Communist entertainers, and how they had dictated the policy of blacklisting, and how employers are plagued by the question whether or not the entertainers they hire are Communists.

Investigation of Communist Activities in the Los Angeles, California, Area—Part V, October 13, 1955; 28 pp., with index.—Includes testimony by Alson A. Bristol and Frank Davis concerning Communist recruiting techniques, as exemplified in the Southern California area.

Investigation of Communist Infiltration of Government—Parts I–II (Part I: December 13, 1955; Part II: December 14, 15, 1955); 153 pp. total, with index to both parts in Part II.—Includes testimony by Herbert Fuchs, a former Communist and former government employee, concerning his activities in government labor agencies. He identified 38 of his associates in the Party. Mortimer Riemer corroborated Fuchs' testimony, and both of them named Frank J. Donner as a Communist. The testimony also revealed the existence of ten hitherto-unknown Communist cells in the Executive and Legislative branches of the U. S. Government during the 1930's and 1940's.

REPORTS

Cumulative Index to Publications of the Committee on Un-American Activities, 1938–1954, January 20, 1955. 1,344 pp. with key.—The most comprehensive publication about the Committee's activities it has ever issued. Included are: the subject and date of each hearing, all witnesses, and all the persons mentioned in testimony since the formation of the Dies Committee in 1939, indexed as to hearing and page. The index reproduces the information contained in Index I (1942, no date), Index II (October 21, 1948), Index III (June 28, 1950), Index IV (April 25, 1952), and Index V (January 19, 1953). Also included: all publications, movies, and organizations ever mentioned in Committee hearings, with page references.

House Report No. 420—Subversive Activities Control Act Amendment of 1955, April 14, 1955; 4 pp.—The amendment proposes that the Subversive Activities Control Board increase from two to three years the period of activities it will study to determine whether the persons controlling Communist-infiltrated organizations are, or have been, members of the Communist Party.

House Report No. 1184—Terms of Subversive Activities Control Board Members, July 14, 1955; 3 pp.—Includes a proposal that members of the Subversive Activities Control Board be allowed to continue to serve the Board, upon expiration of their terms, until the appointment of a successor. The proposal was incorporated into the Subversive Activities Control Board Tenure Act, passed August 5, 1955.

House Report No. 1406—Proceedings Against John T. Gojack, July 26, 1955; 16 pp.—Includes the Committee's citation of Gojack for contempt (refusal to answer questions on First Amendment and pertinency grounds). Gojack's conviction was affirmed, 280 F. 2d 678 (1960).

House Report No. 1648—Annual Report for the Year 1955, January 11, 1956; 53 pp., with foreword, appendices, and index.—An account of the Committee's activities during the year, including sections on each of its hearings and investigations, a list of the year's publications, and a list of recommendations for future legislation based upon its hearings and investigations.

1956—84th Congress, Second Session

HEARINGS

Investigation of Communist Infiltration of Government—Parts III–V (Part III: February 14–16, 1956; Part IV: February 21, 23, 24, 1956; Part V: February 28, 29; March 1, 1956); 394 pp. total, with index to all three parts in Part V.—Includes testimony of James E. Gorham, a former party member and a former government employee, who answered questions concerning Communist cells in four government agencies, and the methods they used to gain access to classified documents.

Investigation of Communist Activities in the North Carolina Area, March 12–14, 1956; 150 pp., with index.—Includes testimony by Ralph C. Clontz,

FBI undercover agent, who exposed the Daniels Defense Committee as a Communist front and named its former Treasurer, Nathaniel Bond, as a Party member. Also the record of an appearance by Bond, who refused to affirm or deny Clentz's allegation.

Investigation of Communist Activities in the Los Angeles, California, Area—Part VII, April 16, 1956; 97 pp. (index to come in Part X).—Includes testimony by Donald Waddilove (and nine other witnesses), a musician and a former Communist, concerning subversive activities in his profession. Waddilove identified his associates.

Testimony of Nikolai Khokhlov (Former Soviet Intelligence Officer), Investigation of Communist Activities in the Los Angeles, California, Area—Parts VIII–X (Part VIII: April 17, 1956; Part IX: April 19, 1956; Part X: April 20, 21, 1956); 316 pp. total, with index to all parts in Part X.—Includes testimony by Khokhlov, who had recently defected from Russia, concerning thought control in Soviet art and literature, and the Russian people's dissatisfaction with their leaders. In the last two parts, the questions concerned Communist influence in the Independent Progressive Party, and in trade unions.

Investigation of Communist Activities in the Rocky Mountain Area—Parts I–II (Part I: May 15, 16, 1956; Part II: May 17, 18, 1956); 228 pp. total, with index to both parts in Part II.—Includes testimony by Bellarmino Duran, an FBI undercover agent, who gave information concerning Communist activities among Mexican-Americans, youth, and labor unions. He named 70 persons as members of the Party.

Investigation of the Unauthorized Use of United States Passports—Parts I–IV (Part I: May 23, 1956; Part II: May 24, 25, 1956; Part III: June 12, 13, 1956; Part IV: June 14, 21, 1956); 588 pp. total, with index to all parts in Part IV.—Includes testimony by Paul Robeson, playwright Arthur Miller, and others, concerning the illegal use of U. S. passports, the falsification of birth certificates to obtain passports, and concerning measures the government might adopt in order to reduce travel abroad by American Communists.

Investigation of Communist Propaganda in the United States—Part I (Foreign Propaganda—Entry and Dissemination), June 13, 1956; 27 pp., with index.—An account of Soviet and satellite propaganda aimed at aliens and refugees in the U. S. in the hope of persuading dissident elements among them to return to their native lands, and to instill dissatisfaction with life in America.

Investigation of Communist Activities in the St. Louis, Mo., Area—Parts I–IV (Part I: June 4, 1956; Part II: June 5, 1956; Part III: June 2, 6, 1956; Part IV: June 8, 1956); 363 pp. total, with index to all parts in Part IV.—Includes testimony of William W. Cortor and Thomas A. Younglove, both FBI undercover agents. Cortor had been a Party member before joining the FBI, and testified concerning his activities in the United Electrical Workers Union, the National Maritime Union, and other unions. Younglove told of his training by the Communists in sabotage techniques.

Investigation of Communist Propaganda Among Prisoners of War in Korea (Save Our Sons Committee), June 18, 19, 1956; 65 pp., with index.—Includes testimony by Anselm A. Czarnowski, Florence Cowgiel, Dale E. Jones, and others, showing that the Save Our Sons Committee was headed by known Communists, and that it made use of fraudulent POW letters from Korea.

Investigation of Communist Infiltration in Government—Part VI, June 20, 28, 1956; 22 pp., with index.—Includes the record of appearances by Ellis George Olim and Frank Donner, both of whom refused to testify on First and Fifth Amendment grounds. Donner had been named before the Committee as a member of the Communist Party by Herbert Fuchs and Mortimer Riemer.

Investigation of So-Called "Blacklisting" in the Entertainment Field—Report of the Fund for the Republic, Inc.—Parts I–III (Part I: July 10, 11, 1956; Part II: July 12, 13, 1956; Part III: July 17, 18, 1956); 244 pp. total, with index to all parts in Part III.—Includes testimony by John Cogley, George E. Sokolsky, Victor Riesel, and others, showing that the Fund for the Republic's report on "blacklisitng" erred in alleging that persons in the entertainment industry had been denied employment merely because of their political affiliations.

Investigation of Communist Propaganda in the United States—Part II (Foreign Propaganda—Entry and Dissemination in Philadelphia, Pa., Area), July 17, 1956; 35 pp., with index.—Includes testimony by U. S. Customs Chief Irving Fishman concerning the amount of Communist printed propaganda that reaches the U. S., and the character of that propaganda.

Investigation of the Award by the Fund for the Republic, Inc. (Plymouth Meeting, Pa.), July 18, 1956; 81 pp., with index.—An account of the Fund for the Republic's award of $5,000 to the Plymouth Meeting (Religious Society of Friends) because it retained a librarian who had refused to take the loyalty oath. The Plymouth Meeting refused the award, and the librarian in question was subsequently cited for contempt by a Senate committee.

International Communism (Testimony of Ernst Tillich), September 10, 11, 1956; 45 pp., with index.—Includes testimony by Ernst Tillich, leader of the Fighting Group Against Inhumanity behind the Iron Curtain, concerning the current European situation, and the giving of possible assistance to anti-Communists in the satellite countries.

Investigation of Communist Activities in the New Haven, Conn., Area—Parts I–II (Part I: September 24, 25, 1956; Part II: September 26, 1956); 225 pp. total, with index to both parts in Part II.—Includes testimony by Harold Kent, a government undercover agent, concerning Communist activities in and around New Haven, with special attention to Communist infiltration of trade unions and industrial plants.

Investigation of Communist Activities in the Los Angeles, California, Area—Part XI: December 16, 1953; June 6, July 5, 1956; 46 pp., with index.—Includes testimony by music composer Jerry Fielding, Judith Poska, Virginia Viertel, Joseph Ayeroff, and John Hubley. Fielding, Ayeroff, and Hubley refused to testify. Miss Poska stated that she had been to numerous Party meetings, but was "stunned" to hear she had been named as a member. Mrs. Viertel told of her own activities while a Party member.

Hearings on Attempts at Subversion and Espionage by Diplomatic Personnel, May 10, 11, 1956; 58 pp., with index.—Includes testimony concerning the use of diplomatic immunity for purposes of espionage by foreign embassies in Washington, with special attention to the case of Sidney Hatkin, whom the Russian embassy had requested to write a report on the aircraft industry in the U. S.

Investigation of Communist Activities in the Youngstown and Northern Ohio Areas, November 26, 27, 1956; 161 pp., with index.—Includes testimony by David W. Garfield, Frank Peoples, and others, concerning Communist activities in the subject area, with special attention to the heavy industries, community organizations, and the trade unions as targets for penetration.

Investigation of Communist Propaganda in the United States—Part III (Foreign Propaganda—Entry and Dissemination in the San Francisco, California, Area), December 10, 11, 1956; 100 pp., with index.—Includes testimony by John C. Caldwell concerning the dissemination of printed propaganda from behind the Iron Curtain, and possible methods of curtailing its circulation in the U. S.

Communist Political Subversion—Part I, dates: Washington, D. C., November 12-14, 1956; Youngstown, November 28, 1956; Chicago, December 3, 4, 1956; Los Angeles, December 5-8, 1956; San Francisco, December 11, 1956; Seattle, December 13, 14, 1956; 958 pp., with index.—Includes testimony by more than 115 witnesses, including Clarence A. Hathaway, Russell Nixon, Frank Wilkinson, Stephen Fritchman, all of whom had been named as Communists, and John Lautner, Barbara Hartle, both former Communists, and experts on Communism.

Communist Political Subversion—Part II, Appendix to Hearings in Part I, dates same as Part I; 1,382 pp., with index.—Contains documents, letters, newspapers, newspaper articles, Communist Party cards, excerpts from the *Daily Worker* and other Party publications, relevant to the Party's program of political subversion.

REPORTS

House Report No. 2189—The Great Pretense, A Symposium on Anti-Stalinism and the 20th Congress of the Soviet Communist Party, May 19, 1956; 173 pp.—A collection of papers, by recognized experts on Communism (among them Whittaker Chambers, Max Eastman, Francis J. Mc-Namara, David J. Dallin), concerning the apparent change in Soviet policy after the death of Stalin.

House Report No. 2240—The Communist Conspiracy, Strategy and Tactics of World Communism—Part I, Communism Outside the United States, with foreword and general introduction, Section A: Marxist Classics, May 29, 1956; 202 pp.—A detailed analysis of Marxist theory, history, and philosophy.

House Report No. 2241—The Communist Conspiracy, Strategy and Tactics of World Communism—Part I, Communism Outside the United States, Section B: The USSR, May 29, 1956; 528 pp.—A concise history of the Soviet Union since the Revolution of 1917.

House Report No. 2242—The Communist Conspiracy, Strategy and Tactics of World Communism—Part I, Communism Outside the United States, Section C: The World Congresses of the Communist International, May 29, 1956; 371 pp.—An analysis of the successive World Congresses of the Communist International, and of their policies and pronouncements.

House Report No. 2243—The Communist Conspiracy, Strategy and Tactics of World Communism—Part I, Communism Outside the United States, Section D: Communist Activities Around the World, May 29, 1956; 553 pp.—A comprehensive history of Communist machines and organizations in non-Russian countries, with special attention to fifth column movements.

House Report No. 2244—The Communist Conspiracy, Strategy and Tactics of World Communism—Part I, Communism Outside the United States, Section E: The Comintern and the CPUS, May 29, 1956; 343 pp.—A history of the Communist Party of the United States, with special attention to the control of its activities by the Comintern.

*A series of Reports (House Report Nos. 2915-2922) of contempt citations (refusal to answer questions on First and/or Fifth Amendment grounds), all of them July 25, 1956.**

Trial by Treason, The National Committee to Secure Justice for the Rosenbergs and Morton Sobell, August 25, 1956; 134 pp., with appendix

---

* Anne Yasgur Kling (1st A. and pertinency, acquitted, appeal by the government dismissed, 252 F. 2d 791 (1958)), John W. Simpson (5th A., case dismissed on a motion of the government), William E. Davis (5th A., acquitted), George Tyne (1st A. and pertinency, tried June 26, 1961, by District Court without jury; decision reserved), Elliot Sullivan (1st A., tried June 19, 1961, by District Court without jury; decision reserved), Peter Seeger (1st A., convicted March 21, 1961; appealing), Otto Nathan (1st A. and pertinency, acquitted, not reported), Arthur Miller (1st A. and pertinency, convicted, reversed, 259 F. 2d 187 (1958)).

and index.—A study of the numerous committees that were organized to demand reprieves for the Rosenbergs and Sobell following their trials for treason, and of the connection between some of these groups and the Communist Party.

Soviet Total War, "Historic Mission" of Violence and Deceit—Volume I, September 23, 1956; 421 pp.—A symposium on specific aspects of Soviet Cold War offensive, with chapters by J. Edgar Hoover, Whittaker Chambers, J. B. Matthews, Capt. Eddie Rickenbacker, David Sarnoff, E. Merrill Root, General Maxwell Taylor, General Nathan B. Twining, General Matthew Ridgeway, Lt. Gen. James H. Doolittle, and others.

Soviet Total War, "Historic Mission" of Violence and Deceit—Volume II, September 30, 1956; 477 pp.—A continuation of the symposium on the Soviet Cold War offensive, with chapters by the Editors of *Life* magazine, Allen Dulles, Ralph de Toledano, Robert Strausz-Hupé, Gen. Albert C. Wedemeyer, Lynn Montross, and others.

International Communism (Revolt in the Satellites)—Staff Consultations with: Dr. Jan Karski, Mihail Farcasanu, Joseph Lipski, Monsignor Bela Varga, Bela Fabian, Stevan Barankovics, Stanislow Mikolajczyk, Ferenc Nagy, October 29, 30; November 1, 17, 20, 1956; 83 pp., with index.—Contains statements by each of several persons who had lived under Soviet-imposed regimes (Hungary, Poland, Rumania), concerning the World Communist movement and the quality of life where that movement has achieved victory.

Guide to Subversive Organizations and Publications (and appendix), January 2, 1957; 151 pp., with index.—Sets forth information about each organization or publication listed as subversive by the Attorney General, by the Committee, or by other government committees and agencies. A revised edition of the May 14, 1951, Guide.

House Report No. 53—Annual Report for the Year 1956, January 2, 1957; 81 pp., with appendices and index.—An account of the Committee's activities during the year, with sections on Communist political subversion, propaganda, the passport conspiracy, the Fund for the Republic, and infiltration of government agencies, together with summaries of each hearing and investigation and the Committee's recommendations for future legislation.

1957—85th Congress, First Session

HEARINGS

International Communist Propaganda Activities, January 30, 1957; 47 pp., with synopsis and index.—Includes testimony by Henry Loomis, S. I. Nadler, Louis J. Doyle, and others, concerning the objectives of International Communism and the effectiveness of Communist propaganda.

*International Communism in Red China and the Far East (Testimony of Chiu-Yuan Hu), February 1, 1957; 14 pp., with synopsis and index.—*Includes testimony by Dr. Hu, adviser to the Chinese mission of the U.N. General Assembly, concerning the Peiping regime and its brutality, and the very considerable resistance it encounters. Also concerns Red China's flourishing narcotics trade.

*Investigation of Communist Propaganda in the United States—Part IV (Foreign Propaganda—Entry and Dissemination in New Orleans, La., Area), February 14, 1957; 53 pp., with synopsis and index.—*Includes testimony concerning the flow of Communist propaganda into New Orleans, none of it declared to U. S. authorities as required by law.

*Investigation of Communist Activities in the New Orleans, La., Area, February 16, 1957; 59 pp., with synopsis and index.—*Includes testimony by Lee Brown, Arthur Eugene, Jr., Theodore R. Means, and Dr. William Sorum. Eugene, a former Communist, told of his activities in the maritime unions, and of the Communist cells he had organized on luxury ocean liners. Sorum, also a former Party member, described his experiences on various levels of the Party's organization, and his Party activities at Tulane University.

*Investigation of Communist Activities in the New Haven, Conn., Area—Part III, February 26, 27, 1957; 69 pp., with synopsis and index.—*Includes the record of appearances by several witnesses whom the Committee sought to question about Communist influence in labor unions and community groups. All the witnesses except Harold Rodgers refused to testify on First or Fifth Amendment grounds, or both. Rodgers denied that he had ever been a Party member.

*Investigation of Communist Propaganda in the United States—Parts V–VII (Part V, New York City area: March 12, 13, 1957; Part VI, New York City area: March 14, 15, 1957; Part VII, Chicago area: March 26, 27, 1957); 358 pp. total, with synopsis to all parts in Part V, index to Parts V and VI in Part VI, index to Part VII in Part VII.—*Includes testimony by several witnesses concerning Communist-controlled foreign language publications and publishing houses in the U. S., including John Lautner, a former Communist, who named 18 persons as Party members. Also the record of appearances by all these 18 persons, each of whom invoked the Fifth Amendment, and by 10 other persons, who refused to testify.

*Investigation of Communism in the Metropolitan Music School, Inc., and Related Fields—Parts I–II (Part I: April 9, 10, 1957; Part II: February 7, 8; April 11, 12, 1957); 179 pp. total, with synopsis of both parts in Part I, index to both parts in Part II.—*Includes testimony concerning the Metropolitan Music School, its control by known Communists, and the incidence of Party members totaling 28, on its faculty. The school, the witnesses stated, was as much concerned with Communism and revolution as with music.

Investigation of Communist Activities in the Baltimore, Md., Area—Parts I–II (Part I: May 7, 8, 1957; Part II: May 9, 1957); 177 pp. total, with synopsis of both parts in Part I, index to both parts in Part II.—Includes testimony by Clifford Miller, a former member of the CPUS and later an FBI undercover agent, concerning Communist plans for the infiltration of industry, and their significance. Miller named as Communists several fellow employees at a Bethlehem Steel plant.

Hearings Held in San Francisco, Calif., June 18–21, 1957—Parts I–II (Part I: June 18, 19, 1957; Part II: June 20, 21, 1957); 256 pp. total, with synopsis of both parts in Part I, index to both parts in Part II.—Includes testimony by several witnesses, among them former Party member Jack Patten and FBI undercover agent Dorothy Jeffers, concerning Communist influence within professional groups. Also the record of appearances by 29 persons who refused to testify.

Investigation of Unauthorized Use of United States Passports—Part V, July 26, 1957; 16 pp., with synopsis and index.—Includes testimony by Susan Warren Frank, who had been named in public documents as a functionary of the Communist Party in New York City. When questioned as to whether she had proposed to Arthur Miller, the playwright, that he join the Party, she invoked the Fifth Amendment.

Investigation of Communist Activities in the Newark, N. J., Area (Supplemental), July 24, 1957; 12 pp., with synopsis and index.—Includes the record of appearances by Mrs. Estelle Laba and Mrs. Perry Zimmerman, both of whom had been named as Party members. Each refused to testify.

Investigation of Communist Penetration of Communications Facilities—Part I, July 17–19; August 2, 9, 1957; 152 pp., with synopsis and index.—Includes testimony concerning Communist influence among the personnel servicing communications facilities, and the dangers involved in allowing Communists to hold jobs that give them access to such facilities. Also testimony by officials of the American Communications Association, which had been expelled from the CIO in 1950 on the grounds that it was Communist-infiltrated.

Investigation of Communist Propaganda in the United States—Part VIII (Buffalo, N. Y., Area), October 1, 1957; 68 pp., with synopsis and index.—Includes testimony by Irving Fishman of the New York Customs Bureau concerning the need for legislation imposing stricter controls on the dissemination of Communist propaganda in the United States. Also the record of appearances by two persons who had been named as Communists and who refused to testify.

Investigation of Communist Activities in the Buffalo, N.Y., Area—Parts I–II (Part I: October 2, 1957; Part II: October 3, 4, 1957); 97 pp. total,

with synopsis to both parts in Part I, index to both parts in Part II.—
Includes testimony concerning the Committee's omnibus security bill
(H.R. 9352), and Communist influence within the steel, mining, and
railroad unions.

*Investigation of Communist Penetration of Communications Facilities—
Part II, October 9, 1957; 24 pp., with synopsis and index.*—Includes testimony by A. Tylor Port and Paul Goldsborough on the dangers of allowing Communists to hold jobs that give them access to communication
facilities.

*Investigation of Soviet Espionage, October 7–9; November 20, 1957; 64
pp., with synopsis and index.*—Includes testimony by Jane Foster Zlatovsky,
John B. Rackliffe, Henry Hill Collins, Jr., William Rossmore, and others,
pursuant to information supplied by Boris Morros, U. S. counterspy, concerning a Soviet espionage ring.

REPORTS AND CONSULTATIONS

*International Communism (Revolt in the Satellites), Staff Consultations
with Janós Horváth, Sandor Kiss, March 20, 1957; 34 pp., with synopsis
and index.*—Includes statements by two of the leaders of the Hungarian
revolt concerning conditions in Hungary subsequent to the repression of
the freedom fighters, and the political attitudes of the Hungarian people.

*International Communism (Communist Control of Estonia), Staff Con-
sultation with August Rei, May 10, 1957; 15 pp., with synopsis and index.*—
Includes a statement by August Rei, sometime President of Estonia, concerning conditions in Estonia and other Baltic countries under Soviet
occupation.

*International Communism (The Communist Mind), Staff Consultation
with Frederick Charles Schwarz, May 29, 1957; 14 pp., with synopsis and
index.*—Includes a statement by Dr. Schwarz concerning the mentality of
those who have accepted the tenets of Communism, and the methods
used by the Communists to enhance that appeal.

*International Communism (Communist Penetration of Malaya and
Singapore), Staff Consultation with Kuo-shuen Chang, May 29, 1957; 16
pp., with synopsis and index.*—Includes a statement by Chang, former
editor of a newspaper in Singapore, concerning Communist preparations
for seizing control of Singapore and Malaya, once British control there
ends, with irregular forces, and concerning the political attitudes of the
Malayan people, with special attention to the incidence among them of
Communist influence.

*Who Are They? Prepared at the Request of the Committee on Un-
American Activities by the Legislative Reference Service of the Library of
Congress—Part I: Khrushchev and Bulganin (USSR), July 12, 1957; 5 pp.,*

with index.—The first of ten parts giving biographies of significant leaders of Communist movements throughout the world.*

House Report No. 1182—Communist Political Subversion, the Campaign to Destroy the Security Programs of the United States Government, August 16, 1957; 85 pp., with appendices and index.—An account of the techniques used by the Communist Party and Soviet agents to circumvent U. S. security programs.

International Communism (the Communist Trade Offensive), Staff Consultations with Joseph Anthony Marcus, Christopher Emmet, Nicholas de Rochefort, June 26, 1957; 28 pp., with synopsis and index.—Includes statements by Marcus, Emmet, and De Rochefort on the fallacy of attempting to trade with the Soviet bloc. Each trade agreement, they insist, is a further avenue for Communist infiltration.

A Series of Reports (House Report Nos. 1239-1241) of contempt citations (refusal to answer questions on First Amendment and pertinency grounds), all dated August 23, 1957.†

The Ideological Fallacies of Communism, Staff Consultations with Dr. S. Andhil Fineberg, Bishop Fulton J. Sheen, Rev. Daniel A. Poling, September 4, 25; October 18, 1957; 25 pp., with synopsis and index.—Includes testimony by prominent religious leaders concerning the clash between Communism and the Jewish, Catholic, and Protestant faiths.

"Operation Abolition," the Campaign Against the House Committee on Un-American Activities, the Federal Bureau of Investigation, and the Government Security Program, by the Emergency Civil Liberties Committee and Its Affiliates, November 8, 1957; 15 pp., with appendix and index.—An account of the activities of the Emergency Civil Liberties Committee, its leaders, and the organizations with which it has co-operated in its efforts to bring about the abolition of the Committee and other government security agencies.

International Communism (the Present Posture of the Free World), Staff Consultation with Constantine Brown, Foreign News Analyst, October 21, 1957; 20 pp., with synopsis and index.—A statement by Constantine Brown, Washington journalist, concerning the attitude of Spain, Western Europe, the Middle East, the Far East, Japan, and Korea toward Communism and the Soviet Union.

International Communism (Espionage), Excerpts of Consultation with Counterspy Boris Morros, August 16, 1957; 21 pp., with index.—Reproduces five articles, published in the *Philadelphia Enquirer,* by Francis E.

* Parts II through VII, published between August and November, 1957, describe, respectively: Mao Tse-tung and Chou En-lai, Georgi Zhukov and Ivan Konev, Walter Ulbricht and Janos Kadar, Josip Broz Tito and Wladyslaw Gomulka, Kim Il Sung and Ho Chi Minh, Maurice Thorez and Palmiro Togliatti.

† Louis Earl Hartman (convicted, appealing), Frank Grumman (convicted, affirmed June 30, 1961), Bernard Silber (convicted, affirmed June 30, 1961).

Walter, the Committee's Chairman, September 29–October 3, 1957, concerning the information presented to the Committee by Boris Morros, a counterespionage agent, and the methods by which he obtained it.

International Communism (Communist Designs on Indonesia and the Pacific Frontier), Staff Consultation with Gen. Charles A. Willoughby, Former Chief of Intelligence, Far Eastern Command, Under General Douglas MacArthur, December 16, 1957; 36 pp., with synopsis, appendix, and index.—Includes a statement by General Willoughby concerning conditions in Indonesia, especially the incidence of Communist influence within its frontiers. General Willoughby emphasized the strategic importance of Indonesia from the standpoint of maintaining Free World unity in the Pacific area.

House Report No. 1360—Annual Report for the Year 1957, February 3, 1958; 90 pp., with appendix and index.—An account of the Committee's activities during the year, including its omnibus security bill, publications it issued, its reference service, its contempt proceedings, its findings about Communism in various localities and about Communist propaganda, and its recommendations for future legislation and other sections. The appendix includes the Court of Appeals majority opinion in the Barenblatt case.

1958—85th Congress, Second Session

HEARINGS

Investigation of Soviet Espionage—Part II, February 28, 1956; February 25, 1958; 50 pp., with synopsis and index.—Includes testimony by Morton Stavis, Esther Auerbach Stavis (1956), Arthur Stein, Herman Zap, and others concerning Soviet espionage, and pursuant to evidence presented by Boris Morros.

Investigation of Communist Infiltration and Propaganda Activities in Basic Industry (Gary, Ind., Area), February 10, 11, 1958; 127 pp., with synopsis and index.—Includes testimony by John Lautner, who had belonged to the CPUS for 20 years until he was expelled in 1950, concerning Communist infiltration of labor unions and Communist colonization of businesses and industries.

Investigation of Communist Activities in the New England Area—Parts I–III (Part I: March 18, 1958; Part II: March 19, 1958; Part III: March 14, 20, 21, 1958); 340 pp. total, with synopsis of all parts in Part I, index to all parts in Part III.—Includes testimony by Armando Penha, FBI undercover agent, concerning Communist organization and operations in New England. Penha named over 200 members of the Party.

Communist Propaganda—Part IX, Student Groups, Distributors and Propagandists, June 11, 12, 1958; 51 pp., with synopsis and index.—Includes further testimony by Irving Fishman of the New York Customs Bureau, who described the propaganda the Communists aim at students and youth groups throughout the world. Fishman named the International Union of Students and the World Federation of Democratic Youth as the two groups most active in disseminating Communist propaganda.

Communism in the New York Area (Entertainment), April 1, 1957; May 8; June 18, 19, 1958; 126 pp., with synopsis and index.—Includes the testimony of John Lautner, a former CPUS member, and the record of the appearances of 19 witnesses who refused to testify.

Communist Infiltration and Activities in the South, July 29–31, 1958; 152 pp., with synopsis and index.—Includes further testimony by Armando Penha, an FBI undercover agent. Penha answered questions about the National Textile Commission, a highly secret entity in the Communist apparatus, whose five members select and train "colonizers" from the North to participate in Communist activities in the South.

Communist Infiltration and Activities in Newark, N. J., September 3–5, 1958; 47 pp., with synopsis and index.—Includes testimony by Robert J. Dixon, Jr., Bernard Zick, and others. Dixon, who had been President of his local of the United Electrical Workers Union before his break with the Communist Party in 1950, testified concerning his activities as a Party member, and named his associates. Dixon named as Communists eight witnesses who appeared but refused to testify. Zick, also a former Communist, named as Communists six other witnesses.

REPORTS AND CONSULTATIONS

Who Are They?—Part VIII: Vincente Lombardo Toledano and Luis Carlos Prestes (Mexico-Brazil), February 21, 1958; 9 pp., with index— Further biographies of Communist leaders.

Who Are They?—Part IX: Enver Hoxha and Gheorghe Gheorghiu-Dej (Albania-Rumania), August 5, 1958; 13 pp., with index.—Further biographies of Communist leaders.

The Erica Wallach Story, March 21, 1958; 80 pp., with index.—Includes a synopsis of testimony to the Committee by Erica Wallach concerning her mistreatment by the Communists in the course of her searching for a friend whom Communist agents had kidnaped. She, too, was in due course kidnaped, and spent five years in Communist prisons and slave-labor camps.

The Communist Program for World Conquest, Staff Consultation with Gen. Albert C. Wedemeyer, January 21, 1958; 35 pp., with synopsis and index.—Includes a statement by General Wedemeyer concerning the deterioration of the world situation through the years of the Cold War.

Communist Psychological Warfare (Brainwashing), Staff Consultation with Edward Hunter, March 13, 1958; 25 pp., with synopsis and index.—

Includes a statement by Hunter concerning Communist psychological warfare techniques, and their implications for the United States.

Chronicle of Treason, Reprint of a Series of Articles by Representative Francis E. Walter, Appearing in the Philadelphia Inquirer, *March 3–9, 1958; 35 pp., with index.*—Reproduces five contributions by Francis E. Walter, the Committee's Chairman, to the *Philadelphia Inquirer,* concerning recent American traitors, among them Rudolf Abel, Judy Coplon, Harry Gold, and the Rosenbergs.

House Report No. 1724—Organized Communism in the United States, May 14, 1958; 153 pp., with index.—A detailed account of the Communist Party's operations and techniques in the field of propaganda, with special attention to the distribution of the operations on various hierarchical levels.

*A Series of Reports (House Report Nos. 2334–2340) of contempt citations (refusal to answer questions on First Amendment grounds, Lehrer and Samter adding pertinency), all dated July 31, 1958.**

Two reports (House Report Nos. 2583–2584), of contempt proceedings (refusal to answer questions on First Amendment grounds), both dated August 13, 1958.†

International Communism (Communist Propaganda Activities in Canada), Staff Consultation with Milan Jakubec, President of the Executive Council of the Mutual Co-operation League of Canada, April 3, 1958; 16 pp., with synopsis and index.—Includes a statement by Jakubec concerning Communist infiltration in Canada. Soviet agents, he assured the Committee, collect $20–30,000,000 each year in the form of customs duties assessed on parcels sent to the Soviet Union.

Communist Psychological Warfare (Thought Control), Staff Consultation with Professor Boldyreff of the National Alliance of Russian Solidarists, April 7, 1958; 23 pp., with synopsis and index.—Includes a statement by Constantin W. Boldyreff concerning the role of propaganda in the Cold War: Soviet concentration on conditioning the minds and hearts of the citizens of Western countries so as to prepare them for continuing Soviet expansion at their expense.

International Communism (Communist Encroachment in the Far East), Staff Consultation with Major General Claire Lee Chennault, United

---

* Edward Yellin (convicted, affirmed February 16, 1961. Filed petition for cert., i.e., requested a hearing before Supreme Court), Robert Lehrer (awaiting trial; case on open calendar), Alfred James Samter (awaiting trial; case on open calendar), Victor Malis (awaiting trial; case on open calendar), Sidney Turoff (convicted, reversed, June 29, 1961), Sidney Herbert Ingerman (indictment dismissed), Paul Rosenkrants (court accepted plea of *nolo contendere;* to reappear before Committee).

† Frank Wilkinson (convicted, affirmed, 365 U.S. 399 (1961)), Carl Braden (convicted, affirmed, 365 U.S. 431 (1961)).

States Army, April 23, 1958; 17 pp., with synopsis and index.—Includes a statement by General Chennault, maintaining that peace can be assured only if the West shifts over to an offensive role.

What Is Behind the Soviet Proposal for a Summit Conference? Staff Consultations with Dr. David J. Dallin, Dr. Anthony Bouscaren, Dr. James D. Atkinson, Francis J. McNamara, April 29, 1958; 29 pp., with synopsis and index.—Includes statements by Dallin, Bouscaren, Atkinson, and McNamara concerning Russia's motives in seeking a Summit Conference, and the gains such a conference would in fact confer on the USSR.

Communist Strategy of Protracted Conflict, Staff Consultation with Dr. Robert Strausz-Hupé, Alvin J. Cottrell, James E. Dougherty, May 20, 1958; 19 pp., with synopsis and index.—Includes statements by Strausz-Hupé, Cottrell, and Dougherty, all experts on the Cold War, concerning the basic theory of protracted conflict, and Communist techniques for turning such conflict to their own advantage.

The Ideology of Freedom vs. the Ideology of Communism, Staff Consultation with Dr. Charles Wesley Lowry, Chairman and Executive Director of the Foundation for Religious Action in the Social and Civil Order, June 5, 1958; 22 pp., with synopsis and index.—Includes a statement by Dr. Lowry, a former clergyman who abandoned the pulpit to devote himself to the struggle against Communism, concerning the points of difference between Communist ideology and Western beliefs.

The Irrationality of Communism, Staff Consultation with Dr. Gerhart Niemeyer, August 8, 1958; 16 pp., with synopsis and index.—Includes a statement by Niemeyer, an authority on Communism and a professor of political science at Notre Dame University, concerning the basic fallacies of Communist ideology, and the parallels between Communism and Nazism.

International Communism in Yugoslavia, the Myth of "Titoism," Staff Consultation with Dr. Alex N. Dragnich, September 15, 1958; 13 pp., with synopsis and index.—Includes a statement by Dragnich concerning his reasons for thinking that Tito is still tied to Moscow, and why the USSR will be victorious in the Cold War.

Legislative Recommendations by the House Committee on Un-American Activities, and Subsequent Action Taken by Congress or Executive Agencies, June 1958; 89 pp., with foreword and appendices.—Lists all the Committee's recommendations for legislation, and subsequent action taken on each one. The report is divided into two parts; the first deals with all recommendations prior to 1958, the second with the 17 principal provisions of the Internal Security Amendments Act of 1958 (H.R. 9937).

The House Committee on Un-American Activities, What It Is—What It Does, July, 1958; 21 pp.—An account of the function and purpose of the

Committee; a revised edition of *This Is Your House Committee on Un-American Activities*, issued September 19, 1954.

Supplement to Cumulative Index to Publications of the Committee on Un-American Activities, 1955 and 1956 (84th Congress), December, 1958; 334 pp., with key.—A listing of all the witnesses and individuals mentioned in testimony during 1955 and 1956, together with publications, movies, and organizations mentioned in testimony, with page references. (Incorporated in the Cumulative Index for the years 1955–1960, issued in 1961.)

Two unnumbered, typewritten Reports of contempt citations (refusal to appear), both dated December 22, 1958.*

House Report No. 187—Annual Report for the Year 1958, March 8, 1959; 104 pp., with index.—An account of the year's hearings and investigations, summarizing each of its reports and consultations during the year. Also included: a synopsis of the publications issued, a statement regarding the Committee's reference service, and a list of recommendations for future legislation.

1959—86th Congress, First Session

HEARINGS

The Kremlin's Espionage and Terror Organizations, Testimony of Peter S. Deriabin, Former Officer of the USSR's Committee of State Security (KGB), March 17, 1959; 16 pp., with synopsis and index.—Includes testimony by Deriabin, a former Soviet security official, concerning the methods and techniques of the two Soviet intelligence services.

The Southern California District of the Communist Party, Structure-Objectives-Leadership—Parts I–III (Part I: September 2, 3, 1958; Part II: September 4, 5, 1958; Part III: February 24, 25, 1959); 295 pp. total, with index to all parts in Part III.—Includes testimony by Dorothy Ray Healey, David Francis Arkin, Horace V. Alexander, Sakai Ishihara, Rosemary Lusher, Archibald MacNair, Jr., and others, concerning the incidence and character of Communist activities in Southern California.

Current Strategy and Tactics of Communists in the United States (Greater Pittsburgh Area)—Parts I–III (Part I: March 10, 1959; Part II: March 11, 1959; Part III: March 12, 1959); 193 pp. total, with index and synopsis in each part.—Includes testimony, among others, by Frank Donner, who had three times been named as a Communist, concerning the problems of security in industrial establishments with defense contracts, and the problems arising in connection with the denaturalization and deportation of Communists.

---

* Harvey O'Connor (awaiting trial; case on open calendar), Donald Wheeldin (convicted, affirmed, October 17, 1960. Cert. denied June 16, 1961).

Passport Security—Part I (Testimony of Harry R. Bridges), April 21, 1959; 80 pp., with synopsis and index.—Includes the record of an appearance by Harry R. Bridges, President of the International Longshoreman's and Warehousemen's Union, who refused to testify regarding his alleged Communist activities. He stated that if the U. S. were to ship arms to Formosa during the war between Formosa and Red China, his union might well call a strike.

Passport Security—Part II, April 22–24; June 5, 1959; 153 pp., with synopsis and index.—Includes testimony by 15 witnesses, all of whom were questioned regarding their passport applications and alleged Communist affiliations.

Communist Infiltration of Vital Industries and Current Communist Techniques in the Chicago, Ill., Area, May 5–7, 1959; 151 pp., with synopsis and index.—Includes testimony concerning Communist "colonizing" of basic industries, especially the meat packing industry and the meat packers' unions.

The American National Exhibition, Moscow, July, 1959 (a Record of Certain Artists and an Appraisal of their Works Selected for Displays), July 1, 1959; 68 pp., with synopsis and index.—Includes testimony by Wheeler Williams, President of the American Artists' Professional League, and others, showing how the Communists use art as a propaganda weapon. One third of the artists represented in the American exhibition in Moscow had, according to the witnesses questioned, extensive Communist affiliations.

Communist Training Operations—Part I, July 21, 22, 1959; 108 pp., with synopsis and index.—An account of methods used to indoctrinate Communist recruits at the Jefferson School of Social Science and its successor, the Faculty of Social Sciences, both of which, witnesses stated, were instruments of the Communist Party.

Testimony by Clinton Edward Jencks, July 22, 1959; 28 pp., with synopsis and index.—Includes testimony by Jencks, named in October, 1952 as a Communist by Kenneth Eckert, working in the capacity of international representative for the International Union of Mine, Mill and Smelter Workers. Jencks refused to testify.

Testimony of Arnold Johnson, Legislative Director of the Communist Party, U.S.A., September 22, 1959; 8 pp., with synopsis and index.—Includes the record of an appearance by Arnold Johnson, the CPUS's Legislative Director, who refused to answer any questions about his recent activities, including alleged Communist lobbying in Washington, participation in the television movie *Dissent in America*, membership in the Faculty for Social Sciences, and a trip around the U. S. for the alleged purpose of gathering information for Khrushchev to use on his visit.

Western Section of Southern California District of the Communist Party—Parts I–III (Part I: October 20, 1959; Part II: October 21, 1959;

Part III: October 22, 1959); 168 pp., total, with synopsis to all parts in Part I, index to all parts in Part III.—Includes testimony by Mrs. Moiselle J. Clanger, Mrs. Marion Miller, Mrs. Adele Kronick Silva, all FBI undercover agents, and others, concerning recent Communist gains in the southern California area.

Communist Activities Among Puerto Ricans in New York City and Puerto Rico—Part I (New York City), November 16, 17, 1959; 99 pp., with synopsis and index.—Includes testimony concerning Communist subversion and infiltration of Puerto Rican groups, with special attention to methods of recruiting Party members in the New York City area.

Communist Activities Among Puerto Ricans in New York City and Puerto Rico—Part II (San Juan, Puerto Rico), November 18–20, 1959; 118 pp., with synopsis and index.—Includes testimony showing that the Communists spend over $100,000,000 per year on propaganda directed at South America, mostly through Spanish-language publications, with Puerto Rico as its main source of dissemination.

REPORTS AND CONSULTATIONS

House Report No. 41—Communist Legal Subversion, the Role of the Communist Lawyer, February 23, 1959; 75 pp., with index.—An account of the Communist legal network, an examination of the role played by Communist lawyers, with case histories of the most active Communist lawyers, among them Frank J. Donner, Bertram Edises, John J. Abt, and Nathan Witt.

House Report No. 259—Report on the Southern California District of the Communist Party Structure-Objectives-Leadership, April 3, 1959; 120 pp., with index.—An account of the CPUS apparatus in Southern California.

Language as a Communist Weapon, Staff Consultation with Dr. Stefan Possony, March 2, 1959; 51 pp., with synopsis and index.—Includes a statement by Stefan Possony, an expert on both Communism and strategy, as to the Communists' use of language as a mask for their objectives (recruiting members, lessening unfavorable reactions to their mischief-making when it is exposed, and softening up the West).

Communist Persecution of the Churches in Red China and Northern Korea, Staff Consultation iwth Five Church Leaders: Rev. Peter Chu Pong, Rev. Shih-Ping Wang, Rev. Tsin-Tsai Liu, Rev. Samuel W. S. Cheng, Kyung Rai Kim, March 26, 1959; 35 pp., with synopsis and index.—Includes testimony by five Protestant leaders from Formosa, Hong Kong, and South Korea, concerning Communist extirpation of all traces of Christianity and other religions in the Far East areas that they control.

Control of the Arts in the Communist Empire, Staff Consultation with Ivan P. Bahriany, June 3, 1959; 24 pp., with synopsis and index.—Includes a statement by Ivan P. Bahriany concerning Soviet cultural expositions, and the absence of "unsupervised" culture in the Soviet Union.

Who Are They?—Part X: Karl Marx, August 28, 1959; 13 pp., with index. —A brief biography of the founder of the Communist movement.

Communist Lobbying Activities in the Nation's Capital, September 3, 1959; 12 pp., with index.—An account of Communist lobbying in Washington, especially by Communist members of the legal profession and Communist front organizations.

The Communist Parcel Operation, September 25, 1959; 17 pp., with index.—An account of Communist extortion of customs duties on relief packages sent behind the Iron Curtain.

The Crimes of Khrushchev—Part I, Staff Consultation with Eugene Lyons, September 4, 1959; 18 pp., with synopsis and index.—The first of a series of consultations with experts on Communism. Lyons provides a biographical sketch of Khrushchev, and analyzes his current maneuvers.

The Crimes of Khrushchev—Part II, Staff Consultations with Dr. Lev E. Dobriansky, Petro Pavlovych, Professor Ivan M. Malinin, Nicholas Prychodko, Constantin Kononenko, Mykola Lebed, Gregory Kostiuk, Professor Ivan Wowchuk, Jurij Lawrynenko, September 9–11, 1959; 69 pp., with synopsis and index.—An account of the mass murders ordered by Khrushchev, with particular stress on his activities in the Ukraine.

The Crimes of Khrushchev—Part III, Staff Consultations with Gen. Bela Kiraly, Joseph Kovago, September 10, 1959; 25 pp., with synopsis and index.—Eyewitness descriptions of Khrushchev's role in the suppression of the Hungarian revolt.

The Crimes of Khrushchev—Part IV, Staff Consultations with Dr. Vilis Masens, Vaclovas Sidzikauskas, September 21, 1959; 18 pp., with synopsis and index.—An account of the repressive measures Russia takes to maintain her control in the Balkans.

The Crimes of Khrushchev—Part V, Staff Consultations with Joseph Pauco, Father Theodoric Joseph Zubek, Nuci Kotta, Arshi Pipa, December 17, 1959; 33 pp., with synopsis and index.—An account of Khrushchev's activities in Slovakia and Albania.

The Crimes of Khrushchev—Part VI, Staff Consultations with Rusi Nasar, Ergacsh Schermatoglu, Constant Mierlak, Vitaut Tumash, Anton Shukeloyts, December 17, 1959; 25 pp., with synopsis and index.—An account of the "Virgin Land Policy," in whose name Khrushchev moved hundreds of thousands of inhabitants from the satellites and resettled them in Siberia and Turkestan.

The Crimes of Khrushchev—Part VII, Staff Consultations with Guivy Zaldastani, George Nakashidse, Dimitar K. Petkoff, Mrs. Cathrine Boyan Choukanoff, January 8, 1960; 48 pp., with synopsis and index.—An account of Khrushchev's terrorism in Georgia, SSR.

Facts on Communism—Volume I, The Communist Ideology, December 13, 1959; 135 pp., with index.—A detailed analysis of Communist ideology, put together with the assistance of Professor Gerhart Niemeyer of Notre Dame University.

House Report No. 1122—Security Program With Respect to Defense Contractors and Their Employees, September 2, 1959; 40 pp.—The record of the Committee's recommendation on how to increase security safeguards in the defense industry. (The proposal was not enacted, and is up again before the present Congress.)

House Report No. 1123—Making Final Orders of the Subversive Activities Control Board With Respect to Communist Organizations Applicable to Successor Organizations, September 2, 1959; 44 pp.—The Committee recommends legislation designed to cope with the practice of Communist-action, Communist front, and Communist-infiltrated organizations, of legally changing their names in order to evade the requirements imposed upon them by the SACB. (The proposal was not enacted. It is again pending before the present Congress.)

House Report No. 1135—Proceedings Against Martin Popper, September 3, 1959; 29 pp.—Includes the Committee's citation of Popper (refusal to answer questions on First Amendment, pertinency, and "lack of authority" grounds). (Convicted May 4, 1961. Appealing.)

House Report No. 1136—Proceedings Against Edwin A. Alexander, September 3, 1959; 34 pp.—Includes the Committee's citation of Alexander for contempt (refusal to answer questions on all constitutional grounds except self-incrimination). (Presented to the Grand Jury: no true bill returned.)

Patterns of Soviet Espionage, January, 1959 (bound in Volume II, 1958); 81 pp., with index.—A report on the nature and extent of Soviet espionage activities, including a record of the names of apprehended Soviet spies, the date when each was caught, the place where, and the action taken in each case.

House Report No. 1251—Annual Report for the Year 1959, February 8, 1960; 144 pp., with index.—A résumé of the year's operations, including a précis of the hearings, a summary of the reports, consultations, and the biographical *Who Are They?* series, contempt proceedings, an explanation of the Committee's files and reference service, and legislative recommendations.

1960—86th Congress, Second Session

HEARINGS

Issues Presented by the Air Reserve Center Training Manual, February 25, 1960 (bound in Volume I, 1959); 36 pp., with index.—Including testimony by Dudley C. Sharp, Secretary of the Air Force, concerning statements in a training manual regarding the Communist front affiliations of certain members of the Protestant clergy, to which representatives of the National Council of Churches, and others, had objected.

Communist Training Operations—Parts II–III (Communist Activities and Propaganda Among Youth Groups): (Part II: February 2, 3, 1960; Part III: February 4, 5; March 2, 1960), bound in Volume I, 1959; 181 pp. total, with synopsis of both parts in Part II, appendix and index to both part in Part III.—Including testimony by Herbert A. Philbrick, Andrew Ilyinsky, Charles Wiley, Paul Robeson, Jr., Stephen Tyler, and others, pursuant to an inquiry into the operations and techniques of the Communist youth movement.

Communist Espionage in the United States, Testimony of Frantisek Tisler, Former Military Attaché, Czechoslovak Embassy in Washington, D. C., May 10, 1960; 9 pp., with index.—Testimony concerning the role played by the Czech Embassy in Communist espionage in the U. S.

Testimony of Anthony Krchmarek and Charles Musil, May 26, 1960; 13 pp., with index.—Both witnesses refused to answer questions concerning their alleged Party affiliations.

Communist Activities Among Seamen and on Waterfront Facilities— Part I, June 6–8, 23, 1960; 107 pp., with synopsis and index.—Includes testimony by Vice-Admiral James A. Hirshfield, Assistant Commandant of the Coast Guard, and others, concerning the dangers of Communist influence on the waterfront.

Communist Penetration of Radio Facilities (Conelrad-Communications) —Part I, August 23, 24, 1960; 46 pp., with synopsis and index.—Including testimony by Robert E. Lee, a member of the Federal Communications Commission, describing Conelrad and its function, and reporting on the granting of radio licenses to Communists.

Testimony of Captain Nikolai Fedorovich Artamonov, Former Soviet Naval Officer, September 14, 1960; 17 pp., with synopsis and index.— Testimony concerning Artamonov's experiences: his life in Russia, his escape to the West, and the capacities of the Soviet Navy.

The Northern California District of the Communist Party, Structure-Objectives-Leadership—Parts I–IV (Part I: May 12, 1960; Part II: May 13, 1960; Part III: May 14, 1960; Part IV: Appendix to all preceding parts, 493 pp., total, with synopsis of all parts in Part I, and index in each part.— Including testimony by former Communist Barbara Hartle, and the record of appearances by Archie Brown, Douglas Wachter, Sol Wachter, and others who refused to answer questions concerning the scope and leadership of Communist activities in the Bay area. The proceedings were constantly interrupted by demonstrators against the Committee. The scene of the famous San Francisco riots that led to the film *Operation Abolition*.

REPORTS AND CONSULTATIONS

Lest We Forget! A Pictorial Summary of Communism in Action: Albania, Bulgaria, Estonia, Finland, Hungary, Latvia, Lithuania, Poland, Czechoslovakia, Rumania, Soviet Union, Ukraine, Staff Consultation with Klaus Samuli Gunnar Romppanen, January 13, 1960; 48 pp., with index.—A series of photographs depicting Russian atrocities with a commentary on each picture.

Soviet "Justice": "Showplace" Prisons vs. Real Slave Labor Camps, Staff Consultation with Adam Joseph Galinski, April 4, 1960; 50 pp., with synopsis and index.—The witness described a typical Soviet prison as prepared for exhibition to foreign visitors, and the contrast with real prison conditions.

Communist Economic Warfare, Staff Consultation with Dr. Robert Loring Allen, April 6, 1960; 23 pp., with synopsis and index.—Testimony by a specialist in international trade on how the Russians exploit foreign trade as a weapon in the Cold War.

How the Chinese Reds Hoodwink Visiting Foreigners, Staff Consultation with Robert Loh, April 21, 1960; 34 pp., with synopsis and index.— A recent escapee from Communist China testifies concerning the means by which the Red Chinese disguise the shortcomings and failures of their social and economic system for the benefit of foreign observers.

House Report No. 2025—Amending the Subversive Activities Control Act of 1950 so as to Require the Registration of Certain Additional Persons Disseminating Political Propaganda Within the United States as Agents of a Foreign Principal, and for Other Purposes, June 28, 1960; 4 pp.—Legislative proposals (still pending before Congress), designed to eliminate loopholes in the Internal Security Act of 1950.

Communist Target—Youth, Communist Infiltration and Agitation Tactics, July, 1960; 18 pp., with index.—A report by J. Edgar Hoover on Communist methods of crowd control, as practiced in the rioting that occurred during the Committee's hearings in San Francisco, May 12–14, 1960.

A Series of Reports (House Report Nos. 2122–2134) of citations for contempt (refusal to answer questions on First Amendment and "lack of jurisdiction" grounds), all dated August 23, 1960. Action on each is pending by the Grand Jury.*

House Report No. 2137—Amending the Subversive Activities Control Act of 1950 so as to Provide That No Individual Who Willfully Fails or Refuses to Answer, or Falsely Answers, Certain Questions Relating to Subversive Activities, When Summoned to Appear Before Certain Federal

---

* José Enamorado Cuesta, Manual Arroyo Zeppenfeldt, Consuelo Burgos de Saez Pagan, Juan Saez Corales, John Peter Hawes, Gertrudis Melendez Perez, Ramon Diaz Cruz, Frank Ruiz, Juan Emmanuelli Morales, Cesar Andreu Iglesias, Pablo M. Garcia Rodriguez, Cristino Perez Mendez, Juan Santos Rivera.

Agencies, Shall Be Employed on Any Merchant Vessel of the United States or Within Certain Waterfront Facilities in the United States, August 23, 1960; 43 pp.—Proposed amendments (still pending before Congress) to the Internal Security Act of 1950.

House Report No. 2228—The Communist-Led Riots Against the House Committee on Un-American Activities in San Francisco, Calif., May 12–14, 1960; October 7, 1960; 22 pp., with index.—The Committee's reasons for believing the San Francisco riots had been Communist-inspired and Communist-led.

Facts on Communism—Volume II, The Soviet Union from Lenin to Khrushchev, December, 1960; 357 pp., with index.—A comprehensive history of the Soviet Union, compiled with the assistance of Professor David J. Dallin.

Legislative Recommendations by the House Committee on Un-American Activities, and Subsequent Action Taken by Congress or Executive Agencies (a Research Study by the Legislative Reference Service of the Library of Congress), December 30, 1960; 132 pp., with index.—A comprehensive survey of the Committee's accumulated legislative recommendations, a summary of each, a description of its purpose, and a report on the action taken by Congress in each case. Includes measures credited to other agencies or subcommittees.

World Communist Movement, Selective Chonology, 1818–1957, Prepared by the Legislative Reference Service of the Library of Congress—Volume I, 1818–1945, published 1960; 232 pp., with foreword and key to sources.—A year-by-year account of the history of the International Communist movement, with special emphasis on shifts in policy, attitudes, and objectives.

House Report No. 2237—Annual Report for the Year 1960, January 2, 1961; 147 pp., with index.—A review of the Committee's work during 1960, and also during the decade of the 1950's, including summaries of hearings, reports, consultations, the use of its reference services, and recommendations for future legislation.

Just before this volume went to press, the Committee held hearings on the Fund for Social Analysis, and during the year has held extensive executive hearings relating to the methods used by the National Science Foundation in making grants and awards for educational purposes. The Committee has plans to make public the executive hearings it held in 1960 on the two National Security Council defectors, Bernon F. Mitchell and William H. Martin; to bring out a new edition of the *100 Things You Should Know About Communism* series; a new *Cumulative Index* covering the years 1955–1960; a new *Guide to Subversive Organizations and Publications;* and an analysis of the charges against the Committee's film *Operation Abolition.*

Ross D. Mackenzie

NOTES

CHAPTER 2

1. For the earliest history of the investigatory power I have relied principally on Marshall Edward Dimock, *Congressional Investigatory Committees* (Johns Hopkins Press, 1929) and Ernest J. Eberling, *Congressional Investigations* (Columbia University Press, 1928).

2. Fletcher Pratt, *Stanton* (W. W. Norton, 1953), p. 154.

3. John Foster Dulles, in a speech delivered in April, 1952, at Louisville, Ky.

4. *Congressional Globe*, 36th Congress, 1st session, Part 2, p. 1102.

5. That is, who refused to testify on the ground—accepted under the prevailing interpretation of the Fifth Amendment—that a truthful answer might tend to "incriminate or degrade" them.

6. Woodrow Wilson, *Congressional Government*, pp. 299, 303.

7. The quotations from the Harper's Ferry debate are taken from *Congressional Globe*, 36th Congress, 1st session, March 12, 1860, pp. 1100-09; and Part 4, June 15, 1860, pp. 3006-7.

8. The most important cases were, in fact, only the four that have already been cited in these pages: *Anderson v. Dunn* (1821); *Kilbourn v. Thompson* (1881); *In re Chapman* (1897); *McGrain v. Daugherty* (1927).

9. *United States v. Bryan* (1947); *United States v. Josephson* (1948); *Barsky v. United States* (1948).

10. Wilson, *op. cit.*, pp. 277-303 *passim*.

11. N. Nelson McGeary, "Historical Development," a contribution to the symposium on Congressional investigations in *University of Chicago Law Review* (Vol. 18, No. 3, Spring 1951), p. 430.

12. The memorandum is reprinted in *The Federal Bar Journal*, Vol. XIV, No. 1, Jan.-Mar. 1954, pp. 73-86.

13. James D. Richardson, *A Compilation of the Messages and Papers of the Presidents* (Government Printing Office, 1896), Vol. 8, pp. 377, 381-2.

14. *The New York Times*, Aug. 17, 1958.

CHAPTER 4

1. Nathaniel Weyl, *Treason* (Washington, D.C.: Public Affairs Press, 1950), p. 30.

2. *Ibid.*, p. 21.

3. Aristotle, *Politics*, Book V, Chapter 8 (Jowett translation).

4. Milton, *Areopagitica*.

5. Edward Gibbon, *Decline and Fall of the Roman Empire*, Chapter XV.

6. Quoted in Weyl, *op. cit.*, p. 62.

7. Zechariah Chafee, *Free Speech in the United States* (Cambridge: Harvard University Press, 1954), p. 271.

8. Macaulay, *History of England*, Chapter VII.

9. Alan Barth, *Government by Investigation* (New York: The Viking Press, 1955), p. 14.

10. Julia E. Johnson (compiler) , *The Investigating Powers of Congress* (New York: H. W. Wilson, 1951) , p. 11.

11. Nathaniel Weyl, *The Battle Against Disloyalty* (New York: Thomas Y. Crowell, 1951) , p. 126.

12. *Idem.*

13. *Idem.*

14. Chafee, *op. cit.*, p. 271.

15. *Ibid.*, p. 319.

16. *Ibid.*, p. 144.

17. Francis Biddle, *The Fear of Freedom* (New York: Doubleday, 1951), p. 112.

18. *Idem.*

19. Telford Taylor, *Grand Inquest* (New York: Simon and Schuster, 1955), p. 71.

20. Donald F. Whitehead, *The FBI Story* (New York: Random House, 1956), p. 46.

21. *Ibid.*, p. 47.

22. Weyl, *Battle Against Disloyalty*, p. 132.

23. Whitehead, *op. cit.*, p. 46.

24. My account of the floor debate, through the adopting vote, is taken from the *Congressional Record—House*, May 22, 1930, pp. 9390-9398.

25. Biddle, *op. cit.*, p. 112.

26. My account of the floor debate, through the adopting vote, is taken from the *Congressional Record—House*, March 20, 1934, pp. 4934-4949.

27. *Congressional Quarterly News Features*, week ending March 13, 1953, p. 321.

28. Robert E. Stripling, *The Red Plot Against America* (Drexel Hill, Pa.: Bell, 1949) , p. 20.

29. *Ibid.*, p. 21.

30. Quoted in Weyl, *Treason*, p. 10.

31. Stripling, *op. cit.*, p. 21.

32. *Idem.*

33. Unless otherwise noted, my account of the floor debate, through the adopting vote, is taken from the *Congressional Record—House*, May 26, 1938, pp. 7568-7586.

34. Stripling, *op. cit.*, p. 22.

35. HUAC, *This Is Your House Committee on Un-American Activities* (Sept. 19, 1954) for figures through 1954. Figures for later years were secured by telephone call to HUAC.

36. *Ibid.*, for years through 1954. Later years' figures also secured by telephone call to HUAC.

37. For HUAC activities through 1944 I have (unless otherwise noted) relied on J. Parnell Thomas, *Ten Years of Vigilance* (extension of remarks in House of Representatives, May 26, 1948).

38. Biddle, *op. cit.*, p. 124.

39. Taken from transcript of HUAC hearing, August 19, 1938, in possession of J. B. Matthews. To this day the passage is notoriously misquoted.

40. Stripling, *op. cit.*, p. 30.

41. *Dies Committee Hearings*, Vol. 6, pp. 3705-3889; Vol. 10, pp. 6043-6124.

42. Stripling, *op. cit.*, p. 26.

43. Martin Dies, *The Trojan Horse in America* (New York: Dodd, Mead, 1940).

44. Stripling, *op. cit.*, p. 32 ff.

45. *Ibid.*, p. 36.
46. Alan Barth, *The Loyalty of Free Men* (New York: The Viking Press, 1951), p. 55.
47. Frank J. Donner, *The Un-Americans* (New York: Ballantine, 1961) , p. 15.
48. Stripling, *op. cit.*, p. 50.
49. My account of the floor debate is taken from the *Congressional Record—House*, January 3, 1945, pp. 11-15.
50. From HUAC annual reports, 1948–1960.
51. *Hearings Regarding Communism in Labor Unions in the United States,* p. 110.
52. *Communist Party of the United States v. Subversive Activities Control Board*, 367 U.S. 38, 39, 61, 84, 94-95, 101, 104.
53. For HUAC activities through 1947 I have (unless otherwise noted) relied on J. Parnell Thomas, *op. cit.*
54. HUAC 1948 annual report.
55. *Congressional Quarterly News Features,* above, p. 323.
56. *Idem.*
57. HUAC 1949 annual report.
58. *Congressional Quarterly News Features,* above, p. 323.
59. Weyl, *Battle Against Disloyalty,* p. 288.
60. *Idem.*
61. *Idem.*
62. HUAC 1951 annual report.
63. Barth, *The Loyalty of Free Men,* p. 72.
64. HUAC 1952 annual report.
65. HUAC 1953 annual report.
66. HUAC 1954 annual report.
67. *Washington Post & Times Herald,* Nov. 4, 1954, p. 15.
68. *Washington Post & Times Herald,* Nov. 17, 1954, p. 2.
69. HUAC 1955 annual report.
70. HUAC 1956 annual report.
71. HUAC 1957 annual report.
72. HUAC 1958 annual report.
73. HUAC 1959 annual report.
74. HUAC 1960 annual report.

CHAPTER 5

1. *Investigation of Communist Infiltration and Propaganda Activities in Basic Industry (Gary, Ind., Area) hearings before the Committee on Un-American Activities, Feb. 10 and 11, 1958.*
Specific authority for the Committee's 1958 activities was embodied in the rules adopted by the 85th Congress, House Resolution 5, January 3, 1957, Rules X and XI.
2. *Committee on Un-American Activities, Annual Report for the Year 1958 (House Report No. 187) March 9, 1959,* p. 19. Hereafter: Annual Report, 1958.
3. *Ibid.,* p. 20.
4. *Investigations of Communist Activities in the New England Area, Parts I–III, hearings before the Committee on Un-American Activities, March 14, 18–21, 1958.*
5. *Communism in the New York Area (Entertainment), hearings before the Committee on Un-American Activities, April 1, 1957, June 18 and 19, 1958.*
6. Annual Report, 1958, p. 28.

7. *Ibid.*, p. 28.

8. *Ibid.*, pp. 29-30.

9. *Ibid.*, 1958, p. 33.

10. *Ibid.*, pp. 34-35.

11. *Ibid.*, p. 35.

12. *Communist Infiltration and Activities in Newark, N. J., hearings before the Committee on Un-American Activities, Sept. 3, 4, and 5, 1958.*

13. Annual Report, 1958, p. 37.

14. *Communist Propaganda—Student Groups, Distributors, and Propagandists, Part IX, hearings before the Committee on Un-American Activities, June 11 and 12, 1958.*

15. *Communist Infiltration and Activities in Newark, N. J., hearings before the Committee on Un-American Activities, Sept. 3, 4, and 5, 1958,* pp. 2796 and 2797.

16. Annual Report, 1958, p. 41.

17. *Chronicle of Treason, Rep. Francis E. Walter, report of the Committee on Un-American Activities, March 3–9, 1958.*

18. *The Erica Wallach Story, report of the Committee on Un-American Activities,* March 21, 1958.

19. In order: *Organized Communism in the United States,* May, 1958; *Who Are They? Part VIII,* February 21, 1958; *Who Are They? Part IX,* August 5, 1958; *The House Committee on Un-American Activities—What It Is—What It Does,* July, 1958.

20. *Patterns of Communist Espionage, Committee on Un-American Activities, January, 1959.*

21. Consultation with the Committee on Un-American Activities, Jan. 21, 1958.

22. Consultation with the Committee on Un-American Activities, March 13, 1958.

23. Consultation with the Committee on Un-American Activities, April 3, 1958.

24. Consultation with the Committee on Un-American Activities, April 7, 1958.

25. Consultation with the Committee on Un-American Activities, April 23, 1958.

26. Annual Report, 1958, pp. 69-70, from Consultation before the House Committee on Un-American Activities, April 30, 1958.

27. Consultation with the Committee on Un-American Activities, May 20, 1958.

CHAPTER 7

1. Statement made by Mayor Christopher to representatives of the St. Paul, Minn., Chamber of Commerce, January 18, 1961.

2. Telegram in files of House Committee on Un-American Activities.

3. Oakland *Tribune,* January 25, 1961. Quoted by Congressman John Rousselot in *Human Events,* "The Truth About Operation Abolition," March 31, 1961.

4. Quoted by W. E. Schmitt and A. O. Hanks, in "San Francisco's Black Friday," *Congressional Record,* May 18, 1961, p. 7836.

5. All quotations from Hoover appear in his report on the San Francisco riots, *Communist Target—Youth.* These appear on pp. 4 and 5 of that document.

6. *In Search of Truth,* pamphlet published by Bay Area Student Committee, p. 3.

7. Statement made, e.g., by Professor Arthur L. Stinchcombe, representing the American Civil Liberties Union, in television debate with the author, August 13, 1961, over station WAVE, Louisville, Kentucky.

8. The Tom Duggan Show, Station KCOP-TV, Los Angeles, September 10, 1960.

9. *Communist Target—Youth*, p. 4.

10. *Ibid.*, p. 5.

11. Quoted by Schmitt and Hanks, *Congressional Record*, May 18, 1961, p. 7840.

12. *The Daily Californian* for May 4, 1960.

13. *Ibid.*, May 12, 1960.

14. Quoted in HUAC report, *The Truth About the Film, "Operation Abolition,"* p. 29.

15. Leaflet photographically reproduced in HUAC report, *Communist-Led Riots Against the House Committee on Un-American Activities*, p. 17.

16. *Communist Target—Youth*, p. 6.

17. *Ibid.*

18. *Ibid.*, p. 5.

19. The statements made in this paragraph are taken from the HUAC report, *The Truth About the Film, "Operation Abolition,"* pp. 20-23.

20. *Ibid.*, pp. 22, 24, 26.

21. Frank J. Donner, *The Un-Americans*, New York, Ballantine, 1961, p. 197.

22. Statement to St. Paul Chamber of Commerce.

23. Hearings before HUAC, "The Northern California District of the Communist Party," Part 3, p. 2091.

24. *Ibid.*, p. 2090.

25. See, e.g., Burton Wolfe in *The Californian*, March, 1961.

26. "The Northern California District of the Communist Party," hearings, Part 3, p. 2138.

27. *Ibid.*, p. 2105.

28. Statement made by Sheriff Carberry over the telephone to the author, mid-January, 1961.

29. *Communist Target—Youth*, p. 8.

30. *The Communist-Led Riots Against the House Committee on Un-American Activities*, p. 11.

31. Oakland *Tribune*, January 25, 1961, quoted by Congressman John Rousselot, *Human Events*, March 31, 1961.

32. See, e.g., the San Francisco *Chronicle*, editorial, May 5, 1961, entitled "Meisenbach Trial Clears Errors."

33. Quoted by William L. S. Mackey, the San Francisco *Examiner*, May 4, 1961.

34. The witness who came closest was James R. Toombs, who said he saw Schaumleffel slip and fall, but who did not say that he saw the officer strike his head. Testimony summarized in San Francisco *Examiner*, May 2, 1961.

35. The corroborating witnesses were John Stansfield, a former investigator for various government agencies, and Albert V. Morris, a retired attorney.

36. San Francisco *Examiner* diagram illustrating testimony, Saturday, April 22, 1961.

37. See, e.g., San Francisco *Chronicle* editorial for May 5, 1961, "Meisenbach Trial Clears Errors."

38. Statement made in a debate with the author by Attorney Merle Miller, representing the Indiana Civil Liberties Union, July 19, 1960, in Louisville, Kentucky.

39. Donner, *op. cit.*, p. 209.

40. *Ibid.*, pp. 209, 210.

41. "The Northern California District of the Communist Party," hearings, Part 1, p. 1949.

42. *Ibid.*, p. 1952.

43. *Ibid.*, pp. 1967, 1969.

44. *Ibid.*, pp. 1969, 1970.

45. *Congressional Record*, May 18, 1961, p. 7836.

46. "The Northern California District of the Communist Party," hearings, Part 3, p. 2103.

47. San Francisco *News-Call Bulletin*, January 31, 1961.

48. "The Northern California District of the Communist Party," hearings, p. 2103. San Francisco *News-Call Bulletin*, January 31, 1961.

49. *The Californian*, June, 1961.

50. "The Northern California District of the Communist Party," hearings, Part 3, p. 2105.

51. *In Search of Truth*, p. 5.

52. Oakland *Tribune*, January 25, 1961, quoted by Congressman Rousselot in *Human Events*, March 31, 1961.

53. *In Search of Truth*, p. 5.

54. *Ibid.*

55. San Francisco *News-Call Bulletin*, January 31, 1961.

56. *Ibid.*

57. "Northern California District of the Communist Party," hearings, Part 2, pp. 2066, 2067.

58. *Ibid.*, p. 2073.

59. *Ibid.*, p. 2075.

60. *Ibid.*, p. 2149.

61. *Communist Target—Youth*, pp. 9, 10.

62. *In Search of Truth*, p. 3.

63. San Francisco *News-Call Bulletin*, January 26, 1961.

64. *Congressional Record*, May 18, 1961, p. 7837.

65. San Francisco *Chronicle*, May 5, 1961, editorial, "Meisenbach Trial Clears Errors."

66. *Ibid.*

67. *In Search of Truth*, p. 1.

68. The Goodwin Knight Show, Station KCOP-TV, Los Angeles, August 9, 1960.

69. Statement issued to radio commentator Fulton Lewis, Jr.

70. *The Reporter*, February 16, 1961, p. 10.

71. *Ibid.*

72. *Ibid.*

73. Quoted by Schmitt and Hanks, *Congressional Record*, May 18, 1961, p. 7838.

74. *In Search of Truth*, p. 6.

75. "Judge Agrees with FBI That Reds Inspired Riot," Washington *Post*, December 25, 1960.

76. *Ibid.*

77. *In Search of Truth*, p. 5.

78. "The Northern California District of the Communist Party," hearings, Part 2, pp. 2000 *et seq.*

79. Braden was identified, during his 1954 trial in Louisville, by Mrs. Alberta Ahearn.

80. See *Louisville Edition of National Review*, Nov. 19, 1955.

81. A photographic reproduction of the story containing this quotation appears in the HUAC report, *The Communist-Led Riots Against the House Committee on Un-American Activities*, p. 21.

82. *In Search of Truth*, p. 4.

83. *Congressional Record*, May 18, 1961, p. 7838.

84. *In Search of Truth*, p. 6.

85. *New University Thought*, Autumn, 1960, issue, pp. 22-23.

86. "The Northern California District of the Communist Party," hearings, Part 2, p. 2067.

87. *In Search of Truth*, p. 2.

88. *The Communist-Led Riots Against the House Committee on Un-American Activities*, p. 7.

89. *Ibid.*, p. 6.

90. *In Search of Truth*, p. 2.

91. See also statement by Congressman Rousselot in *Human Events*, March 31, 1961.

92. *Congressional Record*, May 18, 1961, p. 7837.

93. Reprint of speech distributed by Bay Area Student Committee, p. 3.

94. *Ibid.* Roosevelt stated: "It is not important whether the names were deliberately 'leaked' to the press"—implying that they were.

95. Reprint distributed by Congressman Scherer's office, p. 9.

96. Letter in files of House Committee on Un-American Activities.

CHAPTER 8

1. The remainder of this subsection of the former printed Rules is superseded by House Rule XI 26 (m) which appears on page VII of this document.

2. The Committee seeks factual testimony within the personal knowledge of the witness and such testimony and answers must be given by the witness himself and not suggested to witness by counsel.

3. Statements which take the form of personal attacks by the witness upon the motives of the Committee, the personal characters of any Members of the Congress or of the Committee staff, and statements clearly in the nature of accusations are not deemed to be either relevant or germane.

4. All witnesses are invited at any time to confer with Committee counsel or investigators for the Committee prior to hearings.

5. The House Committee on Un-American Activities is a Congressional Committee, not a court (see pp. IV-VIII). Moreover, the Committee has neither the authority nor the vast powers of a court of law.

A Congressional Committee conducts a search for information, not a trial.

The requirements of time, the nature of the fact-finding hearings, the complications of travel, the realities of expense, and the voluminous duties of Members of Congress all add together to make it impractical for courtroom procedure to be followed.

The Committee has given frequent and diligent consideration to this subject, and has determined that in order to carry out its responsibilities imposed by law, the rules of evidence, including cross-examination, are not applicable.

INDEX

Jan 1966 - Th.S